ADVANCES IN LIBRARY ADMINISTRATION AND ORGANIZATION

ADVANCES IN LIBRARY ADMINISTRATION AND ORGANIZATION

Series Editors: Edward D. Garten, Delmus E. Williams, James M. Nyce, and Janine Golden

Recent Volumes:

ADVANCES IN LIBRARY ADMINISTRATION AND
ORGANIZATION   VOLUME 26

ADVANCES IN LIBRARY ADMINISTRATION AND ORGANIZATION

EDITED BY

EDWARD D. GARTEN
Walden University, Minneapolis, Minnesota, USA

DELMUS E. WILLIAMS
University of Akron Libraries, Ohio, USA

JAMES M. NYCE
Ball State University, Muncie, Indiana, USA

JANINE GOLDEN
Texas Woman's University, Denton, Texas, USA

Emerald

JAI

United Kingdom – North America – Japan
India – Malaysia – China

JAI Press is an imprint of Emerald Group Publishing Limited
Howard House, Wagon Lane, Bingley BD16 1WA, UK

First edition 2008

Copyright © 2008 Emerald Group Publishing Limited

Reprints and permission service
Contact: booksandseries@emeraldinsight.com

British Library Cataloguing in Publication Data
A catalogue record for this book is available from the British Library

ISBN: 978-0-7623-1488-1
ISSN: 0732-0671 (Series)

Printed by MPG Books Ltd, Bodmin, Cornwall

Awarded in recognition of
Emerald's production
department's adherence to
quality systems and processes
when preparing scholarly
journals for print

INVESTOR IN PEOPLE

CONTENTS

v

LIST OF CONTRIBUTORS

Belinda Boon	Kent State University School of Library & Information Science, Columbus, OH, USA
H. Frank Cervone	Northwestern University Library, Evanston, IL, USA
Gary Neil Fitsimmons	Cisco Junior College, Cisco, TX, USA
John Patrick Green Jr.	8916 56th Pl. W, Mukilteo, WA, USA
Deborah Lee	Mississippi State University, MS, USA
Charles B. Osburn	School of Library and Information Science, University of Alabama, AL, USA
Jennifer K. Sweeney	School of Education, University of California, Davis, CA, USA

INTRODUCTION

It is difficult for me to believe that this series has been around for a quarter of a century. But then it is hard to rationalize a belief that I am still a young man. As we begin the 26th volume of ALAO, it seems useful to consider the work that has come before. Twenty-five volumes of research studies and papers focused on library management and organizational issues may be a significant milestone for any monograph series in our profession, but it also represents an opportunity to step back, catch one's editorial breath, and take stock of near-term future directions. Clearly, some monograph series never see a 25th anniversary, while others have been pressed to change focus entirely. Yet others have become less-than-relevant to real-world professional challenges. For better or worse, this series has carried on, and, again, as one of our editors noted a few volumes back, offers the reader "an eclectic collection of papers that convey the results of the kind of research that managers need, mixing theory with a good dose of pragmatism." Since the first volume in 1982, the aim has been to provide a publication venue for those manuscripts that are typically longer than most journal articles but shorter than most books. Moreover, the idea then as now was to relieve authors of the constraints that sometimes attend other genre and at the same time to encourage the presentation of thoughtful pieces that integrate theory and practice. Call me hidebound if you will, but as we offer Volume 26, I would argue that we have stayed true to our tradition of providing good research pieces that are worth reading.

This volume leads off with Jennifer Sweeney's research on skill development among academic reference librarians. Drawing upon the literature of occupational sociology and using the Dreyfus Model, she offers a holistic exploration of skill changes through analysis of reference situations as contextualized and social phenomena. In practical follow-up, Jennifer's findings were used to reorganize the mixed skill levels presented in the Reference and User Services Association (RUSA) *Professional Competencies for Reference and User Services Librarians.*

Next up we have an essay by Charles Osburn, long an observer of our profession and one not unfamiliar to these pages. With his contribution to the series, Charles provides an overview of the literature of organizational development and traces the movement away from bureaucratic systems characterized by authority of position in the hierarchy toward culture-driven systems best characterized by the guided influence of peers working within a flatter structure. Charles argues that, at least for librarianship, a mixture of the conditions and responsibilities of our profession operating in the context of the apparent freedom offered by the organizational culture in which our libraries operate should lead logically to a growth in the importance of the ethical code held by each individual librarian and of the level of trust that exists throughout the library organization. His observations are both provocative and challenging to our profession as we address change.

And with a focus on change and openness to innovation, we complement and follow Osburn with an engaging contribution from H. Frank Cervone. I first encountered Frank's interest in library innovation while serving on his doctoral dissertation committee. The paper here is derived from that dissertation. From the start, I was intrigued with the proposed title of his study *Breaking Out of "Sacred Cow" Culture: The Relationship of Professional Advice Networks to Receptivity to Innovation in Academic Librarians.* After a successful defense, Frank and I worked together to distill the essence of his research in the anticipation that it might be of interest to a broader readership. University libraries have traditionally been the primary caretakers of scholarly resources. However, as electronic modes of information delivery replace print materials, expectations of academic libraries have evolved rapidly. In this environment, academic libraries need to be adaptable organizations. Frank argues that, while librarianship is deeply rooted in strong values and beliefs, which inherently limit receptivity to change and innovation, these constraints are not absolute. His analysis of the nature of relationships within the professional advice networks was based on a combination of quantitative and qualitative techniques, in contrast to the analysis of the respondents' receptivity to innovation, which was based on quantitative measures. The results of this research indicate that there is a relationship between the size of the professional advice networks and individual's receptivity to innovation, but additional aspects of the professional advice network may play a role in an individual's overall receptivity to innovation.

Deborah Lee follows with an important discussion of a range of issues surrounding faculty status, tenure, and wage differentials among members of the Association of Research Libraries. These are areas that have seldom been discussed in the professional literature, and we believe that Deborah has made a significant contribution here to our understanding of a topic that can be contentious at the local campus level. Her study examined 10 years of cross-sectional data drawn from ARL libraries looking closely at both the institutional characteristics of tenure-granting ARL libraries and the impact of tenure on starting salaries. Importantly, Lee explores a number of issues related to both a union wage premium and a compensating wage differential due to tenure. Her findings suggest that tenure, while serving other functions within an academic library, does not have the impact on starting salaries that some might predict.

The next paper is the work of Belinda Boon who provides an intriguing study of professional development among female librarians in small Texas communities. She explores four major topic areas relating to the professionalization of non-MLS library directors: job satisfaction, including library work as spiritual salvation, librarianship and the ethic of caring, making a difference in the community, and pride in professional identity were found to be critical elements in their career choice, and attention was given in her discussions with them to professional development, including hiring narratives, continuing education and lifelong learning, mentoring and professional development, and the importance of the MLS degree; challenges facing small community library directors, including gender-based discrimination, resistance from local governing officials, and geographic isolation. Guidance for success was also offered, including understanding the community, becoming part of the community, making the library the heart of the community, business and managerial skills, and people and customer service skills. We believe Belinda has made an important contribution to rural and small community librarianship, an area of investigation sometimes undervalued.

Then, exploring an area that many of us have long speculated about, but lacked hard evidence to make sense of, Gary Neil Fitsimmons asks the question of *what makes for a good academic library director?* He approaches the topic, not from the perspective of library faculty and staff (where we often have both many and different opinions), but from the perspective of directors' future supervisors, typically vice-presidents for academic affairs or provosts. As Gary candidly observes, the fact of the matter is that librarians seldom hire library directors. They may have input into the hiring decision through search committees, but, in the end, the final decision is made – and subsequent supervision given – by someone outside of the library. He notes, almost through understatement, that library directorships have been in a state of flux, at least since the early 1970s, and wonders if librarians are getting what they need from graduate library schools to be successful library managers. Clearly, a study of the academic administrators who actually hire and then later supervise library directors has long been needed. And as Gary further argues, the opinions of this group should matter to librarians. The implications of knowing the views of hiring administrators of what makes for a good library leadership reach into all areas of a director's work, touching such diverse issues as identification, training, and retention of leaders; dealing with change; campus leadership; and critical decision-making issues in general.

We conclude this volume with what may be the first theoretical study of the application of LibQUAL+-like studies, within a public library and perhaps within any type of library. John Patrick Green, an engineer and management consultant, employs confirmatory factor analysis to analyze the secondary data resulting from a service quality survey conducted by a large metropolitan public library. The library outsourced the development of this survey, which was founded on the well-recognized SERVQUAL and LibQUAL+ service quality models. Applying structural equation modeling and recognized fit indexes to the secondary data, John's study found that the conclusions drawn from the library model did not fit the data and that the data itself were neither reliable nor valid. His study developed a nine-step process for implementing the SERVQUAL model that allowed the data derived from SERVQUAL-type implementations to provide superior information for decision-making. The short paper presented here is derived from his doctoral dissertation, which should be consulted by those who wish an in-depth understanding of this widely used tool for measuring library quality.

Finally, to paraphrase Ecclesiastes: *There is a time and a season.* This editor announces that his time with this publication has drawn to a close. When Delmus E. Williams and I were handed the trust for this series by Gerald McCabe and Bernie Kriessman, following Volume 12, our fond hope was that we would continue to build upon the work of those founding editors. Being a bit superstitious, this editor was a bit fearful that Volume 13 might prove to be both the end of a series and the end to a friendship. Fortunately, luck was with us, and we have continued through this volume (adding our third editor James M. Nyce in 2005). While harboring a few reservations about leaving the series, other editorial opportunities in addition to graduate teaching have nudged this editor to close the door. Replacing me as editor will be Dr. Janine Golden, Assistant Professor at the School of Library and Information Studies at Texas Woman's University. Janine has already demonstrated with this volume that she brings keen editorial insight in addition to a widely acknowledged and growing reputation within the profession. At Texas Women's University, she currently serves on the Faculty Advisory Committee, Doctoral Studies Committee, and is the Faculty Advisor for the university's American Library Association graduate student chapter. Prior to joining Texas Woman's University she was State Library Program Specialist with the State Library and Archives of Florida where she served as state government liaison for libraries in counties throughout Florida and created a formal statewide library leadership mentoring program. Janine's current professional interests include leadership and management of public libraries. More specifically, her research path has focused on factors and strategies related to career development success for emerging library leaders as well as the professional mentoring process. Those interests build on her work with Florida libraries in the creation of a mentoring model, approaches to succession planning, and work on employee retention issues. Janine's PhD in Library & Information Science was completed at the University of Pittsburgh. I expect that her editorial insights and professional contacts will allow this series to continue to grow and be responsive to the interests of its readership. For those who know me, it is not every day that they hear me say that I have been both easily and happily replaced.

Edward D. Garten
Co-editor

TRANSFORMING THE RATIONAL PERSPECTIVE ON SKILL DEVELOPMENT: THE DREYFUS MODEL IN LIBRARY REFERENCE WORK

Jennifer K. Sweeney

ABSTRACT

This study investigated the skill development of academic reference librarians. It has been assumed that skill develops over time through experience, yet workplace competencies are currently described without reference to level of expertise. Drawing on the literature of occupational sociology, the Dreyfus model is an experiential, developmental model rather than a trait or talent model, allowing the holistic exploration of skill change through analysis of reference situations as contextualized and social phenomena. Three aspects of change in skill level were investigated: the shift from reliance on rules and abstract principles to the use of real experience to guide action; the growth in ability to discern relevant information from noise in complex situations; and the increase in engaged, involved performance out of initial detachment. Analysis of interview narratives with 17 reference librarians and two reference assistants suggests that the Dreyfus model is applicable to reference skill development with some differences. Skill characteristics were discerned at

Advances in Library Administration and Organization, Volume 26, 1–39
Copyright © 2008 by Emerald Group Publishing Limited
All rights of reproduction in any form reserved
ISSN: 0732-0671/doi:10.1016/S0732-0671(08)00201-0

four levels: beginner, competent, proficient, and expert. Observed skill criteria in the narratives were used to reorganize the mixed skill levels presented in the Reference and User Services Association (RUSA) Professional Competencies for Reference and User Services Librarians.

INTRODUCTION

This paper presents my dissertation research on the skill development of academic reference librarians (Sweeney, 2006). This study was concerned with finding a language to describe levels of skill across the librarian's career path from novice to expert. What exactly are the differences between the knowledge and abilities of the tentative beginner, fresh from graduate school or professional training, and the intuitive wisdom of the gray-headed individual with 20, 30, and more years of practice in the field? Librarianship, like nursing, teaching, and other professions, draws learning and thus expertise from experience. Yet our discipline has yet to define the knowledge embedded in and the behaviors characteristic of expert practice. Expertise eludes easy description: it is clearly more than an amount of knowledge that can be tested, or an enumeration of tasks successfully accomplished.

A great deal of progress has been made over the past decade in characterizing the basic competencies of reference librarians. This is a significant step forward in light of how quickly our information environments evolve. There is also the urgent need to provide excellent service in a highly competitive industry. Lists of competencies allow us to define the abilities associated with tasks across the scope of work, which is of course vital for human resources in hiring librarians with the right skill sets, for educators in designing relevant training programs, and for managers in creating flexible work organizations. Competencies only provide half the story, however. Even the most comprehensive sets of competencies really provide only a model for superior performance: they do not attempt to differentiate among levels of skill.

This research draws on theoretical advances in the field of occupational sociology, an area which has also made great strides recently in concepts of experiential learning, holistic situational analysis, and community-centered learning, particularly in complex work environments in the midst of rapid social and technological transformation. I particularly focus on the work of Patricia Benner, Stuart and Hubert Dreyfus, Jean Lave, Etienne Wenger, Lawrence Hirschorn, Edward Hutchins, and Yrjö Engeström – theorists whose exciting conceptual findings are new to the library science field. Building on this work is the Dreyfus Model of Adult Skill Acquisition, a developmental model rather than a trait- or talent-based model, offering a framework for analyzing tacit aspects of performance such as judgment and decision making, situational perception, and engagement and involvement with others in the work setting.

Through interviews with reference librarians at different stages in their careers, I attempted to ascertain whether this model might help to clarify the nature of expertise and its development in the librarian's world. The findings suggest quite strongly that on a theoretical level at least, these aspects of analysis are indeed useful for understanding characteristics of librarian skill development from novice to expert. I suggest in my conclusion a reorganization of one of our most comprehensive sets of existing reference competencies, pointing the way toward further increasing our knowledge of the path from novice to expert for reference librarians.

THEORETICAL BACKGROUND

The Purpose of the Study

There has been significant progress in the last decade or so in defining the competencies associated with reference work: the American Library Association (ALA), the Special Libraries Association (SLA), and numerous local organizations and institutions have invested in organizing the knowledge, skills, and abilities associated with the tasks that reference librarians typically engage in (typical examples include *Core Competencies*, Association of Research Libraries, 2002, and *Shaping the Future: ASERL's Competencies for Research Librarians*, Association of Southeastern Research Libraries, 2000). The *Professional Competencies for Reference and User Services Librarians* from the Reference and User Services Association (RUSA) of the ALA represents one of the most comprehensive list (RUSA Task Force, 2003). All of these lists of competencies present complex sets of technical, interpersonal, and communication skills and behaviors: for example, librarians need to build and continually maintain a knowledge base of constantly growing and changing information resources. Librarians need to understand not only a client's information seeking needs and contexts, but also the psychological aspects of the librarian–client relationship (Dervin, 1983; Dewdney & Michell, 1996). There is a vast literature on these various aspects of reference work skills, which has been reviewed extensively by Lynch (1983), Richardson (2002), and Saxton and Richardson (2002).

Given the dynamic and complex nature of the technical and social aspects of the information environment for reference librarians, the work of answering reference questions is clearly an intense learning experience at every level of expertise (Carr, 1983; Mabry, 2003; Wyer, 1930). One becomes a better, more knowledgeable librarian as knowledge is gained through experience over time. But what exactly does the librarian learn over the course of a career? Competencies do provide goals to strive for in excellent performance: the RUSA document states that it is a "model statement of competencies essential for successful reference ... behaviors that excellent performers exhibit more consistently and effectively than average performers" (RUSA Task Force, 2003). Implicitly it is assumed that competencies refer to expertise, not entry-level skill. Common sense, however, tells us that the work performance of beginners is profoundly different from that of experts. The research questions for this study thus center on the general question: What are the characteristics of skill level for reference librarians along the continuum from novice to expert?

What is Skill?

First let us clarify what is meant by skill. Skill can be defined as an attribute or characteristic of personal competence demonstrated through performance, or the "ability to use one's knowledge effectively and readily in execution ... a learned power of doing a thing competently" (Mish et al., 1986). The simplicity of this definition is deceptive, however; sociologist Paul Attewell (1990) noted that concepts of skill across different disciplines and contexts are far more complicated. Research on skill abounds with different theoretical perspectives and ways of measurement, often resulting in inconsistent and contradictory findings (Attewell, 1990; Carnoy, 1997; Vallas, 1990). Inconsistencies and contradictions abound in skill studies within the library field as well, and I will describe some of these later in this article. In general, however, skill is most often associated with the ability to do something, and to do it well. Experience also figures: to be an expert at something implies having had a great deal of practice (Spenner, 1990). Physical skills, or the "skills of the hand" can also be distinguished from (and are often de-valued in comparison to) mental or knowledge-related proficiencies, or the "skills of the head" (Stasz, 2001).

These kinds of assumptions about skill are implicit in all studies of skill, and it is important to realize that different theoretical frameworks will by default emphasize different perspectives. Studies of skill in librarianship throughout the history of the profession have been dominated by a *positivist* perspective, which has been useful for discovering and organizing the tasks involved in work (Ricking & Booth, 1974; US Department of Labor, 2003a; Williamson, 1971). *Ethnomethodological* approaches, in contrast, bring a more holistic, situated understanding of skill in the workplace, which is useful for understanding the developmental aspects of skill in occupations in dynamic environments where ongoing learning occurs as a matter of everyday work. It is important at this point to clarify the differences between these two perspectives.

Positivist treatments view skills as measurable attributes of individuals or jobs, which can be quantified, rated, and ranked (McCormick, Jeanneret, & Mecham, 1969). Job analysis of this type was used to develop the detailed taxonomies of job descriptions in key sources such as the *Dictionary of Occupational Titles* from the US Department of Labor and its more recent online counterpart, the *Occupational Information Network* (*O**NET) (United States Department of Labor, 2003b). In general, these methods rate skills using psychological measures of complexity related to the data, people, or things involved with the task in question. Literally hundreds of constructs defining specific skills and abilities, knowledge, education, occupational values, job characteristics, and so on are listed, evaluated, and ranked in order to calculate the relative importance of each characteristic for a particular job. This was the method used to create the main human resource policy document for the ALA in the early 1970s, a revised version of which is still in effect today (American Library Association, 1998; Ricking & Booth, 1974). This is our positivist paradigm for skill analysis in libraries at the current time.

Problems with positivist approaches to skill analysis have been well documented. The *DOT* was created in the 1940s, a time when the majority of occupations in this country were in manufacturing and agriculture (Cain & Treiman, 1981). As professional and service work overtook these sectors in later decades, it became increasingly apparent that skill measures developed for qualitatively different occupations did not track accurately across different types of tasks (Barley, 1996; Miller, Tremain, Cain, & Roos, 1980). Many of the narrow measures of skill used in the *DOT* thus have little bearing on the complexity of highly technical and dynamic work in the world today, particularly in libraries. This has resulted in inconsistencies and outright nonsensical ratings: for example, the current *DOT* description places a librarian's "trunk strength" and "wrist finger-speed" higher in importance than "problem sensitivity."

Another problem is the social and gender bias that has been conclusively shown to exist in the ratings (Cain & Treiman, 1981; Howe, 1977). Consciously or unconsciously, raters have made assumptions about the prestige or importance of certain tasks. Any job that involves supervision, for example, is rated more complex than a job that involves no supervision. Jobs in predominantly female occupations (such as librarianship, nursing, and teaching) are often rated as less skilled than equivalent jobs in other occupation. Thus, a great deal of obviously complicated and highly skilled work has been ranked lower than much simpler work.

Finally, and most importantly, the constructs in the *DOT* do not address the effect of experience on practice. While the overall *DOT* system has been useful for understanding the scope of tasks involved in library work, it treats skill as a static, unchanging characteristic: it has not been able to account for the developmental differences in skill across levels of expertise. There is strong evidence that experience alters the duties associated with a job along with altering skill (Borman & Ackerman, 1992; Laufer & Glick, 1996).

This "logical/rationalist model of thinking" represented in the *DOT* assumes that the cognitive aspects of skill are embedded in fixed psychological categories, that they are stable, quantifiable things that can be carried around and applied to other situations (Laufer & Glick, 1996, p. 177). Jean Lave (1988) pointed out that the empirical evidence for the transferability of skill from one situation to another is inconclusive at best. The metaphor of skills as tools, with the mind as the toolbox, is too narrow a view for occupations whose everyday tasks involve constant change and ongoing learning. It does not permit consideration of the way dynamic experience in the social world affects abilities and behaviors.

The examples of the logical/rational model in library skill research are numerous. They have been applied to job analysis and beyond, such as in the psychometric measures used in performance appraisal and other evaluation arenas. Examples include the *Individual Rating Scale for Communication Skills* (Hittner, 1981) and the University of Arizona's *Reference Desk Performance Standards* (The Reference Assessment Manual, 1995). The *Reference Assessment Manual* describes many of these instruments. These studies illustrate the breadth of behavioral and task scales that have been used in libraries for some time. None of these provides illumination of the differences between novice and expert performance.

A Holistic Look at Skill

Ethnomethodological studies of skill, on the other hand, draw on the whole of the work environment to produce a completely different view of skill (Attewell, 1990). Mundane activities of everyday life are observed to be highly complicated, requiring close analysis and "thick description" (Geertz, 1973, p. 12). Skill development occurs naturally as a matter of course through everyday practice and experience and interaction with each other and the world. Expertise is demonstrated through unconscious, intuitive performance rather than deliberate effort at individual tasks. In her study comparing math skills in the classroom with those in everyday life, Lave (1988) observed disparities between skill levels demonstrated in the two contexts. Individuals who succeeded in performing complex mental arithmetic in the supermarket often had difficulty with pencil-and-paper calculations of the same type in a classroom environment. Lave concluded that cognition in everyday life is a complex social activity influenced by multiple contextual elements.

The work of Hirschorn (1984, p. 2) and others investigating sociotechnical work environments also helps to clarify our understanding of skill development in occupations that are in the process of being transformed by information technology: "the post-industrial worker ... performs developmental tasks, operating at the boundary between old technical realities and emergent ones". New skills develop as a matter of course during work that is characterized by a constant state of flux and evolution. Lave (1988) showed that the study of practice is concerned with much more than the activities associated with a task: the nature of practice is dialectical in nature and inherently socially constructed. The nature of learning through practice is an iterative process of transformation in which the individual interacts with various elements in the environment – such as people, technology, and social structures. Hutchins (1995) observed that events, actions, and decisions in a multiple-actor scenario were determined by a "set of local computations" rather than by any preset plan, rule, or other single influence. In this way the cognition of the individual transcends the boundaries of the person to encompass the socio-material environment.

We interact in this way with structures in the environment. Performance is mediated through the interaction of the individual not only with artifacts in the environment, but with social actions of others and with cognitive elements as well. Yrjö Engeström (2000) and Engeström and Middleton (1996) noted that collaboration and communication expand the "collective expertise" of the group through debate, negotiation, and combination of different perspectives. Barbara Rogoff (1984) found that interaction with other people is central to the everyday context in which cognitive activity and learning take place: "People, usually in conjunction with each other, set goals, negotiate appropriate means to reach those goals, and assist each other in implementing the means and resetting the goals as activities evolve" (p. 4). This social way of thinking about skill and learning has not been utilized in the library and information studies field, yet it seems readily applicable to the interactive and technological nature of reference work.

Closely related to this are concepts of the "community of practice," which are useful for explaining the social nature of reference skill development. Drawing on *Social Learning Theory* by Albert Bandura (1977), the concept of community of practice was introduced by Jean Lave and Ettiene Wenger in the 1990s to describe groups of individuals with a "shared repertoire" of resources and a sense of "mutual enterprise" (Wenger, 1998, p. 3). Communities of practice share ways of doing things together, and have mutually defined identities. Information flows rapidly through the group, fostering innovation (Holmes & Meyerhoff, 1999). People in these groups benefit through ongoing learning through continual sharing of knowledge; in fact, communities of practice are defined by the "opportunities to learn, share, and critically evaluate what they discover or what may unexpectedly emerge" (O'Donnell et al., 2003, p. 81).

The Social Learning Environment of Library Work

The paradox is that library work has long been seen by librarians as a learning environment. In studies of communication in the reference interaction, for example, learning occurs through a two-sided sense-making process: the client requires an answer to some question, and the librarian has to figure out what the question is (Case, 2002; Dervin, 1976). New search techniques are developed ad hoc and applied in new situations (Rader, 1980).

Coloring this view, however, is the assumption that somehow academic learning is better than everyday learning. In our current library skills paradigm, learning is assumed to be individualized, and separate from other activities. Learning is the specific result of teaching (e.g., teacher–student, librarian–client, or librarian–librarian), and it is also testable (Germain, Jacobson, & Kaczor, 2000; Munson & Walton, 2004; Wenger, 1998). The enduring belief in the worlds of education and work is that people must be taught certain skills, and that they will be unable to do certain tasks without some amount of formal training. The skill that is gained through everyday experience is deemed less important when it is considered at all. Although the ALA human resource policy states that continuous learning is essential for everyone, training and education are the only avenues discussed in the library literature. Indeed, the vast majority of professional reference librarian job openings in this country require (as per ALA guideline) an ALA-accredited professional degree in library studies, rarely permitting the substitution of work experience for this credential.

Also paradoxically, library theorists have long acknowledged the social nature of reference work. Robert Merikangas (1982) and Brian Nielson (1982) suggested that the reference interview was best modeled as a partnership, with the shared goal of empowering the client as an equal partner. Mary Niles Maack (1997) pointed out that the empowerment of the client was a core value of the library profession. Radcliff (1995) noted the paradigmatic shift away from the medical model of communication, in which the professional plays a dominant role over the passive client, toward a mutuality model. Whitlatch (1990) described the shared decision-making and mutual adjustment of both parties in the transformation of both client and librarian. Similarly, Rachel Naismith (1996) urged librarians to look at their relationships with clients, and to encourage sharing of knowledge and development of skills that respect clients' intelligence, acknowledge their needs, and promote collaboration in decision-making. Dervin and Dewdney (1986) and Dewdney and Michell (1997), and Dervin explored ways that librarians contextualize clients' information needs, such as asking "why" and neutral questions. They concluded that librarians and clients need to establish a shared knowledge structure in order to avoid communication failures.

Reflecting on the cooperative aspects of the reference interaction, Celia Hales Mabry (2003) surmised that the learning environment at the reference desk teaches the worker as much as it teaches the client. Cooperative learning requires that participants each bring unique knowledge and assumptions to a situation, and mutually work toward potential solutions. Skill develops throughout this process. Mendelsohn (1997) also noted that the partnership between librarian and client was characterized by a mutuality of expectation, willingness, competence, and satisfaction. Aspects of the social context of the reference interaction are also crucial to client perceptions of the outcome, according to Harris and Michell (1986). Dewdney and Ross (1994) observed that librarian ineffectiveness was a result not only of poor domain knowledge but also of librarian disinterest and unhelpful behavior. Michell and Harris (1987) identified inclusiveness and warmth as necessary for successful reference. Over the years there have been countless descriptions of these types of social skills necessary for reference work (Gers & Seward, 1985; Gothberg, 1976; Kazlauskas, 1976; Mehrabian, 1971; Schwartz & Eakin, 1986).

Reflection in Practice

Beyond this transformation through social interaction is transformation which comes out of the individual's ability to reflect upon one's actions, decisions, and possibilities. Donald Schön (1983) posited that the ability to think about what one is doing and thereby adjust one's approach to fit a situation was a fundamental aspect of skill development through practice. Reflective practice is especially required in environments of uncertainty, change, and unpredictability, where the work consists of problem-setting as much as problem-solving. Professional work in a dynamic environment consists of both the routine and predictable as well as the unique and new, and the worker must confront divergences from the expected with new learning generated through reflection. "Reflective conversation," according to Schön, is the process of *actively fostering learning through engagement with the client*. The professional enters into an active, reflective contract with the client, rather than a traditional contract wherein the client is expected to accept the authority of the professional in a passive manner. The librarian also must be able to draw out from the client what is known as well as what is unknown, to "bring out what is inside, unspoken" (Shulman, 2000).

The difference between reflective and traditional engagement has to do with what Shulman refers to as the difference between "talking at" and "talking with," akin to the Socratic pedagogical tension between lecture and discussion. Both librarian and client must be active participants in the conversation. This may not be easy for clients with varying language skills, low domain knowledge, or a sense of inhibition or insecurity. Librarians do not always get it right either: consider the librarian so focused on explaining the way the search functions in a new database operate that she fails to notice whether her explanation is intelligible or appropriate to the puzzled client.

Finally, reference work is played out in an unpredictable and varied environment. New problems constantly arise. Client knowledge and skill varies from situation to situation, as does that of the librarian. Current assumptions in our field about the predictability and routine nature of reference which emphasize filling an information need and interacting appropriately with the client have not addressed the true nature of the problem-solving skills – the reflection – needed for resolving reference situations.

From Skills to Competencies

From this perspective, the skills of reference really begin with connecting with the client on a close personal level. It is a social activity, enacted through communication (Bunge, 1984; Glogoff, 1983; Harris & Michell, 1986; Kuhlthau, 1994; White, 1985). It is also a mental activity conducted through what Dervin referred to as sense-making (Dervin, 1983; Kuhlthau, 1993). Looking back at earlier conceptions, Mary Jo Lynch (1983) compiled a comprehensive review, updated by Richardson (2002) and Saxton and Richardson (2002). Skills include explicit subject and technical knowledge, communication skills such as active listening and open questioning, and personality characteristics such as friendliness and approachability. These descriptions are consistently well-represented from the earliest textbooks from the 1930s onwards (Bopp & Smith, 1995; Thomas, Hinckley, & Eisenbach, 1981; Hutchins, 1944; Katz, 1982; Mudge, 1936; Wyer, 1930).

A culmination of research on the skills needed for reference work is represented by one of the most comprehensive statements on core competencies for reference work, the *Professional Competencies for Reference and User Services Librarians* (RUSA Task Force, 2003). The list poses behavioral goals to achieve excellent reference performance, organized into specific strategies in five practice domains (the full text of the *Competencies* can be located on the ALA website at http://www.ala.org/ala/rusa/ rusaprotools/referenceguide/professional.htm). The checklists provided in this and similar documents have helped librarians conduct performance appraisal more systematically and educators reorganize training programs to at least keep up with the impact of increased information volume and changing formats.

What has not changed, however, is the lack of actual research on the role of experience in skill development for reference librarians. Research has focused on the effectiveness of various types of training programs (Association of Research Libraries, 1997; Mendelsohn, 1999; Parson, 1988), and librarians' self-directed learning projects (Varlejs, 1996). Educational level is generally substituted as an indirect measure of skill, as it has been historically (Hutchins, 1944; Mudge, 1936; Wyer, 1930).

This is not to say that experience has not been seen as important by library theorists. Wyer (1930, p. 230) described the value of life experience and "learning by doing", affirming that "ten years of varied life and travel are better reference training than a year of library school ... They ought to be; it takes ten times as long to get them." Hutchins (1944, pp. 160–161) agrees, and notes that the reference librarian without formal training but with several years of experience will render better service than the recent, inexperienced library school graduate. In a more recent moment, Juris Dilevko writes:

> the willingness to learn, to continually update and expand one's knowledge in the course of work ... appears to be a key component of what differentiates a highly competent worker from a less adequate staff member. Willingness to learn also assumes ... that an individual realizes that so much information and knowledge is being produced and created that he or she must constantly be in a learning mode (Dilevko, 2000, pp. 4–5).

Rothstein (1983); Grogan (1979); Sherrer (1995, p. 14) all acknowledged that self-directed learning and the ability to grow in the practice of reference work were the "distinguishing characteristics that mark successful librarians." William Fisher (2001) noted how competencies change over time as technology and other factors cause jobs to change. Shaughnessy (1992) pointed out that skills needed to progress beyond the entry level had to be acquired through practice.

Moving beyond theory, how skill actually develops through practice in libraries has not been an easy area to define. In *New Directions for Library and Information Science Education* (also known as the *King Report*), Griffiths and King (1986) attempted to sort out competencies expected of entry-level, mid-, and senior librarians, specifying these categories by certain numbers of years of experience. After establishing lists of work activities and knowledge needed at each level, unfortunately, the study did not achieve what it set out to do. Skills at the mid-level were described as those "listed above [i.e., at the entry level] developed to a greater extent," while skills at the senior level were described the same way, with the addition of some administrative skills such as developing budgets and making projections (pp. 135–136).

Enter the Dreyfus Model of Adult Skill Acquisition

Etienne Wenger (1998, p. 3) asked, "what if we adopted a different perspective, one that placed learning in the context of our lived experience of participation in the world?" Patricia Benner claimed that less was known about the knowledge "embedded in actual nursing practice – i.e., that knowledge accrued over time in the practice of an applied discipline" than the theoretical rules and procedures learned in educational settings (Benner, 1982, p. 1). Consider for a moment the strong parallels between the nature of knowledge and the development of expertise for nurses and librarians. Each starts out with a set of practical skills and theoretical knowledge, formed into preconceptions about these work situations. These preconceptions are continually challenged by new situations and events which change existing foreknowledge (Heidegger, 1962). Expertise develops over time as the individual's perception of a situation changes with experience.

Benner (1982, p. 8) describes how the expert practitioner is able to perceive relevant details and circumstances in a situation because she has experienced similar situations before, whereas the novice has not had the experience and thus is not able to tell relevant from non-relevant details. Problem-solving differs between novice and expert; situations are perceived differently. Reflection in action proceeds differently.

This perspective distinguishes between theoretical and practical knowledge. Aristotle describes the notions of *techné*, or the aspects of practice reflected in formal, explicit knowledge which can be standardized and taught, and *phronesis*, or the situated actions which come about through judgment and wisdom (Benner, 2004, p. 189). Both are needed for practice, but it is judgment which comes out of experience. The differences between expert and novice are distinguished by an increase in explicit knowledge as well as the day-to-day "know-how", demonstrated by progressively more astute perceptual abilities and better problem-solving.

Models of skill development that take this perspective have only recently begun to emerge. Teaching, nursing, and engineering occupations have been the focus of many of these advances (Barab, Barnett, & Squire, 2002; Haag-Heitman & Kramer, 1998; Dreyfus & Dreyfus, 1986; Patel, Glaser, & Arocha, 2000; Trowler & Turner, 2002). In particular, Patricia Benner's (1982) research on the development of nursing skill drew heavily from the model of adult skill development created by Stuart and Hubert Dreyfus.

The Dreyfus model is based on concepts of situated performance and experiential learning, and provides for five levels of skill development from novice to expert: novice, advanced beginner, competent, proficient, and expert. The model describes changes in three areas as skill develops (see Fig. 1). First is a shift from reliance on rules and abstract principles learned in the classroom to reliance on experience for help in understanding what is going on in a situation and in decision making. The second is a transition from the beginner's ability to view the work situation as a confusing collection of equally relevant bits, to the expert's ability to perceive whole situations and intuitively discern the significant elements from the noise.

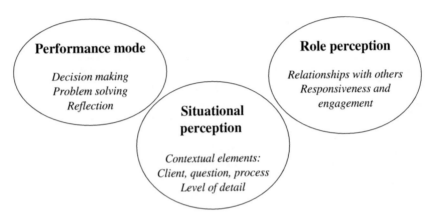

Fig. 1.   Aspects of Skill Development.

The third area of change is the development of the expert's socially engaged, involved role as a performer out of the beginner's passive and detached observation. The characteristics of these changes are outlined in Table 1.

Consider the example of learning to drive. The first-time student drives slowly, taking care to pay attention to many aspects of the situation: the other cars on the road, traffic signals, road signs, the indicators on the dashboard. Coming to a traffic light, he may have to be reminded to use the turn signal and may have to hesitate while he locates it on the steering wheel column. Performance is painstaking because the novice cannot differentiate the most relevant facts among all the things going on in the situation. As the student becomes more adept with experience, performance becomes more relaxed and unconscious. The student gains knowledge of what can happen in different situations by experiencing events and is increasingly able to apply that experience to future decisions.

Similarly, in the Dreyfus model, because the novice does not have experience, she must rely on decontextualized facts presented outside the real task world – such as those learned in the classroom – and is given rules for performing under various conditions. She is taught how to apply these rules in different circumstances. Knowing the rules does not guarantee good performance, because the novice has to think about how to apply the rules in any given situation, and has no sense of how the priorities might change in a new context. The student driver may obtain a perfect score on the written test but not be able to drive well out on the road. She must look to others for instruction when faced with new situations not governed by the

Table 1. The Dreyfus Model of Adult Skill Acquisition.

Dreyfus Level	Performance Mode	Situational Perception	Role Perception
Novice	Follows rules; requires instruction from others; uses structures	Requires help to discern salient aspects	Feels detached from outcome: failure is not "my fault"
Advanced beginner	Comprehends some context; relies on rules and structures, others to bolster performance; learning style is energetic	Recognizes some familiar situations but still requires help in most situations	Beginning to feel some responsibility in familiar situations
Competent	Is analytic, systematic, goal-directed; uses reasoning to cope with overload; develops scripts and tricks to speed performance	Perceives salient aspects after analysis without help in most cases; spurred to organize situational information	Takes more responsibility; involved emotionally in success/failure; engages responsively in some situations
Proficient	Achieves responsive, speedy performance; is immersed and highly situated; decision making is still analytical	Perceives and integrates salient aspects quickly; beginning to understand wider picture	Engages responsively and empathetically; develops deeper moral awareness; beginning to perceive conflicts; encourages client autonomy
Expert	Exhibits deep, tacit understanding of salient aspects; extends the ends of practice through innovation; decision making is intuitive	Perceives salient aspects and appropriate solutions intuitively; sees far-reaching implications of long-term goals	Is highly involved; reflects on practice, and encourages client reflection; resolves conflicts and dilemmas

rules she knows. She likely feels somewhat detached from the outcome of her work: *if I fail, it's not my fault, I am new at this.*

The advanced beginner, on the other hand, has entered into the world of work and has begun to develop an understanding of context. Almost immediately, experience begins to accumulate and the beginner is able to perceive meaningful aspects of certain situations. The beginner creates "maxims" or rules of thumb that are easy to remember (easier than the lists of rules that the novice struggles with), and readily uses these to guide behavior. The beginner still needs to look to others for help and does not take full responsibility for the success of the outcome.

Just prior to reaching the competent level, the practitioner has amassed so many bits of information about so many situations that she is beginning to feel overwhelmed. Dreyfus notes that performance here is often felt to be "nerve-wracking and exhausting" because a sense of what is important within these situations is missing. Competence is achieved as the performer devises ways of coping with this stress, in the form of shortcuts and tricks to guide action. She is starting to organize her experience into strategies to be used in similar situations.

Competent performers are also beginning to feel specific emotions related to success or failure. Enough is known about what to do that remorse is felt at failure, and elation at a job well done. Dreyfus notes that this emotional engagement is intriguing because it seems to contradict the rational, detached, objective action so valued by Descartes. Emotional involvement signals the competent performer's readiness to take responsibility for her actions. Performance at this level is highly goal-oriented, and carefully thought-out. The competent performer is analytical, and while not as rule-bound as the beginner, still considers her choices from among the known rules as well as her experiences.

The proficient level is distinguished from the competent level by a qualitative shift in two areas: perspective and analytical style. Proficient performers have the ability to assess a situation and sort out salient information rapidly, and systematically analyze the factors. The proficient performer sees situations and contexts as a whole and can now sort through them *intuitively*. Intuition develops as a result of the performer collecting so much situational and contextual information over time that the relevant aspects of a situation seem to just occur to her without thinking. Intuition is not guessing, nor is it some kind of mystical occurrence – it is the know-how that is brought to bear through unconscious thought, displayed when something in the new situation triggers a response that was successful in an earlier similar event. The proficient performer does not necessarily see the correct course of action immediately, however, and often needs to fall back on systematic, analytical decision making.

The expert continues on this progression and shares a reliance on intuition with the proficient performers. Continued development of intuition enhances the expert's perceptual awareness; performance is internalized and engrossing. Situations are perceived holistically as they are at the proficient stage. The key difference for the expert is that the most appropriate course of action will come to mind rapidly and intuitively, unlike the proficient performer who must still consider alternatives systematically. The expert perceives more subtle distinctions within situations, and has developed a deep, tacit understanding of the context and its likely outcomes.

The expert sees more long-term goals and impacts related to the present situation. Experts do not need to spend time deliberating on an analysis of alternatives: their innate judgment and wisdom overrides the analytical steps involved with solving problems at the competent or proficient levels. She cannot explain how she knows what to do, she "just knows."

STUDY METHOD

The limits of psychometric and other cognitive measurement devices do not allow for direct measurement of the characteristics of expertise that we have talked about here, such as intuition, judgment, decision-making, or self-awareness (Attewell, 1990; Wenger, 1998). For this reason, a qualitative, interpretive research design was created, centered on the librarian's narrative of the reference encounter.

Narrative analysis is particularly appropriate for studying what it means to develop a sense of identity and self (Mishler, 1995; Riessman, 1993). Psychologists consider the construction of life stories as central to identity formation and sense-making (Daiute & Nelson, 1997; Sarbin, 1986). Narratives can provide an internally consistent view of how an individual understands her past, present, and future (Cohler, 1982). It is one of the basic cognitive and linguistic ways for humans to make sense of things and to express meaning. Stories appear frequently in everyday speech as well as in research scenarios (Mishler, 1986).

Story telling is prevalent throughout library literature, from the case study method of teaching in Galvin (1965), Grogan (1987), and Matarazzo (1971), to reports on talk about reference work (Dilevko, 2000; Mendelsohn, 1997; Radford, 1999). In the study of experience, narrative analysis has proved fruitful: Bell (1999) and Throsby (2002) showed how narrative is used to reshape perceptions of reality. Stevens and Doerr (1997) used narrative analysis in their study of crisis-provoking life events, and of course Benner and many others have called on narrative to study skill (Benner, 1982; Chin, Aligne, Stronczek, Shipley, & Kaczorowski, 2003; Henning, 1998;

King & Clark, 2002; Meretoja, Eriksson, & Leino-Kilpi, 2002; Nicol, Fox-Hiley, Bavin, & Sheng, 1996).

Mischler constructed a typology of the ways narrative is used in research: first, to explain temporal ordering of events; second, to evaluate the linguistic and structural characteristics of a text; and finally, to establish the psychological, social, and cultural functions of description. This latter category concentrates on the way stories are used and the functions they serve. Telling stories about experience reveals in many ways a person's inner sense of self at the moment of telling, and provides clues to help interpret identity. Cain notes that stories contribute to the development of a "collective identity" as interpretation and evaluation of events is shared in a community (Cain, 1991, p. 211). More importantly, narrative has been used to discern aspects of learning and memory by examining changes in forms and structures.

This study drew on this last analytical approach. The stories librarians tell about their experiences provide insight into the evolution of their lives and the meaning they attach to their experiences. Librarians tell stories to help make sense of the meanings embedded in situations, not necessarily as a process-driven set of steps, but as holistic encounters situated in the world of work. These interpretations change over time as individuals gain experience and skill. Perceptions are qualitatively different over the course of development and growth from novice to expert.

Personal narratives were collected through interviews with 19 currently employed academic reference workers (17 professional librarians and two reference assistants). Individuals were invited to participate by email messages sent to various library- and reference-related discussion listservs. Interested individuals were contacted by telephone for a preliminary interview to gather information on education, experience, and availability to participate. The final group selected provided a relatively even spread of ages and years of experience across the participants, from age 20 to 65, with experience ranging from less than three months to over 40 years of experience (see Table 2). In order to assure that sufficient numbers of individuals at each potential skill level were included, an approximate level of experience was assessed at the preliminary stage using the participant's

Table 2.   Average Age and Experience by Skill Category.

	Beginner ($n=3$)	Competent ($n=6$)	Proficient ($n=5$)	Expert ($n=5$)
Age	28.6	41	39.4	55.4
Experience	3	12.2	12.8	23.2

verbal description of experience, documents such as resumes or curriculum vitae, age, and a role-playing exercise.

The main interviews took place in a variety of locations, usually outside the workplace. These took approximately one hour, and were tape-recorded and transcribed. Interview summaries and memos on the interview experience were produced for each interview. The format of the interviews was semi-structured, which means that while the basic questions were the same for each participant, prompts were generated based on the topics of most interest to the participant.

Three general topics were covered in these interviews: recalling recent events, considering past experience, and self rating. First, informants were asked to recall and describe two recent reference experiences: one in which they felt they performed well, and one in which they felt they did poorly. Second, participants were asked about their perception of how they might have handled the situations they described if they were novices: how did they think their skill had changed? Finally, after discussion of the above topics, a simplified version of the Dreyfus model was introduced, and participants were asked to estimate his or her current skill level.

FINDINGS

The narrative evidence of skill level provided by the participants suggested four levels of development on the Dreyfus scale: beginner, competent, proficient, and expert. (The Dreyfus novice level is for students prior to beginning their work experience. All of the participants in this study had been employed for at least three months.)

Beginner

The narratives of the beginners in this study were characterized by several common themes: reliance on rules and structures, asking colleagues for help, and falling back on guesswork when in doubt. They also tended to focus on one aspect of the situation, usually the information need presented by the client, and often mentioned not feeling sure of themselves.

The most prevalent theme across these stories was how they used the rules and structures inherent in the information sources to help the client – specifically, what actions they took to fill the information need or answer the question. One participant described in great detail how she used the

Reader's Guide to Periodical Literature to locate an article on a topic for the client, down to listing the very subject headings she used:

> They [the clients] were looking for articles, primary sources that were written during that time about the coding that was used and how it came about ... I started by going to "coding" and "scripting" and there was another term that we used, it starts with a "p" and I can't remember what it is ... But you know how when you go in and it says "see also", so we did "Native Americans in the war" ... I know we have an online version [of the *Reader's Guide to Periodical Literature*] but ... I like the print version.

Another described using the tables of contents of several issues of a printed journal to locate a specific article requested by a faculty client – an article that the librarian could not find:

> She said she wanted an article that was in [journal name] during the past year that had some to do with employment trends ... So I went to look for that on the shelf. I searched every issue of [journal name] because it's only been coming out for five years or so.

When the librarian tried the same tactic in a different journal, again without success, he turned to his supervisor for help. The beginners frequently talked about how they often were not sure of where to look for very specific information, and how they needed to "check with the person above me to make sure it's the right thing first." These individuals often looked in the wrong types of sources because they simply did not know where else to look, or guessed about what to do next: "It was very very specific ... It's like, okay, where would I find something like that?"

Competent

The competent performers in this study were similar to the beginners in that they, too, focused primarily on the ways they used the information sources at their disposal to satisfy the information need. However, these individuals were clearly much more practiced: their narratives were delivered rapidly and with confidence, and were filled with detail on where they looked, what strategies they used, and why. It was obvious that their experience with different databases, sources, and questions had given them much to draw on for their stories.

Their approach to filling the information need was analytical and systematic, often taking the same approach with each client. The competent performers talked about how they developed scripts for handling frequently asked questions: where is the restroom, how do I find this book:

> Every working reference librarian I think has a repertoire of speeches. Where's the bathroom? How do I update my ID card? How do I find an article? And so we have these pre-set speeches. I've been a librarian for six and a half, almost seven years, and I remember I spent the first three years working out my speeches. So they can be clear, concise, simple. If I have to take too many words, they're gone, I've lost them already, see? Which is tough for me because I'm a talker. And if you have a new question, you're on the fly working out your new speech. If you are new to the job that's probably difficult because you haven't learned your basic speeches ... I think about it as I do it. What do I say? How much do I say? Say too much that time? Okay, I'll say it differently next time.

The very act of picking up a piece of scrap paper as the client is talking, and jotting down a keyword or a database name, becomes for this group an important way to organize what is going in the reference interaction, a way to gain control over what might be for the beginner an overwhelming amount of information:

> I have to write everything down while I'm asking them the questions so I can formulate it in my head ... I need to sit back and think about it for a minute and then here's the approach. Kind of like lining up the plane before it takes off.

These individuals were also confident of their abilities in ways that beginners were not. Several described being able to help a client get started even when they did not know the subject very well:

> Even if I might not know anything about the subject, I can usually get them started on doing their paper ... they've just come from class, and they've got the assignment from the professor. It's a ten-page paper and they need to use some peer-reviewed sources and they need to use journal articles, and this is the topic ... so long as I know that, I'm ready to run with it.

And similarly:

> Even if I'm not familiar with the area, I'll sort of know how to begin looking for the information. I know that every discipline has probably got an index on the computer to search. I can usually find the appropriate database to search in ... Because even if I don't know what I'm doing, I always tend to find something.

The competent librarians were also beginning to engage emotionally with their clients, and to reflect on their relationship with them:

> I think what is most important to me... is some notion of empathy of making the question your own .... A sort of interest in figuring out what is going on ... I become, at least for the time being, interested in what she is looking for.

Proficient

At the proficient stage, there is a qualitative shift in the way these librarians talked about their work. Proficient librarians were no longer focusing primarily on the information process they pursued with the client, as the beginners and competent librarians were. At the proficient level, attention now turns to *how they worked with the client* to come to a mutual understanding and how they empowered the client to act on his or her own. These librarians based their responses closely on the client's conversational cues, and interacted with them on a much closer level. The librarians at this level were deeply immersed in the situation, and were able to adjust their approaches on the fly to changes in situational aspects across information sources and processes and changing client needs. They were attuned to transitional elements in their scenarios in ways the competent and beginner librarians were not.

These librarians talked about how they needed to ask the client questions about many things, such as what they had done so far or what class they were in, in order to understand how best to proceed:

> You have to ask them where they are, and from their answer you know where to start from ... I encourage them to say, now if you already know this, let me know. Because they give you clues, with a frown you know they haven't got it.

Another key aspect of this level is the desire to help the client learn on his or her own, to empower the student by encouraging autonomy. This takes the emerging empathy of the competent librarian a step further:

> I was able to ask them questions that got them to come up with some of the concepts and then think about their topic in a new way.

Expert

At the expert level, this sense of a close, response-based, and immersed relationship with the client continues. This is a shared characteristic across both proficient and expert levels. The general theme of the expert narratives, like the proficient librarians', is how the client and the librarian worked together to come to a mutual solution. The difference for the expert level lies in the expert's ability to see beyond the present moment, to envision possibilities, foster innovation, and in Benner's words, to "extend the ends of practice." Extending the ends of practice includes looking beyond the client's short-term goals to what they might need in the future:

> I also knew that they would feel quite pleased at their success by the end of the class, that they'd learned quite a lot, used and gone through the stuff, and been successful. If they followed the directions they would do it very well. And these would be things they would repeat in the rest of their careers, and in this program. So it was a good stepping stone.

Extending the ends of practice is also helping a client create new connections between himself and the world. One librarian explained that the step of going to college is a significant one for the first-generation children of immigrants, and the library can play a big part in their academic success:

> When I work with people the questions are often not real sophisticated, in terms of the research project. Yet the jump that students make to get into that whole academic way of thinking and working is the most important one they are going to take. Then later on they will go on to run a business, go to graduate school. Whatever they do, the biggest step was the first one. Even though the later ones are more complex.

Innovation was shown in the expert narratives through stories of new and emerging problems in reference work requiring new approaches. One librarian perceived the impact of changes in classroom pedagogy on client behavior with the librarian:

> I think the biggest challenge for our skill set is the evolution of automation. I think we are learning how to search for material faster, more expediently, capture it, show someone how to manage it. There's much more of a full circle situation. I used to tell someone how to find it ... that's not sufficient now. They need to load it into the graphics software, they need to be able to have images that support it .... they need to slice the data twenty-five different ways in a spreadsheet or data management system. So it's not just reading and writing anymore, it's a whole package. I think the role of the librarian has changed quite a lot, and many users today think of themselves using the librarian or seeking the librarian out for the management operation rather than the content.

DISCUSSION

As shown in these narratives, skilled reference practice involves more than applying rules to practical situations, such as using a particular search technique in certain situations, or engaging in a particular communication behavior with a certain type of client. The librarians in this study showed a definite progression from detached, rule-based behavior to increasingly more involved, responsive, situated engagement with the client and environment, and a growing awareness of how the world outside the library influences and is influenced by what goes on in the library. The Dreyfus model integrates these discrete aspects of skill which up until now have been fragmented, and transforms the way reference skill can be analyzed.

While the narratives of some of the librarians in this study had characteristics which placed them squarely in one skill level or another, many more expressed stories which crossed category boundaries in one area or another. Benner notes that this is not unexpected, although it creates complexity. Because of this, it would not be helpful to use strict skill criteria to attempt to standardize expectations about performance and skill development. This is because of the situational nature of skill in the model; the expert responds to unique aspects in each situation, which always require interpretation. Every situation is different and there will always be exceptions to general rules and guidelines which cannot be formulated in advance. The list quickly becomes too long to manage, as the competent librarian knows too well.

The study leaves unanswered questions in several areas. First, there was no evidence offered that might explain why some respondents displayed only competent characteristics despite lengthy experience, or why others progressed to higher levels with less experience. Age itself does not equate to increasing skill either. The average age and years of experience by skill level in Table 2 indicate that although the beginners are in general younger and have been on the job for a shorter time than the experts, there is virtually no difference between the age and experience of the competent and proficient librarians.

What appears to be a key finding for the emergence of expertise is that experience must be varied. Experts have had experience in many different situations, with a multitude of clients, problems, domains, and issues. They are able to bring all this knowledge to bear in their judgment and decision making. Many librarians in this study talked about their affinity for particular fields or types of clients because they have had experience with them, and others talked about their discomfort in certain areas because of inexperience.

REORGANIZING THE RUSA COMPETENCIES

The shift in thinking represented by the Dreyfus model requires us to accept the notion that the reference environment is complex, that the context of each situation is unique and new, and that skill develops across performance mode and perceptual acuity through both situations and in relationships. We need to consider all of these factors together in order to come up with a complete picture of skill. This is a new, integrated perspective – although the findings here are consonant with fragmented body of research on reference, which has touched, tantalizingly, on many of the discrete aspects of skill described by the Dreyfus model.

Richardson's review (1992) identified three separate dimensions for the teaching and learning of reference work: the format of the information, the method of clarification, and the mental traits of both librarian and client. I pointed out earlier that this fragmented view of reference has been perpetuated by the positivist, rational-technical perspectives on work, which have in turn been reinforced by many other factors. The notion of information-as-commodity has influenced library communities to be concerned with efficiency and thus with quantifying distinct elements in the reference environment, such as numbers of questions, question types, clients, and resource usage. The threat of the Internet undermining the need for reference workers (and the libraries that employ them) drew attention to the need to improve librarians' technical skills and increase customer satisfaction.

Professional Competencies for Reference and User Services Librarians (RUSA Task Force, 2003) does an excellent job of enumerating the detailed tasks and functions of reference work within five practice domains (Access, Knowledge Base, Collaboration, Marketing, and Evaluation). The document states that it is to be used to identify "the underlying behaviors that lead to successful performance …. and plans of action that excellent performers typically employ to achieve competency goals." When we examine the competencies through the lens of the Dreyfus model, however, it becomes apparent that the strategies outlined in the RUSA *Competencies* actually foster performance at varying skill levels, depending on the task. The following examples will illustrate.

The *Competencies* document suggests that decision making in reference work occurs systematically in response to the question asked. The examples in the narratives have demonstrated that for experts, decision making is rapid and intuitive. It is at the competent level that practitioners feel compelled to systematically arrange what they know in order to perform more quickly, and to approach their work in a specifically analytical, goal-oriented way.

The RUSA *Competencies* also separate action from outcome: the librarian must first determine the context and question, and then recommend sources. This correspondence view of the way rules are applied to practice is problematic because in reality, rules never quite match up exactly with situations, and one can never account for every possible variation. Each situation is truly unique. While it is sufficient for beginners to look to the rules for the right approach to solving the problem, it is not adequate for competent, proficient, or expert performance. The *Competencies* state in several places that librarians should use the *Guidelines for Behavioral Performance of Reference and Information Services* (RUSA, 2004) when providing reference services. This will be useful for the beginner, but should be fully mastered by the competent stage.

As the librarian becomes more experienced, her abilities shift as she becomes able to accomplish more of the activities in the *Competencies*. In the Access domain, consider the following strategies for achieving the RUSA-stated goal of responsiveness. The *Competencies* state that this goal can be achieved in part when the librarian determines the situational context of user needs, and analyzes and recommends information sources. As the evidence in this study indicates, the ability of the librarian to perceive and assess situational aspects – including client characteristics, information needs, and information resource and process aspects – changes as the librarian gains experience. The expert not only rapidly perceives situational aspects, but intuitively knows which are relevant and which can be ignored. The most appropriate solution presents itself unconsciously and intuitively. The beginner would be able to recognize aspects if they had been taught or experienced; competent practitioners would recognize more situations. At the proficient level, the librarian is able to perceive and sort out contextual information quickly, but still falls back on systematic analysis for decision making.

In another section of the *Competencies*, librarians are required to "engage users in discussions about their experience related to their information needs and communicate interest in every user's experience." Librarians in this study at the competent level were able to rapidly identify resources they believe will meet the client's needs. However, it is not until the proficient stage that librarians demonstrated their affinity for interacting with the client and discerning these more subtle factors.

Another RUSA strategy directs librarians to design and develop information tools and resources, such as bibliographies, displays, tutorials, and so on, to meet the needs of the primary community. These strategies generalize clients, without discriminating between differences within groups, across situations, or other contextual elements. This type of direction is sufficient for competent performers who are keen to organize work this way, but it is not an exemplar of expert performance.

These are just a few examples of the mixed presentation of skill in the *Competencies*. A summary of skill development represented in the

Table 3. Summary of Skill Development within the RUSA *Competencies.*

Practice Domain	Beginner	Competent	Proficient	Expert
Access	Suggests specific materials for clients; creates bibliographies	Organizes/ synthesizes resources; evaluates use patterns	Applies knowledge of info seeking to services; designs services for special needs	Identifies new methods; makes changes
Knowledge base	Reads; attends conferences, seminars	Explores available technology; teaches, presents to clients; discusses issues with colleagues; mentors beginners	Integrates latest technologies; reviews manuscripts for colleagues	Identifies new methods of service; makes changes; experiments with innovation
Marketing	N/A	Determines user focus	Scans environment for new technology; conducts surveys, collects data; develops PR plan to promote services	Networks/consults with other libraries; meets with community leaders; develops partnering models
Collaboration	Uses guidelines; asks for help	Shares knowledge; participates on teams	Evaluates team effectiveness	Identifies outside partners; creates networks
Evaluation	Uses guidelines	Assesses content, authority; reads/ writes reviews	Develops consensus on standards; identifies impediments; finds alternatives; assesses distribution of services	Communicates with information resource designers; assesses new technology; experiments with changes

Competencies follows in Table 3. The appendix provides a detailed breakdown of each of the goals and associated strategies in the *Competencies* by Dreyfus skill level, based on the evidence provided in the narratives.

CONCLUSION

This study of reference skill suggests a new language of expertise for reference work. Whereas before we were limited to a recitation of tasks and behaviors, the Dreyfus model provides a way to describe skill levels for beginner, competent, proficient, and expert librarians. Of the many questions raised by the study, I will mention just a few here, all having to do with what comes next. First, what role should teaching and collaboration play for librarians in academic environments? What are the implications for continuing library education at different skill levels? How can we improve how we organize and manage reference work for individuals at different skill levels?

First, on collaboration and teaching: many librarians actively work with students and teachers in classrooms, developing curriculum that incorporates domain knowledge and resource evaluation. The narratives of this study indicate that this collaboration contributes to closer engagement with client learning and greater perception of problems and influences outside the library. The practical knowledge gained through such collaboration can be used to benefit more clients in new ways – such as expanding the local librarian communities of practice to encompass clients and others. There could be many avenues for expanding reference work beyond library, classroom, and institutional walls.

Second, although this study was not concerned with learning styles per se, the data here suggest that different ways of learning are associated with differences in performance mode, situational perception, and role perception. The observed shift in perceptual acuity, situatedness, and relationships with others suggests that beginners might have learning needs that are different from competent librarians, and so on. Different approaches to teaching might be appropriate. What are these different approaches and how can we incorporate them into the current system?

One example comes to mind. The beginner's comfort level with rules and structures suggests that this group would be able to readily absorb a great deal of learning about information sources and structures. Competent performers who are still engrossed in this systematic approach might be well suited to lead this type of training. Proficient librarians, on the other hand, are beginning to shift their attention to relating to clients on a closer level. Perhaps experts who are more engaged and responsive in this area would be best positioned to help proficient librarians continue to develop these skills.

How might work organization take advantage of this? The study suggests that beginner librarians rely on others to a greater extent than is currently acknowledged. Scheduling, workplace arrangements, and job design are all areas which could benefit from changes based on skill level. Opportunities to share practical knowledge should be developed. Some library studies professional programs and associations already provide informal mentoring for new professionals, but formalized preceptorships would bring librarians at different skill levels together to reflect on practice in a more structured way. One thing is clear: librarians need to share their knowledge and skills with each other, and should have increased opportunities and encouragement to do so.

Finally, I believe the model opens the door to avenues of advancement in the way we organize work, the way we look at performance appraisal, and the way we describe what we do. Much needs to be done to improve how we manage these areas. In the early days of library job analysis – close to one hundred years ago – library work was conceived of in a highly organized, linear fashion which we have carried forward to this day. Our work today is vastly different; the technological environment we work in is no longer simple or straightforward. We have to learn new things, every day, in a much more intellectually intense environment. My hope is that this study will help us envision how to best nurture skill development as the library workplace continues to evolve.

REFERENCES

American Library Association. (1998). *Library education and personnel utilization: A statement of policy adopted by the American Library Association.* Chicago, IL: American Library Association.

Association of Research Libraries. (1997). *SPEC Kit 224: Staff training and development.* Washington, DC: Association of Research Libraries.

Association of Research Libraries. (2002). *SPEC Kit 270, core competencies.* Washington, DC: Association of Research Libraries.

Association of Southeastern Research Libraries. (2000). *Shaping the future: ASERL's competencies for research librarians* (Accessed December 11, 2003 at http://www.aserl.org). Atlanta, GA: Association of Southeastern Research Libraries.

Attewell, P. (1990). What is skill? *Work and Occupations, 17,* 422–448.

Bandura, A. (1977). *Social learning theory.* Englewood Cliffs, NJ: Prentice-Hall.

Barab, S., Barnett, M., & Squire, K. (2002). Developing an empirical account of a community of practice: Characterizing the essential tensions. *Journal of the Learning Sciences, 11,* 489–542.

Barley, S. R. (1996). *The new world of work.* London: British North American Research.

Bell, S. E. (1999). Narratives and lives: Women's health politics and the diagnosis of cancer for DES daughters. *Narrative Inquiry, 9,* 347–389.

Benner, P. (1982). *From novice to expert: Excellence and power in clinical nursing practice.* Menlo Park: Addison-Wesley.

Benner, P. (2004). Using the Dreyfus model of skill acquisition to describe and interpret skill acquisition and clinical judgment in nursing practice and education. *Bulletin of Science, Technology, & Society, 24,* 188–199.

Bopp, R. E., & Smith, L. C. (1995). *Reference and information services: An introduction.* Englewood, CO: Libraries Unlimited.

Borman, W., & Ackerman, L. (1992). Time-spent responses as time allocation strategies: Relations with sales performance in a stockbroker sample. *Personnel Psychology, 45,* 763–777.

Bunge, C. A. (1984). Interpersonal dimensions of the reference interview: A historical review of the literature. *Drexel Library Quarterly, 20,* 4–23.

Cain, C. (1991). Personal stories: Identity acquisition and self-understanding in alcoholics anonymous. *Ethos, 19,* 210–253.

Cain, P. S., & Treiman, D. S. (1981). The *Dictionary of Occupational Titles* as a source of occupational data. *American Sociological Review, 46,* 253–278.

Carnoy, M. (1997). The new information technology: International diffusion and its impact on employment and skills: A review of the literature. *International Journal of Manpower, 18,* 119.

Carr, D. (1983). Adult learning and library helping. *Library Trends, 31,* 569–583.

Case, D. O. (2002). *Looking for information: A survey of research on information seeking, needs, and behavior.* New York, NY: Academic Press.

Chin, N. P., Aligne, C. A., Stronczek, A., Shipley, L. J., & Kaczorowski, J. (2003). Evaluation of a community-based pediatrics residency rotation using narrative analysis. *Academic Medicine, 78,* 1266–1270.

Cohler, B. (1982). Personal narrative and life course. In: P. Baltes & O. Brim (Eds), *Life-span development and behavior* (pp. 205–241). New York, NY: Academic.

Daiute, C., & Nelson, K. (1997). Making sense of the sense-making function of narrative evaluation. In: M. G. Bamberg (Ed.), *Oral versions of personal experience: Three decades of narrative analysis* (pp. 207–215). Mahwah, NJ: Erlbaum.

Dervin, B. (1976). Strategies for dealing with human information needs: Information or communication? *Journal of Broadcasting, 20,* 324–333.

Dervin, B. (1983). *An overview of sense-making research: Concepts, methods and results to date.* Seattle, WA: School of Communications, University of Washington.

Dervin, B., & Dewdney, P. (1986). Neutral questioning: A new approach to the reference interview. *RQ, 25,* 506–513.

Dewdney, P., & Michell, G. (1996). Oranges and peaches: Understanding communication accidents in the reference interview. *RQ, 35,* 520–536.

Dewdney, P., & Michell, G. (1997). Asking 'why' questions in the reference interview: A theoretical justification. *Library Quarterly, 67,* 50–71.

Dewdney, P., & Ross, C. S. (1994). Flying a light aircraft: Reference service evaluation from a user's viewpoint. *RQ, 34,* 217–231.

Dilevko, J. (2000). *Unobtrusive evaluation of reference service and individual responsibility: The Canadian experience.* Westport, CT: Ablex.

Dreyfus, H. L., & Dreyfus, S. E. (1986). *Mind over machine: The power of human intuition and expertise in the era of the computer.* New York, NY: Free Press.

Engeström, Y. (2000). Activity theory as a framework for analyzing and redesigning work. *Ergonomics, 43,* 960–974.

Engeström, Y., & Middleton, D. (1996). *Cognition and communication at work.* New York, NY: Cambridge University Press.

Fisher, W. (2001). Core competencies for the acquisitions librarian. *Library Collections, Acquisitions, and Technical Services, 25,* 179–190.

Galvin, T. J. (1965). *Problems in reference service: Case studies in method and policy.* New York, NY: R.R. Bowker.

Geertz, C. (1973). *The interpretation of cultures.* New York, NY: Basic Books.

Germain, C. A., Jacobson, T. E., & Kaczor, S. A. (2000). A comparison of the effectiveness of presentation formats for instruction: Teaching first-year students. *College and Research Libraries, 61,* 65–72.

Gers, R., & Seward, L. J. (1985). Improving reference performance: Results of a statewide survey. *Library Journal, 110,* 32–35.

Glogoff, S. (1983). Communication theory's role in the reference interview. *Drexel Library Quarterly, 19,* 56–72.

Gothberg, H. (1976). Immediacy: A study of communication effect on the reference process. *Journal of Academic Librarianship, 2,* 126–129.

Griffiths, J., & King, D. (1986). *New directions in library and information science education.* New York, NY: Knowledge Industry Publications.

Grogan, D. J. (1979). *Practical reference work.* London: Bingley.

Grogan, D. J. (1987). *Grogan's case studies in reference work.* London: Bingley.

Haag-Heitman, B., & Kramer, A. (1998). Creating a clinical practice development model. *American Journal of Nursing, 98,* 39–43.

Harris, R., & Michell, B. G. (1986). The social context of reference work: Assessing the effects of gender and communication skill on observers' judgments of competence. *Library and Information Science Research, 8,* 85–101.

Heidegger, M. (1962). *Being and time.* New York, NY: Harper & Row.

Henning, P. H. (1998). Ways of learning: An ethnographic study of the work and situated learning of a group of refrigeration service technicians. *Journal of Contemporary Ethnography, 27,* 85–136.

Hirschorn, L. (1984). *Beyond mechanization: Work and technology in a postindustrial age.* Cambridge, MA: MIT Press.

Hittner, A. (1981). Individual rating scale for communication skills ... in-service training program for library paraprofessionals workshop evaluation and pre-test/post-test. In: D. R. Bafundo (Ed.), *In-service training program for library paraprofessionals: A report.* Fairfax, VA: Consortium for Continuing Higher Education in Northern Virginia. (ERIC Document Reproduction Service no. ED 207 536).

Holmes, J., & Meyerhoff, M. (1999). The community of practice: Theories and methodologies in language and gender research. *Language in Society, 28,* 173–183.

Howe, L. (1977). *Pink collar workers.* New York, NY: Putnam.

Hutchins, E. (1995). *Cognition in the wild.* Cambridge, MA: MIT Press.

Hutchins, M. (1944). *Introduction to reference work.* Chicago, IL: American Library Association.

Katz, W. A. (1982). *Introduction to reference work* (4th ed.). New York, NY: McGraw-Hill.

Kazlauskas, E. (1976). An exploratory study: A kinesic analysis of academic library public service points. *Journal of Academic Librarianship, 2,* 130–134.

King, L., & Clark, J. M. (2002). Intuition and the development of expertise in surgical ward and intensive care nurses. *Journal of Advanced Nursing, 37,* 322–329.

Kuhlthau, C. C. (1993). *Seeking meaning: A process approach to library and information services.* Norwood, NJ: Ablex.

Kuhlthau, C. C. (1994). Students and the information search process: Zones of intervention for librarians. *Advances in Librarianship, 18,* 57–109.

Laufer, E. A., & Glick, J. (1996). Expert and novice differences in cognition and activity: A practical work activity. In: Y. Engeström & D. Middleton (Eds), *Cognition and communication at work* (pp. 177–198). New York, NY: Cambridge University Press.

Lave, J. (1988). *Cognition in practice: Mind, mathematics and culture in everyday life.* New York, NY: Cambridge University Press.

Lynch, M. J. (1983). Research in library reference/information service. *Library Trends, 31,* 401–419.

Maack, M. N. (1997). Toward a new model of the information professions: Embracing empowerment. *Journal of Education for Library and Information Science, 38,* 283–302.

Mabry, C. H. (2003). The reference interview as partnership: An examination of librarian, library user, and social interaction. *The Reference Librarian, 83/84,* 41–56.

Matarazzo, J. M. (1971). *Library problems in science and technology.* New York, NY: R.R. Bowker.

McCormick, E. J., Jeanneret, P., & Mecham, R. C. (1969). *The development and background of the Position Analysis Questionnaire.* Lafayette, IN: Occupational Research Center, Purdue University.

Mehrabian, A. (1971). *Silent messages.* Belmont, CA: Wadsworth.

Mendelsohn, J. (1997). Perspectives on quality of reference service in an academic library: A qualitative study. *RQ, 36,* 544–557.

Mendelsohn, J. (1999). Learning electronic reference resources: A team-learning project for reference staff. *College & Research Libraries, 60,* 372–383.

Meretoja, R., Eriksson, E., & Leino-Kilpi, H. (2002). Indicators for competent nursing practice. *Journal of Nursing Management, 10,* 95–102.

Merikangas, R. J. (1982). Librarian and client: Who's in charge? In: M. D. Kathman & V. Massman (Eds), *Options for the 80's: Proceedings of the second national conference of the Association of College and Research Libraries* (pp. 375–384). Greenwich, CT: JAI Press.

Michell, G., & Harris, R. M. (1987). Evaluating the reference interview: Some factors influencing patrons and professionals. *RQ,* 95–105.

Miller, A., Tremain, D., Cain, P., & Roos, P. (1980). *Work, jobs, and occupations: A critical review of the Dictionary of Occupational Titles.* Washington, DC: National Academy Press.

Mish, F. C., Gilman, E. W., Lowe, J. G., et al. (1986). *Webster's ninth new collegiate dictionary.* Springfield, MA: Merriam-Webster.

Mishler, E. G. (1986). *Research interviewing: Context and narrative.* Cambridge, MA: Harvard University Press.

Mishler, E. G. (1995). Models of narrative analysis: A typology. *Journal of Narrative and Life History, 5,* 87–123.

Mudge, I. G. (1936). *Guide to reference books, 6th edition.* Chicago, IL: American Library Association.

Munson, K. I., & Walton, L. J. (2004). Assessing reference staff competency in the electronic environment. *Medical Reference Services Quarterly, 23,* 33–40.

Naismith, R. (1996). Reference communication: Commonalities in the worlds of medicine and librarianship. *College and Research Libraries, 57,* 44–57.

Nicol, M. J., Fox-Hiley, A., Bavin, C. J., & Sheng, R. (1996). Assessment of clinical and communication skills: Operationalizing Benner's model. *Nurse Education Today, 16,* 175–179.

Nielson, B. (1982). Teachers or intermediary: Alternative professional models in the information age. *College and Research Libraries, 43,* 183–191.

O'Donnell, D., Porter, G., McGuire, D., Garavan, T. N., Heffernan, M., & Cleary, P. (2003). Creating intellectual capital: A Habermasian community of practice (CoP) introduction. *Journal of European Industrial Training, 27,* 80–87.

Parson, L. C. (1988). *Continuing professional education of academic librarians in Massachusetts: Practices, perceptions and preferences.* Doctoral dissertation, Texas Women's University. ProQuest Digital Dissertations, Accession no. AAT 8821416.

Patel, V. L., Glaser, R., & Arocha, J. F. (2000). Cognition and expertise: Acquisition of medical competence. *Clinical and Investigative Medicine, 23,* 256–260.

Radcliff, C. J. (1995). Interpersonal communication with library patrons: Physician–patient research models. *RQ, 34,* 497–596.

Rader, H. (1980). Reference services as a teaching function. *Library Trends, 29,* 95–103.

Radford, M. L. (1999). *The reference encounter: Interpersonal communication in the academic library.* Chicago, IL: Association of College and Research Libraries.

Reference and User Services Association (RUSA). (2004). *Guidelines for behavioral performance of reference and information services professionals.* Also available from: http://www.ala.org/ala/rusa/rusaprotools/referenceguide/guidelinesbehavioral.htm (retrieved December 13, 2005). Chicago, IL: American Library Association.

Reference and User Services Association (RUSA) Task Force on Professional Competencies. (2003). Professional competencies for reference and user services librarians. *Reference and User Services Quarterly, 42,* 290–295. Also available from: http://www.ala.org/ala/rusa/rusaprotools/referenceguide/professional.htm (retrieved December 12, 2005).

Richardson, J. V., Jr. (1992). Teaching general reference work: The complete paradigm and competing schools of thought, 1890–1990. *Library Quarterly, 62,* 55–89.

Richardson, J. V., Jr. (2002). The current state of research on reference transactions. In: *Advances in librarianship* (pp. 175–230). New York: Academic Press.

Ricking, M., & Booth, R. E. (1974). *Personnel utilization in libraries: A systems approach.* Chicago, IL: American Library Association.

Riessman, C. K. (1993). *Narrative analysis.* Newbury Park, CA: Sage.

Rogoff, B. (1984). Thinking and learning in social context. In: B. Rogoff & J. Lave (Eds), *Everyday cognition: Its development in social context.* Cambridge, MA: Harvard University Press.

Rothstein, S. (1983). The making of a reference librarian. *Library Trends, 31,* 375–399.

Sarbin, T. (1986). The narrative as a root metaphor for psychology. In: T. Sarbin (Ed.), *Narrative psychology: The storied nature of human conduct* (pp. 3–21). New York, NY: Praeger.

Saxton, M. L., & Richardson, J. V. (2002). *Understanding reference transactions: Transforming art into a science.* New York, NY: Academic Press.

Schön, D. A. (1983). *The reflective practitioner: How professionals think in action.* New York, NY: Basic Books.

Schwartz, D. G., & Eakin, D. (1986). Reference service standards, performance criteria, and evaluation. *Journal of Academic Librarianship, 12,* 4–8.

Shaughnessy, T. W. (1992). Approaches to developing competencies in research libraries. *Library Trends, 41,* 282–298.

Sherrer, J. (1995). Thriving in changing times: Competencies for today's reference librarians. *Reference Librarian, 54,* 11–20.

Shulman, L. S. (2000). Teacher development: Roles of domain expertise and pedagogical knowledge. *Journal of Applied Developmental Psychology, 21,* 129–135.

Spenner, K. I. (1990). Skill: Meanings, methods, and measures. *Work and Occupations, 17,* 399–421.

Stasz, C. (2001). Assessing skills for work: Two perspectives. *Oxford Economic Papers, 3,* 385–405.

Stevens, P. E., & Doerr, B. T. (1997). Trauma of discovery: Women's narratives of being informed they are HIV-infected. *AIDS Care, 9,* 523–538.

Sweeney, J. K. (2006). *Interpreting skill development in academic library reference work: An application of the Dreyfus model.* Doctoral dissertation, University of California, Los Angeles. ProQuest Digital Dissertations, Accession no. AAT.

The American Library Association Reference and Adult Services Committee (Compilation and Editing) (1995). *The Reference Assessment Manual.* Ann Arbor, MI: Pieran Press.

Thomas, D. M., Hinckley, A. T., & Eisenbach, E. R. (1981). *The effective reference librarian.* New York, NY: Academic Press.

Throsby, K. (2002). Negotiating 'normality' when IVF fails. *Narrative Inquiry, 12,* 43–65.

Trowler, P., & Turner, G. (2002). Exploring the hermeneutical foundations of university life: Deaf academics in a hybrid 'community of practice'. *Higher Education, 43,* 227–256.

United States Department of Labor. (2003a). *Dictionary of occupational titles* (4th ed. Revised). Washington, DC: US Government Printing Office.

United States Department of Labor. (2003b). Employment and Training Administration. *O*Net Online: Occupational Information Network.* Retrieved June 4, 2003 from http://online.onetcenter.org

Vallas, S. P. (1990). The concept of skill: A critical review. *Work and Occupations, 17,* 379–398.

Varlejs, J. (1996). *Librarians' self-directed continuing professional learning.* Doctoral dissertation, University of Wisconsin, Madison. ProQuest Digital Dissertations, Accession no. AAT 9622535.

Wenger, E. (1998). *Communities of practice: Learning, meaning, and identity.* New York, NY: Cambridge University Press.

White, M. D. (1985). Evaluation of the reference interview. *RQ, 24,* 76–84.

Whitlatch, J. B. (1990). Reference service effectiveness. *RQ, 30,* 205–220.

Williamson, C. C. (1971). *The Williamson Reports of 1921 and 1923: Including training for library work (1921) and training for library service (1923).* Metuchen, NJ: Scarecrow.

Wyer, J. I. (1930). *Reference work: A textbook for students of library work and librarians.* Chicago, IL: American Library Association.

APPENDIX. RUSA COMPETENCIES BY DREYFUS SKILL LEVEL

Table A1. RUSA *Competencies* for the Beginner Skill Level.

Practice Domain	Goal	Strategy
Access	Responsiveness	• Uses "guidelines" for interpersonal behavior • Suggests specific works • Analyzes information sources for each user
	Organization and design of services	• Creates bibliographies • Uses "guidelines" for searching
	Critical thinking and analysis	• Connects users with recommended resources • Uses "guidelines" for follow-up
Knowledge base	Environmental scanning	• Reads to keep current in users' relevant areas • Attends exhibits • Reads to keep current on information sources • Reads about materials of interest to users
	Application of knowledge	• Reads literature and applies to improve practice
	Dissemination of knowledge	• Creates web pages • Participates in discussions
Collaboration	Relationships with users	• Uses "guidelines" on listening, searching, follow-up
	Relationships with colleagues	• Recognizes unique knowledge of colleagues • Elicits help when needed
	Relationships within the profession	• Uses "guidelines" for follow-up
Evaluation and assessment of resources and services	Information service providers	• Identifies and uses measures developed by the profession such as "Guidelines for Behavioral Performance"

Source: Reference and User Services Association Task Force on Professional Competencies (2003).

Table A2. RUSA *Competencies* for the Competent Skill Level.

Practice Domain	Goal	Strategy
Access	Critical thinking and analysis	• Synthesizes information resources • Evaluates information use patterns
	Organization and design of services	• Organizes resources to match users' information seeking process • Organizes resources meaningfully
Knowledge base	Application of knowledge	• Explores available technology
	Dissemination of knowledge	• Teaches classes • Prepares presentations • Discusses issues with colleagues • Mentors colleagues
Marketing, awareness, informing	Assessment	• Determines user focus
Collaboration	Relationships with colleagues	• Shares knowledge • Participates in team development • Works effectively as part of a team • Models effective team behavior • Develops shared goals and values
	Relationships with users	• Acknowledges limits of local resources
Evaluation and assessment of resources and services	Information resources	• Assesses content of resources • Determines authority of resources • Identifies bias • Evaluates new information resources • Reads reviews • Writes and publishes reviews
	Information services	• Analyzes and uses resources effectively
	Service delivery	• Determines appropriate technology and delivery channels
	User needs	• Identifies user population • Plans and conducts regular assessments of information needs

Source: See Table A1.

Table A3. RUSA *Competencies* for the Proficient Skill Level.

Practice Domain	Goal	Strategy
Access	Critical thinking and analysis	• Applies knowledge of information seeking to services
	Organization and design of services	• Designs services to meet special needs • Compiles information about community resources
	Responsiveness	• Determines situational context • Talks with users about • Empowers users experiences
Knowledge base	Dissemination of knowledge	• Reviews draft manuscripts
	Environmental scanning	• Scans environment for emerging technologies
Marketing, awareness, informing	Assessment	• Conducts surveys, focus groups • Evaluates background • Implements reference program research
	Communication and outreach	• Develops marketing plan • Develops PR plan • Creates physical environment to encourage use • Promotes reference services via electronic media • Uses print media to communicate reference services • Promotes services through lectures, programs, tours, etc.
	Evaluation	• Conducts meetings and training sessions to gather feedback • Engages users in focus groups, surveys • Evaluates trends and adjusts services • Identifies strengths and weaknesses

Table A3. *(Continued)*

Practice Domain	Goal	Strategy
Collaboration	Relationships with users	• Asks user's opinion • Acknowledges knowledge user brings to the interaction • Involves user in decision
Evaluation and assessment of resources and services	Information interfaces	• Determines if there are alternative resources with better interfaces
	Information service providers	• Develops assessment measures • Develops consensus of service standards • Supports espirit de corps to evaluate and improve service behaviors
	Information services	• Develops and incorporates evaluation measures into new services • Develops service standards • Creates organizational climate for consistent evaluation against standards
	Service delivery	• Assesses distribution of resources
	User needs	• Translates users needs into service plan
	Application of knowledge	• Integrates use of latest technology

Source: See Table A1.

Table A4. RUSA *Competencies* for the Expert Skill Level.

Practice Domain	Goal	Strategy
Collaboration	Relationships beyond the library and profession	• Identifies partners • Communicates effectively with partners • Forms partnerships to improve services
	Relationships within the profession	• Networks with professional organizations • Identifies partners • Participates in collaborative efforts to improve services
	Information interfaces	• Communicates with resource designers
	Service delivery	• Assess new technologies for effectiveness without disenfranchising users • Experiments with services changes
Knowledge base	Application of knowledge	• Experiments with innovations to assist user
Marketing, awareness, informing	Assessment	• Consults with other libraries to network and brainstorm
	Evaluation	• Identifies new methods of service • Decides what changes to make
	Communication and outreach	• Develops partnering models with community groups • Meets with community leaders

Source: See Table A1.

CORPORATE CULTURE AND THE INDIVIDUAL IN PERSPECTIVE

Charles B. Osburn

ABSTRACT

Corporate culture is a spirit formed by the shared values of the individuals in the organization that has potential to make the library more than the sum of its parts, both positively and negatively. It is the vehicle by which the organization defines itself, for both itself and the clientele, with the purpose of providing the best service possible by sharing a vision of the organization as an organic whole. It operates through the power of peer influence rather than direct vertical authority. This paper takes a holistic approach to a concept that is more complex than it first appears; it addresses the molding of corporate culture, not as a management function, but as a complex and deep system, being in effect the soul of the organization, which resides in the motivation of each individual and which, therefore, requires a special kind of leadership.

INTRODUCTION

Especially since the advent of the World Wide Web charged a new infusion of information technologies and services in the mid-1990s, librarianship has manifested a surge of interest in the theory of organization[1] and, more specifically, in organizational development. Behavioral science presents so

Advances in Library Administration and Organization, Volume 26, 41–70
ISSN: 0732-0671/doi:10.1016/S0732-0671(08)00202-2

strong an attraction at this time because its purpose is to help the corporate entity design strategies for coping with change, both evolutionary and deep, the kind of change that envelopes libraries of all types.

At the center of organizational development is the notion of an organizational or corporate culture.[2] For example, just as the quality of the individual assigned to a specific set of responsibilities largely determines the success or failure of that function, so does the quality of the corporate culture hold great potential to determine the extent to which the mission of the entire organization is fulfilled. Corporate culture has the potential to make the organization more than the sum of its parts. Yet, sometimes it can be responsible for making the organization even less than the expected sum of its parts, so it is important to note that there exists a corporate culture whether or not management cares or does anything about it. Management can guide and foster the corporate culture, but, by definition, corporate culture is adopted and maintained by virtually everyone in the organization. As managers of people and ideas, librarians play a very critical part in molding and maintaining the strength of the corporate culture of the library so that the potential of the organic whole[3] can be optimized.

There are many definitions of corporate culture, but most share essential characteristics. Accordingly, corporate culture is generally viewed as the "shared rules governing cognitive and affective aspects of membership in an organization, and the means whereby they are shaped and expressed" (Kunda, 1992, p. 8). Substantial research has led to greater specificity in distilling the definition of culture simply as guidance toward understanding what is important and what is acceptable feeling and behavior in the organization (Pfeffer, 1997, p. 121).

A distinguished research team concludes from their 10-year close analysis of organizations that "cultures can have powerful consequences, especially when they are strong. They can enable a group to take rapid and coordinated action against a competitor or for a customer" (Kotter & Heskett, 1992, p. 8). Of course, as they also point out, cultures can guide action toward results that are not so desirable. The literature of corporate culture has become voluminous, much of it, if not most, having been drawn from research in the field.[4] And although this research focuses almost entirely on the business and industrial setting, it is rich in possibilities for libraries. The generalized findings are particularly applicable to the library, in as much as there is strong consensus that "only cultures that can help organizations anticipate and adapt to environmental change will be associated with superior performance over long periods of time" (Kotter & Heskett, 1992, p. 44). Surely environmental change and its attendant demand for innovation have posed the greatest challenges to librarianship in recent decades. So it is easy to see why considerable attention has been turning to questions of how libraries are organized, how communication should flow, how employees see themselves and their place in the organization, and how decisions are made. Attention has been turning to matters of corporate culture.

This paper synthesizes the most fundamental considerations of corporate culture as they are applied in research and in formal activities like workshops that focus on planning and human resources development. It is my observation that the library profession, while desirous of benefiting fully from the theory and research of organizational development, tends to address the resultant strategies as isolated fragments rather than as an interwoven fabric of principles and ideas, and that this practice can, in the long run, lead to misunderstanding, perhaps even to failure. Furthermore, the literature also suggests that very often the individual is overlooked in the shadows of the broader establishment of the organization as an organic whole since the advancement of the latter perspective is the objective of organizational development. Therefore, throughout this paper a recurrent theme is the disposition of the individual in the life of a library organization, wherein the environment rapidly is becoming more demanding as a result of both the change within it and the organization's planned response to it.

BACKGROUND

To appreciate more fully the current level of attention accorded to the corporate culture of the library, it is useful to understand the context surrounding the relevant theory as it has been formulated over a fairly broad expanse of time. And, in considering the various principles and strategies entailed more generally in organizational development, it is essential to bear in mind that, ultimately, it all has to do with the structuring of employees to accomplish the common goals of the organization's work. The bare essentials of this effort in any organization are well summarized by Gideon Kunda:

> Purposeful collective action, whatever its circumstances, requires the coordination of activities of a diverse and heterogeneous membership. There is, however, an inherent conflict between demands organizations place on the time and efforts of their members and the desires and needs of members when left to their own devices. Thus, the age-old management dilemma: how to cause members to behave in ways compatible with organizational goals. (Kunda, 1992, p. 11)

Theories behind the structuring of people to accomplish the goals and objectives of the organization have abounded for a very long time. Looking back just two centuries, for example, Scottish economist and philosopher Adam Smith gained recognition largely because of his book, which, under its abridged title, *The Wealth of Nations*, advanced theories in 1776 about the value that would be derived from productive labor, meaning labor that would be efficient and effective. Bureaucracy had been a strategy for organizing work for millennia before Smith wrote his treatise, which was timely nonetheless in linking the attributes of the bureaucracy (division of labor, specialization, and mass production) to economic benefit. But the theory that devolved from these ideas focused more on the individual than on the organization as a whole, and certainly did not focus on the organization as an organic whole as we tend to envision it today. In spite of that, it is useful to remember that Smith's focus on the individual more than two centuries ago portrayed the individual as more of a cog-on-the-wheel of production than as a rational, yet sensitive, being.

Theories that emerged during the 19th and 20th centuries reflected Adam Smith's ideas, both by adopting them and by reacting against them. During the 19th century, the form of organization that had come to be known as the bureaucracy found preference in reaction to the communal systems of organization, which had become pervasive. In communal forms of organization, personal matters, such as family, religious, and social associations that emphasized the private side of the individual, tended to account for the level of influence and authority assigned by the organization (Heckscher, 1994, p. 19). When the concept of the bureaucracy, which had been formulated over a long period of time, coincided with the Industrial Revolution, it quickly became the standard, and eventually was adopted even in popular conversation, albeit often derisively.[5]

It is worth noting that, as heavily discussed in the literature of management as bureaucracy has been, Charles Heckscher (1994) finds that the major concepts articulated a century ago by Max Weber[6] are still those "used by most managers in their conscious planning: rationality, account- ability, hierarchy" (p. 19). He also points out that Weber's central concept was the "differentiation of person from *office* ... which was one of the most important breaks with prior tradition ..." (Heckscher, 1994, p. 19). The objectivity of science was to be the efficient and effective replacement for the subjectivity of person in the clockwork organization. During the 20th century, the mounting need for greater resilience of organizational adaptability to the changing environment dramatically revealed the inherent weaknesses of the bureaucratic organization, which are addressed below.

Thus, the flatter, more participatory organization emerged[7] to emphasize the organization as a much more dynamic entity, an organic whole.

This is the barest outline of research and theory in organizational development leading to the present. The remainder of this paper examines more closely some of the key elements of research-based theory that have given and are giving direction to the manner in which organizations are perceived to consolidate their efforts in the interest of enhancing effectiveness.

ENVIRONMENTAL CHANGE

The history of disenchantment with bureaucracy probably goes back as far as bureaucracy itself. In fact, William Starbuck (2003) points out that one of two themes dominating the literature that can be claimed for organizational theory during the century following 1860 had to do with the defects of bureaucracy (p. 161), and he summarizes the writings of the more influential thinkers of the period (pp. 162–166). But it was primarily with the recognition that environmental change was outstripping the pace of managed change in organizations of the mid-20th century that the call for a new order was sounded.

> There is a growing feeling that modern organizations, and particularly the large, bureaucratic business and government organizations, need to increase their capacity to innovate. This feeling stems in part from the obvious fact of the increased rate of change, especially technological change, but also from a rejection of the older process of innovation through the birth of new organizations and the death or failure of old ones. (Thompson, 1965, p. 1)

It is useful to note in this statement that Victor Thompson was contemplating in 1965 the expression of forward-thinking academics and executives of his day. He also prescribed the desired innovative organization pretty much as it is described today in the literature of organizational development (Thompson, 1965, pp. 10–18). In stressing the need for innovation, he observed that the concept implies the capacity to change or adapt, and made the significant distinction that "An adaptive organization may not be innovative (because it does not generate many new ideas), but an innovative organization will be adaptive (because it is able to implement many new ideas)" (Thompson, 1965, p. 2). He stated that "Conflict ... encourages innovations. Other things being equal, the less bureaucratized (monocratic) the organization, the more conflict and uncertainty and the more innovation"

(Thompson, 1965, p. 4). He also related the time-honored debate about reward systems and individual motivation to the demands of organizational change, noting that "the hierarchy of authority stimulates conformity rather than innovation ... Creativity is promoted by an internal commitment, by intrinsic rewards for the most part" (Thompson, 1965, p. 5). More to that point, Thompson (1965) wrote that "The relationship between personal and organizational goals, ideally, would seem to be where individuals perceive the organization as an avenue for professional growth" (p. 11). Again, these were not necessarily Thompson's original thoughts nearly a half century ago, but rather his summary reflection of contemporary thinking.

PURPOSEFUL CULTURE

According to Heckscher, the notion of a strong organizational culture is not a new one, for it developed at least as early as the 1920s in opposition to the bureaucracies that had developed within most corporations. At that time, "corporate leaders began consciously structuring their organizations as *communities*, stressing values of loyalty and cooperation" (Heckscher, 1994, p. 30). Such considerations constitute the most fundamental elements of culture.[8]

So, organizational development, which is founded on the concept of a corporate culture, emerged primarily from the recognition of a higher level of requirements for the organization in its effort to cope effectively and efficiently with a new order of environmental change. This proved to be a capability that the bureaucracy could not achieve, for it had been designed and employed to be effective in a fairly static environment. Whereas "Cultures can be very stable over time, but they are never static" (Kotter & Heskett, 1992, p. 7). And some problems of bureaucracy seem to be inherent even in those that are well managed. The top three among them are that people are responsible only for their own jobs, that bureaucracy fails at effectively controlling the "informal" organization (the systems for accomplishing work without encountering the formal bottlenecks inherent in bureaucratic structures), and that it does not manage processes effectively over time (Heckscher, 1994, pp. 20–23).

In general, the management strategy to move away from the use of power by authority as the lever for organizational change, which characterizes the bureaucratic hierarchy toward the use of peer influence as the means to that end, became the new standard. Peer influence was targeted because "... peers do constitute strong influences on individual behavior, and ... a process of change successfully initiated in a peer group may become self-energizing and self-reinforcing" (Katz & Kahn, 1966, p. 450). An ostensibly grassroots movement to identify and strengthen values held in common by peers as a way to move the entire organization through the onslaught of challenges posed by its environment holds very practical benefits for the organization: it reduces the frequent negative reaction to authority, it enhances communication throughout the organization, and it helps satisfy the need of employees to see their contribution to the greater enterprise. In short, "Culture as a social control mechanism is important because it offers several advantages over external control accomplished through rewards and sanctions" (Pfeffer, 1997, p. 123). But from the strict standpoint of corporate results, the single most significant contribution of the flatter or less rigid hierarchical organization is the greater quantity and higher quality of information that can be brought to bear on any issue.

> "The most important strength is that decisions result from a thorough 'mixing' of the intelligence found throughout the organization. For that reason one would expect the decisions to be better, especially in the long run ... We know that bureaucracies tend to become conservative and inward-focused, missing the implications of important changes. The mixing of intelligence is the best mechanism for avoiding this danger ..." and there is "the probability that an interactive structure is better for the creation of evolutionarily new forms." (Heckscher, 1994, pp. 50–51)

And so, the nurturing of a corporate culture − not just any culture, but a culture attuned to the advancement of the executive vision for the formal organization − became the dominant management strategy in the 1980s. It was to be a strategy whereby everyone could become a winner. But the self-conscious nurturing of a corporate culture was a new and improved plan whose goal nonetheless remained that of maintaining control. Thus, instead of being controlled through manifest administrative force, the culture is managed through the less direct eliciting of "behavior consistent with cultural prescriptions" (Kunda, 1992, p. 218). John Kotter and James Heskett (1992) point out that the ideas embedded in a culture can originate anywhere in the organization, "But in firms with strong corporate cultures, these ideas often seem to be associated with a founder or other early leaders who articulate them as a 'vision,' a 'business strategy,' a 'philosophy,' or all three" (p. 7). In successful examples, the guiding principles come from the top.

Just as corporate culture is the nucleus of organizational development, values constitute the core of culture. Therefore, values figure foremost in molding the ethos of the workplace in an apparently less authority- and power-driven environment than is associated with the bureaucracy. This strategy is commonly called "reengineering." As defined by Michael

Hammer and James Champy (1993), reengineering is "the fundamental rethinking and radical redesign of business processes to achieve dramatic improvements in critical, contemporary measures of performance, such as cost, quality, service, and speed" (p. 32). Reorganization to such an extent was unprecedented in the mid-20th-century America, but its complexities were recognized immediately to be complex, rife with ambiguities, and stressful for all. And its implications went deep, because this effort demanded the adoption of an entirely new perspective on the manner in which the organization functions and how it communicates internally.

> When a company is taking its first steps toward reengineering, no one really knows exactly where it is heading; no one really knows exactly what it will become; no one really even knows which aspects of the current company will change, let alone precisely how. The vision is what a company believes it wants to achieve when it is done, and a well-drawn vision will sustain a company's resolve throughout the stress of the reengineering process. (Hammer & Champy, 1993, p. 154)

The foundation of corporate culture is constructed of the values held formally and promulgated throughout the organization. In fact, according to Jeffrey Pfeffer (1997, p. 121), some researchers have defined culture as a form of organizational control exercised through shared values, while he and Charles O'Reilly conclude from their collaborative research that "A value that is the basis for a set of norms or expectations about what are the appropriate attitudes and behaviors can act as a powerful social control system. This is what organizational culture really is: a social control system in which shared expectations guide people's behavior" (O'Reilly & Pfeffer, 2000, p. 238).

Of course, the work of any organization is performed by individuals, working together, to be sure, but individuals. So, just as the values of the organizational leadership are adopted by the collective workforce, they must be adopted by each individual in that workforce.[9] "For a person to succeed in any organization, he or she has to understand what is really important to that firm — its values ... The policies and practices of the company signal clearly what is valued and important" (O'Reilly & Pfeffer, 2000, p. 233).

The literature of organizational development is comprised of studies of a number of aspects of the change effort it entails, chief among which are leadership and several essential values: motivation and commitment, learning, flexibility, risk-taking, and participation. The most relevant research findings are summarized respectively in the following paragraphs.

Leadership

"The single most visible factor that distinguishes major cultural changes that succeed from those that fail is competent leadership at the top" (Kotter & Heskett, 1992, p. 84). By diminishing the importance of structured authority and power in the organization, the intensity of management supposedly gives way to the prominence of leadership. A useful distinction between the functions of management and leadership is proffered by John Kotter (1990, pp. 103–105), who describes the responsibility of management as coping with the many complexities of daily business, and the responsibility of leadership as orchestrating deeper change. The two functions are not mutually exclusive, of course, but they bear quite distinctive emphases that highlight the differences between the reengineered organization and the bureaucracy. It is clear that the replacement of the bureaucracy with a flatter, less clearly defined organizational structure introduces a less visible order. But, "Structureless does not mean leaderless" (Hammer, 2001, p. 145). And what permits this ambiguity to work well is the likelihood that some in the organization are as much driven to follow as others are to lead.

Most of these descriptive elements seem very positive, of course, because they are consciously determined to improve both corporate competitiveness and the prospects of the individual in the organization. To accomplish these goals requires that they be presented in the most favorable light and certainly without a hint of threat. As will be shown, however, experience with corporate culture as a control mechanism reveals an underlying perspective on management that is no less negative than the image projected by the bureaucratic forms of control and may even lend it a slightly insidious slant on the engineered environment. In 1956, when the memory of the tight bureaucracy was still fresh to make valid comparisons between that form of organization and the nascent reengineered forms and when leadership and management were held in the same few hands, William Whyte wrote in *The Organization Man* that, "No one wants to see the old authoritarian return, but at least it could be said of him that what he wanted primarily from you was your sweat. The new man wants your soul" (Whyte, 1956, p. 327; cited by Kunda, 1992, p. 15).

Motivation and Commitment

The elusive goal of management has long been that of motivating employees using one or both of two routes. Both, however, too often prove to be less than satisfactory. The bureaucratic organization relies on motivational forces such as financial reward, promotion, and sanction that are extrinsic to the individual, while post-bureaucratic theory endeavors to nurture motivation that is intrinsic to the individual through peer influence and an apparent broad distribution of power. The latter is based on the hardly disputable theory that people are driven from within as well as from without and internal motivations were believed to be of greater duration.[10] According to an analysis of the literature on this debate conducted by Judy Cameron and David Pierce (2002), "A prominent view states that rewards and reinforcement decrease a person's intrinsic motivation to engage in an activity" (p. 11). This assessment is well supported by Chris Argyris (1999), a leading scholar in the field of organizational behavior for more than a half century, who concluded that "Individuals whose commitment and motivation are external depend on their managers to give them the incentive to work" (p. 237). Cameron and Pierce (2002), however, take the debate a step further by arguing that the relevant research has not resulted in a discrediting of extrinsic motivation through reward, but rather that "it has revealed conditions under which a negative effect of promised reward will occur, and, inadvertently, it has revealed several conditions that result in positive effects of rewards" (p. 194). The baby need not be thrown out with the bath water.

Among the many hurdles encountered in developing a greater degree of intrinsic motivation throughout the organization, according to Chris Argyris (1999), is one posed by managers who "embrace the language of intrinsic motivation but fail to see how firmly mired in the old extrinsic world their communications actually are" (p. 236). The leadership may not be entirely on board during the voyage from the bureaucratic environment to the culture-oriented environment, and this is at a time when today's employees need to have "as much intrinsic motivation and as deep a sense of organizational stewardship as any company executive" (p. 238). Evidently, what is needed is more of a synergistic balance in extrinsic and intrinsic motivation, for it is not simply that either source of motivation fails to supply the desired result. "Instead, more effort needs to be devoted to the effective management of rewards in applied settings" (Cameron & Pierce, 2002, p. 232), as intrinsic motivation is nurtured. "Effective" is the operative adjective, but the reader is left to assume it means being especially sensitive to the particular nature of the influence that is generated by extrinsic reward when it is employed within the culture-driven organization.

Learning

In a dynamic environment, learning is considered essential to the success of the organization, for it is part and parcel of adaptation and innovation. David Garvin (1993, p. 80) describes the elements behind this notion, characterizing the learning organization as "an organization skilled at creating, acquiring, and transferring knowledge, and at modifying its behavior to reflect new knowledge and insights".[11] He goes on to demonstrate the dependence of continuous improvement on the learning organization, discusses various other definitions of the learning organization, and even lays out a strategy for linking concepts of the learning organization to practical management. But, thwarting the learning organization in the research analyzed by Chris Argyris are once again those pesky extrinsic motivations that in essence are the executive's promises. "Once employees base their motivation on extrinsic factors they are much less likely to take chances, question established policies and practices, or explore the territory that lies beyond the company vision as defined by management" (Argyris, 1999, p. 236). And these attitudes figure among the primary features of the learning organization, which is the ultimate model of choice in the post-bureaucratic environment.

Activation of the learning spirit begins with the individual, but that individual must function within the right kind of environment, one in which the structural, attitudinal, and behavioral trappings, including the unwritten rules of the organization, are conducive to learning. The quality of the organizational environment makes it more or less likely "that crucial issues will be addressed or avoided, that dilemmas will be publicly surfaced or held private, and that sensitive assumptions will be publicly tested or protected" (Argyris & Schön, 1996, p. 28). In summary, fundamental to the learning organization is the understanding among its members that a reasoned inquiry is acceptable to and even encouraged by the organization at no jeopardy to the inquiring member. Trust is the key element in such an environment.

Flexibility

Just as the literature of organizational development touts flexibility of individual responsibilities as a key conduit to the learning organization and, therefore, to the strong corporate culture, it also is a goal expressed by employees. Flexibility offers the individual a break from routine and an opportunity for self-realization through a more broadening experience. But, in spite of the positive intentions behind this condition for both the organization and its individual members, flexibility can be viewed from competing perspectives.

> In the revolt against routine, the appearance of a new freedom is deceptive. Time in institutions and for individuals has been unchained from the iron cage of the past, but subjected to new, top-down controls and surveillance. The time of flexibility is the time of a new power. Flexibility begets disorder, but not freedom from restraint. (Sennett, 1998, p. 59)

And, when pushed to the extreme, flexibility can become merely a tolerance for fragmentation of the work experience in one's life and the development of "a capacity to let go of one's past" (Sennett, 1998, p. 63). For the leadership, the balance required to maintain a healthy culture hinges on being flexible with regard to most practices, but inflexible in matters of core adaptive values (Kotter & Heskett, 1992, p. 148).

Risk-Taking

Argyris (1999, p. 108) places risk-taking fairly high on his list of requirements for success in tomorrow's organizations. Employee risk is closely aligned to trust in the leadership and is central to the strategy of teamwork, which is addressed below. Under the negative rubric "The Sins of Hierarchy," Perrow (1986, pp. 29–30) describes the organizational climate that surrounds risk-taking in the authority-driven bureaucracy, which clearly discourages such initiatives, much to the contrary of the spirit of post-bureaucratic organizations. In fact, not only is risk-taking essential to post-bureaucratic success, the capacity for it no longer is expected just within the executive leadership. "The willingness to risk, however, is no longer meant to be the province only of venture capitalists or extraordinarily adventurous individuals. Risk is to become a daily necessity shouldered by the masses ... The theory is that you rejuvenate your energies by taking risks, and recharge continually" (Sennett, 1998, p. 80). "The mathematics of risk offer no assurances, and the psychology of risk-taking focuses quite reasonably on what might be lost" (Sennett, 1998, p. 82). The willingness to take calculated risks and the trust implied in that willingness are fundamental attributes, if not defining attributes, of a culture-driven organization.

Participation and Teamwork

As shared values constitute the foundation of the corporate culture, so broad organizational participation and teamwork are the means of implementing and building upon that culture. According to Heckscher (1994, p. 46), "there is strong evidence beyond general impressions that participatory systems have been spreading during the past 30 years, and that the shift has been accelerating." That one phenomenon may provide the single most telling reflection of a large-scale trend in organizational change.

A quarter century ago, Tom Peters and R. H. Waterman co-authored a now-well-known analysis of the management of successful corporations, titled *In Search of Excellence*. It broke nonfiction sales records at the time of its publication. On the 20th anniversary of the book's publication, John Newstrom (2002) assessed the astonishing success of the Peters and Waterman's work, and found its importance to reside in the impetus it gave to a two-decade flurry of management activity in which "readers began searching in both the academic and practitioner literature for practical answers to important questions – but only if they were based on substantive, careful research as guided by solid theory" (p. 56).[12] It is of particular note that *In Search of Excellence* identified the key success factor in business to be what the book describes as the "theory of chunks":

> ... simply getting one's arms around almost any practical problem and knocking it off—now ... The small group is the most visible of the chunking devices. Small groups are, quite simply, the basic organizational building blocks of excellent companies ... the small group is critical to effective organizational functioning. (Peters & Waterman, 1982, p. 126)

Today we refer to these chunks or subcultures as teams. They are understood to constitute a formalized method of structuring broad participation in the organizational decision-making required of planning and problem solving.[13] In reviewing relevant research literature for his essay on the value of drawing more fully on the knowledge and expertise found throughout any organization, Jeffrey Pfeffer observes that "Organizing people into self-managed teams is a critical component of virtually all high performance management systems. Numerous articles and case examples as well as rigorous, systematic studies attest to the effectiveness of teams as a principle of organization design" (Pfeffer, 1998, p. 74). And Heide von Weltzein Hoivik (2002, p. 7) finds that the autonomy of "communally mediated control" can even foster motivation and commitment.

With few apparent exceptions, teams are found to offer several advantages over the rigid hierarchical authority of bureaucracy.[14] They substitute peer-based for hierarchical control of work, and frequently are more effective. Teams permit employees to pool their ideas to come up with better and more creative solutions to problems. And, "perhaps most importantly, ... teams permit removal of layers of hierarchy and absorption of administrative tasks previously performed by specialists, avoiding the enormous costs of having people whose sole job it is to watch people watch people who watch other people do the work" (Pfeffer, 1998, p. 77).

But uniformity is not to be found in the scholarly assessment of the relative displacement of authority by participation in the organization. For example, "There have been thousands of studies of the productivity effects of participatory organization, the vast majority of which have claimed significant improvements. Few, however, have established even basic credibility" (Heckscher, 1994, p. 45). And, "Team work is widely touted as a necessary and achievable component of the post-bureaucratic organization. Recent empirical work, however, has found that the transition to teams is slow and painful and the outcomes far less impressive than is commonly thought" (Donnellon & Scully, 1994, p. 64).

The principal reason behind such mixed messages about the value of structured participation is not so much the idea that participation as a strategy is at fault, but rather that its mode of implementation too often is faulty. Recalling an earlier theme about reward in the mixing of bureaucratic and post-bureaucratic systems, participation seems to fall short of expectation when it is applied in an environment that continues much of the old bureaucratic structure. For example, Anne Donnellon and Maureen Scully (1994, p. 64) trace the problem specifically to the meritocratic basis for reward; Heckscher (1994, p. 46) and Katz and Kahn (1966, p. 401) to the apparent anathema of participation and authority; and Richard Sennett (1998) to the sense of irony instilled in the employee as a "consequence of living in flexible time, without standards of authority and accountability" (p. 143). So, the sticking point in broad organizational participation is not so much participation per se, but rather the conflict of systems, each of which contains elements of value to the desired results, but which when harnessed together often prove disappointing. And there remains the seemingly inescapable conflict encountered by individuals who accept compromise that requires them to support wholly a recommendation to which they are only partly committed, because it is their team's recommendation.[15]

In a few sweeping strokes, this is the outline of organizational development centered on culture.[16] As noted previously in several instances, control through culture has proved largely to be a successful strategy for management of the organization, because it appears to have engendered intrinsic motivation and commitment to a culture desired by management and maintained through peer influence. But it may yield a less positive and less obvious result for the individual.

> The evidence suggests that commitment is intentionally built and managed ... Being committed is, almost by definition, to some degree a loss of personal freedom and choice – to be committed to an organization is to stay with it even in the absence of rational reason to do so. (Pfeffer, 1997, p. 120)

The corporate ethos can be guided and nurtured by management, but its raw material still is provided by the worldview and self-view of each individual.

THE INDIVIDUAL

Decades ago, Douglas McGregor (1960) observed that the organization and the individual "are not antithetical. In a genuinely effective group, the individual finds some of his deepest satisfactions" (p. 240). In a "genuinely effective group" this must be true. Moreover, Gideon Kunda (1992) asserts that "work life in general and organizational life in particular are central sources of self-definition" (pp. 161–162). How to harness this potential in the interests of organizational mission and goals has long been a question of prime importance in management; it is one of balancing individual freedom and collective action.

But normative control, however it is couched, remains control. On the positive side, it functions by shaping individuals through "a process of education, personal development, growth, and maturity" (Kunda, 1992, p. 14), thereby rendering them of greater service to the organization, and possibly even making them better people. Interpreted negatively, however, normative control forms a new kind of "bureaucratic personality," for which "identification with the organization overrides all else and leads to the inversion of means and ends, a preference for conformity, a predilection for groupthink, a fear of creativity and initiative, and a dearth of ethics" (Kunda, 1992, p. 15). Accordingly, the normative control of corporate culture can breed a kind of conformity that differs substantively from that produced in the bureaucracy, but is conformity nevertheless.

It should be evident at this point that, while Kunda finds much positive potential in post-bureaucratic systems of management, he also perceives much about which to be concerned, if not wary. And, of course, he is not alone in that regard. Perhaps the most scathing interpretation of the flattening and de-bureaucratization of the organization thus far was authored by Richard Sennett, in a book titled, engagingly, *The Corrosion of Character*. On the subject of the inevitable reaction to change and uncertainty that forever has plagued work groups but which is intensified relentlessly in the post-bureaucratic organization by its adaptation and flexibility, he offers the following thoughts for consideration.

> What's peculiar about uncertainty today is that it exists without any looming historical disaster; instead it is woven into the everyday practices of a vigorous capitalism. Instability is meant to be normal ... Perhaps the corroding of character is an inevitable consequence. 'No long term' disorients action over the long term, loosens bonds of trust and commitment, and divorces will from behavior. (Sennett, 1998, p. 31)

Sennett covers many aspects of the post-bureaucratic workplace, far too many to be addressed here. Essentially, he interprets most or all strategies of organizational development as measures of administrative control that are intended to replace, unobtrusively, those of the bureaucracy, against which they claimed to revolt. It is a provocative essay that did, in fact, provoke a chapter titled "The Corrosion of Character: Capitalist and Socialist Economics," in a book by Chris Argyris (2004, pp. 18–33). The disagreement with Sennett resides primarily in Argyris's (2004) interpretation that "the programs were manipulative, but the designers did not think they were. Many executives genuinely believed these programs would lead to a new flexible capitalism" (p. 21). This may not be knowable, and one would prefer to agree with Argyris. But this particular thought expresses more than a hint of wishful thinking, for what were the executives attempting to achieve if not the operational goals they established?

While both Sennett and Argyris theorize the effects of management strategies on the organization as a whole, they also address the interests of the individual. And their examination of the individual includes attention to what could easily be viewed at first blush as minor considerations, yet which upon closer examination are recognizable as the kinds of thoughts that do occupy one's mind when the more goal-oriented organizational thoughts are not being pressed to the forefront. Two slightly differing perspectives on this phenomenon are portrayed by Sennett and Argyris, respectively:

> In fluid situations ... people tend to focus on the minutiae of daily events, seeking in details some portent of meaning—rather like ancient priests studying the entrails of slaughtered animals. How the boss says hello in the morning ... . (Sennett, 1998, p. 79)

... their boss tells them that the success of the new ideas for solving important business problems is due to their involvement, and that that in turn rests on the opportunity given to them to participate. They are sad and bewildered because their boss does not include as a key factor in the success his own announcement that their jobs are at stake ... Workers do understand the attempts to make work more humane. (Argyris, 2004, pp. 23–24)

So neither the costs nor the benefits of post-bureaucratic systems of organization to either the individual or the organization are as clear as one might wish them to be. But, understandably, considerably less concern for the individual than for the organic whole is to be found in the literature of organizational development. It tends to begin and end with the totality of the organization, when it might more productively begin and end with the individual as the principal constitutive element within the organic whole. And, despite the formally shared culture of the new organization, it is possible that the individual, who, even in a participative setting, remains distant from the executive, is alienated from peers by virtue of his/her own private thoughts about what is happening in the organization. The question remains how that might connect with or disconnect from the individual. It may well be a form of alienation that runs quite deep, yet also is of a nature that renders it quite invisible.[17] With these unknowns and ambiguities as part of the background, we can more productively examine the place of the library in the theory of organizational development.

THE LIBRARY CONTEXT

The environment surrounding each individual in a library today is quite different from that of 50 or even 15 years ago. Attention to the organization as an organic whole, rather than as a mechanism, very likely has been beneficial for most library employees and surely can be credited with the great progress that has been made in meeting the need for swift and profound organizational change and in steering the organization in a direction that will allow it to cope successfully with its environment. The library, as a managed collective, is currently in a better position than ever before to concentrate on the strengths and needs of its individual members, who daily provide the services and public relations of the organization. But, again, this focus should be on the individual as he or she functions in a much more sophisticated organizational dynamic. In the past 50 years, society in general and work in particular have changed considerably, and in a way that makes it likely that management directed at the individual can be more

successful today than then. Movements toward a more flattened organization, toward the flexibility of team approaches, and toward the learning
organization, point in that direction. At the same time, the focus of the kind
of change immediately pertinent to information technologies demands that
individuals become expert and ever adaptable and open to learning
situations. In the final analysis, the burden of change falls on to the back
of individuals.

For many perfectly justifiable reasons, the question inevitably will arise as
to the appropriateness of business models of organization for the library.
That will not be debated here. But it is pertinent to the substance of this
paper to underline just two fundamental distinctions between business
organizations and the vast majority of library organizations. First is the fact
that the library almost always belongs to a host organization. Most often,
however, the library is appended to the host organization, rather than being
firmly embedded in it. Whether or not this should be the case or must
forever remain the case is not argued here.[18] But this situation is a
consequence of the fact that the library is a service to the entire host and, as
such, is not part of the assembly line of daily production, policy, procedure,
goals, and objectives. Instead, the library functions in a consulting,
auxiliary, and/or staff capacity to the host organization. In that regard, it
is useful to bear in mind the counsel of two of the leading scholars in the
field of organizational development:

> The key concept is that of 'fit' … a culture is good only if it 'fits' its context, whether one
> means by context the objective conditions of its industry, that segment of its industry
> specified by a form's strategy, or the business strategy itself. According to this
> perspective, only those contextually or strategically appropriate cultures will be
> associated with excellent performance. The better the fit, the better the performance;
> the poorer the fit, the poorer the performance. (Kotter & Heskett, 1992, p. 28)

"Fit" is a matter of developing the culture that best aligns the library to its
particular setting and that also accommodates the special considerations of
the library profession.

Another feature of libraries that distinguishes them in a most
fundamental way from business and industrial organizations is contained
in the very premise of their existence. The library exists foremost, and in
many cases solely, to engage the cognitive processes of the membership of its
host organization. The implications of this distinction for the management
of the library organization are broad and run deep, and they constitute the
uniqueness of the library. But such implications extend well beyond the
scope of this paper.

Returning to the library culture, the rapid and ubiquitous infusion of innovative technologies in recent years has placed unprecedented demands on the organizational flexibility of the library to fit the shifting contours of its host organization and, at the same time, to meet service standards that are constantly being raised within the profession. These have been challenges that libraries by and large have met through intelligence, dedicated effort, and organizational development. Generally, staff development programs have achieved a high profile in libraries and are becoming well integrated into the daily work and thinking of librarians. The often discussed phenomenon of the "blurring of lines" around functions and administrative units is an indirect consequence of the infusion of information technologies into the library. But it is even more directly the consequence of the organizational development strategies that have been adopted to gain control over the challenges and opportunities that the technologies introduce. It would be difficult for the observer to perceive that the organizational structure that continues to appear from the outside to be very much like that of two decades ago belies the fact that it works in ways that are much different.

Meanwhile, other changes are occurring. As the library organization becomes more horizontal and, therefore, a tad less vertical, direct authority holds less sway, and both authority and accountability become more diffuse. This development creates a set of conditions whereby the role of the individual in the organization takes center stage. Success in the current environment demands greater self-discipline, greater self-accountability, and a much higher level of trust and ethical strength on the part of the individual than was previously required.

Organizational development strategies have helped individuals within these organizations understand more fully their respective roles, and even to gain some insight into the roles of others. Above all, they have helped form individual minds to see that there is a larger picture that incorporates their own responsibilities while placing added demands on them as members of the organization. Thus, the guidelines for individual behavior and attitude in the organization have evolved commensurately with the culture. There are limits to the influence that organizational development can have on the individual, of course, for there are many other influences on behavior and attitude that have formed the individual before entering the workplace, while there are still others that continue outside the workplace. But anyone who has been employed in libraries during the past two decades has surely seen and felt the change in their corporate culture.

Throughout that period, the responsibility of librarianship has been to varying segments of a society that has evolved from a production to a service orientation. Similarly, in the past the profession prepared itself to serve a society that valued knowledge; then it adapted to serve a society that valued nothing very perceptible for a while, and then adapted yet again to serve one that valued information. Now we are returned to meeting the needs and interests of a society that seems to value knowledge, only this time it is a society imbued with a better understanding of the mutual dependence of information and knowledge. We even seem to be on the verge of returning to the notion of library as a place, but not the place that was familiar just a few decades ago. Moreover, while these fairly heavy environmental transformations were in motion, the entire world of knowledge, information, and communication shifted from labor intensiveness to both labor and equipment intensiveness. Our profession has had to make more than a few profound changes in order to remain successful in this tumultuous environment, while its adaptation to the new characteristics of each successive environment definitely required ever greater agility of thought and action.

Consider, for example, the implications of practitioners moving away from the idea of a collection-centered service toward that of a client-centered service. Consider also the shift from viewing library personnel as a group of individuals filling rather discrete slots in rigid bureaucracies to viewing them as a set of teams with a common mission. Then consider that the profession has effected this transformation in a relatively short time. All this was accomplished largely through the process of tacit adoption of a new set of principles — principles of a more qualitative nature that are far more demanding of the individual's total being. "In a turbulent world, the requirement for change is ongoing" (Kotter & Cohen, 2002, p. 183). But note well that this did not come about by fiat of either the profession or the host organization; these principles were not established first and then followed in a neatly ordered fashion. In fact, looking back, it would appear that librarianship quite simply was driven by the desperation of so few trying to do so much in so little time while learning to carry on the business in a changing environment and subsequently in a new kind of organization. In summary, the new qualitative principles are those that have been derived through the culture-driven organization.

The purpose of these qualitative principles in the library is to define how the functional principles are expected to be invoked by individuals, by the organization, and by the profession. Therefore, their implementation hinges on a revised strategy for the deployment of library staff and a raised set of expectations for them. Many of the personal characteristics now in demand formerly were not accorded high value in a formal sense or were considered only as an "icing-on-the-cake" bonus. Such attributes are "flexibility" and "interest in being a team player," and other personal attributes that have become as essential to practice as the functional principles, and in a learning organization may even overshadow some of them. Much like the frequently posted functional hiring criterion of "familiarity with information technologies," they more often are required for success in the profession than just preferred, even if the advertisement fails to make that clear.

> How come human beings are skillfully incompetent and unaware? One answer is that the very action required to become skillful produces unawareness. Once human beings become skilled, they forget much of what they went through to become skillful. Skillful actions are those that 'work', that appear effortless, that are automatic and usually tacit, and that are taken for granted. A consequence of generating skills is designed ignorance. (Argyris, 2004, p. 11)

The point here is not that we are wrong in wanting the skill set, but that we need far more than the skill set. In general, the profession is becoming more interested in the individual as a rational and sensitive being than as a palpable set of skills.

Anyone with much experience in hiring personnel into a large library is familiar with what I have labeled for the past three decades the "bucket brigade syndrome." This syndrome is encountered when those who work closely with the position in question tend to want to hire someone who, posing no disruption, can step into the middle of things and assume the specifics of the vacated position without the need of any training. This is an easily understandable interest, for many reasons. But there are larger considerations. For example, could the bucket brigade be formed in another way, or could it be eliminated entirely in view of some other approach to the responsibilities, while taking other matters into consideration? Probably most of us fall victim to the bucket brigade mentality at some point, but, when the dominant part of the organization functions on that basis, problems arise and opportunities are missed. The question such an organization would do well to raise, if only in the absence of introspection, is, "Do we too often emphasize the skills useful to the maintenance of a particular function in the short term at the expense of an aptitude of value to the mission and goals of the library in the longer term?"

The fact that the library leadership has been directing so much energy to organizational development indicates not only that it has grasped the need to overhaul its organization to fulfill the mission, but also that it has recognized the easily neglected need to project a positive image to the host organization. This involves choices about how the library culture should be perceived from the outside. They are binary choices that could be represented on a sliding scale, such as an inviting and helpful environment, or a forbidding and austere environment; a service orientation or a task orientation; a team spirit or a bureaucratic mentality; an understanding of the culture of the host institution, or a disregard of distinctions among institutions; and manifest respect for clientele and colleagues as individuals, or their treatment as objects and as interruptions on the conveyor belt of daily work.

Similarly, individuals employed by the library have a set of choices for the kind of culture they would choose for the collective mindset of their workplace, where they spend more waking hours than anywhere else: an understanding of the mission and goals of the library and their relation to the individual, or a disregard of the implications of the library's mission and goals for one's responsibilities; knowing how things get done in the organization, or following a mental image only of anarchy; a willingness to test common assumptions, or an acceptance of them; recognition of the benefit of shared values, or protection of insular values; recognition of the value of dialectic, or rejection of the possibility of making improvements and achieving something better through collective reasoning; expectation of change as a normal part of responsibilities, or resistance to change as a distraction from the normal responsibilities; a predominance of continuous planning and evaluation in the work mode, or a predominance of reaction and problem solving; and the adoption of select strategy and tactics because they are congruent with the desired corporate culture, or the acceptance of those that fall outside that norm because they constitute an expedient.

And there are specific implications for choice in one's own behavior and attitude that each individual now should feel responsible to consider: effective and efficient communication, or communication that lacks in clarity, concision, and timeliness; understanding that learning is integral to a successful organization, or seeing it as a specific added task; flexibility and broad vision, or rigidity and narrow focus; initiatives or reactions; identifying and controlling biases and prejudices, or allowing them to become the de facto controls; ability to cope well with ambiguity, or a heavy dependence on specificity; the vision of one's responsibilities as a challenging career, or the reluctant acceptance of them as a job; a generally positive and optimistic outlook, or a generally negative pessimistic outlook; a sense of accountability to the organization and its host, or accountability solely to the supervisor; a process orientation, or a bucket brigade mentality; and the willingness to take risks, or aversion to risk.[19]

These choices all tie together, of course. They are the choices to be made by the individual and by the organization in the interests of service to the community and of earning its support.

SUMMARY AND CONCLUSIONS

Clearly, there is a substantial body of theory in organizational psychology that has been drawn from a considerable accumulation of research, especially in the course of the past half century,[20] yet we still get mixed messages about how best to develop the organization. There are at least two basic reasons why we encounter contradiction and its attendant ambiguities. One reason goes to differences among the approaches used by investigators in the research, some of which is carried out by academics, while some is done by practitioners. In the academic spirit, "hypothesis forming and testing should continue for as long as members of the community of inquiry bring forward plausible competing hypotheses." In the spirit of the practitioner, however, the cycle closes "when their inquiry enables them to achieve their intended result and when they like, or can live with, the unintended side effects inherent in their designing" (Argyris & Schön, 1996, p. 37). Michael Hammer (2001), coiner of the term "reengineering," brings informed common sense to the whole matter by assuring that "there are no silver bullets" (Preface, p. xiv) in determining how an organization should best function.

The other major reason for ambiguity and contradiction in organizational development is the complexity of the organism under the microscope. Nonetheless, even if we really could determine the single best model to follow through a specific intersection of time and place, implementation does not follow easily.

> If the evidence is so consistent about the importance of people to organizational success, why haven't organizations rushed to implement practices that are consistent with the large body of research evidence: The reason is simultaneously simple and complex. The simple response is that for people-centered practices to work, a wide spectrum of management practices, ranging from selection to socialization to compensation, must be tightly aligned with each other. These management practices must then be focused on building and maintaining core capabilities and on devising a business strategy that capitalizes on the capabilities that have been developed. (O'Reilly & Pfeffer, 2000, p. 18)

It is a matter not just of employing select techniques, but of aligning them to work together as a system. The breadth and depth of change required of organizational development is much more complicated, requiring much more time and sustained energy, than is the nature of change required in the bureaucratic organization. But the benefits generally are considered worthy of the costs, if sometimes only on the bases of faith and common sense.

A cynic could well assert that the managed culture shows benefits simply as an example of the Hawthorne effect[21] and, therefore, that they probably will be short lived. Whether this is a valid quibble or to what extent it may be true, would be a complex hypothesis to prove. But what has stirred deeper concern among a number of scholars is the supposed perversion of the concept of authority in the engineering of culture, "when the culture becomes its own object, when the seemingly objective, scientific, concept of culture is expropriated and drawn into the political fray by culture engineers and their various helpers in the service of corporate goals" (Kunda, 1992, p. 222). In the final analysis, whether or not the managed culture does constitute a perversion of authority depends entirely on the executive's intentions, which cannot be known. The mindset of the observer is all but irrelevant to this question.

Perhaps the most radical recommendation for enhancing the corporate culture is that of removing the meritocratic system of recognition and reward, because it conflicts with the intended spirit of the culture (Donnellon & Scully, 1994, p. 64). This would not simply amount to the redefinition of meritocracy or the discovery of a way to make it work in post-bureaucratic systems by shifting merit identified with individuals to one identified with teams. Rather, it would eliminate the individualistic, competitive spirit that characterizes the bureaucracy. The matter of reward strikes directly at motivation and commitment, which are fundamental to work in any situation, but especially in the less supervised, flattened organization, and so presents a most significant connection to all the aspects of a strong culture. But the way this could be accomplished, particularly in a capitalist society, has not yet been clearly defined.

It is the high level of importance some researchers/theorists attach to alignment of effort in managing corporate culture that has led an increasing number to believe it holds the key to longevity of the strong culture. The well-managed corporate culture is more than an assortment of techniques and structures; it is a carefully balanced and dovetailed synergistic package. In their study of eight successful companies, O'Reilly and Pfeffer (2000) found that underlying the complex of initiatives in which those companies engage are three common themes: a clear set of promulgated values; leaders whose primary role is to ensure that the values are maintained throughout the organization; and "a remarkable degree of alignment and consistency in the people-centered practices that express its core values" (p. 232). Changed behavior, stemming from changed attitude, is essential in moving from the rigid authority structure to the less structured system of influence and cooperation. But the changed behavior must show improved and successful results in terms of the organization's mission and goals, because values do not change easily and because there is substantial cost to the organization in bringing that about. In the 10 cases of cultural change studied by Kotter and Heskett (1992), "These new cultures grew in a cycle that was driven by successful results" (p. 99). Measurable success encourages continued success.

It has long been stated, almost as a platitude, that the most important decision made by management is that of determining whom to hire. That decision, more than any other single decision, serves to align all the other efforts in managing corporate culture. "With careful selection, nurturing, and encouragement, dozens of people can play important leadership roles" (Kotter, 1990, p. 103). It starts with hiring: "Organizations serious about obtaining profits through people will expend the effort needed to ensure that they recruit the right people in the first place" (Pfeffer, 1998, p. 69). And, as important as cultural fit may be in hiring, it is of equal importance in matters of promotion and other aspects of the reward system. "In the ten successful cases of cultural change that we studied ... They replaced managers with individuals whose values were more consistent with the cultures they desired ... Even more fundamental, they changed the criteria used in selection and promotion decisions" (Kotter & Heskett, 1992, p. 99).

Pfeffer's interpretation of research he conducted both independently and jointly with O'Reilly supports these findings about cultural fit quite cogently:[22]

> ... organizations should screen primarily on important attributes that are difficult to change through training and should emphasize qualities that actually differentiate among those in the applicant pool. An important insight on the selection process comes from those organizations that tend to hire more on the basis of basic ability and attitude than on applicants' specific technical skills, which are much more easily acquired. (Pfeffer, 1998, p. 71)

O'Reilly and Pfeffer have found that while most companies focus on hiring based on the skills needed for a specific job, people-centered firms hire for how well the person fits the company. They do not ignore a candidate's job-specific abilities, but they do recognize that to contribute substantively in the long term, a person must feel comfortable in the organization; "... the abilities that are important are thus those that help someone grow, change, and develop to meet changing business challenges" (O'Reilly & Pfeffer, 2000, p. 240). And this spirit, they find, carries through to training, where emphasis that usually is placed on specialist skills, they advise, should be transferred to general competence and culture. More than just supervisors, ideally, everyone in the managed culture becomes a leader.

This overview of the literature of organizational development has traced the movement away from bureaucratic systems, which are characterized by authority of position in the hierarchy, toward culture-driven systems, which are characterized by the guided influence of peers in a much flatter structure. Both systems are managed from the top of the organization, but obviously in ways that differ significantly. And both have advantages and disadvantages. It appears highly unlikely that there will be a return to the rigid bureaucracy in libraries at any time in the next quarter century, if for no reasons other than the time required to effect a deep change and the probability that select elements of the bureaucratic system of management will not disappear entirely, but will persist in modified form to serve evolving environmental and internal demands.

In the culture-driven system, the individual bears a great deal of responsibility, because each is responsible, in a formal way, for generating, maintaining, and passing along the culture, while the environment abounds in potential for ambiguity. The mixture of these conditions and responsibilities in the context of the apparent freedom offered by the corporate culture should lead logically to a growth in the importance of the ethical code held by each individual[23] and of the level of trust sensed throughout the organization, for trust is basic to full and effective communication.[24] Increasingly, it will be important for each individual not simply to muster the motivation to accomplish for the organization what must be accomplished, but also to maintain vigilance over one's own inner motivations behind attitude and behavior and the conscious choice of tactics. Ultimately, it is the attitude, the behavior, and the strength of character of each individual, ranging from top to bottom, that determine the quality of the organization of which each is a member.

The Weberian differentiation of person from office, which was founded on supposed objectivity, seems to have been reversed by somewhat less than 180°, but by how much less is still undeterminable. Many questions remain to be resolved about the management structure that can best foster the culture and, therefore, that is most likely to optimize the concerted effort of the organization and the individual effort of each member. Not least among them are those relating to the reward/sanction structure, the balance in functional and personal qualifications of personnel, and the ultimate determination of the costs and benefits of management by corporate culture.

NOTES

1. William Starbuck (2003, p. 144) has traced the origin of the phrase "theory of organization" to Luther H. Gulick, in 1937, but believes it was Herbert A. Simon, in 1950 and subsequently, who most promoted it as a broad category.

2. According to Kotter and Heskett (1992, p. 187, note 22), the first scholarly work to focus on corporate culture was by Andrew Pettigrew, in 1979. They also find that the first known publication to present the English word "culture" in its title is an anthropological study by Edward B. Tylor, in 1887 (Kotter & Heskett, 1992, p. 185, note 1).

3. Starbuck points out that the Latin verb *organizare* meant "to furnish with organs so as to create a complete human being." He believes that the verb in Middle French probably continued to be understood as a biological term, and finds that around 1800, "some writers began to use 'organization' to describe a property of societies" (Starbuck, 2003, p. 156).

4. According to Kotter and Heskett (1992, p. 188, note 32), the earliest publication in English to question explicitly whether corporate culture can, in fact, be managed is that of Thomas Fitzgerald, in 1988. They also (p. 15) attribute the first influential statement of the association of strong cultures with excellence of performance to the work of Geert Hofstede, in 1980, whose book analyzed the work-related values found in forty countries, and revealed four dimensions that differentiate their work cultures: power distance, uncertainty avoidance, individualism, and masculinity.

5. Starbuck (2003, p. 149) attributes the coining of the term "bureaucracy," which was intended as a sarcastic allusion to "government by desk," to Vincent de Gournay, the French Minister of Finance from 1751 to 1758. De Gournay thus ridiculed the government regulators who, in his estimation, knew or cared little about the implications of rules they so rigidly enforced.

6. Considered the most important summary statement of Max Weber's thought, *Wirtschaft und Gesellschaft* was published posthumously in 1922, and was translated into English a quarter century later (Weber, 1947).

7. William B. Given (1950) describes "bottom-up management" in the American Brake Shoe Company from 1919 to 1950.

8. Starbuck (2003, p. 167) writes that not until the 1920s did the literature begin to view organizations as integrated systems, and to discuss the structures of these systems. He points particularly to Edouard Gutjahr, who in 1920 devoted a chapter, titled "L'organisation extérieure de l'entreprise commerciale" (pp. 18–37), to ways in which a commercial enterprise can or should adapt to its economic environment.

9. In a brief account of the management contribution of General Karl von Clausewitz, the famed 19th-century German theoretician of warfare, the authors of a text on organization find that "The maxim that the indoctrinated man who understands principles needs no rules was infused by Clausewitz into the Prussian military system" (Mooney & Reiley, 1939, p. 146).

10. For a particularly informative survey of the thinking on motivation, see the chapter titled "A Sociohistorical Analysis of the Literature on Rewards and Intrinsic Motivation" (Cameron & Pierce, 2002, pp. 177–197).

11. Garvin (1993) elaborates: "Learning organizations are skilled at five main activities: systematic problem solving, experimentation with new approaches, learning from their own experience and past history, learning from the experiences and best practices of others, and transferring knowledge quickly and efficiently throughout the organization" (p. 81).

12. With reference to business and management literature, William Starbuck (2003) finds that "The general norm throughout the first half of the century was that authors said nothing about their sources of data, and this pattern continued into the late 1940s" (p. 172).

13. In fact, according to Starbuck (2003), decision-making in general "remained a marginal theme in organization theory until the late 1950s" (p. 161). He attributes to Chester Barnard (1938) the introduction of the ideas that "decision-making is an important activity performed by executives and that organizations influence executives' decisions" (p. 170).

14. Yet, Charles Heckscher (1994) refers to studies that identify the "successful failure" phenomenon, whereby the team "that appears to fulfill all criteria of accomplishment, from production to employee satisfaction, yet vanishes for undefined reasons after a few years" (p. 46).

15. "Once a decision has been reached by consensus, there are strong motivational forces, developed within each individual as a result of his membership in the group and his relationship to the other members, to be guided by that decision. In this sense, the group has goals and values and makes decisions. It has properties which may not be present, as such, in any one individual. A group may be divided in opinion, for example, although this may not be true of any one individual" (Likert, 1961, pp. 163–164).

16. Jeffrey Pfeffer (1997) provides a concise analysis of the literature on culture as a social control mechanism (pp. 122–126).

17. I am not aware of any studies of this situation, although it is implied by others, most clearly by both Kunda (1992) and Sennett (1998). It may be thought that what goes on beneath the surface has no appreciable effect on organizational results, and therefore is not worthy of attention.

18. Elsewhere (Osburn, 2005), I have suggested community liaison strategies that, in the long term, could be of help in modifying this situation.

19. Chris Aryris was early to study personality and psychological energy in the organization, especially in his chapter on "The Human Personality." This work may be the first book in English to summarize behavioral research in organizations (Argyris, 1957, pp. 20–53).

20. An approach to development of the culture called "positive psychology" (thinking and, consequently, behaving positively and optimistically) is described for the library setting by Brian Quinn. The building of "emotional intelligence," which essentially is the ability to relate well to others and, therefore, is arguably more germane to the corporate culture than to the bureaucratic culture, also is addressed in his essay (Quinn, 2005). For a more general exposition of positive psychology as a developing theory of organizational behavior see Fred Luthans (2002) or Keyes and Haidt (2003).

21. This is the name given to the reported experience in the Hawthorne Plant of the Western Electric Company in Cicero, Illinois, primarily during 1927–1932. The research became influential to the point of legend, and, among other conclusions, demonstrated that almost any special attention paid to workers by administration can result in improved production (Franke & Kaul, 1978).

22. The priority assigned to cultural fit in the organization does not interfere with diversity of membership. It does not relate to race, gender, age, nationality, physical condition, or religion, but rather directly to how the work is to be accomplished.

23. It is difficult to avoid being a bit concerned by the assertion that, in the managed culture, "Value statements have replaced codes of ethics" (Hoivik, 2002, p. 9).

24. "Few organizations can be characterized as having a high level of trust between employees and managers; consequently, it is easy for misunderstandings to develop when change is introduced" (Kotter, 1999, p. 34).

REFERENCES

Argyris, C. (1957). *Personality and organization: The conflict between system and the individual.* New York: Harper & Row.

Argyris, C. (1999). *On organizational learning* (2nd ed.). Oxford: Blackwell.

Argyris, C. (2004). *Reasons and rationalizations: The limits to organizational knowledge.* New York: Oxford University Press.

Argyris, C., & Schön, D. A. (1996). *Organizational learning II: Theory, method, and practice.* Reading: Addison-Wesley.

Barnard, C. I. (1938). *The functions of the executive.* Cambridge: Harvard University Press.

Cameron, J., & Pierce, W. D. (2002). *Rewards & intrinsic motivation: Resolving the controversy.* Westport: Bergen & Garvey.

Donnellon, A., & Scully, M. (1994). Teams, performance, and rewards. In: C. Heckscher & A. Donnellon (Eds), *The post-bureaucratic organization: New perspectives on organizational change* (pp. 63–90). Thousand Oaks: Sage.

Fitzgerald, T. (1988). Can change in organizational culture really be managed? *Organizational Dynamics, 17*(2), 5–15.

Franke, R. H., & Kaul, J. D. (1978). The Hawthorne experiments: First statistical interpretation. *American Sociological Review, 43*(October), 623–643.

Garvin, D. A. (1993). Building a learning organization. *Harvard Business Review, 71*(July–August), 78–91.

Given, W. B., Jr. (1950). Bottom-up management – People working together. *Advanced Management, 15*(February), 2–4.

Gulick, L. H. (1937). Notes on the theory of organization. In: L. H. Gulick & L. F. Urwick (Eds), *Papers on the science of administration* (pp. 1–45). New York: Institute of Public Administration, Columbia University.

Gutjahr, E. (1920). *L'organisation rationnelle des entreprises commerciales.* Paris: Dunod.

Hammer, M. (2001). *The agenda.* New York: Random House.

Hammer, M., & Champy, J. (1993). *Reengineering the corporation.* New York: Harper Business.

Heckscher, C. (1994). Defining the post-bureaucratic type. In: C. Heckscher & A. Donnellon (Eds), *The post-bureaucratic organization: New perspectives on organizational change* (pp. 14–62). Thousand Oaks: Sage.

Hofstede, G. (1980). *Culture's consequences*. Beverly Hills: Sage.

Katz, D., & Kahn, R. L. (1966). Organizational change. In: *Social psychology of organizations* (pp. 390–451). New York: Wiley.

Keyes, C. L. M., & Haidt, J. (Eds). (2003). *Flourishing: Positive psychology and the life well-lived*. Washington, DC: American Psychological Association.

Kotter, J. P. (1990). What leaders really do. *Harvard Business Review*, *68*(May–June), 103–111.

Kotter, J. P. (1999). *John P. Kotter on what leaders really do*. Cambridge: Harvard Business Review Book.

Kotter, J. P., & Cohen, D. (2002). *The heart of change*. Cambridge: Harvard Business Press.

Kotter, J. P., & Heskett, J. L. (1992). *Corporate culture and performance*. New York: Free Press.

Kunda, G. (1992). *Engineering culture: Control and commitment in a high-tech corporation*. Philadelphia: Temple University Press.

Likert, R. (1961). *New patterns of management*. New York: McGraw-Hill.

Luthans, F. (2002). Positive organizational behavior: Developing and managing psychological strengths. *Academy of Management Executive*, *16*(February), 57–75.

McGregor, D. (1960). *The human side of enterprise*. New York: McGraw-Hill.

Mooney, J. D., & Reiley, A. C. (1939). *The principles of organization*. New York: Harper.

Newstrom, J. W. (2002). In search of excellence: Its importance and effects. *Academy of Management Executive*, *16*(February), 53–56.

O'Reilly, C. A., & Pfeffer, J. (2000). *Hidden value: How great companies achieve extraordinary results with ordinary people*. Boston: Harvard Business School Press.

Osburn, C. B. (2005). Collection evaluation: A reconsideration. *Advances in Library Administration and Organization*, *22*, 1–21.

Perrow, C. (1986). *Complex organizations: A critical essay* (3rd ed.). New York: Random House.

Peters, T., & Waterman, R. H. (1982). *In search of excellence*. New York: Harper & Row.

Pettigrew, A. (1979). On studying organizational culture. *Administrative Science Quarterly*, *24*, 570–581.

Pfeffer, J. (1997). Mechanisms of social control. In: *New directions for organization theory* (pp. 100–135). New York: Oxford University Press.

Pfeffer, J. (1998). Seven practices of successful organizations. In: *The human equation: Building profits by putting people first* (pp. 64–98). Boston: Harvard Business School Press.

Quinn, B. (2005). Enhancing academic library performance through positive psychology. *Journal of Library Administration*, *42*, 79–101.

Sennett, R. (1998). *The corrosion of character*. New York: Norton.

Simon, H. A. (1950). Modern organization theories. *Advanced Management*, *15*(October), 2–4.

Starbuck, W. H. (2003). The origins of organization theory. In: H. Tsoukas & C. Knudsen (Eds), *The Oxford handbook of organization theory* (pp. 143–182). Oxford: Oxford University Press.

Thompson, V. A. (1965). Bureaucracy and innovation. *Administrative Science Quarterly*, *10*(June), 1–20.

Tylor, E. B. (1887). *Primitive culture: Researches into the development of mythology, philosophy, religion, art, and custom* (2 vols). New York: Henry Holt.

von Weltzein Hoivik, H. (2002). Professional ethics: A managerial opportunity in emerging organizations. *Journal of Business Ethics*, *39*(August), 3–11.

Weber, M. (1947). In: A. M. Henderson & T. Parsons (Trans.), *The theory of social and economic organization*. New York: Oxford University Press.

Whyte, W. H. (1956). *The organization man*. New York: Simon and Schuster.

BREAKING OUT OF "SACRED COW" CULTURE: THE RELATIONSHIP OF PROFESSIONAL ADVICE NETWORKS TO RECEPTIVITY TO INNOVATION IN ACADEMIC LIBRARIANS

H. Frank Cervone

ABSTRACT

University libraries have traditionally been the primary caretaker of scholarly resources. However, as electronic modes of information delivery replace print materials, expectations of academic libraries have evolved rapidly. In this environment, academic libraries need to be adaptable organizations. Librarianship, though, is deeply rooted in strong values and beliefs which inherently limit receptivity to change and innovation, but these constraints are not absolute. Social network research indicates that professional advice networks play a significant role in how one thinks about and performs work and that individual perspectives are broadened when diverse input is received. Based on social network analysis methods, this study explored the relationship between individual receptivity to innovation and the composition of a person's professional advice network through a purposive sample of academic librarians in Illinois. The group

Advances in Library Administration and Organization, Volume 26, 71–149
ISSN: 0732-0671/doi:10.1016/S0732-0671(08)00203-4

completed a survey that explored two dimensions: (1) the nature of relationships within their professional advice network and (2) the individual's personal receptivity to innovation. Analysis of the nature of relationships within the professional advice networks was based on a combination of quantitative and qualitative techniques, in contrast to the analysis of the respondents' receptivity to innovation which was based on quantitative measures. Based on the information from the 440 respondents, the results of this research indicate that there is a relationship between the size of the professional advice networks and individual's receptivity to innovation, but additional aspects of the professional advice network may play a role in an individual's overall receptivity to innovation.

INTRODUCTION

In an academic environment where "the need for collaboration and greater understanding between parts of the academic silos is necessary for the survival, if not the advancement, of academic work" (Savage & Betts, 2005, p. 4), intra- and interorganizational innovation takes on an even greater importance to reach across "typical academic silos to form mutually beneficial networks for knowledge sharing" (Raines & Alberg, 2003, p. 37) that enable the effective delivery of service to both students and faculty. A lack of innovation in academic units can result in service lapses that may have significant negative implications for individual units within the university as well as the institution as a whole.

Traditionally, the university library has held the role of caretaker of scholarly information on behalf of the academic community. However, as electronic modes of information delivery have begun to overtake traditional print-based formats, the scholarly information environment has been changing rapidly. In an environment where there is a fundamental shift in what people consider a library to be (Shuler, 2005), there is also a significant change in the expectations of academic libraries (Andaleeb & Simmonds, 1998; Baruchson-Arbib & Bronstein, 2002; Harley, Dreger, & Knobloch, 2001; Kroeker, 1999; Lynch, 2003; Pinfield, 2001). As a result, in order to provide a stable and substantive repository of scholarly resources, it is critical that libraries be adaptable organizations that respond to changes in the environment quickly, efficiently, and effectively. Academic libraries need to realign efforts into growth areas and reassess the centrality of other functions (Akeroyd, 2001).

However, even in the face of strong evidence, some academic librarians have persisted in ignoring, denying, and resisting adaptation to environmental changes during a period of time when academic libraries have been "at the center of a revolution ... (that) only hints at the magnitude of changes in information and knowledge production, preservation, and dissemination that are taking place" (Euster, 1995, p. 12). In many ways, this resistance should not be surprising as "people's natural inclination is to hold on to whatever feels familiar, even when there are better alternatives" (Munck, 2002, p. 23). An additional complicating factor is that innovation in libraries is sometimes difficult to detect because innovation in libraries is usually related to services, and innovation in a service-based environment is inherently less obvious than it is in product-based environments (Deiss, 2004).

Nonetheless, the resulting implications of resistance to change can be dire, as "librarians who cannot go forward will find themselves pushed to one side ... (where) the library exists in name but it will become a backwater and an alternative organization will be developed" (Pack & Pack, 1988, p. 130). It is because of this potential for becoming a backwater that authors such as Cluff (1989) have stated that "creativity and innovation are crying needs in the library profession" (p. 185).

It is possible that environmental factors account for a predisposition against innovation. For example, the findings from Luquire's study (1983) may be due to the production orientation (Lewis, 1986) of most academic libraries. On the other hand, lack of innovation may be related to a broader issue. Brodie and Mclean (1995) have observed that libraries, as part of their organizational strategy, seem to encourage those who work in them to accept insularity and to see themselves as victims of circumstances in which they can neither innovate nor change.

These portrayals, however, stand in stark contrast to others, such as the environment Garten and Williams (2000) described in their history of libraries that showed that "librarians placed an early emphasis on the establishment of consortia and networks" (p. 64) as mechanisms for both facilitating cooperation inter-institutionally and for enabling change and advancement. Lack of innovation in librarianship is also at odds with the picture that Dysart and Abram (1997) and Malinconico (1997) painted of librarians as leaders in technological innovation, not just in libraries, but with technology in general. This leads to two simple, but very significant questions: Why does this contradiction exist? Why are there such disparities in innovative practice?

It is possible that part of this paradox is due to the very nature of academic librarianship. Every organization has assumptions about its values and beliefs (Bolman & Deal, 1997) as does every profession (Pavalko, 1988). Librarianship is deeply rooted in a culture of strong values and beliefs: freedom of speech, freedom of access to information, and an overall strong service orientation. Alvesson (1993) has described an institutional culture such as this as a "sacred cow" (p. 20) organizational culture: a culture where the members' internalization of particular ideals and values can cloud the rational acceptance of new or different beliefs because of emotional identification with values. As a result of historical processes in which people gradually accept and internalize beliefs because they have been shown to be successful, cultures operating from this perspective "stress the limits of instrumental reason by focusing on deep value commitments and the stability of the core beliefs and values of the culture" (Alvesson, 2000, p. 33).

Consequently, organizational strategies in this type of culture are tightly coupled to a specific set of values, values which place an inherent limit on change processes. Both Ulrich (2002) and Kanter (2002) have noted that organizations characterized by strong reliance on standards, expertise, and a performance-orientation are less likely to be innovative. These values and rules tend to remain in place, for extended periods of time, because of the general cultural stability that tends to be found in most organizations (Harrison & Carroll, 2006). Eventually, this stability can affect organizational performance (Sørenson, 2002).

Because these beliefs, values, and behaviors become so ingrained in the culture, they are no longer obvious to those within the culture and become unquestioned rules for the organization (Berger & Luckmann, 1966). This is exemplified in the strong group cohesion that develops in this type of organizational context which has negative, rather than positive, consequences (Flynn & Chatman, 2004). One of these negative consequences is that the members of these types of organizational cultures tend to see their core values and beliefs as almost impossible to change because of their unquestioned character and the deep commitment the organization has to them.

Nevertheless, because an organization is a subjective experience (Smircich, 1983), cultural persistence or the transformation of culture is directly associated with how cultural information is transmitted (Cavalli-Sforza & Feldman, 1981). It is well known that social networks affect how people discover and process the information required to do their work (Cross, Rice, & Parker, 2001), so one possible way to affect change in an organization might be by drawing on the knowledge of people in the professional advice networks of the individuals working in the organization in order to increase the amount of external input into the organization.

Yet a more fundamental question must be addressed before it can be said that this approach would be an effective strategy. One needs to know if the professional advice network of a person actually has an affect on their receptivity to innovation. Since the earliest research into organizations, it has been known that the behavior of an individual is "directed by his habitual relations to his fellows in the group" (Veblen, 1909, p. 245) or as Bauman and May (2001) have more recently put it, "how we act and see ourselves is informed by the expectations of the groups to which we belong" (p. 20). That is, everyone is a social construction, formed, sustained, and changed by ongoing interaction (Scott, 1995). It is known that shared experiences can lead to shared meanings (Alvesson, 2000) and that interpersonal connections outside of the immediate environment can substantially broaden ones perspective (Pavalko, 1988). These connections can have a major impact on what we choose to do (Valente, 1995).

Therefore, it would be reasonable to assume that a larger professional advice network could have a greater positive effect on receptivity to innovation than a smaller one. This supposition is based on the increased amount of diverse external stimuli additional interactions would provide (Robinson & Stern, 1998). On the other hand, if professional advice networks were not to have a positive effect on a person's receptivity to innovation and actually inhibited a person's receptivity to innovation, these networks would not be effective mechanisms for increasing innovative input into an organization.

With this in mind, the focus of this study was to determine what influence professional advice networks may have on receptivity to innovation. By using methodologies from social network analysis (Freeman, 2000; Scott, 2000; Wasserman & Faust, 1994), the study explored the relationships between the extent and diversity of professional advice networks and the receptivity of individuals to innovation.

This study addressed three broad areas of inquiry:

1. What is the relationship between receptivity to innovation and the compositional qualities of a person's professional advice network?
2. What are the distinctive characteristics in the composition of the professional advice networks of people with high receptivity to innovation?
3. What are the distinctive characteristics in the composition of the professional advice networks of people with low receptivity to innovation?

These issues were addressed through the investigation of four specific hypotheses:

H_{1A}. People with large professional advice networks are more receptive to innovation than those with smaller networks.

 H_{10}. People with large professional advice networks are not more receptive to innovation than those with smaller networks.

H_{2A}. People with the highest receptivity to innovation have large professional advice networks that are heterogeneous.

 H_{20}. People with the highest receptivity to innovation do not have large professional advice networks that are heterogeneous.

H_{3A}. People with externally focused professional advice networks are more receptive to innovation than those with internally focused professional advice networks.

 H_{30}. People with externally focused professional advice networks are not more receptive to innovation than those with internally focused professional advice networks.

H_{4A}. People with the lowest receptivity to innovation have professional advice networks that are highly homogenous, both demographically and professionally.

 H_{40}. People with the lowest receptivity to innovation do not have professional advice networks that are highly homogenous either demographically and professionally.

In order to answer these, questions in two different knowledge domains were asked. First, it was necessary to understand aspects of the professional advice networks of the people participating in the study. The questions in Appendix A, suggested by Cross and Parker (2004), were used as the basis for this inquiry into both the scope and composition qualities of individual professional advice networks.

For the second knowledge domain, questions from the Rusaw Multi-factor Assessment instrument (Rusaw, 2001) were used to measure the receptivity of individuals to innovation. These questions, outlined in Appendix B, measure the strength of belief in the various principles (defined in Appendix C) which contribute to an environment that fosters the development of innovative products and services.

REVIEW OF THE LITERATURE

The study of formal organizational structure and form, as well as informal structures related to the patterns of relationships and information flows of an organization, lies at the foundation of organization science (Fulk & Desanctis, 1995). One way of thinking about organizational structure or form is to view it as the pattern of connections and interdependencies linking organization members. Together those links may take on a number of forms, and the inherent relationships among the links may reflect (a) the formal organization as defined by authority relationships, (b) the information organization as defined by actual communication and information exchange, (c) the structuring and flow of work, or (d) the social relationships of the members within the organization (Tichy, Tushman, & Fombrun, 1979).

Social network analysis can trace its origins to early developments in organization science. The importance of networks of relations was established in the early 1940s by researchers such as Radcliffe-Brown (2002) who observed that "the interaction patterns describing social structure can be viewed as a network of relations" (p. 33).

Social network analyses are transactional studies of patterned social relationships (Breiger, 1974) where the central guiding tenet is that the beliefs, feelings, and behaviors of people are not driven solely by the attributes of an individual, but also by the patterns of relationships among individuals (Zack, 2000) and the influence they have on one another (Freeman, 2004). As such, it represents an appropriate method for guiding data collection and analysis of groups when the focus is on patterns of interaction over time (O'Reilly & Roberts, 1977; Tichy, 1980a). In this light, social network analysis has taken on an increasing importance as a relevant and highly useful tool for describing organizations and for measuring the effects of organizational systems.

Although social network analysis draws from psychological theory in many ways, it is because of this primary concern with the relationships among individuals rather than the individuals themselves (Degenne & Forsé, 2004; Reffay & Chanier, 2002) that social network analysis is more closely identified with sociological methods. Specifically, social network analysis is most typically classified as a subtype within the general framework of structural sociology (Wellman, 2002). Considered to be a central methodology in the field of structural inquiry (Monge & Eisenberg, 1987), this places it at the center of research in the area of organizational behavior.

Social network analysis is a comprehensive family of analytical strategies, with a rich history, that focuses on how a particular configuration of social ties interacts (Emirbayer, 1997). Tichy (1980b) has traced these origins from three distinct schools of thought:

1. Structural–functional theory as defined by Merton (1968) and Parsons (1956a, 1956b),
2. Exchange theory as defined by Blau (1964) and Ekeh (1974), and
3. Role theory (Katz & Kahn, 1966).

Effective analysis of social networks draws upon the distinctive features that set it apart from traditional approaches to sociological inquiry, which include (a) a focus on relations and the patterns of relations rather than on attributes of individual actors in those relations, (b) an amenability to multiple levels of analysis geared toward providing micro–macro linkages, and (c) an inherent integration of quantitative, qualitative, and graphical data to allow more thorough and in-depth analysis (Kilduff & Tsai, 2003).

Methods for pictorially representing social networks are formalisms based on graph theory. These methods are used to represent relations within a network as nodes and links within an interconnected network structure. However, the primary focus of graph analysis in the majority of social network analysis studies is not the mathematical purity of the network graph, but instead the focus is on the exploration and discovery of the relationships among the nodes of the graph.

While quantitative, qualitative, and graphical data all play important roles in the analysis of the network, quantitative analysis in the form of statistical analysis has an especially vital, although often underestimated, role because the ability to correlate variables is critical in most network studies. Not withstanding the caution that aggregate statistics can be misleading (Downs & Mohr, 1976), the question of how likely it is that one or more things are related to another is a frequent focus of social network analysis research. Together with analysis of network graphs, it forms the basis of virtually every quantitative analysis of data (Trochim, 2001).

Major Traditions of Social Network Analysis

There are two major views or traditions of social network structure: positional and relational (Burt, 1980; Monge & Eisenberg, 1987). The *positional* approach arose in the 1960s due to the increase in availability of computers that could be used to perform analyses of relations in a network based on the mathematics of graph theory. Given its background, it reflects a more formal, mathematical approach to understanding the structure of relations within a network. Before this technological development, it was extremely difficult and time consuming to develop the visual representations of network membership and interaction. The advantages of the positional approach are especially evident in research that attempts to develop theories of network relations. Wellman (2002) states that:

> the use of matrices has made it possible to study many more members of social systems and many more types of ties, and it has fit well with the use of computers to reveal such underlying structural features as cliques, central members, and indirect linkages. (p. 85)

The positional approach is a structural one which first seeks explanations in the regularities of how people and collectivities actually behave rather than in the regularities of their beliefs about how they ought to behave. Structural analysts interpret behavior in terms of structural constraints on activity instead of assuming that internal motivation impels actors toward desired goals; that is, occupants of a given social position or environmental niche may come to share similar attitudes or behaviors if they respond similarly to their conditions. The common conditions these actors play, which may be material or cognitive, are often guided by the economic circumstances and normative guidelines associated with their position or niche within the network (Marsden & Friedkin, 1994a).

Using the positional approach, both the quantity and strength of the relations within the network are analyzed through measures of *structural cohesion*. Structural cohesion is itself defined in terms of *social proximity* – the length and strength of paths that connect actors in networks (Marsden & Friedkin, 1994a). Social proximity can also be defined in terms of the similarity of the functional equivalencies actors may have, that is, the similarity in the role they play within the network. This approach relaxes the relations to and from particular actors to allow definitions of equivalent network environments, in which members are tied to the same types of actors.

Therefore, the positional approach concerns itself primarily with determining how various people cluster together into equivalent "positions" within the structure of the network. People, in the positional approach, may be considered to be linked in the network because they are *structurally equivalent*, even if they do not have direct relations with each other. The pattern of relations a person uses that creates this structural equivalency is called a *role set* (Hammer, 1979).

Given its nature, the positional approach is quantitative. Its methods for representing social networks use formal graph theory to represent the relationships numerically within an $n \times n$ *matrix*, $x = (x_{ij})$, where x_{ij} represents the relation directed from actor i to actor j $(i, j = 1, ..., n)$ and $n =$ number of network members (Snijders, 2001). The matrix is then transformed into a visual representation to facilitate analysis. The resulting graph is created by defining the actors as nodes within the graph and the relations between the actors as links between nodes.

However, the graph should not be an end unto itself. Price (1981) cautions against simplistic analysis that relies primarily on the positional approach in his observation that:

> contemporary network analysts are conducting their research in terms of formal analytical models and at a level of technical complexity which may dismay and discourage as many as it has excited and encouraged. The focus is often exclusively on formal specification of structural aspects of the social relationships in the configuration isolated by the analyst. (p. 298)

Rogers (1987) also cautions that "far too much, I fear, we admire mathematical elegance in our network tools and toolmakers, while largely ignoring what useful objects we can dig up with these tools" (p. 14).

These cautions arise from the concerns both Price and Rogers have as social network researchers who rely on the *relational* approach to social network analysis. The relational approach can be traced back to the 1940s and arose primarily from traditional sociological and anthropological perspectives. In what is considered to be the first reference to social networks, the anthropologist Radcliffe-Brown (2002) noted that "in the study of social structure, the concrete reality with which we are concerned is the set of actually existing relations, at a given moment of time, which link together certain human beings" (p. 28). Furthermore, "social relations are only observed, and can only be described, by reference to the reciprocal behavior of the persons related" (p. 33).

The relational approach suggests that the totality of organizational systems affects the ability of people in the organization to connect and communicate with one another. An underlying assumption of this approach is that greater connectivity and communication can improve organizational performance. In contrast to the positional approach, the relational approach to social network analysis is an inherently comparative methodology for investigation. As is true in qualitative research, comparative research considers how the differences of each case under investigation fit together into a greater whole. However, comparative research diverges from a purely qualitative research methodology because the focus is on the examination of pattern of similarities and differences across a moderate number of cases (Ragin, 1994) rather than the cases themselves. With that understanding, the researcher tries to make sense of each case as well as the diversity and commonality of the set of cases as a whole (Ragin, 1987).

Structuration theory (Giddens, 1979) plays an important role in understanding the differences between these two approaches. Structuration theory suggests that structure contains process and that repeating process creates or adapts structure.

In the positional approach, the network that results from the network analysis represents the existing structure, which is a construct that constrains action (Burt, 1980). The existing structure, therefore, is a limiting factor. However, in the relational approach the network represents the actual interactions within the network that provide a means for potentially defining and redefining existing structure (Monge & Eisenberg, 1987). In this approach, the existing structure is a potentially liberating factor.

Methodological Issues in Social Network Analysis

Given the incredible diversity of disciplines from which social network analysis draws, a great variety of research designs and methods have been used in conducting studies involving social networks. Borrowing theory from mathematics (graph theory) and social psychology (balance theory and social comparison) while incorporating concepts and methods from sociology and anthropology, social network analysis relies on neither qualitative nor quantitative methods exclusively. It is the classic example of the pattern observed by Newman and Benz (1998) that "all behavioral research is made up of a combination of qualitative and quantitative constructs" (p. 9).

The methodological issues in social network analysis, therefore, are complex given its inherently quantitative and qualitative nature as reflected in the positional and relational approaches, respectively. Finding a balance between the two can be challenging, but it is necessary as most research on social networks uses a hybrid approach that draws from each methodology as is appropriate to the nature of the study.

Nonetheless, data collection within social network analysis tends to fall into well-defined patterns. Price notes that "the dominant research strategy in sociology has been to collect data from large representative samples of individuals in a cross-sectional study, with little observation or participation" (Price, 1981, p. 301). In research of this type, Marsden and Friedkin (1994a) have elaborated that these "empirical studies of social influence rarely work with longitudinal data; most researchers study data from cross-sectional designs and infer the operation of social influence from homogeneity among network elements that remains after adjusting for effects of covariates" (p. 11).

As has already been demonstrated, there are many ways in which network studies differ from other types of sociological studies. Perhaps the most obvious difference is that, in a network study, anonymity at the data collection stage is not possible (Borgatti & Molina, 2003). In conventional sociological studies, respondents report on themselves, but in social network studies, respondents report on other people, some of whom may not necessarily wish to be named. While potentially problematic, this is not generally viewed as an ethical problem because what respondents are normally reporting on is their perception of their relationship with another person, "which is clearly something respondents have a right to do: every respondent owns their own perceptions" (Borgatti & Molina, 2003, p. 339).

Social network analysis is often employed as a research methodology within a single organizational unit. Social structure, however, is not necessarily bounded by a formal organization. It also applies to inter-organizational relationships or collections of firms that work together to create networked or "virtual" organizations (Baker, 1993). Wellman and Leighton (1979) have cautioned that descriptions based on bounded groups can oversimplify complex social structures, treating them as well-organized organizational structures when it is the crosscutting memberships of individual network members, in multiple social circles, that weave together the social systems. Alba (1982) has noted that "natural boundaries may at times prove artificial, insofar as individuals within the boundaries may be linked through others outside of them" (p. 43).

Therefore, regardless of scope, establishing the boundary of the network under investigation is one of the fundamental issues that must be addressed when conducting research employing the network perspective (Conway, Jones, & Steward, 2001). In order to provide a defensible methodology for defining the initial boundary of the network in question, data that defines what constitutes the network nucleus is not usually obtained directly from individuals but instead comes from more neutral sources of information such as public listings, external observation, and formal organizational records.

The broadest definition of a personal social network would include all those with whom a person interacts on an informal basis. The average

North American has a maximum of approximately 20 active ties to "significant" individuals where the significance is established by frequent sociable contact and feelings of being supported or being connected (Walker, Wasserman, & Wellman, 1994). Consequently, the average size of a social network and the amount of analysis that will be required can generally be predicted with a high degree of confidence.

Approaches to the Study of Social Networks

Current research in social networks varies considerably in many dimensions from the practical to the theoretical, from strictly quantitative to exclusively qualitative, and from research focused on the structure of the network to that based on understanding the meaning of the network.

The most common method of performing social network analysis is *egocentric network analysis*. This is used to

> build a picture of a typical actor in any particular environment and show how many ties individual actors have to others, what types of ties they maintain, and what kind of information they give to and receive from others in their network. (Haythornthwaite, 1996, p. 328)

In studies of this type, concerns about the size of the study population have not been a major issue because the focus of research is most often on the reactions of individuals and their interactions with the environment and not necessarily on the generalizability of the findings to other contexts.

In contrast, *whole network analysis* is used to describe the ties that all actors in a network maintain within a network. By definition, the entire population of interest is part of the study. Barnes (1979) has noted that these types of "networks are interesting but difficult to study since real-world networks lack convenient natural boundaries" (p. 416). Therefore, except in studies of small populations or studies where the scope of the network is artificially constrained, whole network analysis is impractical because the entire scope of the network must be known in advance.

Within both methodological constructs, a number of qualitative methods can be used within the organizational context, ranging from the ethnomethodological to grounded theory (Strati, 2000). A general distinction between these approaches to qualitative social research is that ethnomethodology relies on *analytic induction* (Znaniecki, 1934), which principally seeks to describe social contexts as they are observed, whereas *grounded theory* (Glaser & Strauss, 1967) primarily seeks to construct theories on the basis of observations made in social contexts (Strati, 2000).

With all of these factors in mind, attempting to address issues related to how the construction of relationships within an individual's professional advice network influences their receptivity to innovation lends itself to egocentric network analysis relying on grounded theory to direct specific questions as the research evolves. Accordingly, qualitative data plays a role in understanding the results of this research; however, unlike other recent studies (Mohrman, Tenkasi, & Mohrman, 2003; Newell & Swan, 2000), the current study does not lend itself to using solely qualitative methods for analysis.

The potential biases inherent in relying on a single method in organizational network research can best be demonstrated by looking at studies on the extremes of the positional-relational spectrum. Faust's (1997) groundbreaking research on centrality in affiliation networks is clearly situated in the positional approach to social network analysis. Her study relied heavily on the mathematical foundations of social network analysis in the form of graph theory to develop a new conceptualization of centrality that builds upon the formal properties of affiliation networks while capturing theoretical insights about the positions of actors and events in these networks. The formality of the study is emphasized by the use of theory to build upon and further extend that theory. By using data from some of the most significant social network studies, Faust furthered the development of network theory by establishing clear ties between the existing research and her new research. While this approach is useful for developing formal theory, it does not provide any insight into the meanings behind these relationships, meanings which are critical to an investigation into organizational behavior within a social network.

On the other hand, while qualitative analysis has great value in case study research and has provided a basis for informing the research of the current study, a completely qualitative approach is often not adequate as it does not provide the data necessary to fully develop theory. This is demonstrated in the study conducted by Macrì, Tagliaventi, and Bertolotti (2002) where they attempted to develop a theory about the process that generates resistance to change in a small organization. Given its use of ethnography and grounded theory, the paper is very exploratory in its approach, but the internal validity is weak because they relied solely on qualitative data that was not transferable to another context.

Looking more broadly, analysis of studies that use a mixed-methods approach exposes patterns of inquiry that are useful in developing methods for studies such as the current one. For example, using mixed-methods Mackenzie (2005) explored how certain segments of a corporate population use their network to obtain information. The study is primarily qualitative, using interviews to capture data for content analysis, so complex statistical analysis was not part of this study. Nonetheless, statistical analysis played a role as simple percentage comparisons of populations falling into various control categories as well as bivariate comparisons of employee type by control category were used to determine the differences in the ways different segments of the population select others from whom to receive information.

Furthermore, Haythornthwaite (1998) investigated the social networking factors that affect the development of an online learning community by looking at how people communicate with each other – the methods, the frequency, the way information flows, and the kind of information being communicated. Relatively simple statistics were applied to control variables. For example, simple counts were used to measure frequency of interaction such as averages (mean and median) that established baseline measures of number of interactions as well as the number of others with whom interaction occurred. Even though the metric is simple, it is critical for creating the interaction measures in the network map.

Expanding the scope to the larger body of social network analysis research regardless of approach, Barnes' (2003) study of neighborhood ties and social resources in poor urban neighborhoods provides a model for how bivariate comparison of relationships between dependent and independent variables can be used to determine differences in the way various population segments interact within networks.

As can be seen from the previous examples, mixed-methods research is well represented in social network research. In fact, the study by Cross, Borgatti, and Parker (2001) on dimensions of an advice network occupies a central position in the theoretical background informing the design of the current study. By blending qualitative and quantitative approaches, the authors addressed how people receive informational benefits when consulting others and if individuals obtain all of the benefits from the same individual or do they create balanced portfolios of complementary contacts.

Ethical Issues Related to the Use of Social Network Analysis

Many of the ethnical issues related to social network analysis have developed based on the corporate environment, the primary context where social network analysis has been used. Purely academic social network organizational research, such as the current study, is relatively rare (Kadushin, 2005).

It has already been noted that "the dominant research strategy in sociology has been to collect data from large representative samples of individuals in a cross-sectional study, with little observation or participation" (Price, 1981, p. 301). If identifying information relating to participants and their associates can be obtained it becomes possible to piece together a picture, so to speak, of social network structure and to better understand implications of different structural properties (Klovdahl, 2005). Research of this type tends to not be longitudinal, for as Marsden and Friedkin (1994a) have elaborated "empirical studies of social influence rarely work with longitudinal data; most researchers study data from cross-sectional designs and infer the operation of social influence from homogeneity among network elements that remains after adjusting for effects of covariates" (p. 11).

It has also been noted that social network analysis is often used as a research methodology within a single organizational unit; however, social structure is not necessarily bound by a formal organization. Social structures apply to interorganizational relationships or collections of firms that work together to create networked or virtual organizations (Baker, 1993) because "natural boundaries may at times prove artificial, insofar as individuals within the boundaries may be linked through others outside of them" (Alba, 1982, p. 43). Caution is warranted as descriptions based on bounded groups can oversimplify complex social structures, treating them as well-organized organizational structures when it is actually the crosscutting memberships of the network members, in multiple social circles, that weave together the social systems (Wellman & Leighton, 1979).

Further complicating matters, in organizational settings, understanding the social network can provide insights that may provide managers with information their employees do not really want them to know. Ties in these networks can provide valuable information and resources related to the structure and control of information, power, and trust among individuals and groups (Stevenson, 2003).

Understanding the composition of a social network can lead to knowledge that impinges on privacy, which is a major concern of research in a closed, corporate network. One small example of this tension is represented by the conflict between knowing who works with whom, which might be a legitimate topic in a corporate network analysis, as opposed to who is friends with whom, which is murky ground, as knowledge of the friendship networks probably lies outside the purview of an employer (Borgatti & Molina, 2003).

Furthermore, some research has indicated that there can be unintended effects of social network analysis in a corporate environment. For example, Kadushin (2005) reported that people who were identified in the social network analysis as leading contributors in the organization were quite happy with this finding; those who were not so identified were not as pleased with the analysis and felt left out.

These issues, however, do not affect this study since it is not based in a corporate or single organizational context. The issues that do apply are more fundamental and are issues that are concerns in all studies that investigate social networks. These concerns arise from the one particularly distinctive attribute all social network research has, the collection of names of either individuals or social units. Typically, social research has focused on protecting the identity of research participants; however, in social network analysis the lack of anonymity is not incidental to the research, but is at its very core (Kadushin, 2005).

As identifying information is essential for effective social network research, confidentiality protection is also essential in such research. While Burkey and Kuechler (2003) observed that "the web survey can incorporate the strengths of personal interviews while maintaining respondent anonymity," (p. 81) some of the factors that are typically considered in a research design include how sensitive the data divulged is to the participants and what the possible value of the information collected may be to someone outside of the study population. Klovdahl (2005) has suggested that people studying social networks can address the foregoing by ensuring two issues are clarified within the research design. The first of these is whether the current work is ethically appropriate and the study, therefore, should proceed.

In the current study, there did not appear to be any violation of ethical issues related to anonymity of participants or others identified by participants. Although the names of individuals were collected, these names are not primary to the purposes of the research, and they were used within the study mainly as a facilitating mechanism for gathering data on the characteristics of the individual respondent's social network rather than as an end unto themselves. The questions did not collect information of a personal nature nor did they require the respondent to make evaluative statements regarding their relationships. The focus of the questions was on broad trends of interaction rather than on the specifics of individual interactions.

The second issue identified by Klovdahl (2005), which has also been discussed by Andrews, Nonnecke, and Preece (2003), is the level and type of confidentiality protection needed to provide a level of privacy appropriate to any given study. It has been suggested that this issue can be addressed by focusing on two major concerns.

First, researchers must ensure that the data collection instrument should keep identifying information separate from other information. In this study, the invitation to participate was kept separate from the instrument itself (Cho & Larose, 1999). In addition, the control numbers assigned to respondents in the invitation were kept in a file that was not associated with the instrument directly. Specifically in regard to social network data, Klovdahl (2005) notes that network data is more secure when each network member is assigned a unique network node that cannot be directly linked back to participant identifiers. Respondents only entered their control number when they completed the instrument; they were not asked for any other identifying information.

The second concern is to restrict the number of project personnel who have access to identifying/linking information. Given the nature of the study, the only person who had access to this linking information was the primary researcher.

The last major issue related to social network analysis concerns who is actually considered a subject of the research and who is not. Given the nature of ethnocentric analysis, it is not surprising that this would be an issue; however, this area has not been extensively explored in the social network analysis literature. What research that has been conducted is primarily in public health environmental studies where disclosure of social network information is a major issue given that compromised privacy could have a significant impact on both the study and participants.

In this context, Klovdahl (2005) noted that most institutional research review boards rely on the Common Federal Rule (Common Rule) to determine who is considered a human subject because research funded by US federal agencies relies on this rule exclusively. It has been argued, using this rule, that the actors in a network who are named by study participants, but who have not been directly interviewed by the study investigator, should not be considered human subjects for purposes of the study. This is because, following the Common Rule, participants are only considered human subjects if they interact directly with the study investigators.

This meshes well with most social network analysis as there is no convenient way of gaining the consent of the people named as part of the network unless an interviewing procedure based on snowball sampling

(Goodman, 1961) is used to contact these people (Thompson, 2002). On the contrary, snowball sampling can often be problematic because there may not be enough individually identifiable information to allow the researcher to contact every identified individual. More importantly, there is often no direct interest (in terms of the study) in contacting the named subjects. Moreover, many social network researchers do not believe the issue of named subjects is a concern at all because what respondents are reporting on is their perception of a relationship with another, not on the other person directly, and people clearly have the right to report on their own perceptions of their environment (Borgatti & Molina, 2003). As a result, when all these factors are considered, social network analysis research typically does not assume named participants are human subjects.

METHODOLOGY

Social network analysis allows a researcher to explore the patterns of relationships among people (referred to as *actors*), to include the availability of resources to these actors, and the exchange of resources between actors (Scott, 2000; Wasserman & Faust, 1994; Wellman & Berkowitz, 1988) in a network of relationships. Through the various methods of social network analysis, it is possible to develop constructs that provide understanding of how relationships within a group are formed and maintained and used. In turn, this can potentially provide the researcher with greater insight into individual behavioral characteristics of the members within a group.

In order to accomplish this, effective analysis of social networks draws upon the distinctive features that set it apart from traditional approaches to sociological inquiry. These features include (a) a focus on relations and the patterns of relations rather than on attributes of individual actors in those relations; (b) an amenability to multiple levels of analysis geared toward providing micro–macro linkages; and (c) an inherent integration of quantitative, qualitative, and graphical data to allow more thorough and in-depth analysis (Kilduff & Tsai, 2003).

When organizational studies investigate related phenomena in several different settings as the current study does, the investigation typically follows one of two strategies: theoretical sampling or purposive sampling. Theoretical sampling, a term coined by Glaser and Strauss (1967), is the process where new research sites or cases are chosen to compare with one that has already been studied. Although theoretical sampling is a method for addressing some of the inherent internal validity concerns of a single case study, it is not appropriate for the current study as there is no original research site or case with which to compare. Derived from theoretical sampling is *purposive sampling*, a method for selecting individuals from a population according to an underlying research interest in a particular group within the larger population. Purposive sampling techniques are not based on probabilistic sampling theory, so they may not generate a sample population that is completely representative; however, given the nature of the current study, purposive sampling is appropriate as it is frequently very effective in predicting patterns of behavior within the general population given a correctly chosen purposive sample (Brewerton & Millward, 2001).

Description of Research Design

The current study was strongly influenced by the dominant strategies used by social network research in the last two decades as well as emerging best practice. That strategy, based on descriptive correlation, has been to collect data from large samples of people (Price, 1981), with longitudinal studies being relatively rare (Marsden & Friedkin, 1994a).

The main hypotheses of this study were investigated using multiple techniques and analytical tools. Justification for selecting specific techniques and tools has been developed by analyzing relevant current research. For example, by using Cross et al.'s (2001) study as a model, the current study incorporated quantitative questions to investigate the number of relationships in social networks in addition to a combination of quantitative and qualitative questions to extract details related to interchanges within the network. However, in contrast to their method, this study gathered data from the participants through the distribution of a three-section questionnaire rather than attempting to perform in-person interviews with all of the actors within any particular network.

While many of the questions were quantitatively based, some of the questions used could not effectively be addressed solely with a quantitative approach as they gathered qualitative data on the nature of the relationships within the network. While acknowledging that many analytical concepts in social network analysis can be presented quantitatively without difficulty, facilitating the comparability, repeatability, and discriminatory power of those concepts, Barnes (1979) has stressed the implications of the standardization of quantitative expression by pointing out that other analytical concepts that are often found in social network analysis remain intractably qualitative. Efforts to make them quantitative are not workable.

Determining the Structural Characteristics of the Professional Advice Network

The scope and size of the professional advice network of each respondent forms the independent variable in this study. Within the relational tradition of social network analysis, there are two possible approaches to determining the scope of the network itself: bounded (whole network analysis) and egocentric (personal) network assessments (Scott, 2000).

The bounded approach is used in situations where the entire network of individuals to be studied is known in advance, for instance, all the employees within an organization. With this approach, each person in the group is asked about their relationship with every other person in the group. In contrast, the more commonly used egocentric approach is employed when the composition of the network is not known in advance. By far, this is the most common method of analysis, because it builds

> a picture of a typical actor in any particular environment and shows how many ties individual actors have to others, what types of ties they maintain, and what kind of information they give to and receive from others in their network. (Haythornthwaite, 1996, p. 328)

In egocentric analysis, every member of the sample population is asked to identify the other people, within the domain of the study, who are important for a specific task or function regardless of whether they are within a particular bound network or not. Follow-up questions are then used to explore the nature of these relationships.

Given the nature of the current study, the egocentric approach was the logical choice. If the current study were focused on the patterns of interaction within a finite network, the bounded approach would be appropriate; however, the current study is concerned with the totality of networks of the individual librarians – within their own institution and within the larger library community. Therefore, the scope of the network cannot be known in advance and the egocentric approach had to be used.

The structural characteristics of the professional advice networks in the current study were solicited via a *name generator* procedure (Burt, 1984; Walker et al., 1994). This process is a rich example of grounded theory in practice, as the name generator procedure provides a means for respondents to specify the significant actors within their network as well as the roles and relationships these people play within that network. In other words, the name generator procedure allows the participant to both define the purpose of their interactions with others and identify the type of support they seek from these people.

In this study, this process was operationalized by asking the respondents to name the people to whom they go for help or with whom they discuss important matters (Campbell & Lee, 1991) and to identify the nature of the relationships they have with these people (Walker et al., 1994).

Measuring the Professional Advice Network

Measuring the size of a social network in the egocentric model is rather straightforward. As the broadest definition of a personal network would include all those with whom a person interacts regularly on an informal basis, the subject is simply asked to list every individual in his or her professional life with whom they interact on a regular basis. As the average North American has a maximum of 20 active ties to significant individuals, this is not as daunting a challenge as it may at first seem. Based on this knowledge, the maximum size of a professional social network can be estimated with a high degree of confidence.

Understanding the scope of a social network is not quite as straightforward. As discussed by Cross and Parker (2004), simply understanding that people interact is not enough to understand the social network. A researcher needs specific information on the ways people interact, which in turn provides data that can aid in understanding the scope of the relationships. Consequently, the survey questions focused on issues related to the scope of collaboration, the information-sharing potential, supportiveness of ties, and the rigidity within the network.

Measuring Receptivity to Innovation

The dependent variable in the current study was the measure of receptivity to innovation. The measure of this dimension provided information about who in the study exhibited attitudinal indicators of receptivity or resistance to organizational innovation.

The use of survey instruments to measure dogmatism and receptivity to new ideas has a long history (Rokeach, 1960; Schulze, 1962; Troldahl & Powell, 1965). One particular instrument in this tradition, which has been used for the measurement of receptivity to innovation in both non-profit and governmental organizations is the Rusaw Multifactor Assessment instrument (2001). Given that "conceptualization of innovativeness as a unidimensional construct is inappropriate" (Damanpour, 1992, p. 641), this instrument measures several attitudinal dimensions (Appendix B) which are operationalized as questions that apply to a particular dimension of innovative behavior (Appendix C). In addition to an analysis of each attitudinal dimension, the instrument provides an overall score indicating the degree of receptivity to innovation an individual has in general. Finally, the version of the instrument used in the current study was adapted specifically to contextualize the questions within the context of academic libraries.

Model for Statistical Analysis

The model for statistical analysis in this study is based on a study by Tenkasi and Chesmore (2003). In the model, they investigated the relationship of network density to the formation of strong personal ties within a corporate-based network by studying 40 organizational units in a large multinational corporation during a time of extensive organizational change. This model study used means and standard deviations to establish baseline measures of population categories and hierarchical linear regression to estimate the effect of the independent variables on the dependent variables.

Power Analysis in the Current Study

The population for the current study was a purposive sample of academic librarians drawn from the membership of the CARLI (Consortium of Academic and Research Libraries in Illinois, 2006). Several factors were considered in choosing this particular sample population for this study and these are discussed more fully in the section *Selection of Subjects.*

The decision to use purposive sampling was based on the widespread use and acceptance of purposive sampling in social network studies. Inherent to the method, study subjects are selected intentionally, based on characteristics that appeared to be related to the overall purpose of the research. Although some researchers question the effectiveness of purposive sampling, Biemer and Lyberg (2003) noted that purposive samples of larger sizes can be quite accurate, as the amount of sampling error goes down in inverse proportion to the number of respondents. The major question in a study based on purposive sample is whether the number of participants in the sample is great enough to ensure adequate statistical power in the study.

The *Normal distribution, 1 sample Power Calculator* (Normal distribution, 1 sample Power Calculator, 2004) was used to determine the minimum sample size needed for the current study. In the study, the receptivity to innovation indicators (the main variable measured) used a 5-point Likert scale. Using Cohen's (1988) recommendation to test for small effect size in the distribution under the alternative hypothesis, the following parameters were assumed:

1. The mean of the distribution under the null hypothesis is $H_0 = 3$,
2. The mean of the distribution under the alternative hypothesis is 2.8 $< = H_1 = > 3.2$,
3. The standard deviation is equal to 1,
4. $\alpha = 0.05$, and
5. The statistical power desired for the test is 0.80.

Based on these parameters, the minimum appropriate sample size for this study was estimated to be 58 people in total to attain a statistical power of 0.80. While there are no fixed rules about how much power is enough, consensus among statisticians is that the power level of a study must be above 0.50 because the study is more likely to fail than succeed when the power level drops below that level. A power level of 0.80 or above is preferred in most studies, with 0.90 being ideal. Although this convention is arbitrary in the same way that significance criteria of 0.05 or 0.01 are arbitrary, a power of 0.80 is typically used as a baseline as it means success (that is, rejecting the null hypothesis) is four times as likely as failure (Murphy & Myors, 2004). To attain a statistical power of 0.90, the minimum number of samples would have to have been 96 people in total. Given there are at least two potential sample members from 178 different institutions, it seemed reasonable to assume the sample pool would be large enough to result in a study with a power of 0.90. In fact, the total number of respondents was 440, well above the required number.

Operational Definition of Constructs and Key Variables

The design of the survey instrument was guided by four principles outlined by Aronson, Ellsworth, Carlsmith, and Gonzalez (1990) as being critical in creating an effective research environment: coherence of elements within the study, simplicity in design, active involvement of the research participants, and consistency in effect among all research participants.

Using these principles, the survey instrument consisted of three sets of questions designed to gather information in three distinct areas: (a) the respondent's receptivity to innovation, (b) the scope and structure of the respondent's professional advice network, and (c) general demographic information about the respondent.

The first section of the survey instrument used an adapted form of the Rusaw Multifactor Assessment (2001) instrument to measure the receptivity of the respondent to innovation. Based on several distinct factors that contribute to innovation (Appendix B), the instrument provided both an individual factor level and an overall score for each individual measuring their degree of receptivity to innovation.

The second section of the questionnaire measured the scope and structure of each participant's professional advice network. These questions (Appendix A) were based on a validated instrument used by Cross and Parker (2004) to measure the scope and structure of individual professional advice networks. In the current study, the questions designed by Cross and Parker were used with only minor language changes designed to tailor the questions to the environmental context of the current study.

The questions in the survey solicited data about the nature of the relationships individuals have with their professional peers, such as how often interactions occur with specific peers and what the hierarchical relationship is between the peer and the respondent, which is a particularly important question in the local organizational context. These data were used to gauge multiple aspects of the professional relations within each participant's network, as well as to determine the scope of network connectivity within the individual networks.

Supplemental questions were added to the second section to gather information about the nature of current and potential organized professional interactions the study participants may have; that is, what professional organizations they belong to and their level of participation in those organizations.

Studies, such as Morrel-Samuels (2002) and Burkey and Kuechler (2003), have suggested that demographic questions should appear at the end of a survey; therefore, the collection of demographic data about the survey participants was deferred in this study to the third section of the survey. The data included the standard demographic control variables typically used in social network studies (age, gender, race, and ethnicity, level within the organization, length of tenure), as well as demographic indicators that are specific to this study, such as the type of academic institution and functional area within the library where the respondent works.

Control Variables

In the current study, as is typical in social network analysis studies that are relationally based, the demographic characteristics of individuals have been used as the control variables, primarily because these represent potential alternative explanations to network-derived sources of social influence.

The first aspect of this is age, which could have been an important factor in relationship to the overall size and density of the professional advice network. Furthermore, length of tenure could also have had the same impact on the size, structure, and membership of that network.

A second aspect is gender, as Ibarra's (1997) research indicates that men, in general, have larger social networks than women. Given that librarianship is known to be profession populated primarily by women, it would not have been surprising if the membership characteristics of the professional advice networks were significantly influenced by gender affinity. This is a particularly reasonable assumption given McPherson and Smith-Lovin's (1986) findings that found members of voluntary associations, such as the American Library Association, tend to be very similar to others in the association. That is, voluntary membership organizations tend to follow gender affinities.

Race and ethnicity could also have played an important role in the same way, either as a potentially inclusive or exclusive factor, because librarianship is a profession that is not especially diverse. As indicated in the demographic analysis of the study population, this lack of diversity was clearly demonstrated.

Similar to age, a person's organizational level has the potential to affect the composition of their professional advice network as "in general, a manager's interactional network with coworkers and outside associates is large and more heterogeneous than a nonmanager's comparable network" (Carroll & Teo, 1996, p. 423).

Finally, anecdotal evidence indicated that type of institution (Carnegie Research Extensive, Carnegie Research Intensive, Masters, etc.) and functional area (such as public services, technical services, collection management, information technology) might well have a significant effect on the membership of individual networks due to the effect of homophily.

Description of Materials and Instruments

The research survey is presented in Appendix D. The construction of the overall instrument was guided by Psacharopoulos' (1980) advice that "questionnaires should be short, containing only questions the answers to which are going to be actually used, avoiding 'interesting' questions" (p. 161). This sentiment is echoed by Lund and Gram (1998). Additionally, the questions were distributed over a several pages design rather than a single, monolithic page (Manfreda, Batagelj, & Vehovar, 2002). Both of these approaches were taken to help ensure a higher response rate. Finally, each of the pages in the web-based survey included an explicit progress indicator, so respondents were able to estimate how close they were to finishing (Dillman & Bowker, 2001).

The first section of the survey instrument is based on the Rusaw Multi-factor Assessment instrument (Rusaw, 2001) as described in Appendix B, with the adapted form of the questions detailed in Appendix C. The second section of the questionnaire is based on Cross and Parker's instrument (2004) that is designed to measure the scope and structure of each participant's professional advice network. This instrument is outlined in Appendix A.

Instrument Reliability and Validity Analyses

As Litwin (2003) noted, "construct validity is the most valuable and yet the most difficult way of assessing a survey instrument" (p. 41). Proof of the validity of a particular instrument only happens, in most cases, after many years of use. Rusaw (2001) and Cross and Parker (2004) both have proven track records in the particular areas they address.

Adapting or adopting questions that have been used successfully in other studies is a technique that can also be used when appropriate (Fink, 2003), and this typically occurs when a researcher is studying a population other than the original population for which an instrument was designed. Given the context of the current study, both instruments used as a basis for the questions were adapted to focus on librarians working in an academic library (Bourque & Fielder, 2003). Assuming that it was possible for these modifications to have introduced reliability or validity issues into the instruments, the researcher chose to conduct a pilot test of the survey to determine what problems respondents might encounter (Forsyth, Rothgeb, & Willis, 2004). As a result, the researcher was able to verify that the language of the survey was appropriate, that the questions were unambiguous, and that the questions could be answered by the target audience without misunderstandings.

Even though the questions in the current study were based on instruments that have been tested, their application in this particular context was not. By performing this test, some issues related to the adaptation of the questions to the current study surfaced and minor modifications were made to the survey instrument.

Given that the bank of questions in the Rusaw (2001) instrument measures each dimension of receptivity to innovation with a set of questions, internal consistency reliability tests using *Cronbach's alpha* were used to provide a quantitative measurement of how well the instrument performed in this particular research context (Litwin, 2003). When *Cronbach's alpha* was run on data acquired during the pilot test, in each of the nine different aspects of innovation along with the overall receptivity to innovation score, the $\alpha = 0.7537$ and the standardized $\alpha = 0.8751$, indicating that the overall innovation score has a multidimensional structure (that is, no one innovation category can be completely correlated to the overall innovation score), but that the instrument overall has adequate internal consistency in the average correlation among all pair items.

In addition, a significant observation was made as a result of the pilot test. Several of the test participants noted that they had difficulty ranking the relationships in their professional advice network because some of their "professional" advisors were not work-related peers at all but family members or people completely unrelated to their profession. This is particularly significant, because there is no indication in the existing social network literature that people regularly include anyone other than professionally affiliated peers in their professional advice network.

Based on the success of the pilot, the researcher used the web-based method for data collection in the actual study. With the complexity of the data gathered, the elimination of manual data rekeying from paper into a statistical analysis tool was a significant help in processing the survey data and ensuring the quality of the collected data was not compromised (Manfreda et al., 2002).

Selection of Subjects

As was previously indicated, the use of the CARLI population as the sampling frame was considered very carefully. Three main considerations argued in favor of this particular purposive sample.

To begin with, the environment within the state of Illinois provided a rich environment for an individual to create a professional advice network outside his/her own immediate institutional environment. Because of the strong tradition of statewide cooperation, academic libraries in Illinois are able to provide greater opportunity for an individual to create a professional advice network than would be possible in most other areas of the United States. Secondly, the population within CARLI is well defined and discoverable, and, because the researcher in this study is employed by a CARLI institution, the population within the CARLI consortium was readily accessible for purposes of this research. This is not the case with other statewide consortia, such as Ohio or Colorado, where membership within the organization was less readily available. Thirdly, the CARLI-member population provided a broad-based representation across all types of academic libraries and library functional areas. The population of CARLI includes institutions from all Carnegie academic classifications, from the very smallest to the largest, as well as both public and private institutions. With at least two institutions of each category being represented within the consortium, using the CARLI-member population as a sample population base provided for the possibility of including representatives of every type of higher education institution.

Procedures

Traditionally, similar types of research have used paper survey forms that were mailed to all the identified participants. The initial mailing would have consisted of a cover letter briefly describing the purpose of the study, the survey itself, and a stamped, self-addressed return envelope. The surveys would not contain any markings to identify respondents; however, the return envelopes would be coded to facilitate follow-up of unreturned surveys.

In contrast, the current study conducted the data collection process through an online instrument. There were several reasons for taking this approach. As indicated earlier, both Smith (1997) as well as Yun and Trumbo (2000) have noted that web-based surveys can outperform paper-based surveys in terms of response rate, particularly with populations that have considerable experience with the Internet. Furthermore, Shannon, Johnson, Searcy, and Lott (2002) have found that online surveys are effective with targeted populations of professionals. Nosek, Banaji, and Greenwald (2002) also noted that web-based surveys specifically have a clear sampling advantage when sample populations cannot easily be interviewed or when the sample population overall is relatively small. Furthermore, with the questionnaire format, the potential problems of courting social approval or generating unduly positive reports from respondents as a method of self-presentation (Wentland & Smith, 1993) are lessened, which is a significant concern within social network research as people may slant their descriptions of organizational reality to their own benefit (Alvesson & Deetz, 2000). An additional advantage is that the dynamic nature of web-based surveys (Baker, Crawford, & Swinehart, 2004) greatly facilitates the collection of social network information.

Potential participants were first solicited via an e-mail that informed them of the study. This initial e-mail was sent to all librarians identified within the local staff directories of each CARLI institution as of August 2, 2006. The message briefly described the purpose of the study and requested that the participant take the web-based survey. In the message, an individual code was included that was useful in correlating responses to institutional participation data as well as facilitating follow-up with non-responders. Three weeks after the initial e-mail, a postal mailing reminding potential participants of the study as well as the URL for the survey instrument was sent to those respondents who had not participated at that point. The use of a regular postal mailing for the reminder was based on Yun and Trumbo's (2000) research that indicates integrating use of regular postal mail and electronic mail can increase response rates by as much as 70%.

Originally, the researcher intended to send a second follow-up US postal mailing to non-respondents. In that mailing, the intention was to omit the response code and the request for the participant to use the code when filling out the survey. This initial plan was predicated on research that has found that foregoing the coding on a survey can improve the return rate for the last group of respondents (Fowler, 1993; Sheehan & Hoy, 1999). However, given the already high response rate, the researcher did not feel it was necessary to follow-up a second time.

Originally, it had been estimated that the total number of invitations to participate would be at least 130 people if the sample population focused exclusively on formal institutional representatives. Assuming a minimum of 130 solicitations to participate, a minimum return rate of 45% would have been required for adequate and reliable research to be conducted. However, since not all CARLI members have formal institutional representatives, the sample population was broadened to include all librarians at the various institutions.

Discussion of Data Processing

Once data gathering is complete, the first step in the analysis of most social networks is to produce a network diagram to demonstrate the structural characteristics of the network based on the relationships reported. The algorithms that are used in the social network graphing software place people with the most ties in the center of the network and those with the fewest ties on the periphery of the network. Other aspects of the relationship, such as those measured by the questions in Appendix A, are used by the graphing algorithms to modify the shape of the diagram by placing individuals with closer relationships in greater proximity to each other while increasing the distance between those less connected.

However, overall network diagrams, while being a useful tool for visually understanding the physical structure of a network, do not necessarily expose the deep structural information of a network. As such, they were not considered to be a primary analytic approach for purposes of this paper. Instead, the underlying matrices upon which these diagrams are built were of more interest for the purposes of the current study.

For purposes of this study, a critical aspect was *network density* – the proportion of relations a person has among the total possible number of relations. This measure indicates how "connected" a person is within a network. The value of network density is arrived at by performing matrix operations on the network data and generating measures of more basic variables such as *degree centrality* – which determines the relative importance of an actor within the network based on the number of relations that that actor has with others in the network (Faust & Wasserman, 1992; Knoke & Burt, 1983). This can be further subdivided by specific types of relations: (a) *in-degree centrality* – those links reported by other group members about the actor under consideration; (b) *out-degree centrality* – those links reported by the actor under consideration; (c) *network proximity* (also known as *network strength*) – a measure of *reciprocated links* – the links where there is both an in-degree and out-degree relation; and (d) *network size* – a measure of the total number of actors within a network.

However, network density is not useful without the consideration of control variables and standard measures, such as mean and median, which were used to analyze these control variables. In the current study, these indicators were critical in analyzing demographic information, such as occupation, occupational level, age, gender, etc., and its effect or role in the composition of the network. For example, to address the first hypothesis, two different approaches were used. To understand the significance of the correlation of network size with receptivity to innovation, the study used descriptive correlation of the size of each individual professional network to the individual's receptivity to innovation. In particular, analyses of the density of the individual professional advice networks were compared to the innovation factor scores to determine if there were any meaningful correlations between the two variables.

Subsequently, to understand the issues related to network diversity and innovation, structural analysis (Wellman, 2002) was used to investigate how, if at all, individual networks differ structurally from each other. Analysis of covariance (ANCOVA) was used to compare the different population segments to see if there were statistically significant differences in relationships or differences between segments.

Addressing the additional hypotheses required additional summarization, analysis, and description of the variables that are correlated with the networks of individuals having high and low innovation receptivity scores, respectively.

Finally, to explore questions related to control variables, such as which occupational categories may be more receptive to innovation than others or whether particular age brackets have more diverse professional advice networks, Spearman's rank correlation was applied to all of the control variables as well as the receptivity to innovation index and network measures, such as network size, centrality, in-degree, and out-degree. In addition, multiple regression analysis was applied to combinations of the control variables that, based on the Spearman rank correlations, appeared to be significantly related.

Methodological Assumptions and Limitations

At a macro level, no single perspective or approach can explain all of the aspects of social and cultural phenomena (Merton, 1975). However, social phenomena can be explained to a great degree by social structure methodologies (Blau, 1977; Mayhew, 1980), such as social network analysis. Descriptive statistics are used widely in organizational studies because "they excel at summarizing large amounts of data and reaching generalizations based on statistical projections" (Trochim, 2001, p. 153). However, this advantage can also be a drawback. Descriptive statistics are inherently a methodology of summation at the expense of detailed analysis of context.

Alvesson (2000) has observed that strict reliance on methods such as descriptive statistics, at the expense of others, leads to situations where research does not provide deep, rich, and realistic understandings of environments. All of these aspects are critical to performing a meaningful analysis of a social network.

FINDINGS

At the time of the survey, there were 178 higher education institutions, in 230 locations, that were affiliated with the CARLI consortium. Of these institutions, 65 (37% of the consortia membership) form a distinct subset known as *I-Share* (see Fig. 1). These institutions are distinguished from the others by their use of a centrally managed consortial library management system (LMS). Use of this centralized LMS provides many opportunities for library staff at the participating institutions to interact with personnel from other libraries through committee work, task forces, and various special interest group meetings.

Library staff at the non-*I-Share* institutions, which account for 63% (Fig. 1) of the total number of member institutions, also have networking opportunities within the consortia, but these are not as extensive as those of the *I-Share* libraries.

It was possible to identify 3,270 current library staff members in the various CARLI-member institutions. Information about staff members was derived from online staff directories found on the member institution web

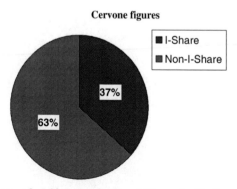

Fig. 1. Percentage of *I-Share* and Non-*I-Share* Institutions in the CARLI Consortium.

sites, which were located from the online CARLI membership directory. Of the staff identified in the various consortia member libraries, 2,036 (62%) people were at *I-Share* libraries (Fig. 2). Further analysis of the *I-Share* staff figures shows that 413 staff members, 13% of the overall staff member total, are *primary contacts*, people who have a formally defined role as an institutional representative to the consortium. The non-*I-Share* libraries account for 1,234 (38%) staff members. This points out an interesting characteristic of the sample population, for while the majority of libraries in the consortium are not *I-Share* members, the majority of academic librarians working in the state are at *I-Share* libraries.

All classes within the Carnegie classification of academic institutions are represented by the 178 members of the CARLI consortium. Using the simplified version of the latest Carnegie classification scheme (The Carnegie Classification of Institutions of Higher Education, 2006), Table 1 demonstrates that although all Carnegie classes are represented within the consortium, the distribution of members among the classes is not equal.

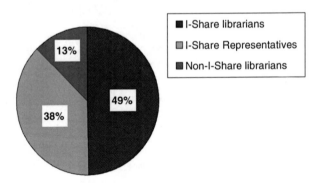

Fig. 2.   Distributions of Library Staff within the CARLI Consortium.

Table 1.   CARLI Institutions by Carnegie Class (*N* = 178).

Carnegie Class	N	P
Associate	58	32.60
Bachelor's	23	12.92
Master's	26	14.60
Doctorate	12	6.74
Special	59	33.14
Total	178	100.00

The largest number of institutions is found in the associate degree granting and special library classes and the smallest number is found at the doctoral level.

The distribution of staff members among the various Carnegie classifications is also not uniform; however, this is not totally unexpected. The number of staff in a library tends to increase as the number and scope of academic programs increases, so it is to be expected that the greatest number of staff will be found at doctoral-level institutions. In fact, this is the case within the CARLI consortium where 48.3% of all staff members in the CARLI consortium work in a doctoral-level institution (see Table 2).

Once the sample base had been identified, e-mails were sent to the 3,270 individuals on August 2, 2006. The initial responses to the survey were received within hours. For those participants who had not responded, a follow-up letter was sent by US mail on August 18, 2006. As a result, 593 responses were received before the end of the data collection period on September 2, 2006. Of the total number of responses received, 440 were complete. This represents a response rate of 11.83%.

Of the 593 responses, 153 responses were discarded for one of three reasons:

1. Seventy-two responses were discarded as the respondent abandoned the survey before answering any questions;
2. Sixty-three responses were discarded as the respondent abandoned the survey after responding to the innovation indicators, but before defining their social network; and finally
3. Eighteen were discarded as they only contained a partial response to the questions related to their professional social network which made it impossible to produce a meaningful analysis.

Table 2. Distribution of CARLI Library Staff by Carnegie Class ($N = 3,270$).

Carnegie Class	N	P
Associate	505	15.44
Bachelor's	151	4.62
Master's	617	18.87
Doctorate	1,581	48.35
Special	416	12.72
Total	3,270	100.00

Table 3.   Institutions Represented by Survey Responses within Carnegie
Class ($N = 92$).

Carnegie Class	N	%	P Represented within Class
Associate	27	29.35	46.55
Bachelor's	15	16.30	65.21
Master's	22	23.91	84.61
Doctorate	11	11.96	91.66
Special	17	18.48	28.81
Total	92	100.00	

Table 4.   Number of Respondents within Carnegie Class ($N = 440$).

	N	P	P Respondents within Class
Associate	48	10.9	9.5
Bachelor's	36	8.2	23.84
Master's	90	20.5	14.58
Doctorate	216	49.1	13.66
Special	50	11.4	12.09
Total	440	100.0	

Responses to the survey were received from staff members at 51.68% of
the CARLI institutions (see Table 3). While responses were received
from all segments within the Carnegie classes, the percentage of institutions
represented within each class was not consistent. The lowest rate of
representation was in the two classes with the largest number of institutions:
associate degree granting and special libraries.

When the individual responses were categorized by potential number of
respondents within Carnegie class, a slightly different picture emerged. As is
seen in Table 4, when compared to the potential number of respondents,
associate level institutions are underrepresented in the respondent pool;
however, bachelor's level institutions are overrepresented.

Notwithstanding, Fig. 3 demonstrates that the overall percentage of
distribution of responses is not dissimilar to the overall distribution of
staff within the consortium which indicates that this unequal distribution
of responses is representative of the characteristics of the sample population.

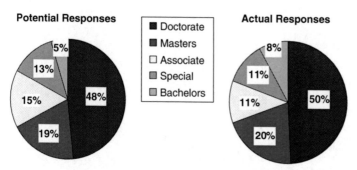

Fig. 3. Population Percentages by Carnegie Class – Potential Versus Actual Responses.

Respondent Demographic Data

In social network analysis studies, control variables are often based on demographic characteristics such as gender, age, race, and ethnicity. In this study, additional demographic characteristics such as type of institution at which an individual works, functional level within the organization, tenure in current job, total career length, and functional area within the library were also considered. This use of additional demographic characteristics in data analysis is consistent with other research based on social network analysis (Watts, 2003).

Of the 440 survey respondents, 312 (70.9%) were female and 128 (29.1%) were male. This gender imbalance is not surprising, as it is a well-known characteristic of the profession (Grimm & Stern, 1974; Joswick, 1999; Pavalko, 1988; Simpson, 2004).

The age range within the sample population (Fig. 4) represents a wide span, from a low of 21 to a high of 79, with an average age of 46.08 years. This bias toward an older demographic is consistent with other studies of demographic patterns within the profession (Lynch, 2002; Pankl, 2004; St. Lifer, 2000; Wilder, 1996, 2003).

Length of time within the profession (Fig. 5) for the survey population ranges from those who have just started (less than 1 year of experience) to people who have been in the profession their entire working life (over 40 years), with the average length of time in the profession being 16.43 years. However, the distribution of career lengths is not normal and has several spikes with many people clustered around 5, 15, and 25 years of career service.

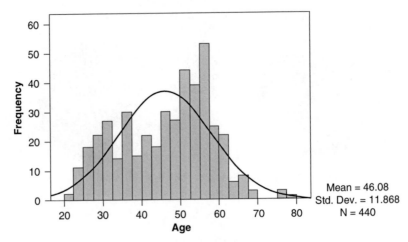

Fig. 4. Age Distribution.

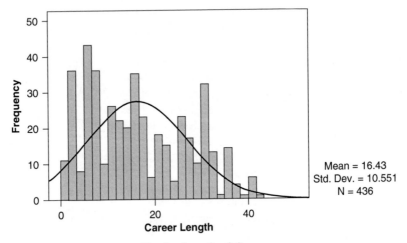

Fig. 5. Length of Career.

The average amount of time members of the survey population have spent in their current position (Fig. 6) is less than half of their average amount of time within the profession. Members of the survey population, on average, have been in their current position for 7.15 years.

Consistent with other studies of demographics within librarianship, the overwhelming majority of respondents are Caucasian (see Table 5), with the

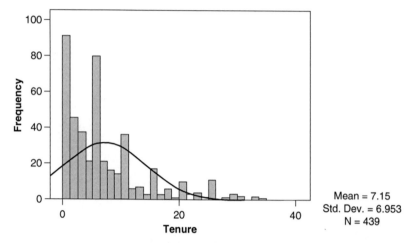

Fig. 6. Length of Tenure in Current Position.

Table 5. Race and Ethnic Identification (*N* = 440).

Identification	*N*	*P*
American Indian/Alaska Native	3	0.68
Hispanic/Latino	3	0.68
Multiracial	3	0.68
Asian	8	1.82
Prefer not to state	8	1.82
Black/African American	16	3.64
White/Caucasian	399	90.68
Total	440	100.0

total number of all minority group members representing less than 10% of the survey population.

As functional level within the organization might have been a factor in both the overall composition of a person's professional social network and their receptivity to innovation, survey participants were asked to identify their position in the library within broad categories of responsibility. Within the survey population (see Table 6), 33.6% of the respondents identified as being in a job category typically considered part of the management structure with 14.5% of the survey population in positions that would be considered senior management level.

Table 6. Sample Population by Job Category ($N = 440$).

Job Category	N	P
Director, dean, or university librarian	38	8.64
Asst./assoc. director, dean, or university librarian	26	5.91
Department head	84	19.09
Librarian – supervisor	76	17.27
Professional staff – supervisor	23	5.23
Librarian – not a supervisor	80	18.18
Professional staff – not a supervisor	30	6.82
Nonexempt library support staff	83	18.86
Total	440	100.0

Table 7. Sample Population by Functional Area ($N = 440$).

Functional Area	N	P
Administration	78	17.73
Archives and special collections	24	5.45
Collection development	23	5.23
Information technology	49	11.14
Public services	181	41.14
Technical services	85	19.31
Total	440	100.0

Finally, functional areas within the organization may also be a factor in the overall composition of a person's social network and their receptivity to innovation. Within the survey population, 41.1% of the respondents identified themselves as being in public services, a job category that is typically the "front line" of the library: the job functions that interact directly with patrons on a daily basis (Table 7).

Measures of Receptivity to Innovation

In the study, the variables used to measure the social networks of the respondent were based on a survey instrument developed by Cross and Parker (2004). The variables measured the types of relationships within the network, various aspects of the physical proximity of the network members, the longevity of the relationship, as well as the number of interactions.

Overall, the majority of the members within the respondents' professional advice network are people in the workplace. As shown in Table 8, coworkers, supervisors, and subordinates make up 54.7% of the typical network. Professional colleagues (34.3%) outside the immediate workplace make up the second largest group of network members.

Physical proximity of other members within the typical professional advice networks of the respondents is high. In the average network, 71.8% of the members of the advice network are at the local workplace, whereas members of the average advice network are external to the local workplace only 28.2% (see Table 9) of the time. This high locality of reference indicates that overall the typical professional advice network is not organizationally diverse.

Table 8.   Network Composition by Type of Relationship ($N = 3{,}522$).

Type of Relationship	N	P
Supervisor/boss	575	16.33
Coworker	1,002	28.45
Subordinate	353	10.02
Mentor	100	2.84
Mentee	8	0.22
Professional colleague	1,209	34.33
Spouse/significant other	82	2.33
Other family member	30	0.85
Personal friend	163	4.63
Total	3,522	100.0

Table 9.   Physical Proximity of Network Members ($N = 3{,}522$).

Proximity	N	P
Same floor, same building	1,412	40.09
Different floor, same building	686	19.48
Different building, same organization	430	12.21
Different campus, same organization	85	2.41
Different organization, same city	198	5.62
Different organization, different city	358	10.17
Different organization, different state	341	9.68
Different organization, different country	12	0.34
Total	3,522	100.0

Table 10.   Organizational Affiliations of Network Members ($N = 3,522$).

Organizational Affiliations	N	P
Within the same department and location	1,100	31.23
Within the same department, but a different location	149	4.23
Outside my department, within the same division or branch	505	14.34
Outside my division or branch, but in the same library	516	14.65
In the same library system	158	4.49
In another library or library system	596	16.92
In another organization that is not a library or library system	498	14.14
Total	3,522	100.0

Table 11.   Frequency of Interactions among Network Members ($N = 3,522$).

Frequency of Interaction	N	P
Two or fewer times a year	314	8.92
Quarterly	507	14.40
Monthly	795	22.57
Weekly	1,105	31.37
Daily	801	22.74
Total	3,522	100.0

Homophily becomes even more evident when the organizational aspects of the relationships are examined. In the average network, 64.5% of the relationships (Table 10) are from within the same library, and 21.4% of the relationships are with people from other libraries. Advice from people not associated with libraries is relatively rare, accounting for only 14.1% of all relationships.

Additionally, interaction within the average network tends to be frequent (see Table 11) with members contacting each other once a week or more over 54.1% of the time. While monthly and quarterly contacts account for 37% of interactions, infrequent interactions of two or fewer times a year only account for 8.9% of the relationship interactions.

Relationships in the average network tend to last longer. Table 12 shows that 51.9% of the relationships reported have been in place for 5 or more years. Only 28.9% of the professional advice relationships have been in place for 3 years or less. This longevity of relationships is not surprising given the previous findings related to average length of career.

Table 12. Longevity of Relationships of Network Members ($N = 3,522$).

Longevity of Relationships	N	P
Less than 1 year	259	7.35
1–3 years	756	21.47
3–5 years	677	19.22
5–10 years	909	25.81
10 or more years	921	26.15
Total	3,522	100.0

Table 13. Relative Hierarchy of Reporting Relationships with Network Members ($N = 3,522$).

Relative Hierarchy	N	P
Two or more levels below	158	4.49
One level below	639	18.14
Equal to mine	1,256	35.66
One level above	854	24.25
Two or more levels above	615	17.46
Total	3,522	100.0

Finally, relationships within the network tend to be formed among peers (35.7%) and those with whom people come into contact as a result of supervision, either receiving or giving. Fully 88% of all relationships reported (see Table 13) were within one level of hierarchy (either above or below) from the respondent.

Assessment of Reliability

The data collected as part of this research and the instrument used to collect that information are both valid and reliable. Based on the power analysis conducted in earlier stages of the research, the minimum sample size appropriate for this study was estimated to be 58 people to attain a statistical power of 0.80. To attain statistical power of 0.90, the minimum number of samples would have had to have been 96 people in total. As the total number of respondents was 440, the number of samples is well above the required number for a power of 0.90. Hellevik (1984) has stated that "the occurrence of interaction may also provide us with clues when we are searching for a deeper understanding of the causal processes underlying the statistical relationships we are studying" (p. 149). Therefore, two analyses of the data were performed to determine the nature of interaction within the survey items.

A test of the overall *Cronbach's alpha* score (Appendix E) for the innovation indicators was performed and found to be 0.853 (0.877 for standardized items). This indicates a reasonably strong model of internal consistency based on the correlation between items (Cronbach & Meehl, 1955; Nunnally & Bernstein, 1994).

Additionally, the innovation indicators were tested using the Kaiser–Meyer–Olkin (KMO) measure of sampling adequacy to determine if factor analysis might be appropriate. In this study, the KMO was 0.896 which is greater than the minimum of 0.70 recommended by Kaiser (1974). According to Hutcheson and Sofroniou (1999), this value indicates that the sample is actually quite good. When factor analysis was performed, however, none of the observed variables had a factor loading value of less than 0.30 (Appendix F); therefore, it is not appropriate to discard any of the variables from the model (Tinsley & Tinsley, 1987).

Analysis and Evaluation of Findings

This study had four major hypotheses, all of which were concerned with the relationship of professional advice networks to the receptivity to innovation individuals demonstrate. In the course of this study, it was demonstrated that people with large professional advice networks are more receptive to innovation than those with smaller networks. This conclusion is supported by a detailed analysis of the data associated with the hypotheses that directed the research in this study:

H_{1A}. People with large professional advice networks are more receptive to innovation than those with smaller networks.

Fig. 7 is a scatterplot of receptivity to innovation and network size (out-degree). As can be seen by the blue line in the diagram, there is a positive linear relationship between the two variables, $r = 0.830$, p (one-tailed) < 0.001. However, given the number of points above the linear regression line in the center of the plot, it does not appear that the relationship is strictly linear.

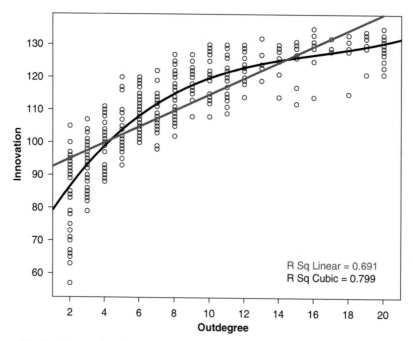

Fig. 7.   Scatterplot of Network Out-Degree and Receptivity to Innovation.

By using an exploratory data analysis approach (Hartwig & Dearing, 1979), it became apparent that the non-linearity of the relationship could be due to non-normal distributions of both variables. Given the potential for each variable to be distribution-free (Sprent & Smeeton, 2001), Shapiro–Wilk tests were performed on both receptivity to innovation and out-degree and proved to be significant in both cases: receptivity to innovation, $D(440) = 0.97$, $p < 0.001$ and out-degree, $D(440) = 0.90$, $p < 0.001$.

Therefore, taking a cue from Ettlie (2006), several other types of functions were applied to the data. With a hyperbolic function (Lewis-Beck, 1995),

$$Y = \frac{a - b_1}{(1/X_1)}$$

the resulting regression line (in red) provides a better fit with this data. One aspect of the relationship that is better demonstrated by the cubic function is the leveling off of increasing receptivity to innovation as the size of the network increases.

While the visual demonstration of the relationship as seen in Fig. 7 is significant, statistical methods also demonstrate there is a positive, non-parametric relationship between network size (out-degree) and receptivity to innovation as $r_s = 0.911$, p (one-tailed) < 0.001. Given the high value of the Spearman correlation coefficient and the high level of significance, there is a strong correlation between network size and receptivity to innovation even though this relationship is not strictly linear.

Given the better fit of a non-linear regression line, it would be reasonable to assume that additional factors beyond out-degree could be correlated to receptivity to innovation. Further analysis of the data indicated that other factors have an effect, although these are small compared to out-degree.

Backward regression analysis of the data was performed to select the most likely variables for further analysis. This process resulted in the selection of two additional variables (in addition to out-degree) that had a significant correlation to receptivity to innovation. The two additional variables that are correlated to receptivity to innovation are

1. the number of professional associations to which a person belongs ($r = 0.39$, p (one-tailed) < 0.001) and
2. length of career ($r = 0.25$, p (one-tailed) < 0.001).

Both of these are less strongly correlated to receptivity to innovation than out-degree ($r = 0.830$, p (one-tailed) < 0.001), which as previously noted had the most significant correlation with receptivity to innovation.

The lesser influence of these variables was demonstrated by an analysis of their fit within the regression model. As demonstrated in Table 14, the first model, using only out-degree as a factor, has an $R^2 = 0.689$. Adding the two other variables to the first model resulted in Model 3 which includes both number of professional associations and career length with $R^2 = 0.711$.

By evaluating the F-ratios of the various models it can be seen that the vast majority of variance is in Model 1 where $F(1/3) = 962.80$. The amount of variance accounted for by the remaining two models is significantly less, $F(2/3) = 25.33$ and $F(3/3) = 7.28$.

Using the formula suggested by Field (2005, p. 196),

$$\overline{\text{VIF}} = \frac{\sum_{i=1}^{k} \text{VIF}_i}{k}$$

where k is the number of predictors, the average variance inflation factor (VIF) of the third model was computed to be 1.074. At this level, there is a small amount of collinearity among the three variables in the third model

Table 14. Model Fit Statistics for Outdegree, Professional Association, and Career Length Regression Analysis.

Model	R	R^2	Standard Error of the Estimate	Change Statistics					Durbin–Watson
				R^2 change	F change	df1	df2	Significant F change	
1 – Out-degree	0.830	0.689	8.312	0.689	962.802	1	434	0.000	
2 – Out-degree and professional associations	0.841	0.706	8.088	0.017	25.332	1	433	0.000	
3 – Out-degree, professional associations, and career length	0.843	0.711	8.030	0.005	7.278	1	432	0.007	2.057

(Bowerman & O'Connell, 1990), but not enough between any two of the variables to warrant exclusion of any of these variables from the model (Myers, 1990).

Therefore, regardless of their lower impact, an argument can be made for keeping both of the lesser influencing variables (number of professional organizations and career length) in the model given the relatively low level of multicollinearity in the third model.

Nonetheless, even though number of professional organizations and career length affect the model, it is safe to say that the model demonstrates that people with large professional advice networks are more receptive to innovation than those with smaller networks.

H_{2A}. People with the highest receptivity to innovation have large professional advice networks that are heterogeneous.

Heterogeneous networks are characterized by interactions that are not limited by proximity or organizational boundaries. Heterogeneity, however, is not directly observable. In order to determine heterogeneity, a network measure must be derived based on other direct network measures. This concept of measuring network interactions via derived variables was first discussed by Homans (1941) and further developed by Marsden and Friedkin (1994b). In this study, the measurement of heterogeneity is derived from a multiplicative vector function, influenced by both Nowak and Vallacher's (2005) "Dynamics of Social Influence" function and Dekker's (2005) pseudo-logarithmic coding scheme, where:

$$\text{heterogeneity} = \sum_{i=1}^{k} \text{proximity}_i \cdot \text{organization}_i \cdot \text{frequency}_i$$

where k is the number of actors in the individual network.

Using this measure, the Spearman's correlation coefficient, $r_s = 0.941$, p (one-tailed) < 0.001, with receptivity to innovation is even higher than that of out-degree.

Based on the high value of the correlation coefficient and the high level of significance, it appears that there is a strong correlation between the heterogeneity of a professional advice network and an individual's receptivity to innovation. However, to determine if those with a high receptivity to innovation have heterogeneous professional advice networks, additional analysis is necessary.

As was noted earlier, neither innovation nor out-degree were normally distributed in this study. Consequently, a Shapiro–Wilk test on heterogeneity, $D(400) = 0.80$, $p < 0.001$ confirmed that heterogeneity was not normally distributed either. A Kruskal–Wallis test was performed to determine if there was a significant relationship between categories of innovation and heterogeneity. The results of the test, $H = 231.41$, $p < 0.001$, confirmed that there was. Subsequently, a χ^2-test demonstrated a significant association between innovation and heterogeneity $\chi^2(9) = 325.62$, $p < 0.001$ with an effect size, as measured by Cramer's V, of 0.497.

However, further analysis of the crosstabulation (Table 15) of the χ^2-test did not provide definitive information that people with the highest receptivity to innovation consistently have large professional advice networks that are heterogeneous. While this was true in 78% of the cases, 16% of the respondents in the highly innovative group had homogenous networks, and 6% of the highly innovative respondents had highly homogenous networks. Therefore, it cannot be said that people with the highest receptivity to innovation always have large professional advice networks that are heterogeneous.

H_{3A}. People with externally focused professional advice networks are more receptive to innovation than those with internally focused professional advice networks.

As was the case with H_{2A}, a Kruskal–Wallis test was performed initially to determine if there was a significant relationship between levels of innovation and network focus. The results of the test, $H = 231.41$, $p < 0.001$, confirmed that there was. A subsequent χ^2-test demonstrated a significant association between innovation and network size, $\chi^2(1) = 80.51$, $p < 0.001$ with an effect size, as measured by Cramer's V, of 0.458.

In this case, further analysis of the crosstabulation (Table 16) of the χ^2-test showed that people with externally focused professional advice networks are more likely to be more receptive to innovation than those with internally focused professional advice networks. Of those respondents with externally focused networks, 50.4% of the respondents are in the high innovation category and 42.2% are in the high average category. This is in contrast with the 10.5% of those with an internally focused network who are in the high innovation category. However, within the internally focused network group, 59.0% are in the high average innovation category. If the high average and high innovation categories are combined, then 92.6% of those with an external focus network are more receptive to innovation and 69.5% of those with an internally focused network are.

Table 15. Cross-tabulation of Innovation and Heterogeneity.

Heterogeneity	Innovation				Total
	Low	Low average	High average	High	
High homogeneous					
Count	10	93	205	6	314
Expected count	7.1	66.4	169.1	71.4	314.0
% within diversity group	3.2%	29.6%	65.3%	1.9%	100.0%
% within innovation group	100.0%	100.0%	86.5%	6.0%	71.4%
% of total	2.3%	21.1%	46.6%	1.4%	71.4%
Low homogenous					
Count	0	0	24	16	40
Expected count	0.9	8.5	21.5	9.1	40.0
% within diversity group	0.0%	0.0%	60.0%	40.0%	100.0%
% within innovation group	0.0%	0.0%	10.1%	16.0%	9.1%
% of total	0.0%	0.0%	5.5%	3.6%	9.1%
Low heterogeneous					
Count	0	0	6	19	25
Expected count	0.6	5.3	13.5	5.7	25.0
% within diversity group	0.0%	0.0%	24.0%	76.0%	100.0%
% within innovation group	0.0%	0.0%	2.5%	19.0%	5.7%
% of total	0.0%	0.0%	1.4%	4.3%	5.7%
High heterogeneous					
Count	0	0	2	59	61
Expected count	1.4	12.9	32.9	13.9	61.0
% within diversity group	0.0%	0.0%	3.3%	96.7%	100.0%
% within innovation group	0.0%	0.0%	0.8%	59.0%	13.9%
% of total	0.0%	0.0%	0.5%	13.4%	13.9%
Total					
Count	10	93	237	100	440
Expected count	10.0	93.0	237.0	100.0	440.0
% within diversity group	2.3%	21.1%	53.9%	22.7%	100.0%
% within innovation group	100.0%	100.0%	100.0%	100.0%	100.0%
% of total	2.3%	21.1%	53.9%	22.7%	100.0%

Table 16. Cross-tabulation of Innovation and Network Focus.

Network Focus	Innovation Group				Total
	Low	Low average	High average	High	
Internal					
Count	10	83	180	32	305
Expected count	6.9	64.5	164.3	69.3	305.0
% within network focus	3.3%	27.2%	59.0%	10.5%	100.0%
% within innovation group	100.0%	89.2%	75.9%	32.0%	69.3%
% of total	2.3%	18.9%	40.9%	7.3%	69.3%
External					
Count	0	10	57	68	135
Expected count	3.1	28.5	72.7	30.7	135.0
% within network focus	0.0%	7.4%	42.2%	50.4%	100.0%
% within innovation group	0.0%	10.8%	24.1%	68.0%	30.7%
% of total	0.0%	2.3%	13.0%	15.5%	30.7%
Total					
Count	10	93	237	100	440
Expected count	10.0	93.0	237.0	100.0	440.0
% within network focus	2.3%	21.1%	53.9%	22.7%	100.0%
% within innovation group	100.0%	100.0%	100.0%	100.0%	100.0%
% of total	2.3%	21.1%	53.9%	22.7%	100.0%

Therefore, while H_{3A} was not validated as stated, it can be said that people with externally focused professional advice networks are more likely to be receptive to innovation than those with internally focused professional advice networks.

H_{4A}. People with the lowest receptivity to innovation have professional advice networks that are highly homogenous both demographically and professionally.

While H_{2A} could not be proved, H_{4A} was found to be true. As can be seen in Table 15, all respondents in the lowest category of innovation also had highly homogenous networks.

CONCLUSIONS AND RECOMMENDATIONS

Social network theory suggests that one way to create change in an organization is to increase the amount of new information made available to the organization by increasing external input (Dewar & Dutton, 1986). The logic behind this is based on research from social psychology that

> suggests that individuals interact, in large part, to construct a shared reality that consists not only of shared information, but also of agreed-upon opinions. In this process, they don't simply transmit information. More importantly, they influence one another to arrive at a common interpretation of information. (Nowak & Vallacher, 2005, p. 90)

Following this logic, one way of potentially increasing the innovativeness of an organization is by increasing the amount of external input brought into an organization. This can be done by expanding the scope and diversity of the professional advice networks of individuals in the organization.

This study focused on determining what influence the professional advice network of an individual may have on their receptivity to innovation. This focus on individual behavior as a means for analyzing the organization is based on Watts' (2003) observation that the networks of personal relationships affect both the behavior of individuals as well as the behavior of the system as a whole.

Based on four hypotheses related to how receptivity to innovation may be related to professional advice networks, two of these hypotheses (H_{1A} and H_{4A} were found to be true:

H_{1A}. People with large professional advice networks are more receptive to innovation than those with smaller networks, and

H_{4A}. People with the lowest receptivity to innovation have professional advice networks that are highly homogenous both demographically and professionally.

The other two hypotheses were also found to be valid, but with qualifications. While it is not true that all people with the highest receptivity to innovation have large professional advice networks that are hetero-geneous, it is true the majority (78% of the cases) of the time. There are cases where people who have high receptivity to innovation also have homogenous professional advice networks.

Additionally, a significant relationship between level of innovation and network focus was found as people with externally focused professional advice networks are more likely to be receptive to innovation than those with internally focused professional advice networks. Of those respondents with externally focused networks, 50.4% of the respondents were in the high innovation category, whereas only 10.5% of those with an internally focused network were high innovators.

Conclusions

The overarching focus of this study, that people with large professional advice networks are more receptive to innovation than those with smaller networks has been shown to be true. Given that people with larger networks tend to have higher levels of support from those network members (Wellman & Gulia, 1993), this seems reasonable.

Even so, it is a rare occurrence when a behavioral characteristic can be completely explained by a single factor. In this study, two additional variables were found to have a positive correlation on receptivity to innovation: the number of professional associations a person belongs to and their length of career.

That there are additional influencing factors is not surprising as the relationship between network size and receptivity to innovation is not perfectly linear. While there is a clear positive linkage between the two factors, there is also a clear correlation between external contact and innovation. Analysis demonstrated that people with externally focused professional advice networks are more likely to be receptive to innovation than those with internally focused professional advice networks. Of those respondents with externally focused networks, 50.4% of the respondents are in the high innovation category, whereas only 10.5% of those with an internally focused network are high innovators.

Therefore, it is in the best interest of library managers to provide opportunities and environments where librarians can develop relationships with other professionals outside of the local work environment. When people belong to one or more professional associations, they inherently have access to a larger pool of potential network members. These network members will be in different contextual settings, thereby creating the possibility to discover new information. In addition, the people that meet in a professional organization provide a mechanism for creating informal contacts, which are known to have a more substantial effect on performance than formal contacts (Weick, 1979). Furthermore, as people progress in their careers the likelihood of engaging with new people through

professional affiliations increases which further argues for active encouragement of continued membership in professional organizations throughout
one's career.

Finally, the fourth hypothesis of the study was found to be true. All
respondents in the lowest category of innovation (the lowest receptivity to
innovation) had professional advice networks that were highly homogenous
both demographically and professionally.

As existing social networks influence subsequent relations (Mizruchi &
Galaskiewicz, 1994), it should be no surprise that highly homogenous
networks tend to have low innovation potential because the links in these
networks tend to be transitive and create a closed off system (Degenne &
Forsé, 2004). This is in opposition to the value of heterogeneous networks,
which are by definition more open and have much greater possibility of
connections to other social systems (Barabási, 2003; Ibarra, 1993). This
openness and potential for connectivity to a larger world is vital to bring in
new ideas, as critical linkages for communicating new ideas into a network
can hinge on just a single person acting as an intermediary from one social
network to another (Friedkin, 1983).

Recommendations

H_{2A} of this study could not be completely demonstrated because while 78%
of the respondents with the highest receptivity to innovation had large
professional advice networks, a significant minority (22%) did not. Further
research should investigate the factors that contribute to a high receptivity
to innovation when professional advice networks are small. Small
professional advice networks can be the result of any number of factors,
some of which are directly modifiable by a person, such as a personal
preference for a smaller set of interaction partners, and some that are not,
such as geographic circumstance. A question worth investigating is what
circumstances create a context where a person with a small professional
advice network is able to maintain a high receptivity to innovation.

As a result of this research, a number of other questions started to emerge
related to the structure and composition of the professional advice networks
and how these factors may influence innovation. While outside the scope of
this study, all of these questions are worth further investigation.

For example, in an average advice network, only 10–25% of network
relations are local (Walker et al., 1994). However, in this study, the overall
proximity of members in the professional advice networks was highly local.

In the majority of cases, 50% of the members of an individual's professional advice network were local. As local proximity is a well-documented indicator of influence opportunities (Festinger, Schachter, & Back, 1950), it is worth investigating if this unusual distribution is peculiar to this sample. If it is not and is indicative of a different type of pattern unique to librarianship, it is worth investigating how this pattern of relationships affects the profession itself.

Another area of inquiry outside the scope of the present study is how the specific composition of individual networks varies. For example, are there more links to people in other professions or specializations within librarianship in the networks of people with high receptivity to innovation than there are in the networks of less innovative people?

Answering the previous question could provide a solid foundation for exploring questions related to larger organizational issues. Given that the majority of members in the professional advice networks of the respondents were fellow librarians, the tendency to reinforce commonalities across organizations should be demonstrable as structural isomorphism or structural equivalence (Scott, 1995). If this is the case, it would be worth discovering if organizations where the majority of professional advice networks are heterogeneous are less structurally isomorphic when compared to their peer institutions. This question could be approached from the opposite direction; that is, looking at organizations that are already less structurally isomorphic than their peers and exploring the characteristics of the professional advice networks of the staff at those institutions.

Finally, an omnipresent question to be explored is whether the staff in larger libraries tends to be more innovative because they have larger professional advice networks than staff in smaller libraries. Ettlie, Bridges, and O'Keffe (1984) have shown that commercial organizations which are more complex, more decentralized and larger tend to be more innovative in producing products. When combined with Damanpour (1992) findings that larger organizations tend to adopt more innovations than their smaller counterparts and that a high degree of specialization of individuals within an organization facilitates innovation (Subramanian & Nilakanta, 1996), it would seem that this is a possibility, yet it remains to be conclusively demonstrated.

The issue of receptivity to innovation in librarianship has not been a topic of systematic inquiry and there has been little written on the aspects of social networks in librarianship. By exploring the question of whether resistance to innovation is associated with the composition of individual professional advice networks and if the networks of resistant individuals are substantively different from those of individuals who embrace innovation, this study makes a unique contribution to the literature. It does this by both addressing these issues as well as providing a model for investigators who wish to study, and perhaps address, the unique organizational issues faced in other academic disciplines and non-profit organizations. Finally, the author hopes that this study facilitates better understanding of the potential for using social networks to foster innovation within libraries and other information agencies.

REFERENCES

Akeroyd, J. (2001). The future of academic libraries. *ASLIB Proceedings*, *53*(3), 79–84.

Alba, R. D. (1982). Taking stock of network analysis: A decade's results. *Research in the Sociology of Organizations*, *1*, 39–74.

Alvesson, M. (1993). *Cultural perspectives on organizations*. New York, NY: Cambridge University Press.

Alvesson, M. (2000). *Understanding organizational culture*. London: Sage.

Alvesson, M., & Deetz, S. (2000). *Doing critical management research*. London: Sage.

Andaleeb, S. S., & Simmonds, P. L. (1998). Explaining user satisfaction with academic libraries: Strategic implications. *College and Research Libraries*, *59*(2), 156–167.

Andrews, D., Nonnecke, B., & Preece, J. (2003). Electronic survey methodology: A case study in reaching hard to involve Internet users. *International Journal of Human–Computer Interaction*, *16*(2), 185–210.

Aronson, E., Ellsworth, P. C., Carlsmith, J. M., & Gonzalez, M. H. (1990). *Methods of research in social psychology*. New York, NY: McGraw-Hill.

Baker, R. P., Crawford, S., & Swinehart, J. (2004). Development and testing of web questionnaires. In: S. Presser, et al. (Eds), *Methods for testing and evaluating survey questionnaires*. Hoboken, NJ: Wiley-Interscience.

Baker, W. E. (1993). The network organization in theory and practice. In: N. Nohria & R. G. Eccles (Eds), *Networks and organizations: Structure, form and action* (pp. 397–429). Cambridge, MA: Harvard Business School Press.

Barabási, A.-L. (2003). *Linked: How everything is connected to everything else and what it means for business, science, and everyday life*. New York, NY: Plume.

Barnes, J. (1979). Network analysis: Orienting notion, rigorous technique, or substantive field of study. In: P. Holland & S. Leinhardt (Eds), *Perspectives in social research* (pp. 403–423). New York, NY: Academic Press.

Barnes, S. L. (2003). Determinants of individual neighborhood ties and social resources in poor urban neighborhoods. *Sociological Spectrum*, *23*(4), 463–497.

Baruchson-Arbib, S., & Bronstein, J. (2002). A view to the future of the library and information science profession: A Delphi study. *Journal of the American Society for Information Science and Technology*, *53*(5), 397–408.

Bauman, Z., & May, T. (2001). *Thinking sociologically* (2nd ed.). Oxford: Blackwell.

Berger, P. L., & Luckmann, T. (1966). *The social construction of reality: A treatise in the sociology of knowledge.* New York, NY: Doubleday.

Biemer, P. P., & Lyberg, L. E. (2003). *Introduction to survey quality.* Hoboken, NJ: Wiley-Interscience.

Blau, P. M. (1964). *Exchange and power in social life.* New York, NY: Wiley.

Blau, P. M. (1977). *Inequality and heterogeneity: A primitive theory of social structure.* New York, NY: Free Press.

Bolman, L. G., & Deal, T. E. (1997). *Reframing organizations: Artistry, choice, and leadership* (2nd ed.). San Francisco, CA: Jossey-Bass.

Borgatti, S. P., & Molina, J. L. (2003). Ethical and strategic issues in organizational social network analysis. *The Journal of Applied Behavioral Science, 39*(3), 337–349.

Bourque, L. B., & Fielder, E. P. (2003). *How to conduct self-administered and mail surveys* (2nd ed.). Thousand Oaks, CA: Sage.

Bowerman, B. L., & O'Connell, R. T. (1990). *Linear statistical models: An applied approach* (2nd ed.). Belmont, CA: Duxbury.

Breiger, R. L. (1974). The duality of persons and groups. *Social Forces, 53,* 181–190.

Brewerton, P., & Millward, L. (2001). *Organizational research methods: A guide for students and researchers.* London: Sage.

Brodie, M., & Mclean, N. (1995). Process reengineering in academic libraries: Shifting to client-centered resource provision. *Cause/Effect, 18,* 40–46.

Burkey, J., & Kuechler, W. L. (2003). Web-based surveys for corporate information gathering: A bias-reducing design framework. *IEEE Transactions on Professional Communication, 46*(2), 81–93.

Burt, R. S. (1980). Models of network structure. *Annual Review of Sociology, 6,* 79–141.

Burt, R. S. (1984). Network items and the general social survey. *Social Networks, 6*(4), 293–339.

Campbell, K. E., & Lee, B. A. (1991). Name generators in surveys of personal networks. *Social Networks, 13*(3), 203–221.

Carroll, G. R., & Teo, A. C. (1996). On the social networks of managers. *Academy of Management Journal, 39*(2), 20–23.

Cavalli-Sforza, L., & Feldman, M. (1981). *Cultural transmission and evolution.* Princeton, NJ: Princeton University Press.

Cho, H., & Larose, R. (1999). Privacy issues in Internet surveys. *Social Science Computer Review, 17*(4), 421–434.

Cluff, E. D. (1989). Developing the entrepreneurial spirit: The director's role. *Journal of Library Administration, 10*(2/3), 185–195.

Cohen, J. (1988). *Statistical power analysis for the behavioral sciences* (2nd ed.). Hillsdale, NJ: Lawrence Erlbaum.

Consortium of Academic and Research Libraries in Illinois. (2006). Retrieved March 11, 2006, from http://www.carli.illinois.edu/

Conway, S., Jones, O., & Steward, F. (2001). Realising the potential of the network perspective in researching social interaction and innovation. In: O. Jones, S. Conway & F. Steward (Eds), *Social interaction and organisational change* (pp. 349–366). London: Imperial College Press.

Cronbach, L. J., & Meehl, P. E. (1955). Construct validity in psychological tests. *Psychological Bulletin, 52*(4), 281–302.

Cross, R., Borgatti, S. P., & Parker, A. (2001). Beyond answers: Dimensions of the advice network. *Social Networks, 23*(3), 215–235.

Cross, R., & Parker, A. (2004). *The hidden power of social networks: Understanding how work really gets done in organizations.* Boston, MA: Harvard Business School Press.

Cross, R., Rice, R. E., & Parker, A. (2001). Information seeking in social context: Structural influences and receipt of information benefits. *IEEE Transactions on Systems, Man, and Cybernetics – Part C: Applications and Reviews, 31*(4), 438–448.

Damanpour, F. (1992). Organizational size and innovation. *Organizational Studies, 13*, 375–402.

Degenne, A., & Forsé, M. (2004). *Introducing social networks* (Rev ed.). London: Sage.

Deiss, K. J. (2004). Innovation and strategy: Risk and choice in shaping user-centered libraries. *Library Trends, 53*(1), 17–32.

Dekker, A. (2005). Conceptual distance in social network analysis [Electronic Version]. *Journal of Social Structure, 6.* Retrieved October 5, 2006, from http://www.cmu.edu/joss/content/articles/volume6/dekker/index.html

Dewar, R. D., & Dutton, J. E. (1986). The adoption of radical and incremental innovations: An empirical analysis. *Management Science, 32*(11), 1422–1433.

Dillman, D. A., & Bowker, D. K. (2001). The web questionnaire challenge to survey methodologists. In: U. D. Reips & M. Bosnjak (Eds), *Dimensions of internet science* (pp. 159–178). Lengerich, Germany: Pabst.

Downs, J. G. W., & Mohr, L. B. (1976). Conceptual issues in the study of innovation. *Administrative Science Quarterly, 21*(4), 700–714.

Dysart, J. L., & Abram, S. K. (1997). What is your information outlook? *Information Outlook, 1*(1), 34–36.

Ekeh, P. (1974). *Social exchange theory: The two traditions.* Cambridge, MA: Harvard University Press.

Emirbayer, M. (1997). Manifesto for a relational sociology. *The American Journal of Sociology, 103*(2), 281–317.

Ettlie, J. E. (2006). *Managing innovation: New technology, new products, and new services in a global economy* (2nd ed.). New York, NY: Butterworth-Heinemann.

Ettlie, J. E., Bridges, W. P., & O'Keffe, R. D. (1984). Organizational strategy and structural differences for radical versus incremental innovation. *Management Science, 30*(6), 682–695.

Euster, J. R. (1995). The academic library: Its place and role in the institution. In: G. B. McCabe & R. J. Person (Eds), *Academic Libraries: Their rationale and role in American higher education.* Westport, CT: Greenwood Press.

Faust, K. (1997). Centrality in affiliation networks. *Social Networks, 19*(2), 157–191.

Faust, K., & Wasserman, S. (1992). Centrality and prestige: A review and synthesis. *Journal of Quantitative Anthropology, 4*, 23–78.

Festinger, L., Schachter, S., & Back, K. (1950). *Social pressures in informal groups: A study of human factors in housing.* New York, NY: Harper.

Field, A. (2005). *Discovering statistics using SPSS* (2nd ed.). Thousand Oaks, CA: Sage.

Fink, A. (2003). *How to ask survey questions* (2nd ed.). Thousand Oaks, CA: Sage.

Flynn, F. J., & Chatman, J. A. (2004). Strong cultures and innovation: Oxymoron or opportunity? In: M. L. Tushman & P. Anderson (Eds), *Managing strategic innovation and change* (2nd ed., pp. 234–251). New York, NY: Oxford University Press.

Forsyth, B., Rothgeb, J. M., & Willis, G. B. (2004). Does pretesting make a difference? An experimental test. In: S. Presser, J. M. Rothgeb, M. P. Couper, J. T. Lessler, E. Martin, J. Martin & E. Singer (Eds), *Methods for testing and evaluating survey questionnaires.* Hoboken, NJ: Wiley-Interscience.

Fowler, F. J., Jr. (1993). *Survey research methods* (2nd ed.). Newbury Park, CA: Sage.

Freeman, L. C. (2000). Visualizing social networks [Electronic Version]. *Journal of Social Structure*, 1, 1–15. Retrieved April 24, 2007 from http://www.cmu.edu/joss/content/articles/volume1/freeman.pdf

Freeman, L. C. (2004). *The development of social network analysis: A study in the sociology of science*. Vancouver, BC: Empirical Press.

Friedkin, N. E. (1983). Horizons of observability and limits of informal control in organizations. *Social Forces, 62,* 54–77.

Fulk, J., & Desanctis, G. (1995). Electronic communication and changing organizational forms. *Organization Science, 6*(4), 337–349.

Garten, E. D., & Williams, D. E. (2000). Clashing cultures: Cohabitation of libraries and computing centers in information abundance. In: L. Hardesty (Ed.), *Books, bytes, and bridges: Libraries and computer centers in academic institutions* (pp. 61–72). Chicago, IL: American Library Association.

Giddens, A. (1979). *Central problems in social theory: Action, structure and contradiction in social analysis.* Berkeley, CA: University of California Press.

Glaser, B., & Strauss, A. L. (1967). *The discovery of grounded theory: Strategies for qualitative research.* Chicago, IL: Aldine.

Goodman, L. A. (1961). Snowball sampling. *Annals of Mathematical Statistics, 32*(1), 148–170.

Grimm, J. W., & Stern, R. N. (1974). Sex roles and internal labor market structures: The "female" semiprofessions. *Social Problems, 21*(5), 690–705.

Hammer, M. (1979). Predictability of social connections over time. *Social Networks, 2*(2), 165–180.

Harley, B., Dreger, M., & Knobloch, P. (2001). The postmodern condition: Students, the web, and academic library services. *Reference Services Review, 29*(1), 23–32.

Harrison, J. R., & Carroll, G. R. (2006). *Culture and demography in organizations.* Princeton, NJ: Princeton University Press.

Hartwig, F., & Dearing, B. E. (1979). *Exploratory data analysis.* Beverly Hills, CA: Sage.

Haythornthwaite, C. (1996). Social network analysis: An approach and technique for the study of information exchange. *Library and Information Science Review* (18), 323–342.

Haythornthwaite, C. (1998). A social network study of the growth of community among distance learners. *Information Research, 4*(1), 49–51.

Hellevik, O. (1984). *Introduction to causal analysis: Exploring survey data by crosstabulation.* London: George Allen & Unwin.

Homans, G. C. (1941). *English villagers of the thirteenth century.* Cambridge, MA: Harvard University.

Hutcheson, G., & Sofroniou, N. (1999). *The multivariate social scientist.* London: Sage.

Ibarra, H. (1993). Personal networks of women and minorities in management: A conceptual framework. *Academy of Management Review, 18*(1), 56–88.

Ibarra, H. (1997). Paving an alternative route: Gender differences in managerial networks. *Social Psychology Quarterly, 60*(1), 91–102.

Joswick, K. E. (1999). Article publication patterns of academic librarians: An Illinois case study. *College and Research Libraries, 60*(4), 340–349.

Kadushin, C. (2005). Who benefits from network analysis: Ethics of social network research. *Social Networks, 27,* 139–153.

Kaiser, H. F. (1974). An index of factorial simplicity. *Psychometrika, 39,* 31–36.

Kanter, R. M. (2002). Creating the culture for innovation. In: F. Hesselbein, M. Goldsmith & I. Somerville (Eds), *Leading for innovation and organizing for results* (pp. 73–86). San Francisco, CA: Jossey-Bass.

Katz, D., & Kahn, R. (1966). *The social psychology of organizations.* New York, NY: Wiley.

Kilduff, M., & Tsai, W. (2003). *Social networks and organizations.* London: Sage.

Klovdahl, A. S. (2005). Social network research and human subjects protection: Toward more effective infectious disease control. *Social Networks, 27,* 119–137.

Knoke, D., & Burt, R. S. (1983). Prominence. In: R. S. Burt & M. J. Minor (Eds), *Applied network analysis: A methodological introduction.* Beverly Hills, CA: Sage.

Kroeker, B. (1999). Changing roles in information dissemination and education: Expectations for academic library web-based services. *Social Science Computer Review, 17*(2), 176–188.

Lewis, D. W. (1986). An organizational paradigm for effective academic libraries. *College and Research Libraries, 47*(4), 337–353.

Lewis-Beck, M. S. (1995). *Data analysis: An introduction.* Thousand Oaks, CA: Sage.

Litwin, M. S. (2003). *How to assess and interpret survey psychometrics* (2nd ed.). Thousand Oaks, CA: Sage.

Lund, E., & Gram, I. T. (1998). Response rate according to title and length of questionnaire. *Scandinavian Journal of Social Medicine, 26*(2), 154–160.

Luquire, W. (1983). Attitudes toward automation/innovation in academic libraries. *The Journal of Academic Librarianship, 8*(6), 344–351.

Lynch, C. A. (2003). Institutional repositories: Essential infrastructure for scholarship in the digital age. *Portal: Libraries and the Academy, 3*(2), 327–336.

Lynch, M. J. (2002). Reaching 65: Lots of librarians will be there soon. *American Libraries, 33*(3), 55–56.

Mackenzie, M. L. (2005). Managers look to the social network to seek information. *Information Research, 10*(2), 216–218.

Macri, D. M., Tagliaventi, M. R., & Bertolotti, F. (2002). A grounded theory for resistance to change in a small organization. *Journal of Organizational Change Management, 15*(3), 292.

Malinconico, S. M. (1997). Librarians and innovation: An American viewpoint. *Program: Electronic Library and Information Systems, 31*(1), 47–58.

Manfreda, K. L., Batagelj, Z., & Vehovar, V. (2002). Design of web survey questionnaires: Three basic experiments [Electronic Version]. *Journal of Computer Mediated Communication,* 7. Retrieved May 5, 2006 from http://jcmc.indiana.edu/vol7/issue3/vehovar.html

Marsden, P. V., & Friedkin, N. E. (1994a). Network studies of social influence. In: S. Wasserman & J. Galaskiewicz (Eds), *Advances in social network analysis: Research in the social and behavioral sciences.* Thousand Oaks, CA: Sage.

Marsden, P. V., & Friedkin, N. E. (1994b). Network studies of social influence. In: S. Wasserman & J. Galaskiewicz (Eds), *Advances in social network analysis: Research in the social and behavioral sciences* (pp. 3–25). Thousand Oaks, CA: Sage.

Mayhew, B. H. (1980). Structuralism versus individualism: Part I, shadowboxing in the dark. *Social Forces, 59*(2), 335–375.

Mcpherson, J. M., & Smith-Lovin, L. (1986). Sex segregation in voluntary associations. *American Sociological Review, 51*(1), 61–79.

Merton, R. K. (1968). *Social theory and social structure.* New York, NY: Free Press.

Merton, R. K. (1975). Structural analysis in sociology. In: P. M. Blau (Ed.), *Approaches to the study of social structure* (pp. 21–52). New York, NY: Free Press.

Mizruchi, M. S., & Galaskiewicz, J. (1994). Networks of interogranizational relations. In: S. Wasserman & J. Galaskiewicz (Eds), *Advances in social network analysis* (pp. 230–253). Thousand Oaks, CA: Sage.

Mohrman, S. A., Tenkasi, R. V., & Mohrman, A. M., Jr. (2003). The role of networks in fundamental organizational change: A grounded analysis. *The Journal of Applied Behavioral Science, 39*(3), 301–323.

Monge, P. R., & Eisenberg, E. M. (1987). Emergent communication networks. In: F. M. Jablin (Ed.), *Handbook of organizational communication* (pp. 305–342). Newbury Park, CA: Sage.

Morrel-Samuels, P. (2002). Getting the truth into workplace surveys. *Harvard Business Review, 80*(2), 111–118.

Munck, B. (2002). Changing a culture of face time. In: *Harvard Business Review on Culture and Change.* Cambridge, MA: Harvard Business School.

Murphy, K. R., & Myors, B. (2004). *Statistical power analysis* (2nd ed.). Mahwah, NJ: Lawrence Erlbaum.

Myers, R. (1990). *Classical and modern regression with applications* (2nd ed.). Boston, MA: Duxbury.

Newell, S., & Swan, J. (2000). Trust and interorganizational networking. *Human Relations, 53*(10), 1287–1328.

Newman, I., & Benz, C. R. (1998). *Qualitative–quantitative research methodology.* Carbondale, IL: Southern Illinois University Press.

Normal distribution, 1 sample Power Calculator. (2004). Retrieved June 15, 2006, from http://calculators.stat.ucla.edu/powercalc/normal/n-1/

Nosek, B. A., Banaji, M. R., & Greenwald, A. G. (2002). E-research: Ethics, security, design, and control in psychological research on the Internet. *Journal of Social Issues, 58*(1), 161–176.

Nowak, A., & Vallacher, R. R. (2005). Social networks applied: Information and influence in the construction of shared reality. *IEEE Intelligent Systems, 20*(1), 90–93.

Nunnally, J. C., & Bernstein, I. H. (1994). *Psychometric theory* (3rd ed.). New York, NY: McGraw-Hill.

O'Reilly, C. A., III., & Roberts, K. H. (1977). Task group structure, communication, and effectiveness in three organizations. *Journal of Applied Psychology, 62*(6), 674–681.

Pack, P. J., & Pack, F. M. (1988). *Colleges, learning and libraries: The future.* London: Clive Bingley.

Pankl, R. R. (2004). Baby boom generation librarians. *Library Management, 25*(4/5), 215–222.

Parsons, T. (1956a). Suggestions for a sociological approach to the theory of organizations, Part I. *Administrative Science Quarterly, 1,* 63–85.

Parsons, T. (1956b). Suggestions for a sociological approach to the theory of organizations, Part II. *Administrative Science Quarterly, 1,* 225–239.

Pavalko, R. M. (1988). *Sociology of occupations and professions* (2nd ed.). Itasca, IL: F. E. Peacock.

Pinfield, S. (2001). The changing role of subject librarians in academic libraries. *Journal of Librarianship and Information Science, 33*(1), 32–38.

Price, F. V. (1981). Only connect? Issues in charting social networks. *The Sociological Review, 29*(2), 283–312.

Psacharopoulos, G. (1980). Questionnaire surveys in educational planning. *Comparative Education, 16*(2), 159–169.

Radcliffe-Brown, A. R. (2002). On social structure. In: J. Scott (Ed.), *Social networks: Critical concepts in sociology* (1st ed., pp. 25–38). London: Routledge.

Ragin, C. C. (1987). *The comparative method: Moving beyond qualitative and quantitative strategies.* Berkeley, CA: University of California Press.

Ragin, C. C. (1994). *Constructing social research: The unity and diversity of method.* Thousand Oaks, CA: Pine Forge Press.

Raines, S. C., & Alberg, M. S. (2003). The role of professional development in preparing academic leaders. *New Directions for Higher Education, 124*, 33–39.

Reffay, C., & Chanier, T. (2002). Social network analysis used for modeling aollaboration in distance learning groups. In: S. A. Cerri, G. Gouardères & F. Paraguaçu (Eds), *Lecture notes in computer science* (Vol. 2363, pp. 31–40). Berlin: Springer-Verlag.

Robinson, A. G., & Stern, S. (1998). *Corporate creativity: How innovation and improvement actually happen.* San Francisco, CA: Berrett-Koehler Publishers.

Rogers, E. (1987). Progress, problems, and prospects for network research: Investigating relationships in the age of electronic communication. Paper presented at the VII Sunbelt Social Networks Conference, Florida.

Rokeach, M. (1960). *The open and closed mind.* New York, NY: Basic Books.

Rusaw, A. C. (2001). *Leading public organizations: An interactive approach.* Fort Worth, TX: Harcourt.

Savage, S., & Betts, M. (2005). Boyer reconsidered: Priorities for framing academic work. Paper presented at the Higher Education Research and Development Society of Australasia Annual Conference. Retrieved January 17, 2007, from http://conference.herdsa.org.au/2005/pdf/refereed/paper_180.pdf

Schulze, R. H. K. (1962). A shortened version of the Rokeach dogmatism scale. *Journal of Psychological Studies, 13*, 93–97.

Schwab, D. P. (2005). *Research methods for organizational studies* (2nd ed.). Mahwah, NJ: Lawrence Erlbaum.

Scott, J. (2000). *Social network analysis.* London: Sage.

Scott, W. R. (1995). *Institutions and organizations.* Thousand Oaks, CA: Sage.

Shannon, D. M., Johnson, T. E., Searcy, S., & Lott, A. (2002). Using electronic surveys: Advice from survey professionals [Electronic Version]. *Practice Assessment, Research, & Evaluation, 8.* Retrieved May 16, 2006 from http://PAREonline.net/getvn.asp?v=8&n=1

Sheehan, K. B., & Hoy, M. B. (1999). Using e-mail to survey Internet users in the United States: Methodology and assessment. *Journal of Computer Mediated Communication, 4*(3), 24–29.

Shuler, J. A. (2005). Creative destruction: Academic libraries and the burden of change. *The Journal of Academic Librarianship, 31*(6), 593–597.

Simpson, R. (2004). Masculinity at work. *Work, Employment and Society, 18*(2), 349–368.

Smircich, L. (1983). Concepts of culture and organizational analysis. *Administrative Science Quarterly, 28*, 339–358.

Smith, C. B. (1997). Casting the net: Surveying an Internet population. *Journal of Computer Mediated Communication, 3*(1), 43–49.

Snijders, T. A. B. (2001). The statistical evaluation of social network dynamics. *Sociological Methodology, 31*, 361–395.

Sørenson, J. B. (2002). The strength of corporate culture and the reliability of firm performance. *Administrative Science Quarterly, 47*, 70–91.

Sprent, P., & Smeeton, N. C. (2001). *Applied nonparametric statistical methods* (3rd ed.). Boca Raton, FL: Chapman & Hall/CRC.

Stevenson, W. B. (2003). Introduction: Planned organizational change and organizational networks. *The Journal of Applied Behavioral Science, 39*(3), 238–242.

St. Lifer, E. (2000). The boomer brain-drain: The last of a generation?. *Library Journal, 125*(8), 38–42.

Strati, A. (2000). *Theory and method in organization studies.* London: Sage.

Subramanian, A., & Nilakanta, S. (1996). Organizational innovativeness: Exploring the relationship between organizational determinants of innovation, types of innovations, and measures of organizational performance. *Omega, International Journal of Management Science, 24*(6), 631–647.

Tenkasi, R. V., & Chesmore, M. C. (2003). Social networks and planned organizational change. *Journal of Applied Behavioral Science, 39*(3), 281–300.

The Carnegie Classification of Institutions of Higher Education. (2006). Retrieved March 11, 2006, from http://www.carnegiefoundation.org/classifications/

Thompson, S. K. (2002). *Sampling* (2nd ed.). New York, NY: Wiley.

Tichy, N. M. (1980a). Networks in organizations. In: P. G. Nystrom & W. Starbuck (Eds), *Handbook of organization design* (pp. 225–247). London: Oxford University Press.

Tichy, N. M. (1980b). A social network perspective for organization development. In: T. G. Cummings (Ed.), *Systems theory for organization development.* Chichester, England: Wiley.

Tichy, N. M., Tushman, M. L., & Fombrun, C. (1979). Social network analysis for organizations. *Academy of Management Review, 4*(4), 507–519.

Tinsley, H. E. A., & Tinsley, D. J. (1987). Uses of factor analysis in counseling psychology research. *Journal of Counseling Psychology, 34*(4), 414–424.

Trochim, W. M. K. (2001). *The research methods knowledge base.* Cincinnati, OH: Atomic Dog.

Troldahl, V. C., & Powell, F. A. (1965). A short-form dogmatism scale for use in field studies. *Social Forces, 44*(2), 211–214.

Ulrich, D. (2002). An innovation protocol. In: F. Hesselbein, M. Goldsmith & I. Somerville (Eds), *Leading for innovation and organizing for results* (pp. 215–224). San Francisco, CA: Jossey-Bass.

Valente, T. W. (1995). *Network models of the diffusion of innovations.* Cresskill, NJ: Hampton Press.

Veblen, T. B. (1909). The limitations of marginal utility. *Journal of Political Economy, 17*, 235–245.

Walker, M. E., Wasserman, S., & Wellman, B. (1994). Statistical models for social support networks. In: S. Wasserman & J. Galaskiewicz (Eds), *Advances in social network analysis: Research in the social and behavioral sciences* (pp. 53–78). Thousand Oaks, CA: Sage.

Wasserman, S., & Faust, K. (1994). *Social network analysis: Methods and applications.* Cambridge: Cambridge University Press.

Watts, D. J. (2003). *Six degrees: The science of a connected age.* New York, NY: W. W. Horton.

Weick, K. E. (1979). *The social psychology of organizing* (2nd ed.). New York, NY: McGraw-Hill.

Wellman, B. (2002). Structural analysis: From method and metaphor to theory and substance. In: J. Scott (Ed.), *Social networks: Critical concepts in sociology* (2nd ed., pp. 81–121). New York, NY: Routledge.

Wellman, B., & Berkowitz, S. D. (1988). *Social structures: A network approach*. Cambridge, England: Cambridge University Press.

Wellman, B., & Gulia, M. (1993). Which types of networks provide what kinds of social support? Paper presented at the International Sunbelt Social Network Conference.

Wellman, B., & Leighton, B. (1979). Networks, neighborhoods, and communities: Approaches to the study of the community question. *Urban Affairs Quarterly, 14*(3), 363–390.

Wentland, E. J., & Smith, K. W. (1993). *Survey responses: An evaluation of their validity*. San Diego, CA: Academic Press.

Wilder, S. (1996). *The age demographics of academic librarians* [Electronic Version]. ARL: A Bimonthly Report on Research Library Issues and Actions from ARL, CNI, and SPARC, 185. Retrieved January 3, 2007 from http://www.arl.org/newsltr/185/agedemo.html

Wilder, S. (2003). *Demographic change in academic librarianship*. Annapolis Junction, MD: Association of Research Libraries.

Yun, G. W., & Trumbo, C. W. (2000). Comparative response to a survey executed by post, e-mail, and web form. *Journal of Computer Mediated Communication, 6*(1). Retrieved April 18, 2006, from http://jcmc.indiana.edu/vol6/issue1/yun.html

Zack, M. H. (2000). Researching organizational systems using social network analysis. Paper presented at the 33rd Hawaii International Conference on Systems Sciences, Maui, HI.

Znaniecki, F. (1934). *The method of sociology*. New York, NY: Farrar & Rinehart.

APPENDIX A. QUESTIONS RELATED TO THE COMPOSITION OF INDIVIDUAL SOCIAL NETWORKS

Questions, suggested by Cross and Parker (2004), which provide information that will allow the researcher to determine the scope of the individual's professional advice network:

- Please identify people who are important in terms of providing you with information to do your work or helping you think about complex problems posed by your work.
- For each person, what is their physical proximity?
  1. same floor
  2. different floor
  3. different building
  4. different city
  5. different state
- Please indicate the organization in which each person works
  1. within the same department
  2. outside department, within the same organizational unit (such as a division or branch)
  3. outside organizational unit, but in the same library
  4. in the same library system
  5. in another library or library system
- How long have you known each person?
  1. less than 1 year
  2. 1–3 years
  3. 3–5 years
  4. 5–10 years
  5. 10+ years
- Please indicate each person's hierarchical level in relationship to yours
  1. two or more levels of hierarchy higher
  2. one level of hierarchy higher than mine
  3. equal to mine
  4. one level of hierarchy lower than mine
  5. two or more levels of hierarchy lower than mine
- Please indicate the frequency with which you typically turn to each person for information on work-related topics
  1. less than twice a year
  2. quarterly
  3. monthly
  4. weekly
  5. daily

APPENDIX B. ATTITUDINAL DIMENSIONS ASSESSED BY THE RUSAW MULTIFACTOR ASSESSMENT INSTRUMENT

Attitudinal dimensions assessed by the Rusaw multifactor assessment instrument measure the strength of belief in the following principles, which provide an environment that fosters the development of innovative products and services.

- *Risk taking* – Employees should be challenged and rewarded for devising novel ways to perform their job functions. Furthermore, they should be encouraged to learn from past mistakes. In this light, standard operating procedures are guides, not rules, for making decisions.
- *Rewards* – People should receive tangible and intangible rewards for trying out new ideas. Employees should receive top-level recognition for their contributions so that they feel a sense of pride and achievement in their work.
- *Empowering* – Employees can be trusted. They should be encouraged to use professional judgment in making non-routine decisions. In addition, they should be encouraged to learn and take part regularly in educational events, both on and off the job.
- *Objective measurements* – Employees should have valid and objectively defined standards that measure their work productivity and quality. These standards are not arbitrary, but are derived from the mission of the organization and assessments of the main programs, products, and services of the organization.
- *Feedback* – An organization should have well-established communication with people both inside and outside the organization. Information should be used to monitor the quality of service and make corrections before problems escalate. Employees are encouraged to know their customer and clients directly and are not impeded from interacting with them as appropriate.
- *Turbulence* – Organizations must be flexible in order to respond to problems and a changing environment. The organization is responsible for communicating with employees and customers to enlist support in solving problems
- *Interdependence* – Checks and balances used to control waste, fraud, and abuse should not interfere with the seamless flow of work. Individual self-interest, whether at the individual, team, department, or divisional level, is deferred in favor of the overall interest of the organization.

- *Decentralization* – Social status differentiation should be minimized. That is, there should be little social status difference between managers and employees in the organization. A variety of ideas should be absorbed from all personnel to find creative solutions and to boost commitment to reaching goals, both individual and organizational.
- *Cosmopolitan* – All employees, but in particular managers, should focus on the "big picture" of customer and client needs. The influx of new ideas by analyzing feedback and soliciting the skills of "outsiders" should be actively encouraged. There is honest enthusiasm for learning about organizations that use "best" practices.

APPENDIX C. QUESTIONS ADAPTED FROM THE RUSAW MULTIFACTOR ASSESSMENT INSTRUMENT

Each question is evaluated on a 5-point Likert scale implying increasing degrees of order (Schwab, 2005) which run the range from complete disagreement (1) to complete agreement (5).

1. People should be rewarded when they challenge standard operating procedures (*risk taking*).
2. A library should prepare its employees to meet the challenges of rapid change in their work (*turbulence*).
3. Managers should make decisions based largely on an understanding of the patron's needs (*cosmopolitan*).
4. Employees should be allowed to use discretion in deciding how they will carry out novel situations (*empowering*).
5. Duplication in the work of various units within the library should be avoided (*interdependence*).
6. Employees should visit other organizations to identify possible practices to adapt (*cosmopolitan*).
7. A library should have measurable work standards for professional work (*objective measurements*).
8. Libraries should regularly gather information from the people it serves and use it to change how things are done (*feedback*).
9. Employees should have numerous opportunities to develop new skills on the job (*empowering*).
10. The library should give adequate financial rewards for work improvement ideas (*rewards*).

11. Managers should help employees try out new ideas (*risk taking*).
12. Managers should resolve "turf wars" between departments through negotiation (*interdependence*).
13. Most workers should have daily contact with their key constituencies (*feedback*).
14. Employees should regularly attend training sessions to learn new skills (*empowering*).
15. Employees should use professional judgment in deciding ethical matters in their work (*objective measurements*).
16. The library should adapt to rapid change in the expectations of patrons (*turbulence*).
17. Managers should use different approaches to motivate employees (*rewards*).
18. Assessment is a critical component to the success of the library (*feedback*).
19. Employees should be encouraged to learn from failure (*risk taking*).
20. Groups should work together to accomplish the major work of the library (*interdependence*).
21. It should be easy to discuss ideas with managers (*decentralization*).
22. Libraries should expect to undergo rapid change in the future (*turbulence*).
23. Employees should use agreed-on standard of quality in performing their work (*objective measurements*).
24. The library should have a vibrant employee recognition program (*rewards*).
25. The library should use teams to develop new approaches to solving problems (*decentralization*).
26. The library should have many professionals who come from other organizations and fields (*cosmopolitan*).
27. Team leadership roles should rotate among members (*decentralization*).

APPENDIX D. SURVEY INSTRUMENT

Question 1 – Indicators. Please read the following statements and then select the answer that best describes your immediate reaction to the statement. Please do not try to overanalyze either the statement or your response. Respond based on how you believe things *should be done* and not on how things may currently be done at your library.

	Strongly Agree	Agree	Neither Agree nor Disagree	Disagree	Strongly Disagree
People should be rewarded when they challenge standard operating procedures					
A library should prepare its employees to meet the challenges of rapid change in their work					
Managers should base decisions largely on the needs of library patrons rather than the desires of staff					
Library staff should be allowed to use discretion in carrying out novel situations					
Duplication in the work of various units within the library should be avoided					
Employees should visit organizations other than libraries to identify useful practices					
A library should have measurable work standards for professional work					
Libraries should regularly gather information from patrons and use that to change how things are done					
Library staff should have numerous opportunities to develop new skills on the job					
The library should provide financial rewards for work improvement ideas					

(Continued)

	Strongly Agree	Agree	Neither Agree nor Disagree	Disagree	Strongly Disagree
Managers should resolve "turf wars" between departments through negotiation					
Most library staff should have daily contact with their key constituencies					
Employees should regularly attend training sessions to learn new skills					
Employees should use their own professional judgment in deciding ethical matters in their work					
The library should adapt quickly to rapid changes in patron expectations					
Managers should use different approaches to motivate individual employees					
Assessment is a critical component of the success of a library					
Employees should be encouraged to learn from failure					
Groups should work together, rather than as distinct units, to accomplish the major work of the library					
The culture of the library should make it easy to discuss new ideas or problems with managers					

Libraries should expect to undergo rapid change in the future				
Employees should use agreed-on standards of quality in performing their work				
The library should have a vibrant employee recognition program				
The library should use teams to develop new approaches to solving problems				
The library staff should include professionals from other types of organizations and fields				
Team leadership roles should rotate among team members				

Question 2 – Colleagues. Please identify the people who are important to you in terms of providing you with information to do your work or in helping you to think about complex problems posed by your work. You may name up to 20 people, but do not feel compelled to do so. Please list only those people who immediately come to mind, whether they work in the same library as you or not. For purposes of the survey, it is important that you list each person's first and last name (i.e., John Smith).

Question 3 – Relationship. For each person listed, please select the answer that best describes their relationship to you

- ☐ Co-worker
- ☐ Supervisor/Boss
- ☐ Subordinate
- ☐ Professional colleague
- ☐ Personal friend
- ☐ Mentor
- ☐ Mentee
- ☐ Spouse/Significant other
- ☐ Other family member

Question 4 – Proximity. For each person listed, please select the answer that best describes their physical proximity to your regular place of work.

- ☐ Same floor, same building
- ☐ Different floor, same building
- ☐ Different building, same organization
- ☐ Different campus, same organization
- ☐ Different organization, same city
- ☐ Different organization, different city
- ☐ Different organization, different state
- ☐ Different organization, different country

Question 5 – Organization. For each person listed, please indicate the organizational unit each person works within.

- ☐ Within the same department and location
- ☐ Within the same department, but a different location
- ☐ Outside my department, within the same division or branch

❑ Outside my division or branch, but in the same library
❑ In the same library system
❑ In another library or library system
❑ In another organization that is not a library or library system

Question 6 – Longevity. For each person listed, please indicate how long you have known the person.

❑ Less than 1 year
❑ 1–3 years
❑ 3–5 years
❑ 5–10 years
❑ 10 or more years

Question 7 – Hierarchy. For each person listed, please indicate the relationship of their position to yours. If you work in different organizations, indicate the relationship as closely as possible.

❑ Two or more levels above
❑ One level above
❑ Equal to mine
❑ One level below
❑ Two or more levels below

Question 8 – Interaction. For each person listed, please indicate the frequency with which you typically turn to that person for information or advice about work- or profession-related topics.

❑ Daily
❑ Weekly
❑ Monthly
❑ Quarterly
❑ Two or fewer times a year

Question 9 – Demographics. This final section consists of standard demographic questions related to you and your environment

What is your current age?

Gender. Are you ...

❑ Female
❑ Male

Ethnicity. If you were to characterize yourself, which of the following would best apply?

❑ *American Indian or Alaska Native* – a person having origins in any of the original peoples of North and South America (including Central America), and who maintains tribal affiliation or community attachment

❑ *Asian* – a person having origins in any of the original peoples of the Far East, Southeast Asia, or the Indian subcontinent

❑ *Black or African American* – a person having origins in any of the black racial groups of Africa

❑ *Hispanic or Latino* – a person of Cuban, Mexican, Puerto Rican, Cuban, South or Central American, or other Spanish culture or origin, regardless of race

❑ *Native Hawaiian or Other Pacific Islander* – a person having origins in any of the original peoples of Hawaii, Guam, Samoa, or other Pacific Islands.

❑ *White* – a person having origins in any of the original peoples of Europe, the Middle East, or North Africa.

❑ *Multiracial* – a person who does not identify solely with any of the categories above.

❑ Prefer not to state

Title. Which of the following categories best characterizes your current position?

❑ Non-exempt library support staff
❑ Librarian – not a supervisor
❑ Professional staff – not a supervisor
❑ Librarian – supervisor
❑ Professional staff supervisor
❑ Department head
❑ Assistant or Associate Director, Dean, or University Librarian
❑ Director, Dean, or University Librarian

Tenure. How long have you been in your current position? Please answer in number of years. If less than 1, please enter 1.

    Years in current position _____

Career. How long have you been working in libraries? Please answer in number of years. If less than 1 year, please enter 1.

    Years in libraries _____

Institution. What institution do you work at?

Area. Within the following list of library functional areas, which most accurately defines your job responsibilities overall?

- ❏ Acquisitions
- ❏ Administration
- ❏ Application and system development
- ❏ Archives
- ❏ Cataloging
- ❏ Circulation
- ❏ Collection development
- ❏ Collection management
- ❏ Computer labs/operations
- ❏ Conservation and preservation
- ❏ Digital media services
- ❏ Digital library development
- ❏ Distance learning services
- ❏ Electronic services
- ❏ Extended services
- ❏ Geographic information systems
- ❏ Government documents
- ❏ Information commons
- ❏ Information technology
- ❏ Instruction
- ❏ Interlibrary loan
- ❏ Media services
- ❏ Microforms
- ❏ Periodicals
- ❏ Public services
- ❏ Reference
- ❏ Reserves
- ❏ Serials
- ❏ Special collections
- ❏ System administration
- ❏ Technical services
- ❏ User services
- ❏ Web development

Associations. Which professional association conferences do you regularly attend?

- ❑ American Association of Law Libraries (AALL)
- ❑ American Library Association (ALA)
- ❑ American Society for Information Science and Technology (ASIS&T)
- ❑ Association for Information Systems (AIS)
- ❑ Association of Research Libraries (ARL)
- ❑ American Theological Library Association (ATLA)
- ❑ Art Libraries Society of North America (ALSNA)
- ❑ Association of College and Research Libraries (ACRL)
- ❑ Association for Library and Information Science Education (ALISE)
- ❑ Coalition for Networked Information (CNI)
- ❑ EDUCAUSE
- ❑ Illinois Association of College and Research Libraries (IACRL)
- ❑ Illinois Library Association (ILA)
- ❑ Library Administration and Management (LAMA)
- ❑ Library Information Technology Association (LITA)
- ❑ Medical Library Association (MLA), Music Library Association (MLA)
- ❑ North American Serials Interest Group (NASIG)
- ❑ Society of American Archivists (SAA)
- ❑ Special Library Association (SLA)
- ❑ Theatre Library Association (TLA)
- ❑ Other

Thanks: Thanks for participating in this research. Please use this space to discuss any questions that were unclear to you, questions where the answer options were not adequate, or any other issue or comment you may have as a result of taking the test.

APPENDIX E. ITEM-TOTAL STATISTICS FOR INNOVATION INDICATORS

Item	Scale Mean if Item Deleted	Scale Variance if Item Deleted	Corrected Item-total Correlation	Squared Multiple Correlation	Cronbach's Alpha if Item Deleted
RiskTaking_1	105.29	88.363	0.450	0.301	0.846
Turbulence_1	104.30	90.600	0.459	0.279	0.847
Cosmopolitan_1	105.07	89.982	0.255	0.147	0.853
Empowering_1	104.73	90.911	0.328	0.208	0.850
Interdependence_1	104.75	90.620	0.277	0.161	0.851
Cosmopolitan_2	104.83	88.227	0.471	0.303	0.845
Objective_1	104.91	89.443	0.374	0.298	0.848
Feedback_1	104.67	88.636	0.498	0.341	0.845
Empowering_2	104.28	90.477	0.472	0.348	0.847
Rewards_1	105.23	87.763	0.382	0.259	0.848
Interdependence_2	104.74	89.559	0.404	0.236	0.848
Feedback_2	104.98	87.952	0.451	0.293	0.846
Empowering_3	104.60	88.545	0.510	0.403	0.845
RiskTaking_2	106.26	88.662	0.123	0.156	0.873
Objective_2	105.41	88.994	0.311	0.223	0.851
Turbulence_2	105.03	87.325	0.477	0.327	0.845
Rewards_2	104.58	89.783	0.471	0.318	0.846
Feedback_3	104.62	89.084	0.496	0.363	0.845
RiskTaking_3	104.57	88.405	0.526	0.358	0.844
Interdependence_3	104.67	88.647	0.441	0.291	0.846
Decentralization_1	104.25	90.672	0.465	0.341	0.847
Turbulence_3	104.59	88.762	0.452	0.310	0.846
Objective_3	104.72	89.818	0.426	0.292	0.847
Rewards_3	104.86	86.961	0.527	0.372	0.843
Decentralization_2	105.07	86.627	0.540	0.382	0.843
Cosmopolitan_3	105.28	88.096	0.421	0.285	0.847
Decentralization_3	105.46	88.358	0.377	0.251	0.848

APPENDIX F. KMO TOTAL VARIANCE EXPLAINED

Component	Initial Eigenvalues			Extraction Sums of Squared Loadings			Rotation Sums of Squared Loadings		
	Total	% of Variance	Cumulative %	Total	% of Variance	Cumulative %	Total	% of Variance	Cumulative %
1	6.706	24.837	24.837	6.706	24.837	24.837	2.879	10.662	10.662
2	1.446	5.357	30.194	1.446	5.357	30.194	2.569	9.516	20.177
3	1.315	4.870	35.064	1.315	4.870	35.064	2.295	8.502	28.679
4	1.264	4.682	39.746	1.264	4.682	39.746	2.035	7.538	36.217
5	1.191	4.410	44.156	1.191	4.410	44.156	1.682	6.229	42.446
6	1.111	4.116	48.272	1.111	4.116	48.272	1.298	4.807	47.253
7	1.020	3.777	52.049	1.020	3.777	52.049	1.295	4.795	52.049
8	0.959	3.551	55.600						
9	0.934	3.460	59.060						
10	0.864	3.199	62.259						
11	0.858	3.177	65.436						
12	0.803	2.976	68.411						
13	0.780	2.891	71.302						
14	0.736	2.727	74.029						
15	0.701	2.598	76.627						
16	0.691	2.560	79.187						

17	0.639	2.367	81.554
18	0.623	2.309	83.863
19	0.598	2.215	86.078
20	0.536	1.987	88.065
21	0.530	1.961	90.026
22	0.513	1.902	91.928
23	0.472	1.750	93.678
24	0.465	1.720	95.398
25	0.443	1.639	97.038
26	0.421	1.559	98.597
27	0.379	1.403	100.000

Extraction method: principal component analysis.

FACULTY STATUS, TENURE, AND COMPENSATING WAGE DIFFERENTIALS AMONG MEMBERS OF THE ASSOCIATION OF RESEARCH LIBRARIES

Deborah Lee

ABSTRACT

The institution of tenure has elicited debate and controversy since its introduction in higher education. Proponents argue the need for tenure based on academic freedom and efficient university governance. Critics argue that it represents inefficiency in the higher education labor market and protects less productive faculty members. The use of tenure in academic libraries has been no less controversial, with only 40–60% of academic libraries supporting tenure track positions for academic librarians. This dichotomy in the labor market for academic librarians represents a natural experiment and allows for the testing of the presence of a compensating wage differential for tenure.

This study examines 10 years' worth of cross-sectional data drawn from member libraries of the Association of Research Libraries (ARL). Models examine both the institutional characteristics of tenure-granting ARL academic libraries and the impact of tenure on starting salaries. Issues related to both a union wage premium and a compensating wage

Advances in Library Administration and Organization, Volume 26, 151–208
ISSN: 0732-0671/doi:10.1016/S0732-0671(08)00204-6

differential due to tenure are explored. The results of this research suggest that tenure, while serving other functions within an academic library setting, does not have the predicted impact on starting salaries.

TENURE

For decades the word tenure has evoked passionate defenses and ardent arguments, both within higher education and in academic libraries. As an institution within academic labor markets, the presence of tenure represents a unique labor arrangement that has generated considerable debate and controversy. In 1940, the American Association of University Professors (AAUP) and the Association of American Colleges (AAC) approved the *Statement of Principles on Academic Freedom and Tenure*, which laid the groundwork for the modern concept of tenure (2003). Tenure grants faculty continuous employment unless due cause is shown for termination. Traditionally tenure is viewed as the prerequisite for academic freedom. While always controversial, the debate over tenure has taken on a renewed fervor since the end of mandatory retirement in higher education, which was eliminated by federal law in 1994 by amendments to the Age Discrimination in Employment Act.

From an American academic labor market perspective, tenure provides a form of employment security. This security, which results in a lifetime employment guarantee (except under rare circumstances), can be viewed as part of the compensation package provided to tenured faculty and therefore, should carry a compensating wage differential. The theory of compensating wage differentials traditionally focuses on the premium offered as part of the wage package to offset certain negative attributes inherent in the job. Positive attributes such as employment security, offered in the form of non-pecuniary compensation, should result in an expected lower wage. Although numerous experiments with non-tenure track options have been introduced within higher education in recent years, much is still unknown about the pricing of non-tenure track positions as alternatives to traditional tenure track professorial positions.

ACADEMIC LIBRARIANSHIP

This study will examine the use of tenure as a compensating wage differential within the case of academic librarianship in American institutions of higher learning. Tenure is no less controversial in academic libraries and the use of tenure within the academic library labor market is not uniformly practiced. Scholars in the field of librarianship have argued for and against the practice for over 50 years. In 1972, the AAUP, the AAC, and the Association of College and Research Libraries (ACRL) released a joint statement on the necessity of tenure for academic libraries. Despite this long-standing endorsement, various studies have placed the number of academic libraries offering tenure between only 20% at research universities and 56% at comprehensive universities (Park & Riggs, 1993).

The appropriate nature of the professional identity of academic librarians has long been debated. As early as the 1950s, ACRL explored this issue through the formation of its Ad Hoc Committee on Academic Status (Branscomb, 1970). ACRL and its parent professional organization, the American Library Association (ALA), formally adopted faculty status and tenure in 1971 as the appropriate standard for the employment of academic librarians (Meyer, 1999). In a 1972 joint statement, the ACRL, AAC, and AAUP define faculty status for librarians as follows: "Faculty status entails for librarians the same rights and responsibilities as for other members of the faculty. They should have corresponding entitlement to rank, promotion, tenure, compensation, leaves, and research funds. They must go through the same process of evaluation and meet the same standards as other faculty members" (Association of College and Research Libraries, 2001). The expectations and responsibilities of faculty status for academic librarians has been more fully developed in subsequent standards issued by ACRL, the latest of which is the reaffirmed June 2002 version (Association of College and Research Libraries, 2002).

Despite the policy statements and standards issued by the major professional organizations within the field, academic libraries have never wholeheartedly adopted the use of faculty status or tenure. Indeed, the exact number of academic libraries offering tenure track positions to its librarians is unknown. Numerous studies have reported conflicting information, depending on the type of sample and the operational definition of faculty status. The academic labor market within academic libraries thus offers both options: those libraries supporting faculty status/tenure track positions for librarians and those that do not. This dichotomy between tenure- and non-tenure-granting academic libraries offers a natural experiment within which the compensating wage differential due to tenure may be studied.

RESEARCH PROBLEM

Despite the extensive debate surrounding the use of tenure within higher education, much is still unknown concerning its economic impact. Economic theory predicts that, all else held constant, compensation at tenure-granting academic libraries will be lower than their non-tenure-granting counterparts, assuming that tenure serves the same function within academic librarianship as in other academic areas. The wage differential should reflect the inherent value of job security provided by tenure. Thus, this study will test the hypothesis that average starting salaries at tenure-granting academic research libraries will be lower, other things held constant, than at their non-tenure-granting counterparts. This hypothesis will be tested using cross-sectional data drawn from the members of the Association of Research Libraries (ARL). The results of this study may have implications for other fields and disciplines evaluating the institution of tenure.

LITERATURE REVIEW

The following literature review is divided into three sections. The first covers the economic theory of compensating wage differentials. Studies discussed in this section concern empirical applications of the theory of compensating wage differentials to a number of different labor market attributes. The second section covers the use and function of tenure within higher education. This section explores the role of tenure within higher education and the ramifications for the academic labor market. And the third section describes the labor market arrangements commonly found within academic librarianship, including the role of tenure and faculty status.

Compensating Wage Differentials

Compensating wage differential models predict wage variations across occupations based on selected job or employee attributes. While some occupations have desirable or agreeable attributes, others have unpleasant or even dangerous ones. Workers and employers agree to a single wage rate that embodies a number of aspects of the employment situation. The theory of compensating wage differentials postulates differences in compensation, which incorporates the negative and positive occupational attributes and equalizes the desirability of disparate occupations.

Adam Smith was perhaps the first proponent of compensating wage differentials, noting the difference in earnings to be found among occupations. In *The Wealth of Nations* (originally published in 1776) he noted: "Pecuniary wages and profit, indeed are everywhere in Europe extremely different, according to the different employments of labour and stock. But this difference arises partly from certain circumstances in the employments themselves, which either really, or at least in the imagination of men, make up for the small pecuniary gain in some and counterbalance a great one in others; and partly from the policy of Europe, which nowhere leaves things at perfect liberty" (Smith, 1976, p. 111).

Nearly 200 years later Rosen (1974) formalized the theory of compensating wage differentials with a model of hedonic prices. In his model the wage rate is thought to embody job characteristics with implicit prices, which reflect the price at which each job characteristic may be bought or sold. These prices reflect the compensating wage differentials. A key feature of Rosen's model is the nature of the matching process between workers and employers. Workers sort themselves into jobs with a given set of attributes based on the workers' individual characteristics and preferences, resulting in a reduction in wage differentials between jobs and an efficient allocation of labor. *The observed differences in wages reflect the positive or negative premium attached to the job attributes by workers* (Rosen, 1974).

Rosen's (1974) article begat a flurry of studies examining any number of potentially negative job characteristics in a variety of labor market settings. The vast majority of these early studies focused on white males and on blue-collar professions. Later studies expanded coverage to other groups and to a broader array of labor market characteristics.

Table 1 summarizes the most significant recent studies examining compensating wage differentials and labor market conditions. Brown's research (1980) is typical of much of the empirical work on compensating wage differentials that was conducted in the 1970s and 1980s. Unlike some cross-sectional studies, Brown used longitudinal data drawn from the National Longitudinal Survey (NLS) Young Men's sample. He examined seven years' worth of data on the labor market experiences of males aged 14–24 in 1966, excluding those with a college education or who were currently enrolled in college. Data on occupational characteristics were taken from several sources and matched to their occupation or industry. Brown chose to use longitudinal over cross-sectional data due to the often-documented problems with empirical results, stating that "the most common explanation is the omission of important worker abilities, biasing the coefficients of the job characteristics" (Brown, 1980, p. 118). Brown used

Table 1. Compensating Wage Differentials: Sample Studies.

Author(s) (Year)	Job Characteristic	Sample
Hamermesh (1977)	Poor working conditions (noise, hazardous materials)	White males
Lucas (1977)	Repetitive working conditions	White males
Abowd and Ashenfelter (1981)	Unemployment spells	White males
McGoldrick and Robst (1996)	Worker mobility	Panel study of income dynamics
Graves et al. (1999)	Unionization	International
Morlock (2000)	Employer-provided insurance	Survey of income and program participation
Gariety and Shaffer (2001)	Flextime	Current population survey
Gunderson and Hyatt (2001)	Job safety	Canadian workers

many of the same variables to be found in other studies: work experience, education, unionization, region, and urbanization. Four job characteristics that were theorized to carry a compensating wage differential were examined: repetitive job functions, high levels of stress, duties requiring physical strength, and "bad" working conditions (based on temperature, vibrations, or other job hazards.) Despite using longitudinal data and attempts to correct for both changing conditions and holding worker characteristics constant, Brown found that "the coefficients of job characteristics that might be expected to generate equalizing differences in wage rates were often wrong-signed or insignificant" (Brown, 1980, p. 131). He suggests that a number of factors may account for this, including job characteristics that are not well measured, additional omitted variables, and varying degrees of competitiveness in labor markets.

Other studies listed in Table 1, while noting some of the empirical difficulties associated with applications of the theory of compensating wage differentials, have had limited success in identifying differentials associated with various job characteristics. Many of these early studies focused on white males in blue-collar occupations. Hamermesh (1977) uses data drawn from an International Survey Research (ISR) survey on working conditions to examine white males aged 21–65, using many of the variables employed by Brown. These included age, education, occupational categorical variables, region, and unionization. Job characteristics examined included noise, weather and heat, "dirty" work, and use of hazardous materials and equipment. While Hamermesh had some success in identifying statistically significant compensating wage differentials, some characteristics ("dirty" work) did not carry the expected sign. Lucas (1977), in a cross-sectional study of compensating wage differentials associated with repetitive working conditions for white males, found similar results. Likewise, other studies have found compensating differentials based on unpleasant working conditions or even the probability of death on the job (Dorman, 1996). Abowd and Ashenfelter (1981) examined the effect of anticipated spells of unemployment on wages. They found that the competitive wage reflects a compensating differential, which varied by industry according to the probability of future layoffs.

Other job characteristics have been examined using the theory of compensating wage differentials. McGoldrick and Robst (1996) examined the effects of worker mobility on the payment of compensating wage differentials for earnings risk. Using the 1979–1984 waves of the Panel Study of Income Dynamics (PSID), they estimated a series of simultaneous equations where both wages and worker mobility were endogenous. Variables used included mean wage, job change, age, education, experience, job tenure, SMSA size, race, marital status, children, unionization, regional categorical variables, and occupational categorical variables. Unlike many of the earlier studies, McGoldrick and Robst included both men and women in their study. This approach allowed them to examine whether workers with greater uncertainty have a greater mobility and whether greater mobility translated into lower compensating wage differentials. They found that workers experiencing uncertainty with a greater degree of mobility did receive a lower compensating wage differential. As they state, "... workers receive compensation for uncertainty and this compensation decreases with mobility" (p. 231). Other authors have examined the interplay between unionization and compensating wage differentials. Interestingly, Graves, Arthur, and Sexton (1999) argued that the returns often attributed to unionization may in fact be due to compensation for poor working conditions.

Recent studies have expanded the coverage of the theory of compensating wage differentials to other types of job amenities. Morlock (2000) examined the employer-provided health insurance and compensating wage differentials. Morlock used wave 1 of the 1990 Survey of Income and Program Participation (SIPP). Variables included in the study mirror those used in other compensating wage differential studies: age, education, unionization, urbanization, training, and occupational categorical variables. Morlock did include both men and women in the study. He found contradictory evidence concerning the theory and empirical results, with the greatest differential accruing to those with the employer-provided insurance.

Gariety and Shaffer (2001) examined the compensating wage differentials due to flextime. Data for women were drawn from the Current Population Survey for 1989 and for both men and women for 1997. They found a positive wage differential associated with flextime for women but not for men.

While the theory of compensating wage differentials has yet to be explicitly applied to the area of tenure and higher education, Zoghi (2000) did address some closely related issues. She examined academic freedom, an attribute of tenure, as an amenity within the academic labor market and modeled the willingness to trade wages for academic freedom. Zoghi found significantly higher wages at universities *without* academic freedom and that public universities fight academic freedom more, based on AAUP data.

Tenure in Higher Education

Historically, the debate concerning tenure in higher education has centered on the concept of academic freedom. In the 19th century, the debate usually focused on dissident religious viewpoints as expressed by faculty members (Cohen, 1998). The late 19th and early 20th century debate centered more on political and economic viewpoints. Interestingly, several noteworthy cases dealt specifically with economic beliefs. In 1892 the president of Lawrence College was fired for free trade remarks; in 1894 economist Richard Ely was fired from the University of Wisconsin, accused of promoting public unrest with his views on labor relations; and in 1895 an economist at the University of Chicago was fired for criticizing monopolies and the railroad industry (Lucas, 1994, p. 194). In 1915 the AAUP was formed, with much of its early work dedicated to the defense of professors claiming unfair dismissal by their employing institutions (Cohen, 1998, pp. 127–129).

Frinz Machlup (1964), economist and president of AAUP in 1964, agreed with critics of tenure when they asserted that tenure introduces inefficiencies into the academic labor market and keeps academic salaries low. Note that this statement inherently accepts the notion that tenure creates compensating wage differentials. However, Machlup argues that the benefits accrued to both society and higher education by the academic freedoms protected by tenure outweighed the costs. In another often-quoted essay written for the AAUP, William Van Alstyne (1971) argues that tenure was never meant to be a lifetime employment contract but merely a guarantee of due process.

McKenzie (1996) argues that the contractual relationship of tenure benefits both the institution and the individual faculty member through the screening of potential employees, and through the protection tenure affords from the ubiquitous internal politics often found in institutions of higher education. Other proponents cite the beneficial role of faculty involvement in the administrative infrastructure of higher education. Accordingly, tenured faculty have greater freedom to actively participate in university governance, serving as a countervailing force to university administrators (McPherson & Schapiro, 1999). Another argument focuses on the role of tenure in the hiring and screening process within academia. Without tenure, potentially less productive, tenured professors would be hesitant to hire applicants with greater promise and productivity than themselves (Carmichael, 1988).

Frustrated with the perceived rigidities and inefficiencies introduced by the tenure system, governing boards and legislative bodies have often been some of the most vocal critics of tenure. The chancellor of the Massachusetts Board of Higher Education, troubled by the higher-than-average number of tenured faculty in the University of Massachusetts system, proposed paying new faculty higher starting salaries to forgo the tenure track (Chronicle of Higher Education, 1999). Again, this supports the contention that tenure results in a compensating wage differential.

The Florida State Board of Regents, in an attempt to incorporate alternatives to tenure in the University of Florida system, established its newest campus, Florida Gulf Coast University, under a system of renewable three- to five-year contracts (Cage, 1995). Florida Gulf Coast University opened in 1997, but reports three years later were not encouraging. As of mid-1999, 22% of the original 155 professors had left the campus. Critics charge that administrators released vocal faculty members, despite prior favorable reviews (Wilson, 2000). Other institutions have experimented with either mixed employment options or have eliminated the tenure altogether. The trustees at the University of South Florida developed 14 actions that could serve as grounds for dismissal, even for tenured faculty. The actions include insubordination and improper conduct. The statement that alarmed faculty the most includes dismissal for "any other properly substantiated cause or action that is detrimental to the best interests of the university, its students, or its employees" (Wilson & Walsh, 2003). Some have argued that such a sweeping statement effectively negates the concept of tenure.

Other questions about the scope of tenure have also entered into the debate in recent years. Concerns in the Texas A&M University system centered on the job benefits guaranteed to faculty members – or exactly what aspects of employment are protected by tenure. New policies enacted by the university system explicitly state that tenure "shall not be construed as creating a property interest in any attributes of the faculty position beyond the ... annual salary" (Wilson & Walsh, 2003). The university system hopes to avoid costly lawsuits over laboratory access, research support, and teaching schedules through the implementation of these policies.

Westark College (located in Arkansas) announced in 1998 that, while retaining tenure for existing faculty, all new faculty appointments would be hired on renewable contracts (Wilson, 1998). According to the AAUP, this reflects a growing trend in higher education. AAUP examined data on employment practices in higher education and found that among full-time professors, approximately 52% held tenure in 1995, the same proportion as in 1975. However, the proportion on tenure track appointments fell from 29% in 1975 to 20 in 1995 (Wilson, 1998).

This increase in the contingent labor force in academic labor markets comes at a price. Ehrenberg and Zhang (2004) studied the effect of part-time and non-tenure track faculty on graduation rates. They found that the increased use of contingent faculty negatively affects the five- and six-year graduation rates of undergraduates enrolled at four-year American colleges and universities.

While many of the strongest criticisms of tenure come from legislators, boards of higher education, or trustees, some criticisms originate from those most familiar with academe. One of the most biting criticisms can be found in Sykes' (1988) bestseller *Profscam*. Sykes, son of a professor and former reporter for the *Milwaukee Journal*, develops a sharply critical analysis of higher education in general, and tenure in particular. He states: "Tenure corrupts, enervates, and dulls higher education. It is, moreover, the academic culture's ultimate control mechanism to weed out the idiosyncratic, the creative, and the nonconformist. The replacement of lifetime tenure with fixed-term renewable contracts would, at one stroke, restore accountability, while potentially freeing the vast untapped energies of the academy that have been locked in the petrified grip of a tenured professoriate" (p. 258).

While less draconian, Breneman (1997) proposes a new examination of the use of tenure in higher education. Breneman is an economist and dean of the Curry School of Education at the University of Virginia. Citing the growing financial disparity between the top 150 institutions and other higher educational institutions, Breneman argues that a one-size-fits-all approach to tenure is no longer viable. Instead, he proposes that many institutions and disciplines would benefit from the introduction of a greater range of employment arrangements. Faculty who opt out of the tenure track system would need to be compensated for the new additional risk they would assume. Breneman notes: "Having argued for the case for a wage premium for new faculty who forgo tenure-track appointments, it is worth considering how large that wage premium must be. No neat calculation exists to guide participants on either side of the market; indeed, the only meaningful answer to that question would be an actual market experiment" (p. 10). This "premium" would be, in economic parlance, the compensating wage differential.

Academic Librarianship and Tenure

Nowhere has the debate concerning the use of tenure within higher education been more intense than in the field of academic librarianship. The appropriate nature of the professional identity of academic librarians dates back to the earliest days of the profession.

Two key themes are consistently intertwined throughout the literature on academic librarianship: faculty status and tenure. As early as the 1950s, the ACRL attempted to shed light on these issues through the formation of its Ad Hoc Committee on Academic Status (Branscomb, 1970). As noted above, ACRL and its parent professional organization, ALA, formally adopted faculty status in 1971 as the appropriate standard for employment of academic librarians (Meyer, 1999). And in its 1972 joint statement, the ACRL, AAC, and AAUP defined faculty status for librarians in the following way: "Faculty status entails for librarians the same rights and responsibilities as for other members of the faculty. They should have corresponding entitlement to rank, promotion, tenure, compensation, leaves, and research funds. They must go through the same process of evaluation and meet the same standards as other faculty members" (ACRL Academic Status Committee, 1974). The expectations and responsibilities of faculty status for academic librarians has been more fully developed in subsequent standards issued by ACRL, the latest of which is the 2001 version (Association of College and Research Libraries, 2001). Note that the definition essentially remains the same. Core to ACRL's definition of faculty status is tenure, which ACRL argues should be available to academic librarians on par with other instructional faculty at the parent institution.

Academic librarians are typically required to have an ALA-accredited master's degree in library science, usually denoted as an MLS degree. In

1975, ACRL endorsed the "Statement on the Terminal Professional Degree for Academic Librarians," which was reaffirmed by the ACRL Board of Directors in 2001 (Association of College and Research Libraries, 2001). This statement explicitly states the minimal requirements for professional librarians, saying: "The master's degree in library science from a library school program accredited by the ALA is the appropriate terminal professional degree for librarians" (Association of College and Research Libraries, 2001). This requirement was challenged in the courts in the mid-1970s by an applicant who did not hold an MLS. The litigant claimed that Mississippi State University, by requiring an MLS and failing to consider other educational alternatives for professional positions in the library, was discriminatory toward women. *Merwine v. Trustees* became a landmark case and established the legality of requiring an ALA-accredited MLS for employment as an academic librarian. Since the original 1975 ACRL statement establishing the MLS as the appropriate terminal degree and the failure of the subsequent legal challenge, there has been minimal debate on this issue (Jones, 1998). Therefore, the MLS is considered the terminal degree for academic librarians, even those with faculty status and tenure. Selected other disciplines also require terminal degrees at the master's level for academic appointment. Examples include creative writing programs (which often require the Master of Fine Arts or MFA) and landscape architecture programs.

Combined with the 1972 statement on faculty status, these proclamations issued by the major professional association set the standards for conferring faculty status (and tenure) on academic librarians. These standards were augmented by the passage in 2002 of the "Guidelines for Academic Status for College and University Librarians" (Association of College and Research Libraries, 2002). These guidelines fleshed out the 1972 statement, explicitly delineating the conditions of faculty status, including such topics as professional responsibilities, governance, contractual relationships, compensation, promotion and salary increases, access to sabbaticals and research funds, and dismissal and grievance procedures.

Despite this overwhelming support by ACRL, the adoption of these standards within academic libraries has been problematic and controversial. Indeed, simply establishing how many academic libraries offer professional positions with faculty status and tenure is not easily accomplished. Numerous studies have been conducted, both prior to the 1972 statement and after. The results from these studies depend in part on how the author(s) operationalized the concept of faculty status. This issue has a long history.

An early 1911 study of 16 "scholarly" libraries found that the head librarian "usually" had faculty status but this status was not extended to the other professional librarians (Henry, 1911). A more empirical study in 1939 of 129 libraries, reflecting a cross-section of academic libraries in terms of geography and size, found that 76% of the head librarians held faculty status while only 40% of the professional librarians held the same status (Maloy, 1939). This reflects, in part, the early tradition of appointing a scholar (usually from the humanities) to head the largest research libraries. The increased emphasis on the professional nature of library science significantly reduced this practice. More contemporary studies no longer find the distinction in status between the library director and the professional staff. Yet these studies vary widely in the resulting number of academic libraries supporting faculty status for librarians.

With the passage of the ACRL standards concerning tenure and faculty status, a spate of studies emerged that examined this issue. Comparing studies of faculty status and tenure are problematic for a number of reasons. Even the area of study can be confusing. In most studies concerning faculty in higher education, researchers in most disciplines would automatically combine the concepts of tenure and faculty status. It would be rare that one would be conferred without the other. This is not the case in academic librarianship, making the need to carefully define the concepts under study paramount.

This variation is due, in part, to the widely differing views librarians have concerning faculty and academic status. As Massman (1972) points out, librarians "have made recommendations which include full faculty status, equivalent rank, identification as academic but without reference to academic rank, a separate classification, and a classification with administrative officers."

Tables 2A and 2B illustrate some of the many studies that emerged during the 1980s as the academic library profession grappled with the issues of faculty status and tenure. Table 2A summarizes the major studies conducted in the decade after the formal adoption of the ACRL standards. Simply identifying who has faculty status and who does not can be a challenge. The numbers range from a low of 35% in a study conducted by Rayman and Goudy (1980) to a high of 80% in Tassin's (1984) study of a small number of southwestern state universities. In some cases, the sample size was perhaps too low to provide results that may be generalized to a larger population. Others have specifically focused on ARL libraries, where almost always the numbers appear on the low end of the spectrum. Table 2B illustrates the major studies concerning tenure that appeared a decade after the 1972

Table 2A.   The Incidence of Faculty Status in Academic Libraries.

Author(s) (Year)	Percentage	Sample
Byerly (1980)	57	Ohio college/university libraries
Rayman and Goudy (1980)	35	ARL libraries
ACRL (1981)	44	Academic libraries
	30	ARL libraries
Benedict, Gavaryck, and Selvin (1983)	72	188 New York university/college libraries
DePew (1983)	79	Academic libraries
English (1983)	46	ARL libraries
Horn (1984)	48	ARL libraries
Payne and Wagner (1984)	59	Non-ARL academic libraries
Tassin (1984)	80	35 southwestern state universities
Mitchell and Swieszkowski (1985)	36	138 academic libraries
Hill and Hauptman (1986)	61	51 academic libraries
Range	30–80	

Table 2B.   The Incidence of Tenure in Academic Libraries.

Author(s) (Year)	Percentage	Sample
Byerly (1980)	48	Ohio college/university libraries
Rayman and Goudy (1980)	57	ARL libraries
Benedict et al. (1983)	58	188 New York university/college libraries
Reeling and Smith (1983)	48	New Jersey academic libraries
English (1983)	42.7	ARL libraries
Payne and Wagner (1984)	61	Non-ARL academic libraries
Mitchell and Swieszkowski (1985)	58.7	138 academic libraries
Range	42.7–61	

ACRL statement. As with the issue of faculty status, researchers found wide variations in the number of academic libraries offering tenure, with results ranging from almost 43 to 61%. Again, variations were due to differences in samples as well as operational definitions of tenure.

Rayman and Goudy (1980) surveyed the 94 ARL member libraries in 1979. With 72% of the libraries responding, they found that 35% reported having faculty status, while another 28% reported that they supported "academic status," a hybrid status offering some but not all of the characteristics of faculty status. In another study of ARL libraries, English (1983) found that 46% of ARL libraries offered faculty status positions to academic librarians. Interestingly, he found a distinction between public and private institutions, with 18.7% of private ARL libraries offering faculty status, compared to 61.4% of public ARL libraries offering the same.

Payne and Wagner (1984) replicated the Rayman and Goudy study in 1983, but chose to expand the study to non-ARL academic libraries. They found that 59% offered "full" faculty status to academic librarians. Unlike Rayman and Goudy, who left it up to the responding ARL library to define faculty status, Payne and Wagner used the published ACRL standards as a working definition for the survey.

The use of tenure and related issues of faculty status for academic librarians have engendered strong comments from both sides. These issues have been debated among researchers and practitioners in the field since the 1972 ACRL statement on tenure. In a study of library directors and the use of faculty status (where faculty status was defined as providing tenure and promotion), one respondent commented: "the whole faculty status issue is a waste of valuable time and energy ... indicative of a profession that is not sure enough of itself to just be librarians" (Park & Riggs, 1993, p. 73). Twenty years earlier, a respondent to a different survey expressed similar reservations: "Let us take pride in what we do, and do it well, and stop all this vain (in both senses of the word) striving for social recognition" (Massman, 1972, p. 189).

Opponents to the 1972 ACRL statement argue that faculty status pulls librarians away from the core elements of librarianship. This argument frequently focuses on the increased need to publish as a result of faculty status and tenure requirements. (Indeed, the 1972 ACRL statement stipulates that the rights and responsibilities of library faculty should be the same as other teaching faculty.) Cronin (2001), for example, states that "if all the time spent writing often forgettable articles for journals of often questionable quality and compiling bloated dossiers were converted into service delivery, we'd be much better off" (p. 144). Even proponents of faculty status admit that "faculty status carries with it a definite set of responsibilities. It requires participation in the library's governance which means that librarians can find themselves immersed in endless committee work, with an inadequate amount of time or energy to devote to library and information services" (Dougherty, 1993, p. 67).

The perception of faculty status and/or tenure as an *additional component* to the core elements of academic librarianship pervades the academic library literature. Furthermore, the need for additional compensation is often noted. Take, for example, Biggs' (1981) discussion of the struggles for faculty status and tenure for the academic librarians in the SUNY New York system. She writes that "some librarians call for the faculty status *without* faculty rank ... to designate a purgatorial state somewhere between the heaven of professorship and the hell of librarianship ... (t)his can mean practical losses in job security and free time without compensating benefits" (Biggs, 1981, p. 195). This statement was inspired by the case of SUNY New York, where academic librarians won the right to tenure and participation in university governance, along with the requirement to publish and eligibility to the academic ranks of instructor, assistant and associate professor. They were not, however, granted academic year appointments, equal salary scales, release time, or access to the highest academic rank of professor, leading one disgruntled librarian to describe the newly acquired faculty status as a hazardous work life (Gavryck, 1975).

An interesting exchange took place in June 2003 in the pages of *American Libraries*, the major trade publication produced by ALA. Michael Gorman, Dean of Library Services at California State University at Fresno, and Mark Herring, Dean of Library Services at Winthrop University in South Carolina, debated each other concerning the use of tenure in academic libraries. Michael Gorman was the incoming president of ALA for 2005. In the exchange, Gorman vehemently defended the use of tenure while Herring was equally adamant concerning the *costs* of tenure to academic libraries. Part of that exchange is reproduced below:

> Herring: I couldn't disagree more. I wish it were the case that we have gained a great deal from it [tenure], but I don't see any of the evidence. Librarians feel as though we need validation from some outside source, as if we really don't belong here. But good, hard work and striving for excellence would probably vouchsafe those same things that we seek through tenure.

> Gorman: The librarians in the California State University system receive far better benefits by virtue of their faculty status and membership in the California Faculty Association than our colleagues in the University of California system, who don't get tenure and are not regarded as academics. When the time comes to make cuts, UC librarians' salaries are always disproportionately cut in comparison to those of people who are considered truly academic (p. 70).

Gorman goes on to argue that tenure increases a professional's involvement with his/her profession, while Herring argues that the need for tenure pushes librarians away from their primary responsibilities. Gorman further comments that "When I came to CSU, I asked to be called dean because I wanted to be a participating member of the dean's council. It's enabled me to be a more useful member of the university. It's also been very good for the library's status within the university" (ALA, 2003, p. 72). Gorman argues that his position as dean was only possible because of the tenure track status of the librarians in his unit. Note that Gorman's argument that benefits and salaries are higher *with* tenure is the reverse of that predicted by the theory of compensating wage differentials.

The use of tenure within the academic library setting has been examined from other perspectives. In a 1993 study, Park and Riggs (1993) examine the variation of tenure across institutional type and find that faculty status and tenure are more likely to be available to academic librarians at doctorate-granting, comprehensive, and liberal arts institutions and less likely at research universities. They conclude that fewer large research libraries may be granting tenure to academic librarians. Given the concern with tenure, some have questioned whether the presence of tenure increases turnover at the institutional level in the academic labor market. However, a study of academic librarians found that having librarians meet tenure track require-ments did not significantly affect the turnover rate (Henry, Caudle, & Sullenger, 1994).

One interesting aspect of the library science literature concerns the relationship between faculty status (and tenure) and compensation. Numer-ous references are made in editorials and trade publications concerning the perception that academic librarians in tenure track positions receive *higher* salaries than other academic librarians, contrary to the compensating wage differential hypothesis. Meyer, in a 1990 study, attempted to study this relationship. When comparing salaries of academic librarians with faculty status at 15 universities, Meyer found that holding tenure had a positive impact on academic libraries. Meyer then more closely examined salary data drawn from Clemson University and found that academic librarians (with faculty status) were paid on par with other faculty members in the humanities and social sciences. However, Meyer measured the impact of holding tenure on an individual's salary and not the effect that the existence of tenure at the institution has on the salary structure (Meyer, 1990b). While Meyer does not explicitly raise the issue of a segmented labor market, this view inherently argues for its presence.

Summary

The compensating wage differential literature suggests a wage premium for non-tenure track jobs. Workers assuming the additional risk of a non-tenure track appointment also assume a greater degree of job insecurity and will require some form of compensation. Workers in a tenure track position trade wages, at least theoretically, for greater job security.

Within higher education, the use of tenure has always been controversial. Some of its strongest proponents (such as Machlup, 1964) acknowledge the potential economic inefficiencies introduced into the academic labor market. These proponents, however, argue that the use of tenure brings with it a higher social good that offsets any potential market inefficiencies. Some colleges and universities have acknowledged the compensating wage premium for non-tenure track jobs, offering a modest premium for non-tenure track appointments.

The institution of tenure has been equally controversial within academic libraries. While reverently championed by some, other academic librarians have expressed a marked reluctance to adopt models of faculty status and tenure, despite its support by the major professional associations. This reluctance springs, in part, from concerns over the perceived additional responsibilities, most notably that of research.

DATA AND METHODOLOGY

This section provides a discussion of the data used and the methodology selected for this study. First, the population is presented and various data resources discussed. The need for additional information is examined and the subsequent survey used to collect the data is presented. A description of the variables is provided. Finally, the hypotheses are presented, along with the models used to test the hypotheses and an explanation of the variables employed in the study.

Data Selection

This study uses cross-sectional data drawn from the member libraries of the ARL. ARL, founded in 1932, is a not-for-profit organization comprised of the largest research libraries in the United States and Canada. Membership is granted only after an extensive application process and documentation of comparable levels of funding and resources. ARL libraries represent an elite group of research libraries. ARL data are frequently utilized in studies on issues pertaining to academic libraries (see, for example, Park & Riggs, 1993). The prevalence of ARL studies is fostered both by the prominent role these libraries play in the academic library community and because of the presence of an extensive amount of institutional data collected on an annual basis.

The original 42 founding institutions were expanded to 72 in 1962. Subsequent changes to the bylaws have allowed other members to join. Member libraries include both public and private university and research collections. The original 1932 constitution stated that "the object shall be, by cooperative effort, to develop and increase the resources and usefulness of the research collections in American libraries" (George & Blixrud, 2002). While ARL has adjusted its mission over the years, the overall focus of the organization has never strayed substantively from that expressed in the original constitution. As such, ARL represents member libraries but not librarians or librarianship per se. As of 2004, ARL has 122 members (Association of Research Libraries, 2004b).

Membership in ARL is based on a membership criteria index. Annually, data on five key areas are collected from ARL libraries: volumes held, volumes added (gross), current serials, total library expenditures, and total professional and support staff (ARL, 2004). Principal component analysis is conducted on the 35 remaining founding ARL members. Weights for each of the five data elements are obtained from this analysis. Data from each ARL library are used along with these weights to develop the annual membership criteria index. This index essentially ranks ARL member libraries and is widely reported in the higher education literature each year (Stubbs, 1980). It is known as the ARL Membership Criteria Index and is computed each year by ARL. (Data from this index were used for the ARL1 variable, discussed below.) The index is also used to evaluate potential new member libraries.

This study includes all U.S. university and college libraries that held membership in ARL during the years 1989 through 1998 for a total of 98 institutions. Due to variations in institutional cultures, Canadian libraries are not included in this study. Institutional and library-specific data for these 98 institutions were collected from the print versions of *The ARL Annual Salary Survey* and *The ARL Statistics*, both published annually by ARL. These data are also available online through the University of Virginia's Alderman Library's GeoStat Center (http://fisher.lib.virginia.edu/arl/).

Survey of ARL Libraries

While published sources provided needed data on variables such as the size of the staff and collections, average starting salaries, and the annual budget, they did not provide critical information on the presence of tenure track library faculty or unionization. To collect these data, a survey was developed that asked seven questions:

- Do librarians at your institution have traditional faculty rank and status?
- For the period 1989–1998, were librarians eligible for tenure at your library?
- For the period 1989–1998, were librarians included in a collective bargaining unit or union?
- Are librarians at your institution required to have an additional advanced degree for appointment at the entry level?
- Do librarians at your institution have research requirements similar to the academic/teaching faculty?
- For the period 1989–1998, how would you rate the research requirements for librarians at your institution?

A complete version of the survey is included in the appendix. The survey was approved by the Mississippi State University's Institutional Review Board for the Protection of Human Subjects in Research prior to distribution.

The survey employs a definition of tenure, drawn from the 1987 policy entitled "Model Statement of Criteria Procedures for Appointment, Promotion in Academic Rank, and Tenure for College and University Librarians" (ACRL, 1987). This statement defines tenure as "an institutional commitment to permanent and continuous employment ... tenure (continuous employment) shall be available to all librarians and in accordance with the tenure provisions of all faculty of the institution" (p. 223). Respondents were asked to use this definition of tenure as the basis for their answers to the survey questions. Questions concerning both tenure and unionization allowed the respondent to specify any variation in status for the library during the time period under study (1989–1998) but *none* indicated a change in status.

The survey was administered to the dean or director of the library via e-mail in the fall of 2001. It was administered to the 98 ARL institutions who were members as of 1998. Two follow-up e-mails were sent to solicit additional responses. ARL libraries are some of the most studied, and surveyed, libraries in the world. Care was taken to ensure a high return rate for the survey. The survey was deliberately short; only data that could not be identified in other sources were solicited. The survey was sent as an e-mail, with the subject line "Tenure Request" and was designed in such a way that respondents could simply "reply" to the e-mail and check off the appropriate answers. A total of 82 surveys were returned. Four of the institutions either

Table 3. Sample ARL Member Institutions by Region.

North Region	South Region	Midwest Region	West Region
Boston University	Duke	Case Western Reserve	Arizona
Columbia	Florida	Chicago	Arizona State
Cornell	Georgetown	Cincinnati	Brigham Young
Dartmouth	Georgia	Illinois, Chicago	California, Berkley
Harvard	Georgia Tech	Illinois, Urbana	California, Davis
Massachusetts	Houston	Indiana	California, Irvine
MIT	Howard	Iowa	California, Los Angeles
New York	Johns Hopkins	Iowa State	California, Riverside
Pittsburg	Kentucky	Kansas	California, San Diego
Princeton	Louisiana State	Michigan	California, Santa Barbara
Rochester	Maryland	Michigan State	Colorado
Rutgers	Miami	Minnesota	Colorado State
SUNY-Albany	North Carolina	Missouri	Hawaii
SUNY-Stony Brook	North Carolina State	Nebraska	New Mexico
Syracuse	Oklahoma	Northwestern	Southern California
Temple	Rice	Notre Dame	Utah
Yale	South Carolina	Ohio State	Washington
	Tennessee	Southern Illinois	
	Texas	Washington University, St. Louis	
	Texas A&M	Wayne State	
	Tulane		
	Vanderbilt		
	Virginia		
	Virginia Tech		

Note: Regional definitions follow U.S. Bureau of the Census conventions.

did not have ARL membership throughout the entire 10-year period under examination or returned incomplete surveys and were ultimately removed from the study. A total of 78 usable surveys were returned, for a response rate of 79.5%. A listing of the 78 institutions included in the study may be found in Table 3, according to their geographic location.

Hypotheses

Two hypotheses will be tested in this study. They are

(1) Everything else held constant, the probability an ARL academic library will offer tenure track positions will be greater if a number of institutional characteristics are present: if there is a research expectation as part of the appointment, if the head of the library holds the title of "Dean," and if the university also supports an ALA-accredited graduate program.

(2) Tenure-granting ARL libraries will offer lower starting salaries, compared to their non-tenure-granting ARL counterparts, other things held constant.

These hypotheses explore the relationship between tenure and beginning wages for ARL academic librarians.

Variable Selection

As discussed above, studies of compensating wage differentials typically use a number of demographic and job-specific variables. The data used in this study are at the institutional level. Therefore, variables often found in compensating wage differential studies (such as job tenure, education, race, and gender) are not an option. Proxies that measure aspects of the library and the university are used in their place. These include measures of size, staffing, and expenditures.

Study Variables

Table 4 lists the variables used throughout the study. The discussion below concerning the two models more clearly defines the variables but further discussion is warranted here. SALARY is the beginning professional salary as reported in the *ARL Annual Salary Survey* (Association of Research Libraries, 2001, 2004a). ARL instructs member libraries to provide these data on an annual basis, even if no new librarians have been hired and to provide the salary that would be paid to a newly hired professional without experience. LSALARY is the natural logarithm of SALARY.

% PROFESSIONALS reflects the number of professionals employed as a percentage of total library employment. Unlike the ACRL, the professional association of most academic librarians, ARL does not provide a definition of a library professional. Instructions to member libraries leave the definition of a professional up to the member library, stating: "each library should report those staff members it considers professional, including, when appropriate, staff who are not librarians in the strict sense of the term, for example computer experts, systems analysts, or budget officers" (ARL, *Instructions*, 2003). Data for expenditures (EXPEND) include all sources of funding, including regularly appropriated institutional support, research grants, special projects, gifts, fees, and endowments. The amount reflects actual expenditures and explicitly excludes encumbered but unexpended funds.

Table 4. Variable Descriptions.

Variable	Description
SALARY	Beginning professional salary as reported in the *ARL Annual Salary Survey*. Salaries represent the starting salaries that would be paid to a newly hired professional without experience
LSALARY	Natural logarithm of SALARY
TENURE	As defined by ACRL
FACULTY STATUS	Professorial rank (i.e., assistant professor, associate professor, etc.)
UNION	Librarians as members of a collective bargaining unit
RESEARCH	Research requirement for librarians
DEAN	Title of chief academic officer in the library
AGE	Years of ARL membership
VOLS	Total volumes held by the library
ARL1	Ranks in the top quartile of the ARL Membership Criteria Index
% PROFESSIONALS	Professionals as a percentage of total library employment
EXPEND	Total library expenditures
TYPE	Private or public institutions
MLS PROGRAM	Presence of ALA-accredited master's program
PHD FIELDS	Number of Ph.D. fields supported by the institution
FACULTY	Number of instructional faculty
URBAN	Location in an MSA
NORTH, SOUTH, MIDWEST, WEST	Regional categorical variables

Doctoral fields (PHD FIELDS) are also drawn from the published ARL data. ARL instructs member libraries to use the same definition as that employed by the U.S. Department of Education's Integrated Postsecondary Education Data System (IPEDS) (ARL, *Instructions*, 2003; National Center for Education Statistics, 2005). The number of instructional faculty (FACULTY) is also based on IPEDS definitions and includes only full-time faculty members.

DETERMINANTS OF TENURE IN ACADEMIC LIBRARIES: A PROBIT ANALYSIS

To address the issue of what factors determine whether or not an institution offers tenure to its academic librarians, Eq. (1) uses a probit model to examine the probability of tenure (T) within ARL library as a function of library (L), institutional (I), and regional (R) characteristics or attributes. Thus,

$$\text{Prob}(T) = f(L, I, R) \tag{1}$$

where L = UNION, RESEARCH, % PROFESSIONALS, DEAN, AGE, ARL1; I = MLS PROGRAM, TYPE, ARL1, FACULTY, URBAN; and R = SOUTH, MIDWEST, WEST.

While Model 2 will examine variables as they relate to beginning salaries, Model 1 uses a probit analysis to examine library and institutional characteristics of tenure-granting academic libraries.

A summary table of the operational variables and their definitions is found in Table 5. The variables chosen are based on factors that are hypothesized to influence an institution's choice to offer tenure to librarians as suggested by the literature review.

Table 5. Model 1: Probit Equation Variables.

Variable Labels	Definition
Dependent variables	
TENURE	Librarian positions are tenure track = 1; otherwise = 0
Library attributes [L]	
UNION (−)	Library is unionized = 1; otherwise = 0
RESEARCH (+)	Librarians have a research requirement = 1; otherwise = 0
% PROFESSIONALS (+)	Librarians (professionals) as a percentage of total library staff
DEAN (+)	Head of library holds title of dean = 1; otherwise = 0
AGE (−)	Years as an ARL member library
ARL1 (−)	Top quartile of ARL members = 1; otherwise = 0
Institutional attributes [I]	
MLS PROGRAM (+)	The university has an ALA-accredited master's program = 1; otherwise = 0
TYPE (−)	The university is private = 1; otherwise = 0
FACULTY (+)	Number of instructional faculty at the institution
URBAN (?)	The university is located in an MSA = 1; otherwise = 0
Region [R]	
NORTH (?)	Library is located in the North = 1; otherwise = 0
SOUTH (?)	Library is located in the South = 1; otherwise = 0
MIDWEST (?)	Library is located in the Midwest = 1; otherwise = 0
WEST (?)	Library is located in the West = 1; otherwise = 0

Note: ( ): Expected value when entered as a right-hand side variable.

A number of library-specific characteristics are hypothesized to influence the use of tenure. The presence of a labor union may be seen as a surrogate for tenure. Unions provide many of the protections and benefits traditionally found in tenure track positions, thus the expected sign for UNION is negative. RESEARCH reflects whether the librarians have an explicit research requirement or expectation as a component of their job. Librarians with faculty status may or may not have a research expectation comparable to other faculty on campus. Librarians with a research expectation as a condition of employment should have a greater likelihood of holding a tenure track position; therefore, the expected sign for RESEARCH is positive.

% PROFESSIONALS measures professionals as a percentage of the total library staff. Larger, more organizationally complex academic libraries are hypothesized to be positively related to the use of tenure. The head of academic libraries may hold various titles. Some have the title of "University Librarian," others "Dean," and some simply are called "Directors." DEAN reports whether the head of the library holds the title of "Dean." It is hypothesized that academic libraries whose administrative head carries the title of "Dean," a traditional academic title, will be positively related to the availability of tenure.

AGE is assumed to have a negative relationship with the probability of tenure. This assumes that the oldest ARL member libraries represent the largest, most elite institutions and that these institutions may have been less likely to adopt the faculty status model when introduced by ACRL in the 1970s. Likewise, ARL1 measures the library's ranking in the top quartile of ARL libraries based on the membership criterion score. The expected sign for ARL1 is also negative.

Data for the variables TENURE, UNION, RESEARCH, and FACULTY STATUS were obtained from the survey administered to the head of each library in the sample. Data for the variables % PROFESSIONALS and AGE were taken from published ARL statistics. Information concerning the title of the library's top administrative officer (DEAN) was obtained from the library's web page.

Institutional variables are hypothesized to play a key role in an academic library's decision to offer tenure track positions. MLS PROGRAM reports on the presence of an ALA-accredited library science program at the university. As discussed above, the accepted terminal degree for academic librarians is the MLS, obtained from a graduate program accredited by ALA. The presence of such a program, with its attendant faculty, may contribute to the perception that academic librarians are faculty. Therefore, the expected sign for MLS PROGRAM is positive.

The number of instructional faculty (FACULTY) is included as a proxy for the size of the institution. It is hypothesized that FACULTY size will be positively related to the probability of tenure track librarians. Note that other measures of institutional size, such as the number of students were not chosen. In matters pertaining to tenure, faculty governance, and academic freedom, larger faculty bodies may have a more developed promotion and tenure process.

Finally, URBAN measures the local environment of the university. Specifically, the variable measures whether the university is located in a metropolitan statistical area, as measured by the Census Bureau. No a priori assumption is made about the relationship of this variable with the probability of tenure.

MLS PROGRAM data were obtained from the ALA's list of accredited programs and the number of instructional faculty is reported in the annual ARL statistics. Again, URBAN was developed using the Census Bureau's regional geographical descriptions.

The final vector of variables are proxies for geographic region. The universities included in the study have been divided into four categories, based on the Census Bureau's geographical divisions: NORTH, SOUTH, MIDWEST, and WEST. NORTH was omitted as the reference variable. Likewise, no a priori assumption is made about the expected signs these regional variables will take.

DETERMINANTS OF TENURE IN ACADEMIC LIBRARIES: A REGRESSION ANALYSIS

The research question central to this study concerns the relationship between wages and tenure within ARL academic libraries. Specifically, this study tests the hypothesis that, all else held constant, compensation at tenure-granting academic libraries will be lower than those at their non-tenure counterparts. A standard log wage equation is often used to examine compensation (Ehrenberg & Smith, 1997). The log wage equation of the following form is estimated where the natural logarithm of starting salaries (W) is a function of library (L), institutional (I), and regional (R) attributes and are assumed to influence starting salaries for academic librarians. Thus,

$$\ln W = f(L, I, R) \qquad (2)$$

where L = TENURE, UNION, VOLS, % PROFESSIONALS, EXPEND; I = TYPE, PHD FIELDS, URBAN; and R = SOUTH, MIDWEST, WEST.

Model 2 is estimated using standard ordinary least squares (OLS) techniques (Greene, 1997). A summary table of the operational variables and their definitions may be found in Table 6. The variables chosen are based on the theory of wage determination and the theoretical literature surrounding tenure in academic libraries.

The dependent variable, LSALARIES, is the natural logarithm of starting salaries as reported in the annual *ARL Salary Survey.* Initial efforts to obtain individual data on salaries collected by ARL proved unsuccessful.

Several library attributes are hypothesized to have a role on average starting salaries. TENURE measures whether or not the library offers tenure track positions for academic librarians. The economic theory of compensating wage differentials leads one to expect that the presence of tenure would serve as a type of non-pecuniary compensation, with a resulting lower wage. Hence, the expected sign for TENURE is negative. Given the vast literature on the presence of a union wage premium (Lewis, 1986), unionization should have a positive impact on the starting salary and thus, the expected sign for UNION is positive.

Table 6. Model 2: OLS Equation Variables.

Variable Labels	Definition
Dependent variables	
LSALARIES	Natural logarithm of average starting salary
Library attributes [L]	
TENURE (−)	Librarians have tenure track positions = 1; otherwise = 0
UNION (+)	Library is unionized = 1; otherwise = 0
VOLS (+)	Number of physical volumes in the library
% PROFESSIONALS (+)	Librarians (professionals) as a percentage of total library staff
EXPEND (+)	Total library expenditures
Institutional attributes [I]	
TYPE (+)	The university is private = 1; otherwise = 0
PHD FIELDS (+)	Number of subject fields supporting a Ph.D. program
URBAN (?)	The university is located in an MSA = 1; otherwise = 0
Region [R]	
NORTH (?)	Library is located in the North = 1; otherwise = 0
SOUTH (?)	Library is located in the South = 1; otherwise = 0
MIDWEST (?)	Library is located in the Midwest = 1; otherwise = 0
WEST (?)	Library is located in the West = 1; otherwise = 0

Note: ( ): Expected value when entered as a right-hand side variable.

VOLS is an aggregate measure of the total number of physical volumes in the library, excluding electronic resources. VOLS is hypothesized to be positive, on the belief that larger libraries would more likely offer higher starting salaries. Likewise, % PROFESSIONALS measures library professionals as a percentage of the total library staff; larger staffs are hypothesized to offer higher starting salaries. (See Lazear, 1998 concerning the relationship between firm size and wages.) Finally, EXPEND measures the total library budget including personnel expenditures. Intuitively, higher expenditures would be positively related to higher starting salaries.

Data for TENURE and UNION were obtained through the survey instrument, while the data for the variables VOLS, % PROFESSIONALS, and EXPEND came from published ARL statistical sources.

Three institutional attributes are also included in the regression equation. TYPE reports whether the university is public or private. TYPE is hypothesized to be positive, reflecting the higher wages often found at private institutions. PHD FIELDS reflect the number of subject fields in which Ph.D. degrees may be awarded in the institution and is hypothesized to be positive. A more extensive and complex graduate program increases the need for more specialized librarians and, should other things held constant, increases average starting salaries. URBAN measures whether the university is located in a metropolitan statistical area, as measured by the Census Bureau. No a priori assumption is made about the relationship of this variable with starting salaries. Rural institutions may have to offer higher salaries to attract applicants. On the other hand, urban areas may offer higher starting wages to compensate for higher costs of living. Data for all three institutional variables – TYPE, PHD FIELDS, and URBAN – were obtained from published ARL data sources.

The final vector of right-hand side variables are proxies for region. The universities included in the study have been divided into four regional categories, based on the Census Bureau's geographical divisions: NORTH, SOUTH, MIDWEST, and WEST. NORTH was omitted as the reference variable. No a priori assumption is made about the expected signs these regional variables will take.

Summary

In sum, this study estimates two models. The first is a probability model, which examines the determinants of tenure within ARL libraries. The second is a wage equation, which examines the relationship between tenure and starting salaries. The sample under investigation is drawn from ARL libraries. Cross-sectional data from 10 years (1989–1998) are analyzed using standard and widely accepted econometric techniques and procedures.

EMPIRICAL RESULTS

This section reports the empirical results of the study. The first subsection provides a descriptive analysis of the variables used in both the probit and OLS regression models. Following this, the results of the probit and OLS regression models are presented, along with additional means of analyzing the results. The section closes with a brief examination of the role of unionization and an analysis of the union wage premium suggested by the findings.

Descriptive Analysis

Tables 7A and 7B report the means and standard deviations by year for the variables used in this study. Reported earlier, data were collected on 78 ARL institutions for the years 1989–1998. As the tables illustrate, some variables were constant throughout the entire 10 years of the study. Some were collected only once and represent the entire time period (RESEARCH, DEAN). Other survey variables allowed for the possibility that the status could change over the 10-year period – attributes such as tenure track options and representation in a collective bargaining unit. However, both TENURE and UNION remain constant for all institutions in the sample throughout the period under analysis. None of the 78 responding institutions reported a change in their status during the 10-year period under study.

A number of variables examine characteristics unique to each library. Approximately 44% of the institutions offer tenure track positions to their academic librarians, with 56% not offering the tenure track option. This number is comparable to other studies reported above. Only 23% were unionized and 33% held professorial rank (FACULTY STATUS). Note that more institutions offer a tenure track option than faculty status and rank. This is counter to the studies from the 1980s reported in the literature review, where typically the reverse was found to be true. This may be a function of the data collection process, given the diverse ways some authors have defined faculty status in the past. Or it may reflect a true change in practice, with more institutions willing to offer tenure than to offer more formal support through the provision of academic ranks. Further

Table 7A.   Variable Means: 1989–1993 ($N = 78$).

Variable	1989	1990	1991	1992	1993
SALARY	21222.70	22426.35	23773.01	24572.83	25344.81
	(2360.35)	(2324.66)	(2293.52)	(2648.83)	(2567.01)
TENURE	0.4359	0.4359	0.4359	0.4359	0.4359
	(0.4991)	(0.4991)	(0.4991)	(0.4991)	(0.4991)
UNION	0.2308	0.2308	0.2308	0.2308	0.2308
	(0.4241)	(0.4241)	(0.4241)	(0.4241)	(0.4241)
RESEARCH	0.3467	0.3467	0.3467	0.3467	0.3467
	(0.4791)	(0.4791)	(0.4791)	(0.4791)	(0.4791)
FACULTY STATUS	0.3333	0.3333	0.3333	0.3333	0.3333
	(0.4745)	(0.4745)	(0.4745)	(0.4745)	(0.4745)
DEAN	0.3462	0.3462	0.3462	0.3462	0.3462
	(0.4788)	(0.4788)	(0.4788)	(0.4788)	(0.4788)
AGE	35.41	36.41	37.41	38.41	39.41
	(18.99)	(18.99)	(18.99)	(18.99)	(18.99)
EXPEND	4092783.22	4395788.40	4715938.68	4903232.05	5193420.87
	(1541772.95)	(1683102.43)	(1817614.31)	(18622185.69)	(2013030.71)
% PROFESSIONALS	0.2657	0.2661	0.2663	0.2687	0.2696
	(0.0380)	(0.0377)	(0.0380)	(0.0419)	(0.0438)
VOLS	2928277.05	3001425.83	3109016.85	3183586.95	3281936.77
	(1883240.24)	(1912773.02)	(1957872.94)	(1994983.08)	(2015630.29)
TYPE	0.3333	0.3333	0.3333	0.3333	0.3333
	(0.4745)	(0.4745)	(0.4745)	(0.4745)	(0.4745)
MLS PROGRAM	0.2436	0.2436	0.2436	0.2436	0.2436
	(0.4320)	(0.4320)	(0.4320)	(0.4320)	(0.4320)
FACULTY	1339.08	1371.85	1401.10	1473.78	1419.08
	(489.30)	(491.86)	(513.62)	(585.04)	(565.53)
PHD FIELDS	58.36	57.26	58.05	57.64	58.49
	(27.3861)	(25.4795)	(25.4568)	(23.9577)	(23.8332)
URBAN	0.7564	0.7564	0.7564	0.7564	0.7564
	(0.4320)	(0.4320)	(0.4320)	(0.4320)	(0.4320)
NORTH	0.2179	0.2179	0.2179	0.2179	0.2179
	(0.4155)	(0.4155)	(0.4155)	(0.4155)	(0.4155)
SOUTH	0.3077	0.3077	0.3077	0.3077	0.3077
	(0.4645)	(0.4645)	(0.4645)	(0.4645)	(0.4645)
MIDWEST	0.2564	0.2564	0.2564	0.2564	0.2564
	(0.4395)	(0.4395)	(0.4395)	(0.4395)	(0.4395)
WEST	0.2179	0.2179	0.2179	0.2179	0.2179
	(0.4155)	(0.4155)	(0.4155)	(0.4155)	(0.4155)

explorations of this issue are beyond the scope of this study but merit research.

Approximately 35% of the library heads held the title of Dean. (Other reported titles included Director, University Librarian, and one Vice Provost.) The role of a dean is unique in the academic organizational structure. Some have argued that serving as a dean enables the library to better serve the university population and enhances the perception of library faculty as members of the university faculty community (ALA, 2003).

Table 7B. Variable Means: 1994–1998 ($N = 78$).

Variable	1994	1995	1996	1997	1998
SALARY	25925.38	27633.46	28606.54	29375.05	30619.44
	(2416.22)	(2552.01)	(2621.69)	(2563.43)	(2905.04)
TENURE	0.4359	0.4359	0.4359	0.4359	0.4359
	(0.4991)	(0.4991)	(0.4991)	(0.4991)	(0.4991)
UNION	0.2308	0.2308	0.2308	0.2308	0.2308
	(0.4241)	(0.4241)	(0.4241)	(0.4241)	(0.4241)
RESEARCH	0.3467	0.3467	0.3467	0.3467	0.3467
	(0.4791)	(0.4791)	(0.4791)	(0.4791)	(0.4791)
FACULTY STATUS	0.3333	0.3333	0.3333	0.3333	0.3333
	(0.4745)	(0.4745)	(0.4745)	(0.4745)	(0.4745)
DEAN	0.3462	0.3462	0.3462	0.3462	0.3462
	(0.4788)	(0.4788)	(0.4788)	(0.4788)	(0.4788)
AGE	40.41	41.41	42.41	43.41	44.41
	(18.99)	(18.99)	(18.99)	(18.99)	(18.99)
EXPEND	5446266.83	5804968.87	6141166.32	6486586.31	6870925.01
	(2148519.06)	(2251562.11)	(2396245.26)	(2614849.99)	(2861764.37)
% PROFESSIONALS	0.2677	0.2697	0.2706	0.2718	0.2762
	(0.0452)	(0.0466)	(0.0479)	(0.0523)	(0.0556)
VOLS	3381733.96	3469798.38	3551291.21	3630706.32	3710892.73
	(2039786.22)	(2071826.27)	(2111995.33)	(2152797.76)	(2191169.64)
TYPE	0.3333	0.3333	0.3333	0.3333	0.3333
	(0.4745)	(0.4745)	(0.4745)	(0.4745)	(0.4745)
MLS PROGRAM	0.2436	0.2436	0.2436	0.2436	0.2436
	(0.4320)	(0.4320)	(0.4320)	(0.4320)	(0.4320)
FACULTY	1433.47	1416.55	1413.88	1415.46	1415.36
	(572.83)	(554.96)	(568.90)	(571.08)	(577.27)
PHD FIELDS	57.86	57.91	56.97	57.27	57.06
	(23.9820)	(24.0104)	(22.1728)	(21.7002)	(21.6366)
URBAN	0.7564	0.7564	0.7564	0.7564	0.7564
	(0.4320)	(0.4320)	(0.4320)	(0.4320)	(0.4320)
NORTH	0.2179	0.2179	0.2179	0.2179	0.2179
	(0.4155)	(0.4155)	(0.4155)	(0.4155)	(0.4155)
SOUTH	0.3077	0.3077	0.3077	0.3077	0.3077
	(0.4645)	(0.4645)	(0.4645)	(0.4645)	(0.4645)
MIDWEST	0.2564	0.2564	0.2564	0.2564	0.2564
	(0.4395)	(0.4395)	(0.4395)	(0.4395)	(0.4395)
WEST	0.2179	0.2179	0.2179	0.2179	0.2179
	(0.4155)	(0.4155)	(0.4155)	(0.4155)	(0.4155)

The percentage of professionals fluctuated minimally during the time period under study, ranging from 27 to 28%. Other variables, such as VOLS and EXPEND, measure the total number of volumes and expenditures, which tended to rise over the sample period. SALARY reports the mean salaries for the time period under study; note that LSALARY uses the natural logarithm of the reported starting salaries. During this time period starting salaries went from $21,222 in 1989 to $30,619 in 1998, in nominal terms.

A number of variables reflect the characteristics of the university. Thirty-three percent of the institutions were privately funded and 67% were public institutions. Twenty-four percent of the sample institutions had a Library

Table 8. Minimum and Maximum Variable Values, 1994.

Variable	Minimum Value	Maximum Value
SALARY	$21,000	$33,312
TENURE	0	1
UNION	0	1
RESEARCH	0	1
FACULTY STATUS	0	1
DEAN	0	1
AGE	6	62
EXPEND	$2,148,519.06	$14,378,067.00
%PROFESSIONALS	0.1809	0.4344
VOLS	1,553,346	12,877,360
TYPE	0	1
MLS PROGRAM	0	1
FACULTY	448	3,193
PHD FIELDS	13	137
URBAN	0	1
NORTH	0	1
SOUTH	0	1
MIDWEST	0	1
WEST	0	1

Science graduate program with a master's degree accredited by the ALA (as of the data collection date, August 2001). The mean number of institutional faculty ranged from 1,339 in 1989 to 1,415 in 1998. The mean number of doctoral programs supported by the universities in the sample fluctuated slightly over time, ranging from 56 to 57.

Other variables examine the geographic aspects of the universities' location. Seventy-five percent of the responding institutions were located in metropolitan statistical areas, as defined by the Census Bureau. Twenty-two percent of the institutions were located in the North, 30% in the South, 25% in the Midwest, and 21% in the West. Southern institutions are slightly overrepresented in the study. (This may reflect willingness to participate in a study generated from a researcher at a Southern institution.) Recall that Table 3 reports participating institutions by region.

Table 8 reports the minimum and maximum values for a selected year of the study, 1994. This year was selected as representative of the study and used for several diagnostic statistics discussed below. Table 8 illustrates some of the wide range of libraries and universities included, even within an elite group such as ARL. The minimum starting salary in 1994 was $21,000, while the maximum was $33,312.

Likewise, the range for expenditures is impressive: the minimum was a little over 2.1 million dollars, while the maximum was in excess of 14 million dollars.

Probability of Tenure Model

Tables 9A and 9B report the results of the probit analysis for Model 1. The probit model examines the library and institutional characteristics that determine the probability that a university offers tenure track academic

Table 9A. Model 1: Probit Results: 1989–1993
(Dependent Variable = TENURE, $N = 78$).

Variable	1989	1990	1991	1992	1993
CONSTANT	−0.2596	−0.2218	0.2321	0.7694	−0.8480
	(1.6871)	(1.7489)	(1.6580)	(1.6596)	(1.6221)
UNION	−0.3563	−0.3962	−0.3384	−0.5127	−0.4648
	(0.5479)	(0.5517)	(0.5566)	(0.5278)	(0.5392)
RESEARCH	1.007***	1.1655***	1.0770***	1.1161***	1.1646***
	(0.3980)	(0.4119)	(0.3979)	(0.3900)	(0.3944)
% PROFSTAFF	−1.8232	−3.0306	−4.7411	−3.3264	0.8642
	(5.5662)	(5.4057)	(5.4815)	(4.8400)	(4.7564)
DEAN	1.0777***	1.1483***	1.1525***	0.9921***	1.0476***
	(0.4200)	(0.4354)	(0.4176)	(0.4234)	(0.4257)
AGE	−0.0212**	−0.0203**	−0.0205**	−0.0199*	−0.0167*
	(0.0132)	(0.0131)	(0.0138)	(0.0140)	(0.0138)
ARL1	−0.1880	−0.7807**	−0.4941	−0.1702	−0.7003*
	(0.4844)	(0.5089)	(0.5501)	(0.5401)	(0.5540)
MLS PROGRAM	0.5099	0.5711*	0.6657**	0.6476**	0.7659***
	(0.4280)	(0.4331)	(0.4421)	(0.4287)	(0.4440)
TYPE	−0.0013	0.0321	0.1910	−0.0170	−0.1075
	(0.5405)	(0.5635)	(0.5619)	(0.5437)	(0.5601)
FACULTY	0.6561E−03**	0.8913E−03***	0.7947E−03***	0.2622E−03	0.6177E−03**
	(0.0004)	(0.0005)	(0.0004)	(0.0003)	(0.0004)
URBAN	−0.0628	−0.1106	−0.0889	−0.1156	−0.1501
	(0.4459)	(0.4415)	(0.4344)	(0.4250)	(0.4382)
SOUTH	−0.5645	−0.5404	−0.4879	−0.5966	−0.6546
	(0.5547)	(0.5782)	(0.5718)	(0.5563)	(0.5592)
MIDWEST	−0.0146	−0.0730	−0.0182	−0.0866	−0.0920
	(0.5671)	(0.6056)	(0.5941)	(0.5686)	(0.5725)
WEST	−0.1777	−0.0755	−0.1530	−0.3841	−0.2935
	(0.6021)	(0.6080)	(0.6028)	(0.5929)	(0.5871)
Pseudo R^2	0.85	0.83	0.86	0.83	0.87

Note: ( ): Standard errors.
*Statistically significant at the .10 level, one-tailed test.
**Statistically significant at the .05 level, one-tailed test.
***Statistically significant at the .01 level, one-tailed test.

Table 9B. Model 1: Probit Results: 1994–1998
(Dependent Variable = TENURE, $N = 78$).

Variable	1994	1995	1996	1997	1998
CONSTANT	−1.289	−0.7738	−0.2894	0.6683	1.3562
	(1.5635)	(1.5408)	(1.5326)	(1.3708)	(1.4359)
UNION	−0.4459	−0.3757	−0.4143	−0.4039	−0.4367
	(0.5399)	(0.5419)	(0.5416)	(0.5352)	(0.5507)
RESEARCH	1.1651***	1.1091***	1.1102***	1.1341***	1.1515***
	(0.3947)	(0.3910)	(0.3902)	(0.3957)	(0.3979)
% PROFSTAFF	3.0374	2.4335	0.2035	−1.9510	−4.5809
	(4.3598)	(4.3597)	(4.3299)	(3.7021)	(3.7393)
DEAN	1.0080***	0.9675***	0.9411***	0.9993***	0.9781***
	(0.4160)	(0.4085)	(0.3975)	(0.4064)	(0.4094)
AGE	−0.0154**	−0.0211**	−0.0163**	−0.0273*	−0.0217*
	(0.0140)	(0.0145)	(0.0137)	(0.0141)	(0.0142)
ARL1	−0.6191	−0.1015**	−0.4322	0.3269	−0.3967*
	(0.5859)	(0.6011)	(0.5467)	(0.5318)	(0.5434)
MLS PROGRAM	0.7366	0.5900*	0.6817**	0.1635**	0.7032***
	(0.4403)	(0.4257)	(0.4363)	(0.4301)	(0.4312)
TYPE	−0.1857	−0.1876	−0.1149	−0.0395	0.0404
	(0.5371)	(0.5375)	(0.5343)	(0.5226)	(0.5324)
FACULTY	0.5293E−03**	0.3723E−03***	0.3630E−03***	0.2351E−03	0.1642E−03**
	(0.0004)	(0.0004)	(0.0003)	(0.0003)	(0.0004)
URBAN	−0.1931	−0.2231	−0.1528	−0.0649	−0.0569
	(0.4423)	(0.4277)	(0.4256)	(0.4252)	(0.4206)
SOUTH	−0.6457	−0.5532	−0.5745	−0.5493	−0.5212
	(0.5519)	(0.5437)	(0.5460)	(0.5501)	(0.5536)
MIDWEST	−0.1199	−0.0028	−0.1038	0.0181	−0.7372
	(0.5744)	(0.5731)	(0.5708)	(0.5799)	(0.5789)
WEST	−0.2876	−0.2455	−0.2591	−0.3966	−0.4408
	(0.5837)	(0.5828)	(0.5894)	(0.5915)	(0.5958)
Pseudo R^2	0.83	0.85	0.81	0.81	0.81

Note: ( ): Standard errors.
*Statistically significant at the .10 level, one-tailed test.
**Statistically significant at the .05 level, one-tailed test.
***Statistically significant at the .01 level, one-tailed test.

positions to librarians. While other studies have examined salaries and wage determination in academic libraries, no prior study has addressed this aspect of tenure in academic libraries.

The results for the 10 years are considerably stable. The pseudo R^2 (the percent of correct predictions) ranges from 81 to 87%. Some of the weakest results are seen in the last year of the study, 1998, as was also true for the OLS model discussed below. This time, however, there are variables that are consistently statistically significant throughout the 10 years. RESEARCH, which measured whether or not academic librarians had a research expectation as part of their appointment, was consistently statistically significant at the .01 level using a one-tailed test. RESEARCH was hypothesized to be positive and the results for 1989–1998 are consistently positive for this variable. This is not a surprising finding, given the centrality of research to many tenure track positions. While there are certainly some colleges and universities where research is not a defining element of the typical tenure track appointment, this was an expectation for the ARL member libraries and their institutions. As mentioned earlier, ARL libraries are found at some of the nation's top research universities. Tenure at these institutions is more likely to be heavily weighted toward the research requirement. While academic librarianship does not necessarily or routinely have research expectations as part of the position description, tenure track positions are more likely to carry this requirement.

Also consistently statistically significant and positive at the .01 level is the variable DEAN. As Gorman mentioned in his debate in *American Libraries*, some heads of libraries consider carrying the title of "Dean" to be an important element both for the viability of the library program and in establishing the parity of library faculty with other faculty members across campus (American Library Association, 2003).

AGE, which measures the years of ARL membership, was hypothesized to be negative. The probit model finds AGE to be statistically significant for 9 of the 10 years (omitting only 1994), although the level of statistical significance varies somewhat. The a priori assumption of a negative sign was confirmed and consistent. Older ARL member libraries are often seen to be the most traditional of research libraries and may have been more resistant to change when the new standards for tenure in academic libraries were introduced in the 1970s. Chressanthis (1994) offers an alternative interpretation, suggesting that older, more established research universities with higher standards for tenure may be less likely to have tenure track academic librarians. This is not entirely supported by another variable, ARL1, which measures the ARL library's placement within the top 25% of the ARL libraries, based on the membership criteria index. While this variable carries the expected negative sign for 9 of the 10 years, it is statistically significant for only two years: 1990 and 1993.

As expected, MLS PROGRAM is positive for all 10 years and statistically significant for 9 of the 10. While the expected sign is positive, the strength and consistency of the relationship is somewhat surprising. It may be that the presence of faculty members in a graduate library science program strengthens the argument for tenure track positions in the library. This synergy between tenure in academic librarianship and library science education has not been explored in the literature and may offer an area ripe for future exploration.

FACULTY is statistically significant for five of the years under study and positive, as predicted. FACULTY measures the number of full-time faculty members at the institution. The variable is not significant for the years 1995–1998, perhaps indicating a shift in the funding priorities of universities at the end of the 1990s.

The only other variable to show statistical significance is % PROFSTAFF, which measures the number of professional employees as a percentage of the total library staff. The variable was predicted to be positive but is negative for 7 of the 10 years, including the only year to show statistical significance, 1998. It would appear that the larger the number of professionals, the less likely the positions will be tenure track. This conclusion seems to be counter-intuitive; one would assume that larger professional staffs would allow for greater labor specialization and ease the burdens on the library of having library professionals pursuing the "extra" duties required by tenure track positions. But the conclusion is supported by some of the literature discussed above, which indicates that non-research/non-ARL libraries (with smaller professional staffs) may be more likely to support tenure track positions.

Other variables impact the model very little. The regional variables are not statistically significant nor are their signs consistent. There is no reason to believe that there would be a strong regional impact on the probability of tenure, so this was not surprising. The effect of unionization, however, is surprising given the role it played in the OLS model below. In the probit analysis, UNION is consistently negative (as predicted) but is never statistically significant. Based on this study, unionization does not appear to be an important factor when universities choose to offer tenure track options to librarians.

Also consistently negative but not statistically significant was TYPE. Chressanthis (1994) found public institutions more likely to offer tenure but that supposition is not supported by this study.

The Wage Model

Originally, the author of this study hoped to incorporate a panel study of wage determination, covering the years 1989–1998 into the project. However, preliminary analysis showed no variability in the variable TENURE, making the panel data approach unviable. An alternative model, using cross-sectional data and utilizing OLS regression was thus employed. As shown in Eq. (2), the natural logarithm of starting salaries (LSALARIES) served as the dependent variable and a number of both library- and institution-specific

Table 10A. Model 2: OLS Cross-sectional Regression Estimates by Year: 1989–1993 (Dependent Variable = LSALARIES, $N = 78$).

Variable	1989	1990	1991	1992	1993
CONSTANT	9.7799	9.9556	9.958	9.9758	10.0405
	(115.477)	(126.143)	(124.762)	(102.396)	(115.984)
TENURE	0.0096	−0.0112	0.0033	0.0103	0.0088
	(0.534)	(0.586)	(0.184)	(0.550)	(0.454)
UNION	0.1230***	0.0933***	0.0987***	0.1108***	0.0923***
	(4.565)	(3.360)	(3.737)	(4.049)	(3.043)
TYPE	0.0666***	0.0586***	0.0553***	0.0745***	0.0637***
	(2.651)	(2.406)	(2.250)	(2.906)	(2.416)
VOLUMES	−0.1150E−07	0.3760E−09	−0.6567E−09	0.1818E−09	0.6490E−08
	(1.172)	(0.050)	(0.076)	(0.19)	(0.679)
% PROFSTAFF	0.1134*	−0.2816	−0.0933	−0.1335	−0.1256
	(0.469)	(1.288)	(0.380)	(0.513)	(0.556)
EXPEND	0.2717E−07***	0.1899E−07***	0.1871E−07**	0.2280E−07**	0.9172E−08
	(2.659)	(2.183)	(1.798)	(2.198)	(0.930)
PHD FIELDS	0.4220E−03	0.1793E−03	0.1525E−03	−0.1603E−03	0.6033E−04
	(0.933)	(0.370)	(0.373)	(0.294)	(0.115)
URBAN	−0.0360**	−0.0200	−0.0169	−0.0144	−0.0209
	(2.004)	(1.069)	(0.880)	(0.715)	(0.890)
SOUTH	−0.0055	−0.0193	−0.0029	0.0012	0.0133
	(0.195)	(0.761)	(0.117)	(0.046)	(0.467)
MIDWEST	0.0082	−0.0024	0.0062	0.6988E−03	0.0101
	(0.265)	(0.088)	(0.231)	(0.024)	(0.314)
WEST	0.0778***	0.0572**	0.0597**	0.0736***	0.0868***
	(2.189)	(1.683)	(2.011)	(2.188)	(2.527)
F-statistic	6.14	5.41	5.04	6.24	3.86
Adjusted R^2	0.4236	0.3864	0.3657	0.4283	0.2901

Note: ( ): Absolute value of *t*-statistic; *t*-statistics are corrected for heteroscedasticity.
*Statistically significant at the .10 level, one-tailed test.
**Statistically significant at the .05 level, one-tailed test.
***Statistically significant at the .01 level, one-tailed test.

variables were used to estimate the model for each year (1989–1998). Only the library-specific variables proved to be consistently statistically significant across the 10 years. Tables 10A and 10B report the empirical results for the OLS wage model. The estimated equations all obtained a significant *F*-statistic and an acceptable cross-sectional adjusted R^2.

Surprisingly, the variable of interest, TENURE, proved to be of little importance in the model, regardless of the year. For all 10 years, the sign is positive, which runs counter to the hypothesis that tenure-granting institutions have lower starting salaries. Compensating wage differential theory predicts the effect of tenure to be negative on wages. However, the lack of statistical significance refutes the common alternative argument in the library science literature – namely, the positive impact tenure has on compensation. The results

Table 10B.   Model 2: OLS Cross-sectional Regression Estimates by
Year: 1994–1998 (Dependent Variable = LSALARIES, $N = 78$).

Variable	1994	1995	1996	1997	1998
CONSTANT	10.1165	10.1700	10.1984	10.3318	10.3547
	(126.922)	(138.260)	(124.777)	(153.480)	(165.277)
TENURE	0.0130	0.0047	0.0165	0.0019	−0.0082
	(0.702)	(0.259)	(0.929)	(0.111)	(0.433)
UNION	0.0550**	0.0635***	0.0573**	0.0458**	0.0237
	(1.743)	(1.943)	(1.737)	(1.660)	(0.752)
TYPE	0.0485***	0.0533***	0.0646***	0.0523***	0.0674***
	(2.094)	(2.184)	(2.613)	(2.157)	(2.462)
VOLUMES	0.9346E−08	0.1387E−07**	0.5012E−08	0.1095E−07*	0.5199E−08
	(1.060)	(1.467)	(0.576)	(1.448)	(0.699)
% PROFSTAFF	−0.1165	−0.0674	−0.2405	−0.4353***	−0.3629***
	(0.578)	(0.344)	(1.030)	(2.225)	(2.114)
EXPEND	0.7360E−08	0.2854E−08	0.7605E−08	0.6363E−08	0.2941E−08
	(0.878)	(0.335)	(0.927)	(1.029)	(0.478)
PHD FIELDS	−0.3910E−03	−0.5607E−03	0.3543E−04	−0.8804E−03**	0.3186E−04*
	(0.754)	(1.067)	(1.160)	(1.821)	(1.247)
URBAN	−0.0120	0.0058	0.0146	0.0216	0.1923
	(0.500)	(0.256)	(0.660)	(1.129)	(0.866)
SOUTH	−0.1980	−0.0156	−0.0088	−0.0148	−0.0254
	(0.699)	(0.586)	(0.291)	(0.604)	(0.809)
MIDWEST	−0.0083	−0.0080	−0.0085	−0.0238	−0.0278
	(0.261)	(0.262)	(0.293)	(0.924)	(0.978)
WEST	0.0321	0.0311	0.0465*	0.0267	0.0274
	(0.995)	(1.015)	(1.670)	(1.068)	(1.046)
F-statistic	2.38	2.51	2.15	3.34	1.89
Adjusted R^2	0.1642	0.1778	0.1415	0.2507	0.1130

Note: ( ): Absolute value of *t*-statistic; *t*-statistics are corrected for heteroscedasticity.
*Statistically significant at the .10 level, one-tailed test.
**Statistically significant at the .05 level, one-tailed test.
***Statistically significant at the .01 level, one-tailed test.

indicate that the existence of TENURE is insignificant in wage formation for academic librarians at ARL institutions, at least at the entry level.

Not so surprisingly, UNION proved to be a more powerful variable in the model. For 9 of the 10 years under study, UNION was statistically significant at either the .05 or the .01 level, using a one-tailed test. UNION was not significant in the last year, which will be discussed below.

The only other consistently significant variable was TYPE. A priori, TYPE was hypothesized to be positive, and the results of the OLS cross-sectional regressions show this to be the case. Private universities are often more heavily endowed, which can substantively increase the financial resources available to the university for salaries. Zoghi (2000) also suggests that public universities are often more constrained in terms of tuition;

private universities can more freely raise tuition, which enhances their ability to offer higher salaries. The present study is consistent with this assumption.

Other library-specific variables included VOLUMES, % PROFSTAFF, and EXPEND. All three were significant in at least one of the years but lack any consistency as to either the sign or statistical significance. The assumption that larger libraries, either in terms of staffing (% PROFSTAFF) or VOLUMES, offer higher salaries does not appear to be substantiated by the results. EXPEND was statistically significant for the early years of 1989–1992 but not for the later years. This may reflect the changing labor market for academic librarians. Due to an apparent labor shortage, many academic libraries are finding it difficult to recruit and retain qualified librarians (Raschke, 2003). If a shortage of librarians persisted throughout the sample period, then wages should be observed to continually rise. Also, jobs should be readily available. This would lesson the need for tenure at least in terms of the job security commonly associated with tenure. Should a job loss occur, the costs of unemployment is less during periods of labor shortage and rising wages.

Other than TYPE, few of the institution-specific variables proved to be statistically significant in the study. For 1997 and 1998, PHD FIELDS was statistically significant but the signs were not stable. PHD FIELDS had been hypothesized to be positive, but was negative for 4 of the 10 years.

No a priori assumption was made concerning the sign of URBAN. For the first six years of the study, it was negative, reflecting a negative relationship between higher starting salaries and urban locations. This may be the result of rural institutions having to offer a positive differential to offset the lack of amenities and job opportunities for spouses and families. Beginning with 1995, however, the sign becomes positive. For 1995–1998, URBAN is positive but lacks statistical significance. This may be a function of the data collected or it may reflect reduced funding to state-supported rural universities.

Of the regional variables, only WEST showed some consistent results in terms of both the sign and statistical significance. The expected signs for the regional variables had been indeterminate prior to the analysis. SOUTH was usually negative, perhaps reflecting lower regional salaries, but the lack of statistical significance makes any conclusions tenuous. MIDWEST was negative for 6 of the 10 years but again lacks any statistical significance. WEST, however, was consistently positive and statistically significant for 6 of the 10 years, including 1989–1993 and 1996. The lack of statistical significance in the latter period of the study, as well as the decrease in the magnitude of the estimate, may be the result of funding difficulties experienced by higher educational systems located in the West, especially in the state of California (Lively, 1992).

The last year of the study deserves additional discussion. The results for 1998 are markedly different than the first nine years. Variables that were consistently significant in the other years are not in 1998 – such as UNION and WEST. Only two variables are found to be statistically significant, TYPE and PHD FIELDS. The overall adjusted R^2 for the model is a modest 11%, substantively lower than the 42% in 1989. Whether this variability in the data for 1998 is a function of the data collection method or an indication of a deeper, underlying trend is beyond the analysis of this study. Additional date for the post-1998 period is needed to address this apparent break in the trend.

OLS regression requires a number of conditions. One of those conditions is that no independent variable be a linear function of one or more other independent variables. Multicollinearity occurs when this condition is not met. Economic data often exhibit some degree of multicollinearity and one of a number of diagnostics is recommended when examining regression data (Studenmund & Cassidy, 1987). One method for examining possible multicollinear variables is to examine the Pearson correlation matrix. The year 1994 was selected as a representative year of the sample and its data were used for further diagnostic examination. Tables 11A and 11B report the Pearson correlation statistics for 1994. An analysis of the Pearson correlation statistics reveals only two variables with a relatively high degree of correlation: EXPEND and VOLUMES. Given the nature of these two variables, some degree of correlation is to be expected and is not cause for removal from the model.

Another diagnostic of multicollinear data is the Variance Inflation Factors or VIFs. VIFs are an indicator of the effect that the other predicator variables have on the variance of a regression coefficient directly

Table 11A. Pearson Correlation Coefficients, 1994.

	TENURE	UNION	TYPE	VOLUMES	% PROFSTAFF	EXPEND
TENURE	1.000	0.009	−0.292	−0.237	−0.124	−0.149
UNION	0.009	1.000	−0.322	−0.114	−0.240	0.004
TYPE	−0.29251	−0.322	1.000	0.120	0.339	0.044
VOLUMES	−0.23739	−0.114	0.120	1.000	−0.002	0.865
% PROFSTAFF	−0.124	−0.240	0.339	−0.002	1.000	−0.100
EXPEND	−0.149	0.004	0.044	0.865	−0.100	1.000
PHD FIELDS	0.050	−0.099	−0.161	0.388	−0.043	0.398
URBAN	−0.075	−0.235	0.041	0.104	0.195	0.047
SOUTH	−0.025	−0.299	0.000	−0.222	0.144	−0.196
MIDWEST	0.075	−0.112	−0.103	0.083	−0.025	0.007
WEST	0.036	0.300	−0.241	−0.047	−0.249	0.057

Table 11B.   Pearson Correlation Coefficients, 1994.

	PHD FIELDS	URBAN	SOUTH	MIDWEST	WEST
TENURE	0.050	−0.075	−0.025	0.075	0.036
UNION	−0.099	−0.235	−0.299	−0.112	0.300
TYPE	−0.161	0.041	0.000	−0.103	−0.241
VOLUMES	0.388	0.104	−0.222	0.083	−0.047
% PROFSTAFF	−0.043	0.195	0.144	−0.025	−0.249
EXPEND	0.398	0.047	−0.196	0.007	0.057
PHD FIELDS	1.000	0.084	−0.152	0.191	−0.012
URBAN	0.084	1.000	0.073	0.075	−0.045
SOUTH	−0.152	0.073	1.000	−0.391	−0.351
MIDWEST	0.191	0.075	−0.391	1.000	−0.310
WEST	−0.012	−0.045	−0.351	−0.310	1.000

Table 12.   Variance Inflation Factors, 1994.

TENURE	1.2158
UNION	1.5975
TYPE	1.6707
VOLUMES	4.9145
% PROFSTAFF	1.2553
EXPEND	4.5734
PHD FIELDS	1.3427
URBAN	1.1187
SOUTH	2.3425
MIDWEST	2.0034
WEST	1.9467

related to the tolerance value (Hair et al., 1995). According to Hair et al. (1995, p. 127), each researcher must set his/her own threshold, but a common cutoff threshold is a VIF equal to 10. Table 12 reports the VIFs for the year 1994. Again, only EXPEND and VOLUMES show fairly high VIFs, with values in excess of 4. However, an analysis of the model with and without one or both variables does not yield substantively different results in either the overall predictive capability of the model or in the statistical significance of the individual regressors. Given the theoretical importance of these two variables, as proxies for institutional support for the library and the total library collection size, the decision was made to keep them in the model.

An Alternative Test

The analysis above assumes that there is no underlying distinction between the librarian labor markets in tenure track versus non-tenure track ARL libraries. In other words, there is no direct evidence of labor market segmentation occurring. But is this conclusion warranted?

A separate analysis of the data examined wage determination across tenure track and non-tenure track ARL libraries. Tables 13A–13E report separate wage equations for the tenure- and non-tenure-granting

Table 13A. Wage Equations: Tenured versus Non-tenured ARL Libraries, 1989–1990.

	1989		1990	
	Non-tenured	Tenured	Non-tenured	Tenured
CONSTANT	9.8863	9.5760	10.0501	9.7076
	(93.147)	(62.382)	(94.119)	(61.515)
UNION	0.1344	0.0822	0.1041	0.0823
	(2.977)	(1.703)	(2.482)	(1.822)
TYPE	0.0603	0.0422	0.0251	0.0361
	(1.763)	(0.870)	(0.822)	(0.769)
VOLUMES	$-0.5984E-08$	$-0.1187E-07$	$0.2013E-08$	$0.1379E-08$
	(0.332)	(0.570)	(0.149)	(0.068)
% PROFSTAFF	-0.1952	1.0993	-0.4395	0.8535
	(0.610)	(1.943)	(1.477)	(1.353)
EXPEND	$0.2544E-07$	$0.2794E-07$	$0.2363E-07$	$0.8132E-08$
	(1.212)	(1.264)	(1.587)	(0.432)
PHD FIELDS	$-0.3039E-03$	$0.6823E-03$	-0.0010	0.0013
	(0.463)	(1.002)	(1.772)	(1.861)
URBAN	-0.0382	-0.0668	-0.0240	-0.0557
	(1.264)	(1.614)	(0.909)	(1.483)
SOUTH	0.0120	-0.0518	-0.0089	-0.0725
	(0.283)	(0.972)	(0.227)	(1.395)
MIDWEST	0.0210	-0.0754	0.2465	-0.0348
	(0.508)	(0.143)	(0.648)	(0.697)
WEST	0.0812	0.0482	0.4190	0.0412
	(1.669)	(0.871)	(0.961)	(0.793)
N	44	34	44	34
F-statistic	5.19	2.36	5.54	2.30
Adjusted R^2	0.4936	0.2919	0.5138	0.2822

Note: ( ): Absolute value of *t*-statistic.

universities. A Chow test was performed to evaluate whether the coefficients of different regressions are equal (Chow, 1960; Pindyck & Rubinfeld, 1981). Testing the null hypothesis that the regressors are equal for tenure track and non-tenure track ARL libraries, yields the F-statistics found in Table 14. The critical value for an F-statistic with 11 restrictions and 56 degrees of freedom is 1.95. Since the value of the F-statistic is consistently less than the critical value of the F-distribution at the 5% level, the results fail to reject the null hypothesis. Therefore, based on the data in this study, it is safe to assume that the coefficients are equal across tenure, the tenure and non-tenure sub-samples, and that the single equation estimated above for the full

Table 13B.   Wage Equations: Tenured versus Non-tenured ARL Libraries, 1991–1992.

	1991		1992	
	Non-tenured	Tenured	Non-tenured	Tenured
CONSTANT	10.0167	9.8617	10.1427	9.8329
	(90.938)	(64.063)	(99.696)	(55.327)
UNION	0.0859	0.1024	0.0493	0.1267
	(1.954)	(2.485)	(1.238)	(2.697)
TYPE	0.0395	0.0348	0.0480	0.0608
	(1.211)	(0.757)	(1.569)	(1.071)
VOLUMES	−0.8027E−09	0.9003E−08	−0.5570E−09	0.6960E−08
	(0.056)	(0.515)	(0.041)	(0.324)
% PROFSTAFF	−0.1869	0.3282	−0.414	0.4235
	(0.626)	(0.555)	(1.536)	(0.693)
EXPEND	0.2139E−07	0.1135E−07	0.2239E−07	0.1724E−07
	(1.357)	(0.589)	(1.563)	(0.839)
PHD FIELDS	−0.7377E−03	0.8614E−03	−0.0013	0.5618E−03
	(1.180)	(1.203)	(2.231)	(0.697)
URBAN	−0.0120	−0.0424	0.0014	−0.0354
	(0.426)	(1.154)	(0.053)	(0.889)
SOUTH	0.0064	−0.0443	−0.0274	−0.0138
	(0.159)	(0.900)	(0.735)	(0.250)
MIDWEST	0.0266	−0.0318	−0.0075	−0.0206
	(0.678)	(0.651)	(0.207)	(0.369)
WEST	0.0737	0.0500	0.1001	0.0531
	(1.630)	(0.989)	(2.388)	(0.930)
N	44	34	44	34
F-statistic	3.68	2.12	7.28	1.78
Adjusted R^2	0.3838	0.2536	0.5936	0.1911

Table 13C. Wage Equations: Tenured versus Non-tenured ARL Libraries, 1993–1994.

	1993		1994	
	Non-tenured	Tenured	Non-tenured	Tenured
CONSTANT	10.1706	10.0537	10.1838	10.1440
	(86.969)	(55.916)	(97.744)	(59.894)
UNION	0.0102	0.1202	0.0127	0.0840
	(0.216)	(2.584)	(0.287)	(1.750)
TYPE	0.0340	0.0804	0.0149	0.0690
	(0.983)	(1.363)	(0.455)	(1.081)
VOLUMES	0.1406E−07	0.6848E−08	0.1328E−07	0.1161E−07
	(0.894)	(0.339)	(0.873)	(0.548)
% PROFSTAFF	−0.2509	−0.2209	−0.1405	−0.2381
	(0.871)	(0.335)	(0.527)	(0.345)
EXPEND	0.2508E−08	0.5094E−08	0.7852E−08	−0.1964E−08
	(0.160)	(0.258)	(0.566)	(0.103)
PHD FIELDS	−0.0011	0.7760E−03	−0.0015	0.7205E−03
	(1.507)	(0.944)	(2.273)	(0.803)
URBAN	−0.0057	−0.0393	−0.7490E−03	−0.0367
	(0.184)	(0.926)	(0.026)	(0.797)
SOUTH	−0.0211	0.0061	−0.0219	−0.0404
	(0.496)	(0.107)	(0.524)	(0.707)
MIDWEST	−0.0085	0.0156	−0.0065	−0.0046
	(0.208)	(0.278)	(0.159)	(0.079)
WEST	0.1197	0.8851	0.0417	0.5606
	(2.638)	(1.526)	(0.032)	(0.928)
N	44	34	44	34
F-statistic	3.49	1.42	2.32	1.08
Adjusted R^2	0.3663	0.1119	0.2355	0.0244

sample is valid. Given this, there appears to be no evidence of a segmented labor market for ARL libraries, based on the use of tenure.

Union Wage Premium

Of significant interest is the impact unionization has on starting salaries. Given the significance of UNION in Model 2, one could reasonably assume the existence of a union wage premium. The existence of a union wage premium has been extensively explored across a wide number of occupations (Lewis, 1986). This issue has been less well studied for librarians, although

Table 13D. Wage Equations: Tenured versus Non-tenured ARL Libraries, 1995–1996.

	1995		1996	
	Non-tenured	Tenured	Non-tenured	Tenured
CONSTANT	10.1588	10.2901	10.0693	10.4828
UNION	0.0468	0.0849	0.0636	0.0594
TYPE	0.0347	0.0783	0.0802	0.0977
VOLUMES	0.1655E−07	0.2336E−07	−0.4680E−08	0.1760E−07
% PROFSTAFF	0.0544	−0.5788	−0.0113	−1.0984
EXPEND	0.5483E−08	−0.1177E−07	0.1858E−07	−0.6729E−08
PHD FIELDS	−0.0016	0.6721E−03	0.4039E−04	0.1314E−03
URBAN	0.0130	0.0015	0.0163	0.0150
SOUTH	0.0059	−0.0418	0.0323	−0.0459
MIDWEST	0.0114	−0.0111	−0.0034	0.0018
WEST	0.0581	0.3783	0.8451	0.3429
N	44	34	44	34
F-statistic	2.95	0.97	2.40	0.91
Adjusted R^2	0.3117	0.0000	0.2451	−0.0289

Table 13E. Wage Equations: Tenured versus Non-tenured ARL Libraries, 1997–1998.

	1997		1998	
	Non-tenured	Tenured	Non-tenured	Tenured
CONSTANT	10.2447	10.5418	10.2456	10.5223
UNION	0.0538	0.0694	0.0288	0.0276
TYPE	0.0528	0.0843	0.0917	0.0692
VOLUMES	0.9493E−08	0.2983E−07	−0.1284E−08	0.2143E−07
% PROFSTAFF	−0.1925	−1.3157	−0.2252	−0.8939
EXPEND	0.9487E−08	−0.4699E−08	0.8650E−08	−0.6648E−08
PHD FIELDS	−0.0012	−0.4803E−03	0.3683E−04	0.0003
URBAN	0.0208	0.0213	0.0466	−0.0210
SOUTH	0.2275	−0.0308	0.0081	−0.0611
MIDWEST	−0.0058	−0.0196	−0.0186	−0.0346
WEST	0.0527	0.0306	0.0690	0.0154
N	44	34	44	34
F-statistic	3.11	1.62	1.50	1.17
Adjusted R^2	0.3292	0.1589	0.1043	0.0479

Table 14.   Chow Test Results, 1989–1998.

Year	F-statistic
1989	0.7391
1990	1.2167
1991	0.5833
1992	0.9048
1993	0.6164
1994	0.7123
1995	0.8696
1996	0.7917
1997	0.9643
1998	0.7848

Note: F-statistic tests the null hypothesis that the coefficients are equal across the tenure-granting and non-tenure-granting wage equations.

some effort has been made to analyze the wage premium in public libraries (see, for example, Rosenthal, 1985). Other studies that have focused on academic libraries have examined the issue of job satisfaction (Hovekamp, 1995).

The union wage differential may be estimated using the data collected for Model 2. The adjusted union wage differential is the percentage by which union membership increases the wage rate from what it would have been in a market without unions (Pindyck & Rubinfeld, 1981). Assuming a competitive labor market D^* can be written as

$$D^* = \frac{W_U - W_N}{W_N} \qquad (3)$$

where W_U equals the beginning wage the librarian receives if the academic library is unionized and W_N equals the competitive beginning wage the librarian would have received in the absence of a collective bargaining agreement. The non-union wage can be specified as

$$\ln W_N = \alpha + \beta_1 I + \beta_2 L + \beta_3 R + e \qquad (4)$$

where I is the vector of institutional characteristics, L is the vector of library-specific characteristics, and R represents the regional categorical variables. Assuming the relative wage differential for beginning salaries due to unionization is the same for all ARL librarians, the beginning wage for union positions can be written as

$$W_U = (1 + D^*)^U W_N \tag{5}$$

where $U = 0$ if the academic library is not unionized, and $U = 1$ if it offers professional positions covered by a collective bargaining agreement. Eq. (5) may be rewritten as

$$\ln W_U = \ln(1 + D^*)U + \ln W_N \tag{6}$$

or expanded as

$$\ln W_U = \alpha + \beta_0 U + \beta_1 I + \beta_2 L + \beta_3 R + e \tag{7}$$

where $\beta_0 = \ln(1 + D^*)$. The regression equation yields estimates of β_0. To obtain the exact value of D^*, the antilog of the estimates must be calculated, such that

$$D^* = e^{\beta_0} - 1 \tag{8}$$

Table 15 reports the estimated coefficients for UNION for each of the 10 years of the study (1989–1998). For example, D^* for 1989 is .13, indicating that union ARL libraries offered average starting salaries 13% higher than their non-union ARL counterparts, other things held constant.

Table 15. Estimated Union Wage Premium.

Year	Union Wage Premium		Tenure Differential	
	β_u	D^*	β_T	D^*
1989	.1230***	.13	.0096	.01
1990	.0933***	.10	−.0112	−.01
1991	.0987***	.10	.0033	0
1992	.1108***	.12	.0103	.01
1993	.0923***	.10	.0088	.01
1994	.0550**	.06	.0130	.01
1995	.0635***	.07	.0047	0
1996	.0573**	.06	.0165	.02
1997	.0458**	.05	.0019	0
1998	.0237	.02	−.0082	−.01

Note: β_u = OLS coefficient on UNION; β_T = OLS coefficient on TENURE.
*Statistically significant at the .10 level, one-tailed test.
**Statistically significant at the .05 level, one-tailed test.
***Statistically significant at the .01 level, one-tailed test.

This union wage premium steadily declines throughout the period under study, ranging from a high of 13% in 1989 to a low of 2% in 1998 (the only year where the UNION variable was not statistically significant). Note that this range and decline are consistent with the union literature. For comparison purposes, a similar analysis is presented for the variable TENURE, even though this variable was not statistically significant. Had it been statistically significant, D^* would have represented the compensating wage differential due to tenure. As Table 15 reports, the compensating wage differential is considerably smaller than the union wage premium, and takes the expected negative sign in only two years (1990 and 1998). These results are not surprising, given the lack of statistical significance in the OLS model above.

In the sample under study, the presence of a union clearly has an impact on starting salaries. It is possible that the resulting differential (or premium) due to tenure is not apparent at the entry level but only manifests itself after a period of years. The presence of a union would more likely have an impact on *starting* salaries, given the role unions typically play in setting hiring wages.

SUMMARY AND CONCLUSIONS

Based on the data analyzed in this study, *tenure does not appear to either positively or negatively affect starting salaries for academic librarians.* This fails to confirm either the hypothesis of compensating wage differentials or the alternative theory, the popular belief among academic librarians that there is a positive relationship between tenure track positions and compensation. There are several factors that may contribute to this finding.

One concern is the type of data used in this study. It may be that *institutionally reported* starting salaries, as collected by ARL, do not capture the complex relationship between wages and tenure. Efforts to secure individual level data, as reported by the ARL member libraries, proved unsuccessful and library-wide starting salaries were selected as the only viable alternative. However, the starting salary data may reflect reporting errors, and individual effects could obscure the true relationship between salaries and tenure. Tenure studies in academic libraries is problematic, in part, due to widely varying definitions of both tenure and faculty status used by individual libraries. Brown (1980) also identified methodological problems with compensating wage differential studies, citing the noise and errors inherent in the analysis that often obscure the ability to identify a differential.

In addition, non-pecuniary compensation unique to tenure track positions is not captured in the starting salaries variable. It may well be that tenure track librarians have access to additional travel funds, research support, and on-the-job training opportunities beyond their non-tenure track counterparts. This type of compensation is not reflected in starting salary figures.

An alternative explanation may lie in the true differential for tenure track positions. The differential, whether positive or negative, may not exist at the point of hire, but only manifest itself upon the award of tenure. More extensive data reflecting compensation after tenure might provide valuable insight on this topic.

Tenure Probability Model: Conclusions

The probit model identifies a number of library and institutional characteristics related to the use of tenure. Of particular note, the AGE variable indicates a marked difference in the use of tenure between older, "founding" ARL members and newer member libraries. The availability of tenure track ARL positions is also highly correlated with faculty status and rank, and the expectation of research as a condition of employment. The use of the title "Dean" for the head of the library is also highly correlated, although this may in fact be a function of tenure. ARL libraries with tenure track librarians may be more likely to have an organizational head with the title of Dean.

The other statistically significant variable, at least in most years, is LIS PROGRAM. While the various contributions of library science faculty members and practitioners to the library science literature are a frequently studied topic, little attention has been paid to the impact, if any, the presence of a library science graduate program has on the hiring and retention practices of the university library. This study indicates that the presence of a library science graduate program may enhance the view of librarians as faculty and increase the likelihood of the library supporting tenure track positions.

Little research exists on the institutional characteristics of tenure. While the present study attempts to contribute to this understanding, additional research clearly needs to be pursued in this area.

OLS Wage Model: Conclusions

Surprisingly, the wage model failed to support either the more formal hypothesis concerning the presence of compensating wage differentials or the more popularly held belief concerning a positive relationship between wages and tenure. The variable TENURE was never statistically significant over the

10 years under study, and failed to maintain a consistent sign. Other than the potential data problems described above, why might this be the case?

Some scholars argue that tenure does not serve the same function for academic librarians as it does for other faculty (Hill, 1994). The ACRL standards go to great lengths to equate the need for tenure and faculty status for both academic librarians and classroom faculty. However, if tenure serves a different function for academic librarians, then the results may not be empirically identifiable through a study of wages. As one avowed proponent of tenure states, "... for academic librarians, because faculty tenure is not the overwhelming norm, there is no stigma attached to being untenured, and institutions that do not offer tenure do not need to offer higher salaries to make up for it" (Hill, 2005). (Note the implied positive relationship between tenure and wages.)

The most robust findings concern the relationship between union representation and wages. This is hardly a surprising finding, given the voluminous research on union wage premiums. However, the lack of empirical research on the use of unions in academic libraries is noteworthy. While many of the typical wage equation variables proved to be erratic at best (including variables related to size, region, etc.), the union variable was consistently statistically significant, with the exception of 1998.

Summary of Major Findings

This study results in a number of major findings, summarized below:

- Forty-four percent of ARL member institutions offer tenure track academic positions to librarians.
- Institutional characteristics influence the probability that ARL members use tenure. Ceteris paribus,
  - Older ARL members are less likely to offer tenure track positions.
  - Institutions with stated research expectations for librarians are more likely to offer tenure track positions.
  - The number of faculty members employed by the university is positively related to the probability that librarians have access to tenure.
  - Institutions with degree-granting library science programs are more likely to offer tenure track positions to librarians.
  - Librarians headed by an academic dean are more likely to offer tenure track positions.

- The existence of tenure track positions for librarians does not significantly affect the starting salary for librarians at ARL member institutions.
- A positive and significant union wage premium existed for librarians employed by ARL institutions during the 1990s.
  - This wage premium fell from more than 10% to only 2% over the decade under study.
- Starting salaries for librarians at private universities belonging to ARL are greater than those at their public cohorts.
- Higher levels of overall expenditures at ARL member libraries are associated with higher starting salaries.
- Starting salaries are higher for ARL librarians in the Western United States than those located elsewhere.

Limitations and Future Research

As indicated earlier, there are a number of limitations inherent in this type of study. Data availability severely limited the ability to measure the relationship between tenure and wages beyond starting salaries. Given the aggregate data available, no individual characteristics were observable, but these might very well prove to be important.

The true differential due to tenure, whether positive or negative, may not be observable at the point of hire and only become apparent at some later point. In addition, other job attributes, not measurable in starting salaries, may be important. Tenure track positions may include greater access to on-the-job training, research, and professional development opportunities, all of which would theoretically result in higher wages at some later point.

This study did not support the hypothesis of segmented labor market based on tenure *within* the sample of ARL institutions. However, there may well exist a segmented market *between* non-ARL academic libraries and ARL libraries. Tenure may play a role in this segmentation. At least some prior studies indicate a higher use of tenure in non-ARL academic libraries (Chressanthis, 1994). Non-ARL academic libraries may use tenure as a way to attract candidates to less prestigious environments. While beyond the scope of this study, a natural extension of this analysis to a non-ARL sample would be beneficial to the understanding of the relationship between tenure and salaries in the academic library labor market.

The last year of the study proved to be the most problematic. Both the probit and OLS models were weakest in this year, and even the union wage premium was noticeably smaller by the 10th year of the study. Whether this is a function of the data or represents a shift in compensation patterns is beyond the scope of this study and will be addressed in future research.

This dissertation sought to examine the use of tenure in ARL academic libraries, and by extension, the compensating wage differentials due to tenure. While more robust findings would have been desirable, the lack of either a positive or negative relationship contributes to the understanding of the academic labor market in ARL libraries. The strong union wage premium illustrates the need for additional research into the use of unions both within academic libraries and in the academic labor market in general.

Unanswered Questions

While the OLS model used in this study does have some explanatory power for wage determination, that clearly wanes over the 10-year period under examination. What accounts for this change? What other elements affect wage determination, if not tenure, in academic libraries?

While some authors have indicated the importance of gender in the study of compensating wage differentials (Gariety & Shaffer, 2001), given the type of data used for this study, it was not possible to study issues related to gender. But gender is clearly an issue in a profession dominated by female workers. Future work must take this into account.

While the existing literature sheds little light on the characteristics of tenure-granting academic libraries, the probit model examined in Model 2 raises some interesting questions. Why are older ARL libraries less likely to offer tenure track positions? What is the relationship between staffing and tenure in academic libraries?

Most importantly, if tenure is not a critical determinant of wage determination in academic libraries, what role does it play? Its presence in 44% of the institutions studied indicate that it must play some role for many large, research institutions to invest in its use. The examination of the institutional characteristics of tenure lays the groundwork for further research into the institutional uses of tenure for academic libraries.

As one author points out, the debate surrounding tenure in academic libraries is based on a good deal of emotion and considerably less empirical analysis (Hill, 2005). Empirical studies such as this one, however, can dispel some popularly held myths concerning the role tenure plays and lay the groundwork for a more meaningful discussion of the institution of tenure in higher education, and specifically in academic libraries.

REFERENCES

Abowd, J. M., & Ashenfelter, O. (1981). Anticipated unemployment, temporary layoffs, and compensating wage differentials. In: S. Rosen (Ed.), *Studies in labor markets* (pp. 141–170). Chicago: University of Chicago Press.

ACRL Academic Status Committee. (1974). Joint statement on faculty status for college and university librarians. *College and Research Libraries News, 35*(February), 223–225.

ACRL Academic Status Committee. (1981). Academic status survey. *College and Research Libraries News, 42*(June), 171.

ACRL Academic Status Committee. (1987). Model statement of criteria procedures for appointment, promotion in academic rank, and tenure for college and university librarians. *College and Research Libraries News, 48*(May), 247–254.

American Association of University Professors. (2003). *Statement of principles on academic freedom and tenure.* Available online at: http://www.aaup.org/statements/Redbook/ 1940stat.htm. Accessed December 1, 2004.

American Library Association. (2003). Do librarians with tenure get more respect? *American Libraries, 34*(6), 70–72.

Association of College and Research Libraries. (2001). *Joint statement on faculty status of college and university librarians.* Available online at: http://www.ala.org/ala/acrl/ acrlstandards/jointstatementfaculty.htm. Accessed December 1, 2004.

Association of College and Research Libraries. (2002). Guidelines for academic status for college and university librarians. *College and Research Libraries News, 63*(October), 664–665.

Association of Research Libraries. (2001). *ARL annual salary survey 2000–2001.* Washington, DC: Association of Research Libraries.

Association of Research Libraries. (2003). *ARL annual statistics: Instructions.* Washington, DC: Association of Research Libraries. Available online at: http://www.arl.org/stats/ coordinator.html. Accessed December 8, 2004.

Association of Research Libraries. (2004a). *ARL annual salary survey.* Available online at: http://www.arl.org/stats/salary/. Accessed December 8, 2004.

Association of Research Libraries. (2004b). *ARL Membership Criteria Index.* Washington, DC: Association of Research Libraries. Available online at: http://www.arl.org/stats/index/ indxdesc.html. Accessed July 7, 2004.

Benedict, M. A., Gavaryck, J. A., & Selvin, H. C. (1983). Status of academic librarians in New York state. *College and Research Libraries, 44*(January), 12–19.

Biggs, M. (1981). Sources of tension and conflict between librarianship and faculty. *Journal of Higher Education, 52*(2), 182–201.

Branscomb, L. C. (Ed.) (1970). *The case for faculty status of academic librarians.* Chicago: American Library Association.

Breneman, D. W. (1997). Alternatives *to tenure for the next generation of academics.* New Pathways Working Paper Series, no. 14. American Association for Higher Education, Washington, DC.

Brown, C. (1980). Equalizing differences in the labor market. *Quarterly Journal of Economics, 44*(February), 113–134.

Byerly, G. (1980). The faculty status of academic libraries in Ohio. *College and Research Libraries, 41*(September), 422–429.

Cage, M. C. (1995). New Florida University to offer an alternative to tenure. *Chronicle of Higher Education,* June 2, p. A15.

Carmichael, H. L. (1988). Incentives in academics: Why is there tenure? *Journal of Political Economy, 96*(June), 453–472.

Chow, G. C. (1960). Tests of equality between sets of coefficients in two linear regressions. *Econometrica, 28*(July), 591–605.

Chressanthis, G. (1994, May). The *effect of faculty status for librarians on the cost structure of academic libraries at American Research Universities*. Unpublished paper.

Chronicle of Higher Education. (1999). Massachusetts official proposes bonuses for professors who forgo tenure track. *Chronicle of Higher Education*, May 14.

Cohen, A. M. (1998). *The shaping of American higher education: Emergence and growth of the contemporary system*. San Francisco: Jossey-Bass Publishers.

Cronin, B. (2001). The mother of all myths. *Library Journal, 126*(3), 144.

DePew, J. N. (1983). The ACRL standards for faculty status: Panacea or Placebo? *College and Research Libraries, 44*(November), 407–413.

Dorman, P. (1996). *Markets and mortality: Economics, dangerous work, and the value of human life*. Cambridge: Cambridge University Press.

Dougherty, R. M. (1993). Faculty status: Playing on a titled field. *Journal of Academic Librarianship, 19*(2), 67.

Ehrenberg, R. G., & Smith, R. S. (1997). *Modern labor economics: Theory and public policy*. Reading, MA: Addison-Wesley.

Ehrenberg, R. G., & Zhang, L. (2004). *Do tenured and tenure-track faculty matter?* NBER Working Paper Series, no. 10695. National Bureau of Economic Research, Cambridge, MA.

English, T. G. (1983). Librarian status in the 89 U.S. academic institutions of the Association of Research Libraries: 1982. *College and Research Libraries, 44*(May), 199–211.

Gariety, B. S., & Shaffer, S. (2001). Wage differentials associated with flextime. *Monthly Labor Review, 124*(March), 68–75.

Gavryck, J. A. (1975). The SUNY librarians' faculty status game. *Journal of Academic Librarianship, 1*(July), 11–13.

George, L. A., & Blixrud, J. (Eds). (2002). *Celebrating seventy years of the Association of Research Libraries, 1932–2002*. Washington, DC: Association of Research Libraries. Available online at: http://www.alr.org/pubscat/pubs/celebrating70/. Accessed December 4, 2004.

Graves, P. E., Arthur, M. M., & Sexton, R. L. (1999). Amenities and the labor earnings function. *Journal of Labor Research, 20*(3), 367–376.

Greene, W. H. (1997). *Econometric analysis*. Upper Saddle River, NJ: Prentice Hall.

Gunderson, M., & Hyatt, D. (2001). Workplace risks and wages: Canadian evidence from alternative models. *Canadian Journal of Economics, 34*(2), 377–395.

Hair, J. F., et al. (1995). *Multivariate data analysis with readings*. Upper Saddle River, NJ: Prentice Hall.

Hamermesh, D. S. (1977). Economic aspects of job satisfaction. In: O. Ashenfelter & W. Oates (Eds), *Essays in labor market and population analysis*. New York: Wiley.

Henry, E. C., Caudle, D. M., & Sullenger, P. (1994). Tenure and turnover in academic libraries. *College and Research Libraries, 55*(September), 429–435.

Henry, W. E. (1911). The academic standing of college library assistants and their relation to the Carnegie foundation. *Bulletin of the American Library Association, 5*(May), 259–269.

Hill, F. E., & Hauptman, R. (1986). A new perspective on faculty status. *College and Research Libraries, 47*(March), 156–159.

Hill, J. S. (1994). Wearing our own clothes: Librarians as faculty. *Journal of Academic Librarianship, 29*(2), 71–76.

Hill, J. S. (2005). Constant vigilance, babelfish, and foot surgery: Perspectives on faculty status and tenure for academic librarians. *Portal: Libraries and the Academy, 5*(1), 7–22.

Horn, J. (1984). Peer review for librarians and its applications in ARL libraries. In: *Academic libraries: Myths and realities* (pp. 125–140). Chicago: Association of College and Research Libraries.

Hovekamp, T. M. (1995). Unionization and job satisfaction among professional library employees in academic research institutions. *College and Research Libraries, 56*(July), 341–350.

Jones, P. J. (1998). Academic graduate work in academic librarianship: Historicizing ACRL's terminal degree statement. *Journal of Academic Librarianship, 24*(6), 437–443.

Lazear, E. P. (1998). *Personnel economics for managers*. New York: Wiley.

Lewis, H. G. (1986). *Union relative wage effects: A survey*. Chicago: University of Chicago Press.

Lively, K. (1992). California colleges worry about how to live with deep state cuts. *Chronicle of Higher Education, 39*(September), A25.

Lucas, C. J. (1994). *American higher education: A history*. New York: St. Martin's Press.

Lucas, R. (1977). Hedonic wage equations and psychic wages in the returns to schooling. *American Economic Review, 67*(4), 549–558.

Machlup, F. (1964). In defense of academic tenure. *AAUP Bulletin, 50*(Summer), 11–124.

Maloy, M. C. (1939). Faculty status of college librarians. *ALA Bulletin, 33*(April), 232–233, 302.

Massman, V. F. (1972). *Faculty status for librarians*. Metuchen, NJ: Scarecrow Press.

McGoldrick, K., & Robst, J. (1996). The effect of worker mobility on compensating wages for earnings risk. *Applied Economics, 28*, 221–232.

McKenzie, R. B. (1996). In defense of academic tenure. *Journal of Institutional and Theoretical Economics, 152*, 325–341.

McPherson, M. S., & Schapiro, M. O. (1999). Tenure issues in higher education. *Journal of Economic Perspectives, 13*(Winter), 85–98.

Merwine v. Board of Trustees for State Institutions of Higher Learning, 754 F. 2d 631, n. 3 (5th Cir. 1985).

Meyer, R. (1990). Earnings gains through the institutionalized standard of faculty status. *Library Administration and Management, 4*(Fall), 184–193.

Meyer, R. (1999). A measure of the impact of tenure. *College and Research Libraries, 60*(March), 110–119.

Mitchell, W. B., & Swieszkowski, L. S. (1985). Publication requirements and tenure approval rates: An issue for academic librarians. *College and Research Libraries, 46*(May), 249–255.

Morlock, R. J. (2000). *Compensating wage differentials in the presence of employer provided health insurance: An empirical inquiry*. Ph.D. dissertation, Wayne State University.

National Center for Education Statistics. (2005). *IPEDS web-based data collection.* Available online at: http://nces.ed.gov/ipeds/webbase.asp. Accessed February 15, 2005.

Park, B., & Riggs, R. (1993). Tenure and promotion: A study of practices by institution type. *Journal of Academic Librarianship, 19*, 72–77.

Payne, J., & Wagner, J. (1984). Librarians, publication, and tenure. *College and Research Libraries*, *45*(March), 133–139.

Pindyck, R. S., & Rubinfeld, D. (1981). *Econometric models and economic forecasts*. New York: McGraw-Hill Book Co.

Raschke, G. K. (2003). Hiring and recruitment practices in academic libraries: Problems and solutions. *Portal: Libraries and the Academy*, *3*(1), 53–67.

Rayman, R., & Goudy, F. (1980). Research and publication requirements in university libraries. *College and Research Libraries*, *41*(January), 43–48.

Reeling, P., & Smith, B. K. (1983). Faculty status: A realistic survey. *New Jersey Libraries*, *16*(Fall), 17–25.

Rosen, S. (1974). Hedonic prices and implicit markets: Product differentiation in pure competition. *Journal of Political Economy*, *82*, 34–55.

Rosenthal, M. (1985). The impact of unions on salaries in public libraries. *Library Quarterly*, *55*(1), 52–70.

Smith, A. (1976). *The wealth of nations*. Chicago: University of Chicago Press.

Stubbs, K. (1980). *ARL library index and quantitative relationships in the ARL*. Washington, DC: Association of Research Libraries.

Studenmund, A. H., & Cassidy, H. (1987). *Using econometrics: A practical guide*. Boston: Little, Brown and Company.

Sykes, C. (1988). *Profscam: Professors and the demise of higher education*. Washington, DC: Regnery Gateway.

Tassin, A. G. (1984). Faculty status for librarians: Progress and perplex. *LLA Bulletin*, *47*(Fall), 83–86.

Van Alstyne, W. (1971). Tenure: A summary, explanation, and 'defense'. *AAUP Bulletin*, *57*(Autumn), 329–351.

Wilson, R. (1998). Contracts replace the tenure track for a growing number of professors. *Chronicle of Higher Education*, June 12.

Wilson, R. (2000). A new campus without tenure considers what it's missing. *Chronicle of Higher Education*, May 12.

Wilson, R., & Walsh, S. (2003). Tears in the fabric of tenure. *Chronicle of Higher Education*, January 10, p. A8.

Zoghi, C. E. (2000). *Labor markets in higher education*. Ph.D. dissertation, University of Texas, Austin.

APPENDIX

Survey of Tenure and Academic Librarians

Date: Contact:
Institution:

The following survey is being conducted as a part of my dissertation research. Participation is voluntary. The survey will take less than 10 min to complete. I will ask several questions concerning the use of faculty status and tenure in your library.

The 1987 ACRL guidelines governing the appointment, promotion, and tenure for academic librarians defined tenure as "an institutional commitment to permanent and continuous employment ... tenure (continuous employment) shall be available to all librarians and in accordance with the tenure provisions of all faculty of the institution."

Using this definition, please answer the following questions:

1. Do librarians at your institution have traditional faculty rank and status (e.g., assistant professor, associate professor, etc.)?
   ____ Yes ____ No

2. For the period 1989–1998 were librarians eligible for tenure at your library?
   ____ Yes ____ No

   If tenure eligibility changed during this 10-year period please indicate the years for which librarians were eligible for tenure.

3. For the period 1989–1998 were librarians included in a collective bargaining unit or union?
   ____ Yes ____ No

   If union representation changed during this 10-year period, please indicate the years for which librarians were represented by a union.

4. Are librarians at your institution required to have an additional advanced degree for appointment at the entry level?
   ____ Yes, a Masters in addition to the MLS
   ____ No, an additional degree is not required
   ____ Other:

5. Are librarians at your institution required to have an additional advanced degree for tenure?
____ Yes, an additional Masters degree
____ Yes, a Ph.D.
____ No, an additional degree is not required
____ Other:

6. Do librarians at your institution have research requirements similar to the academic/teaching faculty?
____ Yes ____ No

7. For the period 1989–1998, how would you rate the research requirements for librarians at your institution?
____ Librarians are not required to conduct research.
____ Research requirements have increased over time.
____ Research requirements have remained the same over time.

Thank you for your response to this short survey. Your assistance is greatly appreciated and will be duly acknowledged in my completed dissertation. Results of the survey will be made available to all participants.

Approved by the Mississippi State University Institutional Board.

THE PROFESSIONAL DEVELOPMENT OF SMALL COMMUNITY LIBRARIANS IN TEXAS: A QUALITATIVE STUDY OF THE FEMALE EXPERIENCE

Belinda Boon

ABSTRACT

In 2005, a qualitative study was undertaken to explore the educational events, personal experiences, and job circumstances that a selected group of non-MLS library directors working in small Texas communities believed were significant in contributing to their professional development. Face-to-face interviews were conducted with 17 female library directors working in Texas communities with populations of 25,000 or less using open-ended questions, and interviews were recorded and transcribed for later analysis. Four major topic areas relating to the professionalization of non-MLS library directors were identified from the data: (1) job satisfaction, including library work as spiritual salvation, librarianship and the ethic of caring, making a difference in the community, and pride in professional identity; (2) professional development, including hiring narratives, continuing education and lifelong learning, mentoring and professional development, and the importance of the MLS degree; (3) challenges facing small community library directors, including

Advances in Library Administration and Organization, Volume 26, 209–264
ISSN: 0732-0671/doi:10.1016/S0732-0671(08)00205-8

gender-based discrimination, resistance from local governing officials, and geographic isolation; and (4) guidelines for success, including understanding the community, becoming part of the community, making the library the heart of the community, business and managerial skills, and people and customer service skills.

BACKGROUND

Since the inception of public librarianship in the mid-nineteenth century, librarians have worked collectively and individually to establish the professional status of the field. To become a professional librarian, one must earn a master's degree in library and information science (MLS), preferably in a program of higher education accredited by the American Library Association. Yet, in small communities of 25,000 or less – which constitute 79% of America's public libraries – an MLS degree is not required of library directors. Most small community library directors are women who grew up and now reside in their communities. Non-MLS female library directors may have a high school, college, 2-year business school, or master's degree in another field, and generally are expected by their governing entities to work part-time for lower pay in what is often perceived as a clerical position.

Although state library agencies in most US states are responsible for the professional training and education of small community librarians through continuing education events and programs, participation in this training by the librarians is voluntary and not mandated by law. Despite recent efforts to create a unified approach to training,[1] continuing education programs are developed by individual state library agencies and do not conform to any national standards. Consequently, the professional development process for non-MLS library directors working in small communities is inconsistent, and little is known about the elements that influence this process. To date, only one non-published qualitative study (Bushing, 1995) has attempted to define the formal and informal elements that contribute to the professional development of non-MLS female library directors; however, participants in that study worked in rural communities with populations of 5,000 or less.[2] The study reported on in this paper provides data about the personal experiences of 17 Texas public library directors[3] working in small communities, including some rural areas. Data resulting from this study may aid library consultants at the regional and state level to develop more effective continuing education events, and can provide useful information to other women considering a career as a small community library director.

Small Community Library Directors

Small community public libraries tend to be managed by well-meaning and dedicated individuals – mainly underpaid women between the ages of 40 and 60 working part-time – who love to read, have a high regard for literacy and education, and enjoy helping others (Vavrek, 1984, p. 12; Flatley, 2000, p. 9). Most of these women do not have a formal library education, and often get their jobs because of their previous experiences in education, management, or working with computers. In many instances people in small communities still view the librarian's job as a sort of glorified clerk position, yet non-MLS library directors are expected to perform professional work such as preparing and justifying budgets, hiring and managing staff, building and maintaining collections, and developing policies. These "non-professional" librarians also may have to handle materials challenges from individuals or groups in the community; confront inappropriate behavior or computer usage by children or adults; and navigate a hostile political environment when working with their board, city council, or county commissioners. Non-MLS library directors working in small communities face many of the same challenges as their degreed counterparts working in large urban and suburban areas, but often lack professional knowledge and skills coming into the job.

In Texas, many non-MLS library directors seek out training and continuing education opportunities provided by the ten regional library offices of the Texas Library System[4] and the state library to gain the necessary competencies and skills. Often, a mentor or predecessor will informally train a non-MLS librarian in library procedures and operations. As a result, many small community library directors become competent librarians and managers without earning a MLS,[5] becoming "librarians by experience rather than by training" (Plummer, 1899, 1976, p. 2). Moreover, since many of these librarians were born or raised in the communities they serve, local residents perceive them as a member of their community – a friend and neighbor – as well as a knowledgeable information provider. But in the larger field of librarianship, their degreed colleagues do not consider non-MLS library directors to be professional librarians or even library professionals.

The process of professional development is essential for library managers in all types of libraries, but is particularly important for small community librarians. Non-MLS library directors often work in geographically isolated areas without the support of colleagues and the larger profession, but, as managers and librarians, they must still provide quality library services and handle complex management issues.

METHODOLOGY

The Texas study attempted to discover what elements in educational events, personal experiences, or job circumstances that a select group of library directors working in small Texas communities believed to be significant in contributing to their professional development. Much of the previous research about rural librarians, in particular studies conducted by the Center for Rural Librarianship at Clarion University, focused on the needs of and challenges inherent in rural communities (i.e., communities of 5,000 or fewer people). Prior studies relied mainly on survey data to determine the circumstances within which small community libraries operate and challenges facing library staff. To date, less than a handful of qualitative studies, including the one conducted by Bushing (1995), have explored the attitudes and perceptions of the librarians working in small communities. None have been conducted in Texas prior to this study.

Based on my experience working with small community library directors during 10 years as a continuing education consultant for the Texas State Library & Archives Commission, I anticipated that external influences – such as challenges related to the authority and competence of small community library directors because of their gender and the assistance of mentors – would emerge during the interviews as significant factors in some participants' professional development. In addition, I assumed that internal influences such as the librarians' personal characteristics – learner motivation, perseverance, determination, and self-confidence – also would influence the study participants' professional development. I also antici-pated that librarians in the study would demonstrate their agency and authority in a number of ways, such as choosing to participate in continuing education workshops and programs in an effort to achieve some level of professional certification.

In the summer of 2005, 17 female library directors working in small Texas communities were interviewed to determine what factors had contributed to their professional development. Fourteen of the librarians interviewed did not have MLS degrees. Specifically, the study explored educational events, personal experiences, and job circumstances these librarians believed to be significant factors in their professional development. A stratified random sampling technique (Miles & Huberman, 1994, p. 32) was used to identify two library directors from each of the ten regional library systems constituting the Texas Library System. Data indicating libraries with service populations of less than 25,000 and managed by directors without MLS degrees were obtained from current (2003) statistics provided by the Texas State Library & Archives Commission. The interview data were analyzed to identify patterns or factors contributing to the process of professionalization, focusing mainly on non-MLS librarians working in small Texas communities.

The study relied on naturalistic research methods to obtain narrative data addressing the research question. Using an interview protocol, I asked each librarian in the study about her experiences as a female library director using open-ended questions. Topics of inquiry included hiring experiences, job satisfaction, challenges experienced as a woman in a position of authority, events that influenced her professional development, what advice she would give to first-time small community library directors, and what it meant to her to be a librarian (for a complete list of questions, see Appendix B). Interviews were recorded on audiotape and as digital recordings. Data emerging from the interviews indicated many common attitudes, experiences, and perspectives shared by the study participants despite differences of economic status, educational background, job experience, involvement with professional organizations, geographic region, and local government and community support.

After an independent transcriber transcribed 20 hours of recorded interviews, both the study participants and I reviewed the interview narratives for errors and omissions. I further analyzed the interview data to determine patterns and themes relating to the study objectives, which resulted in the coding of 250 quotations. After an initial data analysis, I developed a verification form listing themes and sub-themes emerging from the narrative data (see Appendix A). Study participants were asked to review and give feedback on the verification form. Study participant feedback included indicating agreement or disagreement with each of the themes and sub-themes and adding further comments. Study participants also were instructed to add additional information, if desired, to the interview transcripts. Allowing the study participants to review and respond to the interviews and themes created a process of triangulation for the study and gave the librarians an opportunity to verify, comment on, and modify my initial analysis. Themes were modified based on the participants' input as "indicators of evidence."

The Librarians

The library directors interviewed for the Texas study were as diverse as the regions they represented. They ranged in age from late 30s to nearly 80, and their education levels included high school, business school, some college, and in one case, a master's degree in theatre. Three of the 17 study participants were Hispanic, reflecting the statewide percentage of Hispanic small community library directors in Texas (15%) identified in a pilot study I conducted in 2004. The remaining participants were Caucasian. All but two librarians were born or raised in the communities they now work in, and all but one had been a librarian for more than 5 years. Some participants had husbands and young children; others were widowed, divorced, or single. The personalities expressed in the interviews were gregarious, outgoing, friendly, warm, reticent, detail-oriented, scattered, unassuming, proud, engaging, abrasive, funny, serious, energetic, and apathetic, making it impossible to generate a stereotype of a "typical" small community librarian. Nevertheless, with one exception all of the librarians shared three outstanding qualities:

Sensitivity to the needs of a small community:

> Well, small communities are completely different than, like, a large town, so I would say that you definitely have to make it personable. You can't just be, just, "Okay, here's your book. Here, check this out." And, you know, you do have to make it a personal place to come.

Dedication to their job:

> You gotta put a lot into it. You've got to put a lot, a lot of thought, a lot of feeling, and a lot of caring into it. You can't just do it without that.

> Well, being crazy helps a whole lot to start out with 'cause you don't mind working yourself to death, and you like what you're doin'.

An enormous feeling of gratification from helping others:

> And so you get such a sense of satisfaction, you know, such a gratification from people. It is a re*ward* you know, every *day* because if nothing else you've helped someone learn to read.

> It's a chance to make a *difference* ... You never know who you're gonna touch or where they're gonna go.

> *Everybody* is an enrichment to me – everybody. No matter if they're even surly and angry, you know, they're offering me something.

Indicators of Evidence

The following indicators of evidence summarize the themes emerging from the interview process and confirmed by study participants who reviewed the Theme Verification Form:

(1) *Evidence of job satisfaction* – Factors that have contributed to the personal and professional satisfaction of women managing small community public libraries.
(2) *Positive influences on professional development* – The experiences women managing small community public libraries perceive as having contributed to their professional development.
(3) *Challenges facing small community librarians* – The nature of the challenges facing women managing small community libraries, including gender-based discrimination related to the women's authority.
(4) *Guidelines for success* – Qualities and characteristics that women managing small community libraries believe are essential for successful librarianship.

Table 1 summarizes the study themes and sub-themes described as "indicators of evidence" in the *Findings* section of this paper.

FINDINGS

Findings in the Texas study reveal much about the caring behavior of female librarians. Librarianship often is thought of as a caring profession that relies on human contact and interaction. The role of caring in librarianship is even more evident in small communities where library patrons are also neighbors, friends, and even relatives. The prevalence of female librarians in small communities may in part be due to the low pay and the perception of librarianship as unskilled labor by local governments, but this prevalence also may be the result of people's perceptions that women are more caring than men, and, therefore, better able to fill a public service role.

Findings in the Texas study support Bushing's (1995) conclusions that the concept of being a librarian arises not only from the self-perceptions of non-MLS librarians working in rural communities but also from "the various definitions, expectations and stereotypes imposed by family, friends, communities, and others in the library community – peers, MLS librarians, consultants, and educators" (Bushing, 1995, p. 74). For example, the library

Table 1. Themes and Sub-themes Identified in the Texas Study.

Evidence of job satisfaction
   Library work as spiritual salvation
   Librarianship and the ethic of caring
   Making a difference in the community
   Pride in professional identity
Positive influences on professional development
   Hiring narratives
     Accidental librarianship
     Intentional librarianship
   Continuing education and lifelong learning
   Mentoring and professional development
     Networking with peers
     Regional library system staff
     Other mentoring relationships
   Importance of the MLS degree
Challenges facing small community librarians
   Gender-based discrimination
   Resistance from local governing officials
   Geographic isolation
Guidelines for success
   Understanding the community
   Becoming part of the community
   Making the library the heart of the community
   Business and managerial skills
   People and customer service skills

directors interviewed in Bushing's study perceived the following factors as contributing to the process of their professionalization:

- help from others (such as mentors) and networking with peers
- relevant continuing education topics
- experienced educators with good communication skills and knowledge of circumstances in a small community library
- support from local government and community and
- organizational skills, self-confidence, and assertiveness

Participants in the Texas study identified at least four of these same factors – help from others and networking, continuing education, support from the community and local government, and personal qualities such as organizational skills – as contributing to their professional development.

Evidence of Job Satisfaction: I Just Love Being a Librarian!

Job satisfaction is a major theme emerging from the Texas study, reflecting one aspect of professionalization: a positive self-image related to one's work. As the interviews progressed, a pattern of personal satisfaction related to the job became clear. All of the librarians in the study expressed positive feelings associated with their work resulting from the daily variety and diversity of the job. The following statement is typical:

> I have a lot of fun working here and there's just lots of things. It's never dull and [there is] always something you can laugh about everyday, and sometimes there's things that you want to cry about. But you do, you know, it's good. It's a good place to work.

Another librarian working in a community with a dwindling population remarked, "Well, in the thirty-two years I've been here, no two days has [sic] ever been alike."

Study participants frequently commented that they enjoyed being librarians and had difficulty envisioning themselves doing any other kind of work. The following comment from another librarian illustrates a common sentiment expressed by librarians in their interviews:

> [Being a librarian] was the highlight of my life, besides my two kids, and my husband. I couldn't have thought of a better position. I always wanted to be a librarian, and I can't think of anything else I'd rather do.

Library Work as Spiritual Salvation

Several librarians in the study described a strong attachment to their work that might be thought of as a kind of spiritual salvation. Study participants who expressed strong emotional attachments to their work also spoke of severe personal losses they had experienced, usually the death of a spouse or parent. These librarians articulated a fervent sense of gratitude for their work and, in some cases, an almost desperate desire to cling to their jobs to keep from being overwhelmed with and immobilized by grief. Comments like, "It's been real good for me. You know, my husband died, so … it, you know, it seems like it's become my *life*" and "It kept me *sane*. It kept me from going *crazy*. 'Cause I had that money to raise and I had that *[work]* to do" indicate these librarians' delicate mental and emotional states and the succor they gained from their work. The quotes below clearly reveal these librarians' perceptions that their work provided them with a concrete sense of purpose and a reason to continue participating in the life of the community rather than withdrawing from public view:

> I don't know what I'd *do* without the library ... during the last six years of my life if I hadn't had this library to *come* to ... it would've been very hard. Because this was kinda my balance, *this* is where I could *fix* things where I couldn't fix [my husband's terminal illness]. So I could come down here and I could make something work.

> So it's, you know, kinda my world. My husband died. That left me, you know, by myself ... so, you know, my life just kind of revolves around the *lib*rary. I get to where I can't *talk* unless they talk about books ... and the library.

> I just can't *im*agine not being here. I thank God every day for me being able to get up and get across here. And, as long as I can, I, you know, I want to be [at] it because I'm, I'm interested in the library.

Not everyone participating in the study agreed with the premise that library work could offer a kind of spiritual salvation to directors who were grieving over the death of loved ones. A few study participants disagreed with this premise on their Theme Verification Forms, including one librarian who had lost her mother – whom she was very close to emotionally and geographically – within the previous 6 months. However, this particular librarian currently is happily married and enjoys a close and supportive relationship with her husband, suggesting that it is the loss of one's primary emotional support that causes a woman to seek solace in her work.

The sense of spiritual salvation from library work seems to occur more often with women who have lost the person who provides the majority of their emotional support, whether this is a husband, in the case of married women, or a parent, in the case of unmarried women. Yet mourning is not the only condition that supports the sense of spiritual salvation found in one's work. Also essential to this experience are a sense of duty and responsibility to the job on the part of the librarian, and a sense of personal satisfaction that comes from the feeling that she makes a difference in the community. Having a profession or vocation offers strong emotional and mental support to a person who has lost the focus of her feelings and efforts.

Librarianship and the Ethic of Caring

Librarianship often is described as both a caring and helping profession, and nowhere is this more evident that in a small town. One librarian interviewed in the current study summed up this attitude of caring by saying, "In a small town, people care so much." Another recent proclamation of this label comes from the deputy director of the Harris County Public Libraries system in Houston speaking about relief efforts by local librarians for library patrons displaced by hurricanes Katrina and Rita:

> The incredible part of how well Houston area librarians responded is that they do this work every day. The extraordinary response is all in a day's work for the library community. We are a caring profession – we help people (Meraz, 2005, p. 90).

Most of the librarians interviewed in the Texas study articulated feelings of caring and concern for library patrons, especially children, illustrated by the following comment from a librarian working in a geographically isolated community: "And you've got to love your little town. You've got to want to help those kids get educated in your own town." This same librarian also expressed strong feelings of caring for her patrons in another remark:

> You get attached to your – I have a lot of elderly patrons, and you just get so attached to them. They're so nice, and you just, you just fall in love with them. Well, you get attached to a lot of the patrons and you are concerned about 'em.

The librarian quoted above clearly demonstrates the caring role of librarianship in the following statement:

> From the little kids that, that want me over there to sit down with them and read a book to the high school kids ... and then the older people ... that just want to talk about the day's events. You know, you get to know ... who expects what from you. Combine all of that, and it makes your day.

Many study participants described the purpose of the library as helping the community in some way, either through satisfying patrons' information needs or, more often, by improving patrons' – and by extension, the community's – social welfare. All of the librarians in the current study clearly articulated the library's helping role, and related the helping aspect of library work to their own self-esteem and sense of accomplishment:

> You know, it does make you feel good when you know that [the patrons are] really working hard at [improving themselves] and that you have something in here that can help them. And that makes your day, too. It makes you feel as good as it does them.

> Well, I think it has such great rewards because you can see the people you're helping, and in life, the goal – you should always be helping somebody.

> I just think it's a, a great way to help people and enrich them and enlighten them, or help them do all that for themselves, actually. Really, you're just giving them the mechanisms to go on and showing them how to use what's there, help them figure it out. And that's that.

As evidenced in the quotes above, library directors in the current study view their roles as librarians in terms of caring and helping members of their communities. In one interview with a librarian working very near a large metropolitan city, the ethic of caring took on a quality of social work:

> I'll tell you, the people that I reach out to the most and that's when they come in looking the most dejected. You know, they're obviously substance abusers, maybe they're homeless, they're, you know, their situation is worn on their person. And, you know, I just go out of the way to welcome them, let them know that we're only there because they've come needing help, and really try to show them what we have that can help them.

The librarian quoted above described herself as a very caring person. She also elaborated on how their caring roles gave her and her staff a sense of personal satisfaction and fulfillment:

> It's the people. It's the people that come in, and they need something and, you know, we work with them individually to determine what they need and when we're able to give them that and give it to them completely and with a good attitude and that, you know, we're here to help you. That's what makes – it makes me feel good, and I must say that my entire staff embraces that.

In the comment below, this same librarian articulates self-knowledge about her propensity to care for others:

> It's very personal to me, to me as a person. I really see it as a way to reach strangers' lives. You know, people that, they come to me and then it's my opportunity to show them what is here. And I … personally, I receive a lot of gratification from it.

Librarianship, along with the vocations of teaching and nursing, is founded on an ethic of caring. Librarians, particularly in small communities where people often know or are related to each other, often become personally involved in the lives of their patrons, sometimes unwillingly. The following quote from a former hair dresser who is now a librarian illustrates her sense of humor as she describes people's tendencies to tell the librarian all about their personal lives:

> They don't really want my opinion, but they do want me to listen. I have people come in and, oh, they want to tell me about the argument they had with their husband and how they settled that or not settled it or, you know, their in-laws are complaining about their troubles, you know, and what's bothering them. They want somebody to listen to them.

The study participants often described feelings of concern for their patrons, and the satisfaction they gained from their patrons' response to this caring behavior. Noddings (1984, p. 47) describes situations in which people perceive bonds or relationships with others as "chains of caring," and notes that caring behavior:

> ... is conditioned not by a host of narrow and rigidly defined principles but by a loosely defined ethic that molds itself in situations and has a proper regard for human affections, weaknesses, and anxieties (Noddings, 1984, p. 25).

The passage above has implications for the ways in which small community librarians interact with people in their communities in a professional capacity. The librarians in the study noted their willingness to remain open to each patron's needs and provide assistance on a level to best meet those needs. Additionally, most of the study participants expressed affection toward the people in their communities, in particular for people who visited the library. Study participants identified young children, the elderly, non-English speaking populations, people who actively seek their assistance in the library, and those who seem "lost" in the library as deserving of special care from library staff.

Making a Difference in the Community
Closely related to the ethic of caring described in the previous section is the idea of "making a difference." Most of the study participants felt that making a difference in the community through improving the intellectual and social skills of the citizens was of paramount importance:

> When you see those people it's like, well, that's why I work here, you know. I do make a difference. It's kind of like a teacher. You make a difference here. That's the way I feel.

> Especially since I've been here almost 12 years, watching the kids grow up and seeing them grow, and seeing them progress, and seeing them become better citizens and better people because of their library experience and because of what they read. That type of thing. That's where the fulfillment comes in.

> It's a rewarding [job]. I'll tell you that because I – most days I can go home feeling good about things. Very seldom do I not feel, you know, good about today.

> That is the goal of this library. We want to help those kids graduate from high school. How do we do that? We want them to be better citizens. How do we do that? *We get them involved in reading.* We get them involved in reading.

Almost every librarian in the study expressed feelings of satisfaction and fulfillment resulting from "having made a difference in the community" by providing library services. The narratives reveal that these feelings most often arise from giving children a safe place to congregate after school or from contributing to the education of children, helping adults improve themselves by locating needed information, and acting as an intermediary who connects people in the community (usually adults) with the civic and social services provided by other agencies and organizations. Some of the study participants adamantly emphasized – through their voice inflections and choice of words – how much it means to them to have contributed to the improvement and well being of their fellow citizens. "That's why I work here ... I *do* make a difference" is a sentiment often expressed in the interviews, along with "you never know who you're gonna to touch or where they're gonna go."

A few of the study participants also described the feelings that members of the community have for library staff, illustrated in the following comment from a 40-something librarian who emphasized the importance of reciprocal caring throughout her interview: "People come in the library, Belinda, because ... they want to. So they have good attitudes. They have good, good feelings for you." Another librarian articulated the reciprocal nature of the caring relationship between librarian and library patrons when she described the reactions of a "winter Texan" to the personal service she provided:

> And so I helped her set up her browser. I stepped her through it, and then she said, "Oh, thank you so much!" And, "You went beyond the call of duty!" And so they gave me that card and a plant. And they stayed for, like, about a month. So we have a lot of that return.

It is common for a person involved in a caring profession like librarianship to feel that her work has contributed to the well being and growth of her community, by helping one person at a time. This phenomenon is apparent in small towns where the librarian identifies herself as a member of the community and considers her patrons also to be her friends and neighbors. In small communities, "everybody knows everybody else." This sense of closeness and relationship, coupled with the civic responsibility inherent in being a community leader and an intrinsically caring nature on the part of the librarian, engenders in her a sense of accountability for the well being of the community, both for individuals and for the community as a whole.

Pride in Professional Identity – "It's the Library Lady!"
Most of the librarians in the study expressed pleasure at being identified as the librarian by people in the community, especially children. Remarks like, "Oh, it is great 'cause, you know, whenever I'm going anywhere, they recognize *me* as the *librarian*, you know" and "When I go to get something at the Legion or when I go to church, uh, or I'm just out and about or I'm with my son, 'Oh, you're the librarian'" were typical. When asked to *Tell me*

about your experiences as a person of authority in your community, study participants from all areas of the state spoke with pride about how children recognized them as "the library lady" during their comings and goings around town:

> In the last two years the elementary school has brought the third-graders in during their library hours. At the end of the school year, they'd bring them over here on a little field trip. And so, when I would see them, they were especially, "You're the *library* lady. I re*member*"

> When I walk around the town and someone's little kid doesn't know my name, but he'll go, "There's the library lady!" It makes me feel like I've contributed to them.

> I'll have kids look at me and, you know, if they're by themselves they'll usually go to mamma or daddy or whoever they're with, and I see some of them tugging on slacks or skirts or whatever, and they point. And some of them will come and they'll say, "Yeah. He said it was the library lady."

Several of the librarians interviewed for the current study spoke of the responsibility they felt as a public servant to set a positive example for their community even in their personal behavior. This is evident in the following comment:

> Who I am and how I present myself is important because I am now looked up to and a point of that community. And I will try to keep my life and who I am and my understanding in a respectable frame of mind and always try to remember that who I am – it helps you keeps your temper a little bit.

The study participant quoted above also articulated this sense of responsibility to the community when she said, "There's a *trusting* factor that I feel is *very* important." Working in a town nearly 300 miles away, another librarian quietly echoed this belief when she declared that the "librarian position [is] a sacred trust and a great responsibility" (Theme Verification Form response). Her comment exemplifies the spirit of dedication inherent in small community librarianship. Yet another librarian articulated her pleasure with the sense of authority she gained from her position as the library director:

> ... you know, I'm listened to. I, you know, they pay attention, so ... that's good. That's a good feeling of having respect of your coworkers or your peers ... so that's been a good thing.

In a small community, the librarian is as much of an icon as the teacher, the fire marshal, the mayor, the coach, and the police chief. Participants in the Texas study indicated that they enjoyed and appreciated being identified as librarians. The librarians in this study did not refer to themselves as information specialists, information brokers, or information architects, and were not ashamed to be identified with what the literature sometimes terms the "L-word." Rather, these librarians reported gaining status and respect from others through their roles as librarians.

Positive Influence on Professional Development

The process of becoming a library professional is a complex progression that includes many facets, beginning with hiring narratives, that describe how an individual came into her job as a library director. Other factors that influence professional development – continuing education, mentoring from other professionals, and peer interaction – also are discussed in this section.

Hiring Narratives

In an effort to make the study participants more comfortable while being interviewed and recorded, and to encourage the librarians to talk freely about their experiences, I began each interview with a general, open-ended question about the librarian's background, *Tell me how you became a librarian, and how you became the library director.* None of the participants hesitated to answer the question, and many began their narratives with a smile as they recalled the events leading up to their current employment. Several of the librarians expressed a love of books and reading that manifested at a very early age; others recounted how they had, almost serendipitously, "fallen into" their jobs as librarians. The stories of how each study participant came to be a librarian are significant in that they provide insights into the attitudes these librarians have toward their work. These attitudes may shift over time as the librarian begins to identify with her role as a library professional and perceive herself as a community leader.

Accidental Librarianship. Bushing (1995) describes the phenomenon of landing a job as a rural library director without knowing beforehand that it would become a vocation as "accidental librarianship." She observed that in many cases a woman would apply for a general job with the city or county without intentionally seeking a job as a library director. This phenomenon also arose in the Texas study. Many of the participants described their experience of becoming the library director as happening "by pure accident" or from being "in the right place at the right time." One librarian in the study commented, "Yeah, so it was like, you know, the job – I tell people the job found me. I wasn't looking for it. The job found me." Another librarian joked, "That's how I got my job. I was just ... sittin' on the *cor*ner one day and *got* it!"

Based on the content of many informal conversations with small community librarians during workshops and other continuing education events when I worked as a continuing education consultant, I expected to hear a number of study participants describe how they became a librarian as an accident or fluke. This assumption is supported by the narrative data gathered during the interviews, which often describe a woman applying with the city or county governing entity for part-time work in order to earn extra money or as a way to keep busy. Several study participants mentioned how their relationships with others, such as library board members or previous librarians, were instrumental in obtaining their positions. One such story came from a librarian who held a master's degree in theatre and had worked primarily in financial institutions who said, "I've always loved to read, and the lady that had been library director here for like 20 years virtually handpicked me as her successor." Another study participant, a warm and friendly elderly librarian working in a town of fewer than 900 people, explained it this way: "When the librarian – the other one – was sick down there, well, they [city officials] asked me to come fill in for her." Following are similar narratives from other librarians in the study:

> I saw the position for desk clerk advertised in the local newspaper, and so I came and filled out an application just like everybody else and was hired for that position. I think probably through the influence of one of the library board members, who I knew personally, although I didn't know it at the time.

> I had gone to city hall one day and just put in an application as a general – just, as working. And they said they really didn't have any openings. But then when I turned around about two or three weeks later I was downtown and we were getting ready to build the square for Jambo*ree,* which is a celebration, and the librarian came out of City Hall and she said, "Are *you* still looking for a job?" and I said, "Yes I *am*" and she said, "Well, I'm gonna have a part-time opening at the *li*brary." So that's how I got my job.

> I had worked for the school for twelve years, and I had just quit the school and the librarian wanted to retire, and she asked me if I would be interested. I'd come in and we'd visit and talk, and then I started substituting for her and filling in when she needed time off or whatever.

Most of the study participants recounted that they were seeking any available clerical position, and had not intended to become the library director. A few of the study participants were hired as library assistants or circulation staff and worked in the library for several years before applying for the director position when it became available. One librarian described being pursued for the director's job by members of the library board. She finally relented in the face of persistent entreaties by board members and agreed to fill out an application "in pencil." This woman might be better described as a "reluctant librarian" than as an accidental librarian.

A number of study participants described their hiring experiences as "falling into the job" or "being at the right place at the right time," indicating an element of serendipity or chance in the hiring process. This phenomenon could be described as "occupation encountering." At least one librarian attributed landing her job to the intervention of Providence, but most of the librarians interviewed credited the assistance of others in the community with whom they had some kind of established relationship, however casual. The hiring narratives of several of the librarians in this study corroborate findings in Bushing (1995) study concerning accidental librarians:

> None ... indicated that they had any particular interest in working in the library before the job opportunity was available to them. They did not seem to have any prior knowledge of what a librarian does beyond checking out books, nor did they have any ambitions to become a librarian. Their first initiation into librarianship and what a librarian is or does came only after they were hired (Bushing, 1995, pp. 79–81).

Accidental librarianship is a common hiring experience reported by the small community librarians in the Texas study. Although small community library directors in general may seem to find their jobs in a haphazard fashion, the study participants' long tenure in their jobs (between 3 and 40 years) suggests that "accidental" librarianship may be the most advantageous means of filling library director positions in small towns.

Intentional Librarianship.   Only a small number of the study participants indicated an aspiration to be librarians from an early age, although many recalled fond experiences of visiting libraries when they were children. The three librarians in the intentional librarianship category all related having positive childhood experiences with libraries or librarians. One of the participants became a librarian at the same library she went to while growing up, where her mother had been the director for 23 years. Two other librarians spoke of wanting to be librarians since their young childhood, and one described in detail the encounter with a bookmobile collection and librarian that became the defining moment of her life's direction. Still, these librarians were in the minority, and all seem to have experienced a positive encounter with a librarian at a very early age.

One librarian in the study, a woman who originally earned an education degree and went into teaching because she could not afford to move to other regions or states to go to library school, made the following comment:

> I couldn't have thought of a better position. I always wanted to be a librarian ... So, if I'd had a first choice, it would've been to be a librarian. So I think that worked out really well.

Another librarian explained how a negative experience with a librarian she had as a child made her determined to provide a different level of service for the children in her community:

> Well, I wanted to change it because I had had a bad experience as a child ... with a librarian. I have dyslexia. I was a little behind on everything, but I loved to read, I loved to study. But I had went and took some, picked some books up that were below my – [I] was probably [in] junior high, and they were probably *early* chapter books, maybe even some children's books, picture books, but it was on a specific study. I had took 'em up to the desk and she looked at me and she said, "Aren't these a little too young for you?" And I, of course, defended myself and said, "No." But at that point in time, I never went back. That didn't discourage me from learning, but it did discourage me from using the library.

One small community library director working in a growing bedroom community near a large urban center described the powerful impact of her first encounter with bookmobile library services in rural Washington state:

> One day I was out playing and the bookmobile came. And they drove up in the yard and there was this great big van and my mother came out of the house and we were invited *into* the bookmobile. And I was *surrounded by books*, it was the most *exciting*, truly the most exciting thing that had ever happened to me. That was my first adventure with libraries and library books and it was a focal point in *my life*. And I always wanted to be a person who worked on the bookmobile.

This inspiring quote is an anecdotal example of one woman's compelling drive to become a librarian.

Continuing Education and Lifelong Learning

Prior research has established that most small community librarians will not pursue master's degrees due to geographic distance, family commitments, inadequate education, limited time and funds, or for other reasons (Bushing, 1995; Fitchen, 1991; O'Neill, 2005; Vavrek, 1980, 1982a, 1982b, 1984, 1990, 1997, 2004a, 2004b; Zaltman & Duncan, 1977). The experiences of one librarian in the current study reflect these findings:

> I always wanted to be a librarian. But when I was going to college, it was in the '70s, and it was like, you had to go to East Texas or New Mexico. But it just wasn't accessible. So,

that was the reason I went into education because I thought, well, that was pretty close. And, with being one of four children, I didn't have that option of going off that far to go to school.

Yet, many small community librarians, hired for management positions but possessing little or no practical library experience, find themselves desperately in need of training and instruction. Librarians interviewed in the present study often cited well-established continuing education programs offered by the Texas Library System and the Texas State Library & Archives Commission as being essential to their professional development. Typical comments included, "I couldn't have done this job without that training, by any means ... I've learned *every*thing I know about libraries from those workshops" and "But without that additional training, I could not have done it 'cause you can't, I mean, you're flying basically by the seat of your pants." This latter librarian also remarked:

> Yes, undoubtedly, it's been the training I've received through the State Library and the Library Systems, the Texas Library System. Without that ... I, I would not have been qualified to do the job that I've done.

The Small Library Management Training Program, an ongoing, basic skills program for non-MLS librarians developed by the Texas State Library & Archives Commission, was singled out by many of the study participants as being a significant factor in their professional development. Responses to the program ranged from complimentary to enthusiastic:

> Yes, and I got in on the first round of those [Small Library Management Training Program workshops] which I found *extremely* helpful. Those were all wonderful.

> And I also was extremely fortunate when I came in January of '94 that in March of '94 is when the Small Library Management Program [started]. I was the first graduate from that, and it was a huge help.

> The small library management [program] – I felt like – I thought, "It should just have my name on it." "Dorothy, this is for you." "Dorothy, welcome! This is for you. We made this *just* for you."

Also noteworthy in the interview comments is the enthusiasm for ongoing learning shown by the small community librarians in the study. Several participants spoke of their willingness to learn through any available avenue, be it workshops, colleagues and mentors, listserv postings, library patrons, or mass media. One librarian working in a community of nearly 10,000 that is rapidly being subsumed by a major metropolitan area stated frankly, "I'm not shy about asking for help. I can really admit that I don't know. I don't have a problem with that. That I don't know and let me see what I can find out." The quote below from another librarian working in a community of similar size indicates both her inner drive and willingness to learn and her ability to disseminate useful information:

> And being a small library, that's what you have to do. You have to say, "Okay, let me go to this workshop and pick something out of it." "Well, okay, what can I learn? What can this person teach me? What can *this* person teach me?" You have to be willing to be taught.

Mentoring and Professional Development

Almost every librarian interviewed for the current study credited outside help for her success as a library director. The library literature identifies mentoring as a key element in the professional development of librarians working in academic, public, school, and special environments. Mentoring is especially important for non-MLS librarians working in small community public libraries, particularly for new librarians who are unfamiliar with library procedures and the professional expectations of the larger library profession. As Burrington (1993) pointed out:

> ... mentors teach skills, give advice, provide encouragement by example, and help those they mentor to develop sound judgement and gain confidence. They pass on their enthusiasm to those they guide. They encourage personal growth and development" (Burrington, 1993, p. 226).

Field's (2001) observations sum up the need for mentoring for non-MLS librarians when she states, "This rapidly changing information environment has increased the necessity for developing mentoring activities, making them more available to all information professionals" (Field, 2001, p. 270). Although librarians in the western, northern, and southern regions of Texas more often indicated that they relied on the assistance of regional system consulting staff for instruction in library procedures, small community librarians in all areas of the state cited assistance from mentors as a key element in their professional development. One librarian spoke of being "hand picked" by the librarian she succeeded; another credited the person who hired her with her success as a library director; still another expressed gratitude toward professional librarians and others that she could "lean on" and who would help her learn to do her job.

Study participants distinguished between assistance from peers – with whom they felt themselves to be on equal footing – with assistance from mentors, those they considered to be in positions of greater knowledge and positions of authority. One librarian's comment that her mentors "treat me as an equal, and I'm not one" illustrates a common type of positioning expressed by the librarians in their interviews. Study participants credited mentors with getting them their jobs, teaching them how to manage a library, and encouraging them to believe in themselves as librarians.

Networking with Peers. Networking with peers was identified by many study participants as an intrinsic component of their professional development. Small community librarians often take advantage of informal mentoring relationships with more experienced peers. Most of the peer interaction cited by the library directors in the Texas study took place during breaks, lunches, or other informal periods scheduled during structured meetings and continuing education workshops. An experienced librarian who was the director of a public library that she and several other interested citizens took the initiative to establish made the following comment:

> You get what the expert has to impart, and you go to lunch with the bunch, and you go talk to somebody. The best ideas in the world are the ones you steal from your colleagues because they've already tried them. They either worked or they didn't. But that's where good ideas live is among your colleagues.

Another long-time library worker and director voiced a similar opinion:

> And typically, I learned it from the instructor, but if nothing else, you could always learn from other librarians. And I am a firm believer in the, "Don't invent the wheel," you know, just...cheat!

Two other librarians in the study commented on the value of informal learning from peers and the capacity of networking to alleviate feelings of professional and geographic isolation:

> I think the workshops are really good in one aspect. Even though we like our jobs here, we get exposed to how other libraries do things. And I've enjoyed that. Because you can always ask somebody else how they do it and get a little bit of input. And...your library will benefit from that.

> You know, I learned so much at these workshops. And then I learn just as much sometimes at *lunch* as you do at the workshop. Because you learn how to network...and you just hear people talking, well, about this or that, and you're going, "Well, how did you do this?" or "How did you do that?" and there's so much of that.

> And then you say, "Okay, my situation," you know, you're here working by yourself, and you think, "I'm the only person that's in this situation." And you find out you're not. You know, so many people just kinda jump in and this one could be a second career for them or a first career or, you know, whatever. And you're not as isolated as you think you are.

Study participants also cited the professional benefits of networking that occurred within the framework of the continuing education event but that was unrelated to the topic of instruction:

> And it seems like in all of them [the workshops] we've had discussions to where something will come up that I'll think, "Oh, that's a good idea" and then kind of implement it from that.

> I'm not even sure where all the people were from, but the networking that we did, or the information that was shared about this topic that had nothing to do with [the workshop topic] – or at least it was kind of out in left field – was really helpful to me.

Several librarians described how they sought help for specific problems from their peers outside of continuing education events; for example, during regional and library system meetings: "You know, when there's a question or a problem or an issue, we do talk and visit and compare notes or ask for help." Others commented that they would rather "pick up the phone and call" their colleagues in other libraries rather than communicate through listservs or email, like the librarian who stated, "I know even if I don't see them [other librarians] at workshops or if the issue doesn't come up at workshops, I can phone, you know."

The comment below provides another example of the importance of networking with colleagues during organized events:

> We met monthly, we compared notes, anecdotes about situations and how it was handled. And that was very valuable to me in my early years when I was, you know, still trying to figure out what was going on.

According to the study participants' narratives, networking seemed to be most effective after the librarians had a chance to become acquainted with and establish relationships with their peers. In many cases, the demonstration of caring behavior on the part of a more experienced colleague helped establish these relationships. The following remark indicates the value study participants place on caring behavior from their peers:

> [A peer] made a remark at the other library. And I needed to follow up on that. I can call her and she'll go into detail and explain to me what she's doing. She is such a cheerful person, you know, more than happy to take time out of their day and help somebody else.

Regional System Staff. The Texas Library Systems Act, passed by the state legislature in 1969, authorized the formation of ten regional library systems to provide cooperative library and consulting services to staff working in Texas public libraries. Funded by service grants through the Texas State Library & Archives Commission, the ten regional systems vary in the size of their budgets and consulting staffs, and in the variety of services available to their member libraries. Inequalities also exist between the needs of larger public libraries, such as those in Houston and Dallas, and the smallest community libraries. Larger, urban libraries employ many professional librarians while staffs in small community libraries often lack education, experience, and knowledge of library procedures.

Consulting services provided by the ten regional system offices are crucial for staff of small community libraries. Comments like, "[System staff] are great. I can call them and ask them about anything. The System is really what makes the, this library function" and "[The System is] what saved my life!" were common responses to the interview question, *What has contributed most to your professional development?*

Perhaps the most heartfelt response to the assistance provided by system consulting staff comes from an elderly librarian working in a community of less than 900 people. This woman became the library director after substituting for the former librarian during a serious illness. She exuded warmth and friendliness to me and to members of the community both before and during the interview. She also insisted on taking me to lunch at the local senior center and introducing her to people she knew well. Both her actions toward me and her discourse in the interview reflected the importance this librarian placed on friendships and personal relationships. She later identified these qualities as being important personal traits for small community librarians. This librarian came into the library director position with no prior knowledge of or experience in library work. She described how consulting staff from her regional system office – she mentioned them by name several times during the interview – personally taught her library skills and procedures such as collection weeding, purchasing and collection development, and book processing during onsite visits over the course of her first year on the job. Her feelings toward the consulting staff are evident in the following quote:

> They've [System staff have] been ... I just can't tell you how *good* they've been to me. I just love *all* of them. They've *all* helped me *so much*, and I feel like I'm good *friends* with them all.

Other Mentoring Relationships.   Almost every librarian interviewed for the current study credited outside help for her success as a library director. The quote below from a librarian in south Texas is typical:

> That's the other thing that I will always do is I will give my boss the credit because, you know, it's just like I always thank the mayor, and I always thank [my mentor]. I will *always* thank [the System coordinator] and people at Texas State Library.

Study participants also emphasized the important role played by their mentors and the gratitude they felt for the assistance of the people who taught them to work in the library, while acknowledging the ongoing assistance they still receive:

> I can think of mentors whose names that I will bless forever. There's no way for me to ever pay back *all* the people that have helped me. For instance, look at [names a workshop instructor], look at Belinda, who offer *practical advice* for librarians with dusty shoes who are really gonna get out there and do it.

> Course, I did have some *dim* idea of how to do it [manage a library] because my mentors were there, I could – had somebody to lean on, I had continuing education that I could go into and … well, it's been people who have held my hand.

The following statement, made by the experienced small community librarian quoted above, sums up the feelings of gratitude toward more experienced professionals who have taken the time to guide and educate their non-MLS colleagues: "It's just one lucky day that he [my mentor] walked into my life."

Importance of the MLS Degree

Although I did not specifically ask study participants about their attitudes toward earning an advanced degree, several of the librarians in the study mentioned the importance of having a MLS. Some librarians in the study expressed mixed attitudes toward the MLS degree. At times, individual librarians displayed contradictory feelings in the same passage of their narrative, first citing the MLS as a necessary qualification for a professional librarian, but in the next breath assuring me that they themselves did not require the degree in order to do a professional job as a small community library director. Several study participants felt compelled to explain why they did not have an MLS degree, going into some detail about the life experiences (illness, childbirth, etc.) that had prevented them from earning an advanced degree. Almost all of the study participants who mentioned the MLS in their narratives said that the library director hired as their successor should hold a professional degree, although they felt that cataloging knowledge, business and management skills, and a love of people and willingness to provide service were adequate qualifications for the director of a small community library. The following statement is typical:

> I don't have a college degree or anything. I don't think you could pay me enough to go there. And if my three years, if that's all that I've accomplished, and the person that takes over after me then can build upon that and actually maybe have a real librarian's degree.

All of the study participants who discussed the MLS were aware of state and national efforts to upgrade standards and require the MLS degree for library directors in small communities; however, none of them agreed that this was a good idea. Study participants cited inadequate compensation and the propensity of MLS librarians to become frustrated and want to move onto other, more challenging work as reasons why the MLS should not be required of small community librarians.

The study participants went on to elaborate on the reasons they felt they did not need a master's degree to be a competent small community librarian. The following comments typify the feelings of the small community librarians in the study about the necessity of having an MLS degree to competently manage a library:

> But I don't think [the MLS degree is] really necessary. I think if you have the background – basic cataloguing and organizational skills. But, as far as the day-to-day activities, I think you can pick it up.

> To get the Master's – I think you learn from that, but you really do learn onsite. You learn more, you know, there's a lot of things I figured out on my own way more than I probably would've learned there [in library school]. And I know they don't teach you everything.

> There's things that I know by not having an MLS I don't, didn't know and probably don't know, but experience is a wonderful teacher, and if you have the experience, you know, I said to some people that, you know, when I retire, when I quit, I think they'll need to hire somebody with an MLS degree.

One librarian who worked in a community of 11,000 people embedded in the suburbs of a major city pointed out the availability of alternative education opportunities for librarians without the MLS degree. This librarian had served both as a library board member and library volunteer before taking the job as the library director. In her view, continuing education is just as valuable as formal education for small community librarians:

> But if you don't have a degree and you're willing to learn, there's so many avenues that you can learn from. From your state library, the continuing education, to the [regional library] system for the workshops that they offer you, to going and becoming a member of [a regional group of public library administrators]. You don't have to have an MLS degree to do it. You just have to go.

Another librarian articulated what she perceived as reluctance on the part of MLS librarians to share information or mingle with their non-MLS counterparts:

> I'm a little bit surprised at how the line is drawn within the library profession among MLS and non-MLS because I really see that non-MLS, we stick together and we are more forthcoming. I have seen exceptions to the rule on both sides, but there seems to be a little line drawn that MLS is over here and if I'm not MLS, over here.

One librarian working in a more rural region commented favorably on the camaraderie she enjoyed with MLS librarians, while at the same time downplaying her own worth as an non-MLS librarian: "But all these people that I have talked about treat me as an equal, and I'm not one, but they have treated me as an equal." Despite a successful career as a library director that has spanned more than 40 years, this librarian spoke with some bitterness about her inability to gain admittance to an accredited Texas library school in the 1950s. This negative experience galvanized her to return to her hometown and, with several other people, including her mother, establish the first public library in her community:

> When I got to [the university], I was going to library school. That was my goal. And I worked for [the university] library for 6 weeks, and I found out they wanted warm bodies not...not gonna teach you anything. So I got married and went on with my life ... If I was gonna be a librarian, I was gonna have to start on square one. And so, that was the motivation.

As the interview progressed, this librarian recognized and valued her experiences as a non-MLS small community library director. Far from regretting her rejection by the library school, she dismissed the MLS degree as something that would qualify her to be only a kind of "worker bee" in a larger institution by saying, "If I had gone and had the MLS, I would have been working on the bottom of the pile somewhere still."

The majority of the comments in this section show an awareness of the MLS degree as the benchmark for professional librarians. Another librarian in the study spoke of the scrutiny she felt she was under from people in the community she believed were watching and judging her performance as a library professional. In the comments below she equates professional competence with advanced education while describing her determination and self-confidence to do the best job possible without an advanced degree:

> I think probably even today that there's still some that say, "Well she doesn't need that job." And so that's been my biggest problem. I *knew* I could do it. But it made me better. Because I knew I had these people watching me. And I knew they would con*tinue* to watch me. Because I didn't have an MLS. That I wasn't a *cert*ified librarian.

Other librarians in the current study echoed the study findings of earlier researchers by pointing out how difficult it is for small community librarians to obtain master's degrees, and the lack of compensation they would receive even if they managed to obtain this level of education:

> And you know, county librarians are not required to have degrees. You know, just, and for small libraries, I doubt it's, you know, pay scale being like it is, I doubt if anybody, you know, that's not fair to ask a person with a degree to take a job that wouldn't pay 'em for the time that they spent learning.

> I know [state certification requirements are] leaning that direction [requiring the MLS]. But I'm afraid the small counties can't afford to pay the salaries that they might want. And if they had a degree, they'd probably move on to some other [community]. I think it'll hurt the small libraries.

The issue of low pay for small community librarians emerged during several of the interviews. Each of the librarians who brought up the subject mentioned they had some alternative means of support (for example, a husband with a good salary or retirement income) that allowed them to work for low wages at a job they enjoyed and from which they gained personal satisfaction. I heard comments like, "Luckily, my husband had a job where it didn't matter. I wasn't working because I needed to work. So it made a difference" and "We're all *women*. We don't get *paid* what the men do. They're *trying* to build it *up*. They've tried to get us a little *closer*. But we don't get *paid* like they do." Another study participant observed:

> There's been…an interesting exchange going on, uh, it's been on PUBLIB in the last few days. It's one about the high-flown ideas of librarianship, and I have really had to close my mouth about, you know, like, the good pay doesn't matter and all this stuff, and I want to say, "Folks, that's not where it is anymore. You've still got to live. I don't care what your high-flown ideas are, somebody's gotta pay the rent."

While the small community library directors in the Texas study recognize and acknowledge the MLS degree as a valuable credential for professional librarianship, many non-MLS library directors working in small communities remain unconvinced of the necessity for earning an advanced degree. While the non-MLS librarians' attitudes toward education in general are positive, they believe the time, expense, and effort required to earn an MLS degree far outweigh the compensation and opportunities available to use the degree as a small community library director. Yet, the three librarians in the study who had MLS degrees were willing to take on the challenges of lower pay, smaller buildings and collections, and less staff in exchange for the personal satisfaction of providing quality library service for people in small towns who might otherwise not have had it, and from the chance to be part of a close-knit community.

Challenges Faced by Female Librarians in Small Communities

Nationally, women manage more than 90% of rural and small community libraries. In Texas, male librarians make up only 4.5% of the total number of small community library directors (*Texas Public Library Summary for 2004*). All participants in the Texas study were female, reflecting the predominance of women managing small community libraries. I expected to hear a number of examples of women treated as second-class citizens in their often rural and geographically isolated communities, demonstrated by the attitudes and behavior of patrons, governing officials, and others toward the library directors. In the interviews, I asked study participants to describe their experiences – positive or negative – as women in positions of power in their communities.

The library literature provides many examples of challenges facing small community librarians, particularly in studies conducted by faculty and staff of the Center for Rural Librarianship (Vavrek, 1980, 1982a, 1982b, 1983, 1984, 1989, 1990, 1995, 1997). Data gathered for the current study describe three main areas, two of which – resistance from governing officials and geographic isolation – have been identified in the library literature. The current library literature does not cover gender-based discrimination – an area of challenge identified in the present study – but this phenomenon has been increasingly documented in the sociology literature (Caprioli, 2005; Gorman, 2005; Jerby, Semyonov, & Lewin-Epstein, 2005).

Gender-Based Discrimination: Working Within the Established Patriarchy

Most of the librarians interviewed for the Texas study insisted they were not treated differently because of their gender by people in their communities or by local (city or county) governing officials. One librarian working in a town of nearly 9,000 people who had held the director position for more than 10 years noted that there were "quite a few women in positions of authority" in her town, including a doctor, a county judge, a curriculum director with the school district, and a human resources director. Another librarian in a town lying within 45 miles of a major metropolitan city commented almost as an afterthought on the unequal pay scales for male and female department heads in her town: "of course, we don't get *paid* what the men do." This librarian made the preceding comment after first responding that being a woman in a position of authority had "never been an issue" for her. Instead, this librarian experienced challenges to her authority because of her lack of formal education credentials (i.e., not having an MLS degree). However, another librarian in the study commented, "Women are not looked at as equals in a, in a small town. It's always the male directors, you know, the Chief of Police or the Fire [Chief] or the Public Works [Director]."

Murrell and James (2001) acknowledged, "one of the most widely studied areas that examines the barriers to women's career advancement are the consequences of discrimination in the workplace" (Murrell & James, 2001, p. 244). Only one library director, working in a predominantly Hispanic community of just over 4,500, said she had experienced challenges and overt job discrimination because of her gender. This librarian, like most of the study participants, had grown up in the community where she now works but had gone to college in a large metropolitan city in another region of the state. After earning a bachelor's degree and working for several years in the education field, the librarian returned to her hometown to work. In the quote below she describes losing the library director position to a less-qualified male candidate who benefited from the established "good ol' boy" network in that community:

> It took me a long while 'cause most of the jobs here are political. It's probably like that in most places. But here it's literally who you know or who you don't know. I have a degree. A young man that did not have a degree but had about forty relatives that vote in the county, he got the job. Okay? So, and that's...how I really found out how the things work here.

This librarian later benefited from her own network when she was hired to be the assistant library director by a male mentor she had worked with previously in a major metropolitan city. Her mentor, who was well known and respected in their small community, held a dual position as the town's City Administrator and the library director. This study participant – one of three Hispanic women interviewed for the study – felt strongly that women in positions of authority experienced overt discrimination in her community. It is interesting to note that the biased attitudes described in the quote below, while typical in a traditional Hispanic culture, are described in terms of gender rather than culture by the librarian:

> I think, still, people, especially in this community and rural communities, they don't like to see a woman in an authority, in a position that they're the head of a department. I think it's threatening to a lot of the male population.

This same librarian wryly provided specific examples of what she perceived as gender-based discrimination from local governing officials, describing the events below as "comical":

> Just like at the city council, my ideas or whatever were dismissed. And I was challenged. In fact, when I became Library Director, I would submit travel reimbursements, and I would submit claims for things that I would buy for the library. Two Council members, two of the ones that were always after me – not any other department, not *any* other department, and I was the only female head of any department.
>
> Finally I asked them – I said, "Are you trying to imply that I'm trying to cheat the city out of money?" And that's when the Council members on the other end of the table said, "No. No, we don't mean" – and one of the Council members, the male Council member said, "Uh, no, we're doing this across the board [with] all of the city personnel," which I knew didn't happen.

The preceding quote was pared down to its main points, emphasizing the librarian's confidence in her own abilities and willingness not only to defend herself but also to go on the offensive in the face of antagonism from authority figures. One last comment reflects this librarian's perceptions of gender-based resistance to attitudes of female assertiveness: "And see, I think that was another thing that *stuck* in these male councilmen. That I would not back down." This librarian's confidence, grounded in her education and professional experience, substantiate Foster's claims that "women should be likely to act out against discrimination when their social identity as women is salient" (Foster, 1999, p. 167).

Nearly 500 miles away in a town of just over 5,000, a soft-spoken librarian described overtly hostile behavior exhibited by some male library patrons toward the library staff:

> I do have some problems – I hate to say this – mostly with males. They just don't want to... look at me as telling them what to do. And they get real angry. Or you can't, uh, get a certain book for them or they're not allowed to look at certain materials on the computer – different things like that. And I've, we've had one that, or two that had to be banned from the library because they were so violent toward us.

The librarian quoted above grew up in the town she worked in and had taken over the library director's job from her mother after working as a library volunteer for several years. Unlike the previous librarian, who, though small of stature, exhibited a strong, self-assured, and confident nature, the second librarian exhibited a timid, shy manner, and unassuming personality. Seeming embarrassed, she volunteered information about her experiences with gender-based hostility reluctantly and declined to elaborate on the experience when prompted.

The data gathered from this study indicate that some small community librarians in Texas do not perceive themselves as experiencing gender-based discrimination from people in their communities or from their city or county governing entities. At the same time, the librarians in the study are aware of their governing entities' prejudice in favor of male department heads regarding pay and political influence. This bias also may be the result of the perception that certain departments, such as police, fire, and public works – generally staffed and directed by men – provide more essential city services than the library. Study data also indicate that some small community librarians experience strong resistance to their authority from men in their communities. The accounts of gender-based discrimination by one of the study participants are difficult to substantiate, as the actions she described could be based on personal rather than gender discrimination. Nevertheless, this librarian's perceptions of discrimination based on her gender are genuine. More study is needed to determine if gender-based discrimination is prevalent in small Texas communities.

Resistance from Local Governing Officials

Vavrek (1984) identified perception of low prestige from both the public and funding entities as a challenge facing librarians working in small communities. Several participants in the Texas study described occurrences of resistance and even antagonism experienced with their local governing officials. One librarian working in a large, well-supported library in a town with a thriving economy lamented the perception of low prestige exhibited toward the library by its governing authorities:

> I … just wish there was some way that we could figure where we could show our worth as a service to the Powers that Be. I mean, I know – like, firefighters and police with the criminals and saving lives and things – it doesn't necessarily play along that line, but we're saving people's lives by helping them live better lives and enriching the quality of what life that they have. And I *wish* we could make more people see that.

Most of the study participants indicated that their libraries enjoyed the enthusiastic support of their city and county governing officials. Several spoke of the good relationships they had established with their city managers, county commissioners, and chief financial officers, and the respect they were accorded by these officials as the library director. Only two librarians in the study described negative experiences with their governing officials. One librarian who has been on the job for more than 40 years spoke frankly about the suspicious attitude of the library staff and advisory board toward county officials over the issue of outside funding. In the passage below, she assumed my understanding since I had previously worked as a small community library director:

> And we don't ever say much about [the private funding and donations the library receives]. Because you well know what governmental bodies do if they think you've got some money somewhere else.

This same librarian spoke also about the dismissive attitude of county governing officials toward the library, which she believes they perceive as a non-essential community institution:

> My idea is to run a superb institution when the governing body doesn't care whether you do anything. They wish you would go away; they would be so happy if you would just go away. I mean, we're not painted yellow, and we don't say "Caterpillar" on the side, and we're not a pile of caliche. And therefore, we're not important.

Even the kind-hearted, elderly librarian working in the central Texas community of fewer than 900 people admitted that relations between the library board and city officials had been tense in the past, although she did not share her board's current distrust of the present city government:

> We used to just kinda, didn't trust the city at *all*, but, you know, I've gotten along with them so *well*. That board wouldn't forgive 'em for the way they'd treated 'em in a way, you know. I [of] course, I, you know, could forgive and forget.

Geographic Isolation

Geographic isolation was cited by several of the study participants as a factor negatively influencing their ability both to take advantage of continuing education opportunities and to elicit assistance from their more experienced colleagues and peers. Texas is well known for its vast geographic distances and varied population areas with terrain ranging from dense forests along the Louisiana border, to the high plains of the Panhandle to the flat grasslands and sandy seashores of the coastal bend. In the western half of the state, most communities lie more than 40 miles apart. Due to the semi-arid and, in some cases, mountainous environments in the far western reaches, some of the larger counties in these areas have only two or three small towns. It is common for librarians in this region to travel more than 200 miles to attend continuing education workshops or to shop at large urban retail centers. By contrast, the eastern half of the state is more densely populated and small communities in this region rarely lie farther than 10 or 15 miles from one another.

Several librarians expressed their unwillingness to travel long distances to attend training workshops that lasted less than three hours or for only half a day. Librarians working in less populated areas of the state expressed frustration because their travel time often was twice as long as the duration of the continuing education event they wanted to attend. Some study participants spoke of feeling isolated from other librarians. Several librarians stated that early in their careers they often felt they were the only ones experiencing certain problems and situations. This sense of "being the only one" tended to disappear once the librarians had an opportunity to meet with and share information with their peers at workshops and regional meetings. One study participant working in the western region of the state described how geographic distances precluded her from networking with colleagues in other communities. Her comment below also reveals the importance she places on face-to-face relationships with peers:

> I communicate with the lady that is the director in [a town 30 miles away], but since we're so far apart, it's hard for us to communicate with the other librarians in our system ... It's hard for us to get together and just talk.

The well-established political tradition of local governance in Texas, coupled with variations in population, ethnicity, and topography, contribute to the vast differences in building size and condition, quality of materials collections, and local support of public libraries in small communities. Librarians working in these communities may or may not have the resources or, in some cases, permission from their governing officials to attend workshops and professional conferences. Many librarians, particularly those who are new to the library field, experience a strong sense of isolation from their colleagues in other areas of the state and from the larger library profession. Although most small community librarians recognize the need for continuing education and are willing to travel to attend workshops, the comments below demonstrate an unwillingness to spend more time traveling than in training:

> Part of the problem here is the isolation, and you're a good many miles from the next workshop ... because to go to a workshop here, you're talking four hours [driving time].

> [Geographic distance] is ... a challenge. Because they put on a two-hour workshop in Abilene, I'm not driving an hour and a half and back to go to a two-hour workshop.

In contrast, continuing education workshops and programs that were centrally located so that librarians from several regions could attend and that lasted for one day or longer received high praise from study participants:

> It was so, you know, kind of centrally located for a lot of libraries and easy to get there, and I liked the idea of the two days in a row because you could, if you missed anything

or didn't understand anything that first day, you could get caught up on it or ask questions. I loved it. And being new to ... everything, I needed that.

Most of the small community librarians participating in this study, particularly those in less populated areas of the state, experienced a sense of geographic isolation from their colleagues and peers and from the larger library profession that negatively impacted their professional development. Study participants indicated a preference for meeting with their colleagues in person rather than communicating online, and favored telephone conversations over email correspondence. Although librarians in western areas of the state have fewer opportunities to meet in groups than librarians in more populated regions, library directors in all areas of the state would benefit from structured and unstructured opportunities to exchange information with each other in person, which could be scheduled during meetings and continuing education workshops.

Guidelines for Success

In her interviews with 24 rural librarians in six states, Bushing (1995) concentrated a portion of her study on identifying the characteristics of effective rural librarians. The Texas study covers broader issues influencing the professional development of small community librarians, and assumes that the study participants had accumulated enough professional experience to offer advice to new library directors. One component of professionalization covered in the Texas study is the participants' perceptions of which job skills and knowledge are important for managing a small community library. In the course of each interview, study participants were asked, "*What advice would you give to someone coming into a small community library as the director for the first time?*" Responses revealed the librarians' attitudes toward their jobs, but also indicated either a broad (social) or narrow (personal) perception on the part of each individual toward librarianship.

Understanding the Community

Every librarian in the current study cited understanding the social construction of small communities – in particular, the tendency of people in small communities to be suspicious of and resist change – as being vital for a successful librarian. Resistance to sudden change was most often cited by study participants as the reason for a new librarian to get to know her community before making any drastic changes in the library's operations.

Eighty percent of the library directors interviewed for the Texas study were raised in the communities they currently work in. Although some of these women moved away from their communities for a few years either to attend school or to work, all eventually returned to their home towns to live. Consequently, their experiences provided insight into the dynamics of small community life. The following advice from one librarian embodies the study participants' belief that librarians must try to understand the communities they serve: "That [new] person needs to *know* their patronage, *know* the area, feel the, the atmosphere of it, and really take that into consideration." Another study participant advised new librarians to:

> Learn your community. Be a part of your community. You may have worked for a place and know all about libraries. The most important thing you need to know is all about your community.

Many of the librarians interviewed for this study emphasized that people in small communities are resistant to and suspicious of change. Most of the study participants cautioned new library directors not to make any changes when first coming into their jobs, and spoke of their communities' resistance to change:

> Get to know the people and don't bulldoze things at your patrons. Take it easy. I know with this community, you don't bring things up; you ease it in. You ease it in. We had a guy here that was director for about nine months, and he tried to shove it down everybody's throats. That's one reason why he didn't last as long as he did. And then, the next guy that came along, he was a little more patient with it. He was here for 14 years.

> I think the biggest mistake a person can make is when they move to a new community or a new area, just to go in and try to change everything that's been done in the past. Maybe small towns are more … they want things kept the same more than big towns do. But small communities, they don't like [change]. I still get complaints about the automation.

> Before you start making your mark, learn everything that you can however it's done. First, before you start changing things. I think that's what worked for me is that I didn't go in and try to change everything right away to fit mine. You know, I'm the one that's in charge. I was, like, no, I'm going at this, and I need to learn all that I can learn from whoever I can learn it from before I could put my mark.

The study data clearly indicate that a new library director working in a small community should spend several months becoming acquainted with the needs, attitudes, and opinions of the people in the community before implementing any changes in library structure or operations. Even librarians who have lived and worked in their communities for a number of years were advised to allow others to become comfortable with them in their new roles as library managers before making any changes. A small community library director who wishes to keep her position for a period of more than two years needs to gain the support and trust of her coworkers and patrons. Taking the time to do this will help ensure that the community will accept the librarian's suggestions and alterations to the library's materials and services.

Becoming Part of the Community

Another recommendation from study participants, closely aligned with their advice to get to know the community, is for the librarian to become part of her small community. Study participants recommended activities such as shopping in the community, going to church, participating in community functions, and taking every opportunity to become acquainted with people in the town where the library resides, even if they did not live in the town itself.

Nearly every study participant mentioned at some point in her interview how vital it is for librarians to become part of their local communities. As one librarian put it, "If I were, did *not* know anybody, I'd certainly try to get acquainted in town. 'Cause you need to know people." Another energetic and dynamic librarian who successfully championed her community's new library building described how her strategy of becoming part of the community led to a successful vote in the general bond election:

> So I decided, number one, to win the staff in the city. Whatever it took, I was going to win those people, to get 'em on my side, and then I was going to win the City Council ... We just became involved in everything the town did – very supportive and got out to people who didn't know us...And so, the library just became the focal point of the town.

This same librarian encouraged her employees to take part in community activities to further raise the library's profile among the townspeople:

> I work to involve [the library] in the community. So we have, you know, these big celebrations. I tell my staff to go. And, and the reason is, I want people to know them, who they are. It may cost you a few hours. You may have to work a little harder, but I'd rather you be out in the community, at a community function, where people can *see* you than sitting at home going, "Oh, no, I don't want to do that."

Two librarians, working in different regions of the state, exhibited their awareness that the library would benefit from maintaining a positive image in the community, stating, "You need to know the community. Know what you can get away with and what you can't" and "*Get* to know your people. And *keep* it as *flexible* as you can, because that goodwill is more important than even worrying about losing a piece of material." Other study participants advised new librarians to network in their communities and become acquainted with people who can offer assistance in an effort to establish themselves as a community leader. The belief that participation in community affairs leads to positive feelings toward the library and its staff is illustrated in the following comments. These remarks also illustrate this librarians' political astuteness:

> Just become involved in your community. Remember that you're not trying to reach the world. Your job is to reach your community. So whatever your community is, find out what they do and do it with them. And *then*, you can get them to come do what you want them to do. You've got to be willing to do what they do first, whether you like it or not.

> The first piece of advice that I would give [a new director] really does not have much to do with the science of administration of the library. It would be to network within the community, get to know people, you know. Let yourself be known and find out who exactly it is that can help you, and start moving toward establishing yourself as a community leader. And then all that other stuff kind of comes with it.

Establishing herself as a member of the community can be advantageous in several ways for the small community librarian. Being active in the community can help the librarian gain support for her projects and promote good will toward the library, acting as a kind of marketing strategy for the small community librarian. Political networking is vital if the librarian is to become a leader in her community. People who are personally acquainted with the librarian are more inclined to offer their time and energy to support library causes and are more likely to become library advocates. The small community librarian's active participation in community activities demonstrates her interest in and caring for the town, which in turn will encourage others to care for the library.

Making the Library the Heart of the Community
Tangential to the idea that the community's needs come before the wishes of the librarian is the concept that the library is an extension of the community in which it resides. The small community librarians participating in the Texas study perceived the library as a public institution and felt strongly that the wishes of the people in the community should guide the library's services and operations. Librarians who perceive the library as being a vital part of their community will try to create an inviting and welcoming environment and encourage library use among all members of the community. An outgoing and sociable librarian working in a recreational community said, "I feel like libraries are a vital part of the community and especially in a small community. Because, I mean, we're the hub." In the comment below, a soft-spoken librarian working in a community of fewer than 500 people articulated her belief that the library not only belongs to the

community, but also is the very center of community life, a place to exchange news and visit with neighbors:

> The midday is the – that's the time the mothers come in. Their kids may be in school and they needed a little time, maybe it's computer time or whatever, and they don't wanna have to, you know, watch their little kids. And sometimes that's the only place they have to visit. They don't see their neighbor, so they'll visit in here a lot of times. And, I think that's important, you know, to keep contact with what's going on in your community. And this is a good place for it.

Comments from other study participants echoed this belief:

> I think that no matter what's going on everywhere else, a library should be the one place they [people in the community] can come in and feel comfortable. And that it belongs to them. It's their library. Not ... how *they* want it, not how I want it so much.

> The people that are here and involved with the community, this is an important part of it because not everybody goes to the same church, not everybody belongs to the civic center, not everybody belongs to the Legion. But see, this is a place that people can come.

Business and Managerial Skills

Leaders in the library field have long emphasized the importance of business and managerial skills for women in librarianship. A paper presented at the 14th American Library Association annual conference in 1892 insisted that "the librarian must be both a good business woman and an educator in the highest sense of the word" (Proceedings, 1892, 1976, p. 13). Six years earlier, Melvil Dewey warned that female librarians were handicapped compared to their male counterparts, in part because "women lack business and executive training" (Dewey, 1886, 1976, p. 10). Librarians interviewed for the Texas study also were convinced that business skills – which may include bookkeeping experience, organizational skills, personnel management, and budgeting skills – were valuable in their work. One librarian remarked, "I think getting any kind of bookkeeping experience you can get is important with all the state reports, and organizational skills." Another library director echoed this sentiment: "If you don't have some experience with preparing and administering budgets, that is very, very important." Others commented:

> I think a lot of times, sometimes librarians that wind up being in *small* libraries like this get into it for the love of the books and things like that, but if they don't have a whole lot of business experience, I think that sometimes that can hamper them.

Well, but that also takes, you know, business skills. I mean it takes some sort of management and budgeting skills, too. So, you know, you can't just make it up without knowing.

Additionally, several of the library directors credited their business-related backgrounds and skills with making them better library managers:

I had worked in banks and things like that – and handling money and different things like that in the real world, and then coming in and being able to appreciate all the different aspects of librarianship plus the fact that it's a business. I think that made it easier, in some ways, to handle the money from the grants, to handle all these different things.

I had a business. I had been in private business all my life. I am business-minded...Our library had gone down to about 900 people coming in a month. It had really decreased. It just didn't have the excitement. You know, you just have to have someone generating that. And that's what I am. I'm a promoter/generator. Marketing is kinda my deal, so that's one reason they hired me – and I can use power tools.

I've been in the book business all my life. I run a library on the side and do research and write a little bit ... I've been in the rare book business, I've been in retail book business, I've been in the library business. You have to have a little piece of all of 'em, keep it all going, because it's so interrelated.

I was a terminal manager for the seventh largest trucking company in the United States. So anyway, so when I got the [library director] job, I said, "Okay, what do you need to know?" You need to know who your patron is, what they like to read, and how you can service them. Because there's not much difference between moving freight than there is in moving books.

Several study participants had managed, worked in or owned their own businesses, or had completed a 2-year business school certification program. Evidenced by the comments above, even librarians who did not have corporate work experience or business backgrounds were cognizant of the value of business skills such as budgeting, supervising, and planning in their roles as library managers. The librarians with knowledge of business procedures described instances in which they were able to transfer this prior knowledge to specific situations in the library. Those who lacked these skills initially realized their need and sought out learning opportunities early in their careers as library directors.

People and Customer Service Skills
Customer service skills or "people skills" are essential for anyone working in an environment that requires greeting and interacting with the public. Interacting with people – the public, governing officials, state and system staff, and other librarians, is an essential part of small community

librarianship. Without exception, every librarian in the Texas study emphasized the importance of developing people skills for managing a small community library. Weingand (1997) asserts that:

> The nature of a public library...creates an environment that tends to be rather personal in terms of public relations. Many customers are regular users and become very well known to the staff. It is a milieu in which a high standard of customer service can flourish (Weingand, 1997, ix).

One enthusiastic, vivacious librarian in the Texas study who worked in a retirement and recreational community described her own interpersonal skills with frank good humor:

> And talk about the stereotype of, you know, everybody's shy ... Well, I haven't met one yet. And, in fact, I got so much grief from my friends and family. And I got, "You're a librarian now? You're gonna, *you*? I just can't see it." And then my brother – one of my brothers said, "You're a librarian? Oh, how many times a day do the patrons tell *you* to shush?"

Perhaps the most vital qualification is simply enjoying being around people, a concept articulated by the same librarian: "You know, I love to read. I love people. And I try to make – when people come in – a warm and inviting place for kids as well as adults."

Study participants described in their interview narratives what they considered to be good customer service skills. Foremost among the qualities articulated was friendliness and the ability to maintain personal relationships with library patrons. One librarian in the study remarked that library patrons had described her to her supervisor in the following way: "She's really friendly. She always got a smile for you." Other comments included:

> At the beginning when I was working, I was real shy, and I've slowly come out of that shyness because of the patrons that come in, like I said, [they] need more than just a librarian. They need you to be [their] friend.

> You're not just a librarian, you listen to their stories and their problems. And I guess that's one of the advantages of being in a small library in a small community 'cause you know everybody.

> Small communities are completely different than, like, a large town, so I would say that you definitely have to make it personable. You can't just be, "Okay, here's your book. Here, check this out." And, you know, you do have to make it a personal place to come.

Several librarians added comments to their Theme Verification Form reiterating that people skills were the most important qualities for a small community librarian to have, including comments like, "To know your people, be friendly and helpful" and "Openness to interact with people; approachability."

SUMMARY

The study findings provide a conceptual framework for understanding the attitudes and perceptions of 17 small community librarians in Texas. The findings both corroborate and expand on earlier findings by researchers studying the professional development of rural librarians in other states. These findings are summarized in two sections following: (1) The Importance of Personal Relationships and (2) Evidence of Professional Development.

The Importance of Personal Relationships

The ability to establish and maintain personal relationships with patrons is a major factor in the small community librarian's sense of job satisfaction. As revealed in the sections titled *Making a Difference in the Community* and *Librarianship and the Ethic of Caring*, relationships with others are of paramount importance to librarians working in small communities. Librarians in the Texas study who articulated a deep love for and enjoyment in their work during their interviews were more likely to enjoy interacting with people from all walks of life and working with the public on a daily basis.

While libraries in larger cities experience a much higher volume of visitors and librarians often are not always personally acquainted with their patrons, librarians in small communities are able to offer more personalized service. This personalized service may be a leading reason that small community libraries continue to exist and even thrive in the age of iPods, instant messaging, and Internet access. The caring relationships between library staff and people in the community also may be the small community library's best asset to emphasize when seeking community support for building expansions, bond elections, and increased funding.

Findings in this study reveal that small community libraries in Texas exist within complex social environments that are supported by caring relationships between the librarian and people in the community in which the library is embedded. Caring relationships are based on trust and, in many instances, affection. Coupled with a sense of civic responsibility on the part of the library director, caring relationships allow small community librarians to determine the information and library services needed by the people in their communities on a case-by-case basis. At the same time, the establishment of prior relationships and acquaintanceship are not necessary for the librarian to exhibit caring behavior toward library users. Several librarians in the study described their concern for strangers, especially those who exhibited a need for assistance through their words, body language, or behavior, and for children of all ages.

A willingness to establish relationships with the public and even feeling some affection toward people in general, were cited by almost every study participant as vital skills for librarians working in small communities. Librarians in the Texas study provided numerous examples of their interaction with adults and children. Further, several study participants were interrupted by their staff, patrons, or members of the public either in person or over the telephone during their interviews. In every instance, the librarian apologized to me and spent the necessary time to assist or visit with the person who interrupted the interview while the recording equipment was turned off. This behavior demonstrated as well as any narrative the value that small community library directors place on human relationships and interactions.

The importance of relationships also extends to the professional arena. Small community librarians, particularly those working in geographically isolated areas, rely on informal networking opportunities with peers for problem solving and to gain insights into their work. Thus, the professional development of small community librarians is positively influenced by the advice and information shared with peers. However, despite having access to email and online discussion or news groups, small community librarians would rather communicate with others in person or "with a real voice" over the telephone. Even so, the librarians in the Texas study indicated that they tend to only contact people they have established relationships with or who work in towns nearby.

The attitudes expressed by librarians in many of the interviews reflect a predilection for personal, relationship-based interactions with others over text-based electronic communication. One reason for this bias may be that the regional computer-based listservs subscribed to by Texas public librarians are not active discussion venues; instead, they are used mainly by state library and regional library system staff to relay announcements about grant and continuing education opportunities. Discussion on national library listservs – which generally includes between 20 and 50 postings per day – often is driven by a handful of outspoken individuals. To date, this phenomenon has not taken hold among small community librarians in Texas. The predilection for establishing personal relationships and reluctance to use electronic communication exhibited by the study participants may indicate prevailing attitudes among small community librarians. These attitudes can negatively influence small community librarians' willingness to participate in online learning venues, which can have an impact on the kinds of continuing education programs developed by continuing education providers.

Evidence of Professional Development

Rather than being unaware of "what competent library service should be" (Luchs, 2001, p. 54), the narrative data gathered for the current study reveal that small community librarians are motivated by their understanding of their communities' needs for quality library service to gain the expertise and skills necessary to do their jobs well. Small community librarians in Texas seek training in areas like budgeting, collection development, and maintenance, Internet and database searching, handling intellectual freedom challenges, establishing programming for children and youth, providing business services, and maintaining computer hardware and software. Findings from this study reveal that small community librarians in Texas feel they have received adequate training and education to qualify as library professionals, if not as professional librarians.

Study participants identified four main sources of professional development:

(1) continuing education events such as workshops organized by the Texas State Library & Archives Commission and the Texas Library System, and events offered during the annual conference of the Texas Library Association
(2) information shared by more experienced peers and colleagues during formal and informal meetings, and hands-on instruction from previous librarians or library staff
(3) assistance provided by regional library system consulting staff, especially through onsite training and offering advice on issues affecting day-to-day and long-term library operations and
(4) personal experience gained after years working in a small community library as a desk clerk or library director

The small community library directors participating in the Texas study were well aware of the need for skills relating to fiscal management, supervising staff, project management, and planning. Data indicate that librarians with management certification or prior experience in business-related industries such as accounting or who have managed their own businesses have an advantage over their less experienced colleagues. The wide gaps in experience and education among library small community library directors indicate that continuing education programs targeting non-MLS librarians should include a substantial management component. Study data further indicate that small community librarians in Texas learn about the issues facing small community libraries and begin to identify with the larger library profession by attending continuing education events, visiting with more experienced colleagues, and through the mentoring of regional library system consulting staff, colleagues, and experts in the field.

Without exception, all of the participants in the Texas study identified their participation in continuing education events as a major factor in their professional development. Most credited the workshops developed and provided by their regional library systems and the Texas State Library & Archives Commission – especially the Small Library Management Training Program – with providing the necessary skills and knowledge for managing a small community library. Most of the study participants also expressed a willingness, and even eagerness, to take advantage of every available organized learning opportunity. One librarian, concerned about the challenges of working in a rapidly changing profession, expressed a sense of urgency when she said, "the industry is moving, and you can't do it like you did it 10 years ago. And I have gotten behind *again*, and I need to be up there." Her comment reflects Abbott's assertion that "the major cultural force affecting librarianship is internal intellectual change" (Abbott, 1998, p. 437) and indicates an awareness of a professional's responsibility to continually gain new knowledge and expertise.

It is interesting to note that only one librarian interviewed for the current study expressed a belief that training should specifically relate to small community library issues. In the following quote, this director cites time constraints imposed by her job responsibilities as the reason for her unwillingness to attend continuing education events not directly related to her situation: "It's hard to get out of here, you know, so it's gotta be – it *must* be something that is gonna apply to what we are doing or want to do or plan to do." In contrast, one experienced librarian with more than 10 years of experience as a library director wrote on her Theme Verification Form that continuing education is "valuable even when not applicable to small libraries." This librarian also telephoned me three months after her interview to express her beliefs about the benefits of continuing education. During this conversation, the librarian emphasized how important she felt it was for small community librarians to take advantage of every training opportunity because "you never know when you'll learn something you can use" and "even if [the training is] geared toward larger libraries, you take what you can use and apply it to your situation."

Study data indicate that continuing education programs and events provided by the Texas Library System and the Texas State Library & Archives Commission are essential to the professional development of small community library directors in Texas. Whether through printed flyers mailed out by the regional system offices and the state library or through email announcements posted by the consultants working in these organizations, small community librarians seem well informed about the number and variety of continuing education opportunities available in their areas. Small community library directors are motivated to attend continuing education workshops by two primary needs: (1) the need to learn basic library procedures and (2) a desire to gain organizational and management skills. (It should be noted that the data gathered in this study only concern small Texas community library directors' attitudes toward onsite continuing education events and do not reveal any insights about their willingness to take part in online training.)

All of the study participants working in the western and southern areas of the state cited assistance from regional library system consulting staff as a major factor in their professional development. The interview narratives indicated that consulting staff in the West Texas, Texas Trans-Pecos, Texas Panhandle, North Texas Regional, and South Texas Library Systems[6] often made site visits to instruct new librarians on library procedures such as collection development, weeding, and filling out reports mandated by the system office or the state library. Interview data also revealed that system consulting staffs in these regions provide extensive telephone, email, and, in some cases, Web-based assistance to both new and experienced librarians in a variety of areas including computer problems, difficult reference questions, and grant writing. Study participants in the western, southern, and northern regions of the state articulated a high level of comfort when approaching their regional library system consulting staff with questions on routine matters or to help solve minor problems. The assistance provided by regional library system consulting staff is vital to the professional development of small community librarians in Texas, particularly in areas of the state where librarians are geographically isolated. While continuing education workshops provide necessary training and opportunities for networking with peers, onsite assistance and training provided one-on-one between consulting staff and librarians are essential for many small community librarians to gain hands-on knowledge of library operations. In-person visits also help to establish personal relationships between regional library system staff and small community library directors, which in turn encourage the librarians to ask for help when it is needed. Librarians in the Texas study who have benefited from mentoring articulated a better understanding of the roles and responsibilities of a public library director.

For some small community library directors, guidance provided by more experienced colleagues, supervisors, governing officials, and others is key to their professional development. Mentors not only provide instruction in day-to-day library operations, but also inspire the small community librarian to believe in herself, instilling in her a sense of confidence and helping her perceive herself as a library director. Psychology literature has established that professional development is enhanced by mentoring; for example, in a qualitative study conducted by Chovwen (2004) it was determined that:

> ...although [the] protégé/mentoring relationship was not formally constituted in most organizations it was found to be a significant predictor of growth and participants with mentors perceived they experienced higher growth than those without mentors (Chovwen, 2004, p. 126).

Librarians in the current study who mentioned the influence of mentors also exhibited proactive leadership and a high degree of self-confidence in their abilities as librarians. For example, one librarian overcame personal disappointment and found a library in her hometown. In succeeding years, she became very active in the state's library association and established herself as a historian by publishing several historical indexes and writing for a professional history journal. Another librarian overcame serious injuries sustained in a car accident to establish her authority in the face of overt resistance from city officials, and later launched a successful campaign to open branch libraries in two nearby towns in the county. A third librarian spearheaded a successful effort to build a new, state-of-the art library building, and later participated on a statewide public library task force. Mentorship played a fundamental role in the professional development of each of these small community librarians.

Many times, small community librarians are women who are already members of the community, are willing to work for low pay, and have no expectations about the job other than a vague idea that libraries are quiet and safe places and that librarians spend most of their time reading, stamping books, and shushing noisy patrons. The remarkable transformation from library worker to librarian occurs only after these women make connections with other librarians and mentors, are identified as "the librarian" in their community, and, perhaps most importantly, gain a sense of personal satisfaction from providing library services.

CONCLUSIONS

Exploring the perceptions and beliefs of non-MLS librarians working in small Texas communities through qualitative case study methods has confirmed findings in previous studies relating to professional development and identified motivations not previously recognized. The Texas study reveals that small community library directors are motivated to improve their knowledge, skills, and abilities by a number of factors, including:

(1) A strong service orientation.
(2) A love of and devotion to literacy, libraries, and learning.
(3) A willingness to learn from more experienced and knowledgeable individuals, including colleagues, outside experts, and regional library system consulting staff.
(4) A sense of ownership for the library building, collection, and services.
(5) A feeling of pride in being identified as a person of authority in the community.
(6) A feeling of professional achievement gained from having a career rather than a job.
(7) A sense of civic responsibility toward improving the quality of the community and contributing to the education and self-actualization of all individuals, particularly children and adults with less education and fewer life skills.
(8) Caring relationships among the library's community of users and within the community where the library is embedded.

These motivations, coupled with positive experiences related to professionalization – such as gaining knowledge and skills from continuing education events and guidance from mentors – contribute to the process of transformation inherent in professionalization that distinguishes a worker from a working professional.

Despite dire warnings in the literature that small community public libraries will cease to exist without the direction of MLS librarians

(Luchs, 2001; Vavrek, 1992, 1997), public libraries continue to be established in areas that are unserved and underserved by larger institutions. This study suggests that the librarians participating in the study are dedicated and caring individuals who recognize the value of building and maintaining personal relationships. Most of these librarians are women over the age of 40 who draw from their life and occupational experiences to guide their current work. Librarians who have at least one year of experience in their jobs, who have participated in some kind of library management training, and who have been mentored by regional system consulting staff or by their more experienced colleagues exhibit a strong professional identity. Face-to-face continuing education programs and events appear to be the most valuable tools for professional development, but hands-on assistance from regional library system consulting staff, mentoring by more experienced colleagues, and networking with peers also greatly contribute to the professionalization process.

Since the MLS degree remains the standard measurement of professional ability, small community librarians are not acknowledged as professionals in the library field. Yet all of study participants exhibited traits associated with professional librarians: knowledge of information sources and tools, research skills, business and management skills, and customer service skills. Further, the librarians in the study articulated their awareness of a sense of duty inherent in being a public servant, the seriousness of the responsibility for maintaining trusting relationships with library patrons, and a willingness to act as a community leader. As Weingand (1992) observed, "In these smaller towns, 'professional' must rightly apply to dedication and attitude, regardless of educational preparation" (Weingand, 1992, p. 362). Some of the study participants perceived themselves as visionary leaders whose responsibility it is to guide the library staff and community through rapid technological and sociological changes. Others viewed their work on a more personal, immediate level, and relished the personal satisfaction that comes from helping one individual to achieve her goals. All expressed a belief that they were performing rewarding work that made a difference in their communities. For some, what began as a job became a vocation.

The small community librarian is on call 24 hours a day. She supplies information; provides a comfortable environment for children and adults to visit with each other or to pursue intellectual interests; teaches patrons how to use the library's resources, including computer skills such as database searching and email; repairs broken steps and furniture using her own power tools; and, on occasion, rescues small crustaceans from toilets.[7] She is accustomed to having people give her lengthy explanations about why they have not returned their library materials while standing in line at the grocery store, and having neighbors and relatives ask her to let their child into the library after hours so he can finish a school report. The small community librarian will forever be known as "the library lady" in her community, and she wears this title as a badge of honor.

The Texas study emphasizes that non-MLS library directors working in small communities have much to offer to the larger library community. Unfortunately, many small community librarians operate almost invisibly on the fringes of the library profession, and their voices remain absent from discussions held on national listservs and at state and national committee meetings and conferences. Library leaders, particularly those working in state library agencies, state library associations, large urban libraries, and on college and university faculties should make more efforts to mentor non-MLS public librarians, and to include them in the mainstream profession.

NOTES

1. For example, the Western Council of State Libraries Library Practitioner Certification Program initiative (http://www.westernco.org/wcsl/minutes/index.html).
2. Rural libraries constitute 44% of the total number of public libraries in the United States according to the National Center for Education Statistics publication, *Public Libraries in the United States 2003* available at http://nces.ed.gov/pubs2005/2005363.pdf (Accessed 23 Aug, 2005).
3. Fourteen of the librarians interviewed for the study did not have MLS degrees.
4. The Texas Library System comprises ten regional library systems established throughout the state and funded by contract with the Texas State Library and Archives Commission (TSLAC). More information about the Texas Library System is available at http://www.tsl.state.tx.us/ld/pubs/libsysact/index.html (Accessed on 14 August, 2005).
5. In this study, the MLS degree is used generically to mean any professional master's program in librarianship, including the master's in library science (MLIS), master's in information studies (MIS), and master's of science in information studies (MSIS).
6. The regional library systems in the western part of the state have fewer member libraries than their counterparts in the eastern half of the state, but cover much broader geographic areas. These systems also have only one or two consulting staff, where more populated systems often employ three or more consulting staff.
7. This last situation is a reference to my own experience as a small community library director.

REFERENCES

Abbott, A. (1998). Professionalism and the future of librarianship [revision of a paper presented at the 1993 ALA Conference]. *Library Trends, 46*(3), 430–443.
Burrington, G. (1993). Mentors – A source of skill, strength and enthusiasm. *Library Association Record, 95*(4), 226–227.

Bushing, M. C. (1995). *The Professionalization of rural librarians: Role modeling, networking and continuing education.* Doctoral dissertation, Montana State University Bozeman, UMI® Dissertation Services.

Caprioli, M. (2005). Primed for violence: The role of gender inequality in predicting internal conflict. *International Studies Quarterly, 49*(June), 161.

Chovwen, C. O. (2004). Mentoring and women's perceived professional growth. *IFE Psychologia: An International Journal, 12*(1), 126–132.

Dewey, M. (1886, 1976). Women in libraries: How they are handicapped. In: K. Weibel & K. M. Heim with assistance from D. J. Ellsworth (Eds), *The role of women in librarianship 1876–1976: The entry, advancement, and struggle for equalization in one profession* (pp. 10–12). Oryx Press.

Field, J. (2001). Mentoring: A natural act for information professionals?. *New Library World, 102*(1166/1167), 269–273.

Fitchen, J. M. (1991). *Endangered spaces, enduring places: Change, identity, and survival in rural America.* Boulder, CO: Westview Press.

Flatley, R. (2000). Characterizing the role of the rural librarian: A survey [of 441 directors of rural libraries]. *Bookmobile and Outreach Services, 3*(1), 24–43.

Foster, M. D. (1999). Acting out against gender discrimination: The effects of different social identities. *Sex Roles, 40*(3/4), 167–186.

Gorman, M. (2005). The greatest challenge. *American Libraries, 37*(3), 5.

Jerby, I., Semyonov, M., & Lewin-Epstein, N. (2005). Capturing gender-based microsegregation: A modified ratio index for comparative analyses. *Sociological Methods and Research, 34*(1), 122–136.

Luchs, M. (2001). The education of the rural librarian: Advantages and obstacles. *Rural Libraries, 21*(1), 51–64.

Meraz, G. (2005). In times of trouble. *Texas Library Journal, 81*(3), 90.

Miles, M. B., & Huberman, M. (1994). *An expanded sourcebook: Qualitative data analysis* (2nd ed.). London: Sage Publication.

Murrell, A. J., & James, E. H. (2001). Gender diversity in organizations: Past, present, and future directions. *Sex Roles, 45*(5/6), 243–257.

Noddings, N. (1984). *Caring: A feminine approach to ethics and moral education.* University of California Press.

O'Neill, L. (2005). A small public library and its community: Case study of Churchill county library. *PNLA Quarterly, 69*(4), 12–32.

Plummer, M. W. (1899, 1976). The training of women as librarians [Women librarians: Excerpts from the international congress of women of 1899 …]. In: K. Weibel & K. M. Heim with assistance from D. J. Ellsworth (Eds), *The role of women in librarianship 1876–1976: The entry, advancement, and struggle for equalization in one profession* (pp. 26–29). Oryx Press.

Proceedings of the 14th American Library Association conference: The woman's meeting. (1892, 1976). In: K. Weibel & K. M. Heim with Assistance from D. J. Ellsworth (Eds), *The role of women in librarianship 1876–1976: The entry, advancement, and struggle for equalization in one profession* (pp. 13–17). Oryx Press.

Vavrek, B. (1980). Information services and the rural library. *Library Trends, 28*(4), 563–578.

Vavrek, B. (1982a). Profession needs a new entry level: Non-MLS workers in rural libraries are isolated from the mainstream. *American Libraries, 13*(4), 271–272.

Vavrek, B. (1982b). *Reference service in rural libraries.* School of Library Science, Center for the Study of Rural Librarianship, Clarion State College.

Vavrek, B. (1983). A Struggle for survival: Reference services in the small public library. *Library Journal, 108,* 966–969.

Vavrek, B. (1984). Rural library services. *The Bookmark, 42*, 245–248.

Vavrek, B. (1989). Rural library service. *Wilson Library Bulletin, 63*, 29–31, 34–38, 40–47.

Vavrek, B. (1990). *Assessing the information needs of rural Americans*. Center for the Study of Rural Librarianship.

Vavrek, B. (1992). Educating rural library staff. *Library Mosaics, 3*(1), 7–9.

Vavrek, B. (1995). Rural information needs and the role of the public library. *Library Trends, 41*(1), 21–48.

Vavrek, B. (1997). A national crisis no one really cares about. *American Libraries, 28*, 37–38.

Vavrek, B. (2004a). The challenge of starting a rural library. *American Libraries, 35*(3), 77.

Vavrek, B. (2004b). Rural and small libraries: Providers for lifelong Learners. http://www.ala.org/ala/olos/outreachresource/servicesrural.htm. Accessed November 22, 2005.

Weingand, D. E. (1992). Continuing professional education. In: T. W. Sineath (Ed.), *Library and Information Science Education Statistical Report, 1992* (pp. 343–362). Chicago: American Library Association.

Weingand, D. E. (1997). *Customer service excellence: A concise guide for librarians*. American Library Association.

Zaltman, G., & Duncan, R. (1977). *Strategies for planned Change*. Wiley.

APPENDIX A. THEME VERIFICATION FORM

Below are several themes I identified during our interviews. Please indicate whether you agree or disagree with each, and feel free to add your own themes in "Other themes/salient points?" (You may want to rank the lettered items in #6, 7, and 8 from most important to least important.) I welcome your input!

	Themes	Agree	Disagree
1.	Becoming a small community librarian/library director often happens by accident or through serendipitous circumstances, but it eventually becomes a vocation.		
2.	Assistance from others (mentors, library board, Friends, colleagues, System and TSLAC staff, foundations) contributes greatly to the success of libraries and librarians in small communities.		

	Themes	Agree	Disagree
3.	Continuing education is valuable when it is practical and applicable to the small library situation.		
4.	Networking with other librarians is one of the best ways to learn and grow professionally.		
5.	Working at the library can become a kind of "spiritual salvation", giving direction and purpose to one's life after the loss of a loved one.		
6.	Small community librarians gain the most satisfaction through:		
	a. Helping children and adults find information.		
	b. Helping children and adults improve their lives.		
	c. Making a difference in the community.		
	d. Receiving both formal and informal recognition from the community.		
7.	The biggest challenges facing small community libraries are:		
	a. Geographic isolation.		
	b. Lack of funding.		
	c. Rapid changes in the field.		
	d. Rapidly changing technology and low computer skills.		
	e. Being undervalued by city and county officials.		
8.	Important characteristics for small community librarians to have include:		
	a. Business and management (people and money) skills.		
	b. Knowledge of library procedures and organization.		
	c. Getting to know and being active in the community.		

Themes	Agree	Disagree
d. A love of books and reading.		
e. Vision and leadership skills.		
f. Political savvy.		
g. People skills and a willingness to help others.		

OTHER THEMES/SALIENT POINTS?

Becoming/being a librarian:

_____
_____
_____

Continuing education:

_____
_____
_____

On the job:

_____
_____
_____

Job satisfaction:

_____
_____

Challenges and frustrations:

_____
_____
_____

Essential characteristics:

_____
_____
_____

Other:

_____

APPENDIX B. INTERVIEW PROTOCOL AND QUESTIONS

Introduction

Thank you for agreeing to be interviewed today. I want to reiterate that this interview is part of a formal research study, and that your participation in this project is entirely voluntary; you are free to stop at any time. I also want to assure you that no one will profit materially from this study, and that there are no physical risks involved.

With your permission, the interview will be recorded digitally or on audiotape to avoid my misinterpreting or misquoting your words after the fact. I am the only person who will listen to the tape besides the transcriptionist, and although I will identify you at the beginning of the interview for my records, I will refer to you, your library and community by descriptive characteristics (age, education, region, population) in the study. Your identity and the location of your library will be kept confidential, although the library will be described in general terms (e.g., population, geographic region), and no information will be shared with other researchers or the general public without your written permission. You will also have an opportunity to look over a summary of our interview, and to add or modify any of the information. If you agree to all these terms, please take a moment to read and sign the Informed Consent Form. Thank you.

As a researcher I am interested the kinds of experiences that have influenced your professional development. During the interview I will ask you about your background – how you became a librarian, for example – and also about your present situation. I have several questions written down, but please feel free to tell me anything you think is relevant to this topic.

INTERVIEW QUESTIONS

1. Tell me how you became a librarian, and became the director here.
2. Describe what it is like to be a woman in a position of authority in your community.
3. How has your job given you a sense of personal or professional satisfaction or accomplishment?
4. What has contributed most to your professional development?

5. What advice would you give to someone coming into a small community library?
6. What does being a librarian mean to you?
7. Is there anything else I should have asked, or that you would like to share?

Thank you for your time and willingness to be involved with my research project. Even though I will touch base with you over the next several weeks, please feel free to call or email me if you think of anything else that might be relevant, or if you would like to add to any of the topics we discussed.

ACADEMIC LIBRARY DIRECTORS IN THE EYES OF HIRING ADMINISTRATORS: A COMPARISON OF THE ATTRIBUTES, QUALIFICATIONS, AND COMPETENCIES DESIRED BY CHIEF ACADEMIC OFFICERS WITH THOSE RECOMMENDED BY ACADEMIC LIBRARY DIRECTORS

Gary Neil Fitsimmons

ABSTRACT

Librarians have traditionally looked to academic library directors (ALDs) to list those qualities that make them good at what they do. Little research has sought the input of institutional administrators (who are the ones who hire ALDs) about what they look for when hiring ALDs. This study presented a list of qualities that had been rated by ALDs as being important for the position to these senior institutional administrators and asked them to rate the relative importance of these qualities

Advances in Library Administration and Organization, Volume 26, 265–315
Copyright © 2008 by Emerald Group Publishing Limited
All rights of reproduction in any form reserved
ISSN: 0732-0671/doi:10.1016/S0732-0671(08)00206-X

and to add to the list any qualities they felt should be there. Their ratings were then compared with those of the library directors to see how closely they correlated. The results showed not only that there was statistically significant agreement between the two groups, but also that there were important differences, with the hiring administrators placing more priority on ideological attributes (attributes based on professional orientations and ideals) while ALDs emphasized the need for experience. The hiring administrators also added several attributes to the original list, including managing multiple priorities, being learning/student oriented (especially toward low achievers), being self-directed with a good work ethic, being able to relate effectively to all constituencies, and experience in the same type of institution as the one the person was being hired to lead.

THE PROBLEM AREA AND ITS SIGNIFICANCE

What makes a good academic library director (ALD)? The answer is more elusive than one might think. Academic library directorships have been in a state of flux at least since the early 1970s (McAnally & Downs, 1973; Woodsworth, 1989; Hernon, Powell, & Young, 2001, pp. 116–117). The assumption pointed out and refuted by Totten and Keys (1994) – that librarians are getting what they need from library education to be successful library managers – may indeed no longer be the case. The responsibilities of ALDs have grown considerably more varied in recent years with the influx of information technology and the demands of an information-rich society. This complexity in the ALD position has provided fodder for a mass of research and opinion in the library world, much of it centering on what qualities, attributes, and competencies should be found in an ALD (for example, O'Brien, 1989; Piccininni, 1995). Recent studies (such as Hernon et al., 2001, 2002) have delved into the qualifications that current ALDs say are essential for their positions, yet none of these lists have ever been matched against the requirements and expectations of others at institutions of higher education (Hernon et al., 2002, p. 89).

The simple fact of the matter is that librarians seldom hire or supervise library directors in academia or any other venue. Librarians in higher education sometimes have input into the hiring process through search committees, but nevertheless, the final decision is made and subsequent supervision done by someone outside the library. A study of the academic administrators who actually select library directors was warranted in order to include these important voices in the discussion of what makes a good ALD.

The opinions of this group should matter to librarians, since the libraries serve the institutions that the administrators represent. The implications of knowing the views of hiring administrators of what makes a good academic librarian reach into all areas of the ALD's work, touching such diverse issues as identification, training, and retention of leaders (Kaufman, 1993), dealing with change (Cargill & Webb, 1988), campus leadership (Williams, 1998), staffing issues (Plate, 1970), and critical decision-making in general (Allen & Weech, 1995).

RESEARCH QUESTIONS

This research addressed two questions:

1. What attributes, qualifications, and competencies do hiring administrators look for most in prospective ALDs?
2. How do these expectations of hiring administrators compare with those of current ALDs?

The purpose of the study was not really to develop yet another list of attributes or qualities that library administrators need, but rather to determine if current lists have any validity with hiring administrators. If librarians knew what qualifications hiring administrators see as essential for the position of the library director, they could then work much more effectively with their supervising administrators by gaining additional relevant competencies and working to resolve any differences of opinion, if possible. Library education could make appropriate curriculum changes to better prepare librarians to be ALDs, and those aspiring to such positions would know how better to prepare themselves. By simply knowing the expectations of institutional administrators, current ALDs would be better equipped to evaluate their own ideas of what is crucial to their positions and to identify areas of library administration that may be presently misunderstood. Many institutional administrators also may find this research useful in evaluating their expectations of their current library directors and in hiring new ones.

A CONTEXT FOR THE STUDY

There are numerous writings in the library literature setting forth lists of qualities or credentials that all effective library administrators should have (such as O'Brien, 1989; Piccininni, 1995; Rooks, 1994; Sweeney, 1994).

Traditionally, research into what makes a good ALD has looked to library professionals as the recognized experts in library management, with ALDs themselves being the most common primary sources for research on what it takes to make someone good at what they do (as in Farey, 1967). Some researchers have surveyed perceived library leaders (such as Sheldon, 1991; Hernon et al., 2001, 2002) for their opinions of what makes an effective leader or library director.

Research in the profession has resulted in lists of desirable technical competencies (such as Bundy & Wasserman, 1979), managerial skills (as in Cooney, 1952), or personal attributes (for example, O'Brien, 1989). Other writers deal with specific conditions with which they feel an ALD must be able to deal effectively (Anonymous, 1991; Curran & Davidson, 1999; Hernon, 1998; Newman, Dibartolo, & Wells, 1989). One researcher compared library leader attributes to those of corporate leaders (Sheldon, 1992). These lists have been developed over several years, and most are at least 10 years old.

THE STAKEHOLDERS

All of this material is useful in describing what makes a good ALD, but the voices of other major stakeholders relative to how an ALD performs his or her duties should be considered in this discussion. These stakeholders include the library staff (librarians and paraprofessionals working in the library), the institutional leaders (trustees and administrators), and the users or constituencies (faculty, students, parents, taxpayers, etc.) (Eggleton & O'Dell, 1981, p. 1). A few studies include these important voices. The perception of the effectiveness of the ALD's leadership patterns in the eyes of library staff was investigated by Suwannarat (1994). Euster (1986) garnered the views of dean-level peers in addition to those of the ALDs and middle managers under the ALDs. Carlson (1989) actually went so far as to interview the superiors of five Association of Research Libraries (ARL) library directors in his case studies as did Holmes (1983). However, these and similar studies tended to evaluate the perceived effectiveness of ALDs and their activities rather than gather data on which attributes made them effective.

Search Committees

In the hiring process, most or all of these other stakeholders are traditionally represented on the search committees for the director position

(Stussy, 1989), described by Euster (1987) as "'rainbow' bodies representing a spectrum of special interests" (p. 105). She goes on to note that "the less successful the library has been in the past in fulfilling its mission, the more likely that each constituency – faculty, students, library staff, administrators outside the library – will have a unique agenda." Search committees can vary widely not only in which groups of stakeholders are represented and by how many members, but also in the myriad of other external circumstances affecting each committee member. Such committees will almost never be comprised of the same persons twice, even in the same institution. Nevertheless, Perez (1990) asserts that the academic search process is now more inclusive and responsive to its constituents, and according to Parsons (1976), "the advent of acting positions may be an indication of the care with which new appointments at this level are made and perhaps of wider participation in the selection process" (p. 613).

Most literature on the subject of search committees in general consists of "how to" papers, covering everything from choosing committee members to instructing them about updating a job description for the position. The few studies on search committees that exist center on how effective they were at choosing a successful candidate or what aspects of the committee or process contributed most toward this success (Bromert, 1984; Twombly, 1992; Person & Newman, 1988, 1990). One study (Johnson, 1987) found notable procedural differences in how six departments of one university handled the hiring process. There is little doubt that search committees have some influence in the process if only because they often write or update the job description (or at least should, per Sager, 2001, p. 70) which determines the selection criteria or because they screen candidates and give administrators far fewer possibilities from which to choose. One study of presidential search committees (Boccaccio, 1993) determined that faculty at four-year institutions and those at private institutions had more influence in the process than their respective counterparts at two-year, research, and public institutions.

The ALDs in Hernon et al.'s (2001, pp. 138–139) study involving ARL directors shared their impressions of how search committees for ALD positions work. One director

found it difficult to generalize about search committees. In some instances, the provost works closely with a committee and prefers to make the final selection. In other instances, the committee makes the decision. In that case, a member's preference may color the outcome. She remembered that she once failed to get a job because she did not get along with one of the committee members. Thus, a single committee member may wield "a lot of power and influence." In some instances such as at the University of

Notre Dame, the search was turned over to an executive search firm. In that case, a
search committee would not see the list of applicants. In either situation, the library staff
was not powerless. If they objected strenuously to a particular candidate, they could
influence the process. After all, the committee would not want to see a bad situation if
that person were hired.

Another ALD stated that a provost deferring to the committee's decision
was not common in his experience, where "a committee generally produced
an unranked list of acceptable candidates and the provost made the
selection." Others said that "ARL's executive director and others may be
asked to comment on the final slate of candidates for an ARL position."
This literature search, however, encompassing the ERIC, Education
Abstracts, Worldcat, and Dissertation Abstracts databases, revealed no
research on the amount of influence wielded by any given committee
member or that of the committee as a whole.

Hiring Administrators

The higher education administrators who hire library directors indirectly
represent all of the stakeholders because they are the ones charged with
seeing that the libraries are directed capably on behalf of all of the
stakeholders. If this charge were always taken seriously, then all
administrators would be more likely to choose an ALD on the basis of
what is good for the organization and its stakeholders. Although there is no
research showing how often this is the case, it is a professional expectation
and since ALDs must work closely with their supervisors once hired, their
"ability to meet institutional leaders' selection criteria may, in the long run,
best serve the needs of all groups with a stake in the process [of selecting a
library director]" (Eggleton & O'Dell, 1981, p. 8).

Many directors feel that a close working relationship with their superiors
is vital to their success (Eggleton & O'Dell, 1981, p. 8), even though that
relationship may be one of the lowest priorities for the institutional
administrators (Chapin & Hardesty, 1995). There is also a feeling that some
hiring administrators may not know what they should be looking for or
what they want (Snyman, 2001; Woodsworth, 1989; Hernon et al., 2001,
p. 138). Few ALDs become upper-level academic administrators (Garten,
1988) even though many institutional administrators think of library
directors as one of them in many ways (Craddock, 1986, p. 233). This might
lead some to assume that the views of the hiring administrators must be the
same (as appears to be the case in Ivy, 1984).

However, McElrath (2002) found both similarities and differences in the views of the two groups on the most important challenges facing ALDs. In terms of the means both groups rated the challenges of user satisfaction, diversity, and hardware similarly. A difference showed up in the rating of the challenge of "training" that varied with the size of the budget. Age and length of tenure also seemed to affect the ALDs' rating of the training, organizational change, and crime challenges more than the administrators' ratings of these challenges. Both groups added challenges of their own, in similar categories (staffing, technology, library role, and miscellaneous), but with the ALDs adding staffing issues the most while the administrator's added the library's role within the institution more often.

GLEANING FROM THE LITERATURE

What can be found in existing research that might indicate the views of others, and particularly the hiring administrators? Some case studies (such as Brittingham, 1997) and informal research (as in Hernon, 1998) on single campuses may add something to our knowledge in this area. For instance, Brittingham (1997) found that "because of the substantial changes underway in libraries and technology," the provost was looking for someone with "a broad range of experiences" who could offer "an independent look at the challenges and opportunities" as an interim Dean of University Libraries (p. 60). The idea of the ALD being a scholar-librarian was important to deans and faculty members whom Hernon (1998, p. 111) interviewed. Such insights cannot be generalized to the entire population of institutional administrators however, without a great many more similar studies.

Career Path Studies

Studies of how individuals advance to academic library directorships could indicate some of the traits administrators are seeking (Metz, 1978, 1979; Moran, 1982, 1983). Research points out that directors of academic libraries, both large and small, have usually been hired from outside the institution, presumably for qualities that could not be found in persons occupying lower-level positions within the library (Hardesty, 1997, p. 285; Metz, 1977, p. 101; O'Keeffe, 1998, p. 144), often with no previous supervisory experience (O'Keeffe, 1998, p. 144). In ARL libraries the average number of years of professional experience figures prominently as a possible credential desired by hiring administrators, increasing steadily from 21 years in 1958 (Parsons, 1976, p. 615) to 28.46 in 1998 (Hernon et al., 2001, p. 117). Assistant/associate library directorships – a common feeder position for directorships – often require broad-based knowledge of library operations, with a specialization in one area of responsibility (Bailey, 1992b, p. 193). Although this and other studies and papers list attributes possessed by or needed by assistant/associate library directors (Bailey, 1992a; O'Connor & Duchon, 1993; Shaughnessy, 1987; Veaner, 1984), there is little indication of which attributes will help them to advance to the director position. Moran's study (1982, p. 135) did find a connection for males between reaching the academic directorship and advanced degrees, participation in library organizations, some publishing, and experience in different academic libraries, but no such connection for females.

One measure of how directors advanced to their positions and hence an indication of hiring administrators' opinions could be the most common attributes or qualifications that current library directors have, assuming that they were hired specifically for those attributes or qualifications. The qualification that library directors have that has been studied most is their degrees. Most institutions desire or require a director to hold a doctorate and doctorates were found to be no more common among library directors at larger institutions than smaller ones (McCracken, 2000). Unlike the number of ARL directors holding a doctorate (which actually dropped), the number of ARL directors holding a professional degree increased consistently up to 1973 (Cohn, 1976; Parsons, 1976), and became 100% by 1981 (Karr, 1984). McCracken (2000, p. 403) makes the point that the lack of a doctorate among ARL directors does not necessarily mean that a second master's degree – often held – was considered an acceptable substitute as theorized first by Karr (1984) and later by Myers and Kaufman (1991). He also notes that this situation might also have changed in the time since those studies. Other studies of the qualities or credentials that current directors exhibit include studies of their creativity (Aldridge, 1992) and several general surveys (such as DePew, 1984).

Role Studies

Some researchers have looked at the roles of ALDs (Craddock, 1986; Mech, 1990; Metz, 1979; Moskowitz, 1986; Pugliese, 1985) and how they seem to be changing (Karr, 1984; McAnally & Downs, 1973; Myers & Kaufman,

1991), which could indicate some of the desires of hiring administrators for certain qualities in ALDs. Among these are shifts from internal to external functions indicating a possible desire for an external orientation (Cottam, 1994, p. 15) and an increase in fund-raising duties indicating a possible desire for that ability (Martin, 1998; Winston & Dunkley, 2002). That the role of ALDs is changing implies a change in at least some of the desirable qualities for future directors, which several authors have attempted to predict or promote (as in Martin, 1997; O'Brien, 1989; Orenstein, 1999; Rooks, 1994; Sweeney, 1994). However, as Parsons notes (1976, p. 617), the differences that he found between 1958 and 1973 may reveal "the effects of changing roles and pressures, rather than changes in the kind of person who seeks and attains these important library positions."

Content Analysis Studies

Probably the most direct existing measure of what hiring administrators think makes a good ALD is what they ask for in their position announcements. Post-MLS degrees were found by this measure to be increasingly important, especially in universities, until 1976 and then began to decline (Olsgaard & Olsgaard, 1981). Martin (1997, pp. 50–51) looked for signs of increasing demand for leadership qualities as opposed to management skills and found it in one-third of the postings for 1995. Lin (2001) looked for trends in changes shown in job announcements between the years 1992 and 1997, and found increasing demands for more advanced degrees, more technological skills, and skills needed for external purposes (especially fund-raising), while looking for fewer years of experience.

As Euster (1987) puts it, one difficulty with studies based on position descriptions is that "increasingly, those announcements are laundry lists of an impossible array of expertise in every aspect of library operations, as if what was lacking in the past was knowledge of specific applications" (p. 104). The inadequacy of LIS position advertisements was observed by Lary (2005), who noted that even in advertising for LIS faculty there is a lack of definition concerning the subject expertise sought. A common language was not evident in the ads, making it difficult to compare position requirements between jobs. It is also important when using job ads for content-analysis research (which has been done extensively in the area of library science) to be aware that they are primarily designed as a recruiting/marketing tool that puts the best possible face on the requirements for a position. There is always the possibility that some highly desired attributes might not make it into the position announcement because of space constraints or some other reason. (Examples of research experimenting with what works best in position announcements in higher education include Fowler-Hill (2001) and Winter (1996a, 1996b).) Also, the source of the description (hiring administrator, personnel director, search committee, current ALD, etc.) is not easily determined, so the researcher cannot be sure of whose desires are actually being listed.

Perceptions of Others

A final category of existing research to review for possible expressions of what hiring administrators look for in ALDs is the perceptions of the hiring administrators' colleagues. The ARL directors have given their views of what their presidents, provosts, and library director search committees looked for in new library directors (Hernon et al., 2001, pp. 138–139), which include "someone who doesn't make waves (e.g., likely to make the faculty complain)," fund-raising ability, "'chemistry' between the candidate and provost/president/chancellor," leadership abilities, and knowledge about budgets and technology. In short, according to another ARL ALD, "they want someone who (1) can function with minimal attention and direction; (2) can be trusted financially, politically, and socially; and (3) is acceptable to the faculty."

A host of studies exist regarding the perceptions of others about the roles of upper-level administrators, perceptions of these administrators about departmental deans, and even a few tackling the relationships between these positions. Other professional positions that are subordinate to upper-level administrators are facing the same challenge of defining what makes them good at what they do and discerning their hiring supervisors' desires for those positions. The role of community college division chairman in the eyes of supervisors, colleagues, and themselves was studied in 1974 by Hutchins. Another study asked Chief Student Affairs Officers (CSAOs) about their critical skills based on their guiding philosophies (Davis, 2002) and another paper advocated understanding of the Chief Academic Officer (CAO) position by CSAOs in order to promote collaboration with them (McKee, 1993). A study supportive of this idea by Krasowski (1997) found that an important perception of trust existed between CAOs and those they most closely supervise in two-year colleges in Minnesota. The position of enrollment manager was recently studied and defined as being a "visionary, facilitator, and collaborator" (Stewart, 2004).

One study, similar to this research, sought to investigate the current role of Chief Information Officers (CIOs) in higher education by comparing the perceptions of the CIO, the Chief Financial Officer, and the CAO (Fowler, 2003) starting with previous research as a template. The CIOs thought of themselves as executives while the other two groups looked at them as more of a technical position reacting to the needs of other administrators in the institution and having a limited understanding of the overall higher education environment. The CIOs also felt that elevating their position to a senior-level position would be an important step in increasing their effectiveness and all three groups agreed that better communication would also help with that goal. Another, more generic version of this research asked chief administrators at two-year institutions what they looked for in prospective administrative staff members, finding the number one priority to be junior/community college work experience followed by other experience-related credentials or specialized junior/community college training (Prather, 1980). The necessary skill sets for administrative positions in general have also been studied (for example, Skipper, 1979; Crawford, 1982).

The available data described so far paint a complex picture of possible attributes and credentials that might be desired in ALDs by their hiring supervisors, peers, and subordinates. The difficulty in ascribing most of these desires to any of these groups is that the desires are only implied by the data if no other circumstances are considered. There may be other intervening variables involved that are not readily apparent, especially since most of the described research was not performed with the express purpose of illuminating this area. For instance, the data about the increasing years of professional experience of ARL ALDs in the study by Parsons (1976, p. 615) and Hernon et al. (2001, p. 117) may indicate that hiring administrators look explicitly for years of professional experience, that they want specific traits that only come with years of experience, that qualified applicants for ALD positions just happen to have more experience now than they used to, or a number of other possibilities. The high turnover rates, first observed by McAnally and Downs (1973), that still mark the ranks of ALDs (Woodsworth, 1989; Hernon et al., 2001, pp. 116–117) may be an indication that there are serious disagreements between what ALDs think is essential to their positions and what their superiors seek from them (McElrath, 2002, p. 305) or they may be due to one or more factors that are entirely unrelated to the expectations of the hiring supervisors. Euster (1987, p. 67) found that the supervisors of ALDs consistently rated them as more effective in six management roles than did the middle managers under them. She came to the conclusion that "internal and external raters will tend to evaluate performance differently." In short, librarians really cannot guess what hiring administrators or anyone else consider as important qualities for ALDs by looking at their own perceptions or circumstantial evidence. The most direct way to really find out what hiring administrators think is to ask them.

A BASIS FOR COMPARISON

In order to ensure that the opinions of hiring administrators could be validly compared to those of ALDs, it made sense to start with a data set from the ALDs and ask the administrators the same questions. The work of Hernon, Powell, and Young (2003) yielded a list of desirable attributes, competencies, and credentials (Tables 1–3) from the library director's perspective, divided into the three categories of managerial attributes, personal attributes, and areas of knowledge (technical competencies). Using multiple methods they refined separate sets of the three lists for ARL directors, ACRL directors of four-year institutions, and public library directors, repeating roughly the same process for each of these three groups. Although Hernon et al. developed a combined set of categorized lists from these three groups studied, the ACRL four-year institution lists (pp. 70–71) proved to be the most useful, since they are ranked, and did not include public library

Table 1. ALD-rated Managerial Attributes.

Managerial Attributes	Rating
Supervisory experience	9.00
Personnel, fiscal, budget, program, management	8.90
Plan, implement, assess strategic goals	8.70
Work in collegial, networked environment	8.70
Commitment to institutional mission	8.70
Facilitative leadership skills	8.60
Team building and participatory management	8.50
Record of innovative and effective leadership	8.50
Firm commitment to quality	8.50
Integrate print and electronic resources	7.80
Positions of increasing responsibility	7.70
Commitment to diversity	7.50
Demonstrated ability to identify trends	7.20
Experience developing digital libraries	6.60

Note: 1 = unimportant, 10 = very important now and in the future.
Source: Hernon et al. (2003, pp. 70–71).

Table 2. ALD-rated Personal Attributes.

Personal Attributes	Rating
Integrity	9.80
Strong interpersonal skills	9.50
Ability to serve as an advocate for the library	9.50
Excellent oral and written communication	9.50
Work collaboratively w/campus colleagues	9.30
Articulate vision for library w/in institution	9.10
Exercise mature judgment	9.10
Have MLS degree	9.00
Flexible	9.00
Listening skills	9.00
Commitment to professional development	9.00
Respect for scholarship and learning	8.90
Strong service orientation	8.50
Enthusiasm for work in educational environment	8.50
Sense of humor	8.40
Documented record of problem solving	8.30
Creative	8.00
High energy level	7.90
Dynamic	7.50
Second advanced degree	6.60

Note: 1 = unimportant, 10 = very important now and in the future.
Source: Hernon et al. (2003, pp. 70–71).

director data, which was outside the scope of this research. The present research made use of their three lists of qualities, identified by ACRL library directors to establish the base list to be used in the survey. The survey also allowed institutional administrators to add any qualities they felt were needed that were not covered in the ACRL list. This allowed for comparisons of like sets between the two groups so that the degree of congruence between them also could be determined.

The decision to use the Hernon et al. research was not without caveat, however. Their research exhibited some characteristics that diminish the usefulness of their findings and may have caused their findings not to be entirely representative of the groups studied or of library directors as a whole. While some of the items are attributes based on professional orientations and ideals (ideological) others would be better described as "experience" (experiential) or "credentials." This lumping of unlike items together and the use of the natural language terms of their participants allowed for some richness in the data while sacrificing precision of definition.

Table 3.   ALD-rated Areas of Knowledge.

Areas of Knowledge	Rating
Knowledge of library operations	8.90
Experience with change management	8.20
Current technology/info systems in libraries	8.10
Program assessment and evaluation	7.90
Experience with information technology	7.80
Experience with long-range planning	7.50
Collaboration w/other campuses/institutions	7.50
Experience with scholarly communication	7.30
Experience with public relations	7.30
Knowledge of collection development	7.20
Experience with marketing services and resources	7.20
Record of scholarly achievement	7.20
Experience with facilities planning	7.10
Fund-raising and securing funding support	7.00
Experience with information literacy	6.90
Knowledge of bibliographic control	6.90
Managing/planning digital libraries	6.70
Experience with grant writing	6.40
Planning/coordinating new library building	6.30
Expertise with distance education	5.10

Note: 1 = unimportant, 10 = very important now and in the future.
Source: Hernon et al. (2003, pp. 70–71).

The decision was also made with this research to lay the groundwork for more comprehensive comparisons in subsequent studies by aiming for the broadest sweep possible in order to obtain a fuller, more accurate picture of hiring administrators' views across the entire range of academic institutions in the United States. This limits the validity of the comparisons made with the data from just the ACRL directors.

DATA COLLECTION AND ANALYSIS

The population for this study was administrators of American colleges and universities, both public and private, granting associate or higher degrees, who have direct hiring responsibilities for the library director in their institutions. These positions, as expressed in the 2005 edition of the *Higher Education Directory*, were contacted at the general fax number given for each institution by name and title, using (in order of preference) the 05 field (Chief Academic Officer), the 02 field (Chief Executive

Officer within a system-President/Chancellor), the 03 field (Executive Vice President), or the 01 field (Chief Executive Officer-President/Chancellor). The faxed letter invited participation in the survey and asked for the invitation to be forwarded to a more appropriate person if the fax recipient would not directly participate in hiring for the library director position. The invitation directed each participant to use a specified password at the web address of the online questionnaire.

Participating administrators were asked to rate the qualities from the Hernon et al. study individually on the same scale (i.e., rather than ranking them in comparison to one another). Space was given for listing and rating other qualities not on the list that were deemed important by participants. A few other questions dealt with institutional characteristics in order to categorize responses. A final question offered an opportunity for general comments. To increase participation an incentive was included at the end of the questionnaire, where participants were given an e-mail address, which they could use to request a summary of the survey results in a way that was not tied to their anonymous answers on the survey.

Statistics describing institutional characteristics were calculated as were means for each attribute within each category for four sets of institutional characteristics: Carnegie class, funding type, enrollment size, and whether there were extenuating circumstances. The resulting means for each attribute were then used to rank a list for the combined responses as in the Hernon et al. (2003) study. Lists were also ranked for each of the institutional characteristics. The Spearman rank correlation coefficient test (Faculty of Health and Social Care, 2002) was chosen to show the strength of the correlation between the rankings of the hiring administrator participants from each Carnegie class and the library directors. Responses from each class, funding type, and institution size were compared separately with the combined rankings and those of the library directors. Although conventional wisdom holds that the necessity of using a non-parametric test limits the confidence in the resulting correlations, the confidence level (overall 94.7% at a confidence interval of $\pm 5\%$) is as high as practically possible for this type of research.

RESULTS AND DISCUSSION

How Representative Are the Results?

The response rates and an idea of how much of the population might have been missed in the invitation process, stratified by broad Carnegie class

Table 4.   Contact Numbers and Response Rates.

Class	No. in Class[a]	Contact Failures	Failures: % of Class	Response Freq'cies	Responses: % of Class	Responses: % of Contacts	Error Level (±5) (%)
PhD	261	2	0.8	28	10.7	10.8	17.5
MA	607	1	0.2	72	11.9	11.9	10.8
BA	609	2	0.3	68	11.2	11.2	11.2
AA	1,669	8	0.5	126	7.5	7.6	8.4
Spec'l	768	8	1.0	15	2.0	2.0	25.1
Tribal	28	0	0.0	3	10.7	10.7	53.5
Total	3,942	21	0.5	320	8.1	8.2	5.3

[a]Figures from Carnegie Foundation for the Advancement of Teaching (corrected), 2004.

(Carnegie Foundation for the Advancement of Teaching, 2001), are shown in Table 4. Of the 4,364 separate entries in the 2005 *Higher Education Directory*, 3,942 discrete institutions with separate governance were identified and 3,921 of these were successfully contacted, resulting in 320 usable responses and an overall response rate of 8.2%. Eight of these responses did not answer the demographic questions at the end of the survey, so were usable only in the overall response category. At a confidence interval of ±5% the response rate shows error levels for the classes as ranging from 8.4 to 53.5%, with an overall error level of 5.3%. For the purpose of comparisons between classes, the class with the highest error level determines the error level for each comparison. The error levels for some of the comparisons discussed below will therefore be considerably worse than for others.

The question might be posed as to whether some busy administrators had someone else fill in the survey. All but a handful (9 or 2.59% of actual respondents) filled in the position title and indications from those who did are that the survey did actually reach its intended audience of administrators with responsibility for hiring an ALD.

Tables 5 and 6 show the numbers and percentages in each funding type and size of the participants' respective institutions, broken down by Carnegie class. All funding types and sizes of schools in each class seem to be at least nominally represented among the participants. The divisions between publicly and privately funded schools in each class appear to roughly represent the proportions of existing schools in these categories as do the different sizes. Empty categories such as larger tribal and specialized schools represent institutions that, for the most part, simply do not exist.

Table 5. Class Respondents by Institution Funding Type.

Class	Of Total	Funding Type	
		Public	Private
PhD	28	14	14
	9.0%	50.0%	50.0%
MA	72	26	46
	23.1%	36.1%	63.9%
BA	68	10	58
	21.8%	14.7%	85.3%
AA	126	110	16
	40.4%	87.3%	12.7%
Spec'l	15	2	13
	4.8%	13.3%	86.7%
Tribal	3	3	0
	1.0%	100%	0.0%
Total	312	165	147
	100%	52.9%	47.1%

Ranking the Attributes by Carnegie Class

Participants were asked to rate each item as to its importance for the position of library director on a scale of 1–10 (1 being unimportant and 10 being extremely important). After the means were calculated from participant responses for each category and then for each type of institution within each category, the researcher placed them in the overall rank order within the categories (represented by the "total" column). For the sake of brevity in the tables the names of some of the longer items have been shortened.

Managerial Attributes

The category of managerial attributes, consisting of 14 items was placed in the rank order by the means of all responses. Table 7 gives the means broken down by Carnegie class for each item. This category showed the narrowest range of the three categories, from an overall low of 7.51 for experience developing digital libraries to a high of 8.90 for the ability to work in a collegial, networked environment. The tribal class was the most extreme (possibly due to the small number of responses in this class) rating the items with its highest overall scores high and most other items at the lowest rank. Otherwise, the highest ranking of each item was almost always in the

Table 6. Class Respondents by Institution Size.

Class	Of Total	Size in FTE							
		0–999	1K–2,499	2,500–4,999	5K–7,499	7,500–9,999	10K–14,999	15K–19,999	20K+
PhD	28 9.0%	3 10.7%	7 25.0%	1 3.6%	3 10.7%	1 3.6%	2 7.1%	3 10.7%	8 28.6%
MA	72 23.1%	12 16.7%	21 29.2%	20 27.8%	7 9.7%	2 2.8%	6 8.3%	3 4.2%	1 1.4%
BA	68 21.8%	28 41.2%	26 38.2%	8 11.8%	3 4.4%	1 1.5%	0 0.0%	0 0.0%	2 2.9%
AA	126 40.4%	21 16.7%	33 26.2%	37 29.4%	12 9.5%	6 4.8%	11 8.7%	2 1.6%	4 3.2%
Spec'l	15 4.8%	10 66.7%	4 26.7%	1 6.7%	0 0.0%	0 0.0%	0 0.0%	0 0.0%	0 0.0%
Tribal	3 1.0%	3 100%	0 0.0%	0 0.0%	0 0.0%	0 0.0%	0 0.0%	0 0.0%	0 0.0%
Total	312 100%	77 24.7%	91 29.2%	67 21.5%	25 8.0%	10 3.2%	19 6.1%	8 2.6%	15 4.8%

Table 7.   Means for Managerial Attributes by Broad Carnegie Class.

Managerial Attributes	PhD	MA	BA	AA	Sp	Tr	All
Work in collegial, networked environment	9.29	9.19	8.79	8.68	8.93	8.67	8.90
Commitment to institutional mission	9.18	9.03	9.04	8.65	8.47	9.67	8.87
Firm commitment to quality	9.29	8.96	8.72	8.79	8.60	9.33	8.84
Integrate print and electronic resources	8.64	8.86	8.63	8.40	8.80	7.67	8.59
Plan, implement, assess strategic goals	9.04	8.86	8.44	8.21	8.73	8.00	8.50
Personnel, fiscal, budget, program, management	9.25	8.84	8.09	7.96	8.27	9.33	8.30
Supervisory experience	9.11	8.46	8.00	8.13	7.93	8.67	8.23
Team building and participatory management	8.32	8.49	8.12	8.12	8.13	8.00	8.22
Facilitative leadership skills	8.39	8.41	8.04	7.93	7.93	7.67	8.12
Commitment to diversity	8.54	8.03	7.37	8.03	7.13	9.00	7.88
Demonstrated ability to identify trends	7.86	8.06	7.74	7.81	7.33	7.33	7.82
Record of innovative and effective leadership	8.36	7.99	7.59	7.52	7.73	7.73	7.73
Positions of increasing responsibility	8.11	7.96	7.57	7.57	6.87	7.00	7.66
Experience developing digital libraries	7.25	7.76	7.59	7.51	6.67	8.33	7.51

Note: 1 = unimportant, 10 = very important now and in the future. Sp = special, Tr = tribal.

doctoral or master's classes followed by the specialized, baccalaureate, and associates, in that order. Doctoral and tribal administrators rated personnel, fiscal, budget, and program management nearer the top than the others and commitment to diversity was much less important to baccalaureate and special administrators than to the others with tribal colleges understandably rating it the highest. Most of the baccalaureate schools were private, but this probably did not contribute to this lower score because, on the whole, the private schools actually rated this item slightly higher. Notably, the lowest rating by any subgroup (i.e., as designated by their Carnegie class, funding type, or institution size) on any of the managerial items was between six and seven, indicating that all of these items were considered at least somewhat important.

Personal Attributes
One respondent highlighted the number one choice in the category of personal attributes (Table 8) with a comment: "There is no greater attribute than personal integrity." Integrity was rated the highest of any item in all three categories by all but tribal administrators, and a second advanced degree came in a distant last on all ranking lists in the personal attributes

Table 8.   Means for Personal Attributes by Broad Carnegie Class.

Personal Attributes	PhD	MA	BA	AA	Sp	Tr	All
Integrity	9.82	9.74	9.38	9.49	9.53	8.67	9.56
Work collaboratively w/campus colleagues	9.36	9.33	9.00	9.08	9.07	8.67	9.15
Exercise mature judgment	9.04	9.19	8.85	8.93	8.93	9.00	8.97
Strong interpersonal skills	9.04	9.03	8.79	9.02	8.73	9.00	8.96
Enthusiasm for work in educational environ.	9.14	9.04	8.87	8.85	9.47	8.00	8.95
Strong service orientation	9.00	9.17	8.96	8.75	9.27	8.33	8.93
Articulate vision for library w/in institution	9.11	9.07	8.88	8.80	8.73	8.33	8.90
Excellent oral and written communication	8.64	8.99	8.56	8.99	8.80	8.33	8.86
Respect for scholarship and learning	9.18	9.10	8.82	8.60	8.93	9.00	8.82
Ability to serve as an advocate for the library	8.89	8.87	8.59	8.76	8.73	8.67	8.75
Listening skills	8.96	8.73	8.40	8.85	8.67	8.33	8.73
Have MLS degree	8.57	8.51	8.72	8.63	8.67	6.33	8.58
Flexible	8.68	8.50	8.28	8.65	8.47	9.00	8.54
Commitment to professional development	8.82	8.59	8.26	8.40	8.60	7.33	8.45
High energy level	8.29	8.09	8.13	8.18	7.60	7.67	8.12
Documented record of problem solving	8.11	8.14	7.94	7.93	7.53	9.00	7.97
Sense of humor	7.57	7.83	7.63	8.06	7.20	8.33	7.97
Creative	7.79	8.17	7.90	7.89	7.53	7.00	7.91
Dynamic	7.79	7.40	7.50	7.69	7.13	7.67	7.55
Second advanced degree	6.39	6.37	5.09	4.77	5.07	3.00	5.33

Note: 1 = unimportant, 10 = very important now and in the future. Sp = special, Tr = tribal.

category. In fact, if it were not for the extremely low scores for the second advanced degree, ranging from 3.00 for the tribal to 6.39 for the doctoral administrators, the range would have been much closer to that of the management attributes. Understandably, the highest ratings for a second advanced degree came from the two classes that offer such degrees. Once again, the tribal ratings seemed the most extreme overall with the MLS degree being notably less important to tribal administrators while flexibility, a record of problem solving, and a sense of humor were more important to them. One small public community college administrator who rated the MLS degree requirement as a 6 wrote, "I hired a[n] M.Ed. in Library Media, so Masters is 10 but not MLS." The same administrator added this telling statement in the comments section:

> Perhaps it was just the applicant pool, or the fact that our college is rural and associate degree, or maybe we just didn't pay enough to attract a bunch of hot dogs. But, I was interested in finding someone who had energy, wanted to take our dull library and make it exciting to students, someone who was willing to hound even our technical faculty and say 'when can I come over and visit with your students regarding our library offerings, and can I help you by suggesting research you might assign'. She is modern and up to date with databases and understands learning theory. Now, were we a graduate research

institution I might feel differently, but the MLS had no appeal to me. I surveyed a number of other colleges in my state to determine that a number of them had hired and were satisfied with their M. Ed. in Library Media degreed professional. My last librarian retired after 34 years. This past 18 months has been a breath of fresh air to me!

Areas of Knowledge

Knowledge areas (Table 9) came out with a more even spread with an overall low of 5.03 and a high of 9.15, indicating once again that all were considered important, although some to a far lesser degree than others. The more specific the knowledge areas, the fewer institutions there are that may see a need for that particular area. Fund-raising and grant writing which appeared at the bottom of the list overall were rated higher by doctoral administrators and somewhat higher by the tribal administrators.

Table 9. Means for Areas of Knowledge by Broad Carnegie Class.

Areas of Knowledge	PhD	MA	BA	AA	Sp	Tr	All
Knowledge of library operations	9.00	9.24	9.13	9.17	9.20	9.00	9.15
Current technology/info systems in libraries	8.96	9.13	8.79	8.94	9.00	9.33	8.96
Experience with information technology	8.54	9.06	8.62	8.67	8.87	9.33	8.73
Knowledge of collection development	8.00	8.33	8.50	8.18	8.60	8.00	7.26
Experience with information literacy	7.50	8.24	8.09	7.90	8.07	9.00	7.98
Program assessment and evaluation	7.82	8.20	7.99	7.89	7.73	7.00	7.95
Experience with long-range planning	7.93	8.10	7.88	7.82	8.47	7.00	7.93
Knowledge of bibliographic control	7.50	7.96	7.96	7.72	8.07	5.67	7.79
Experience with change management	7.50	8.10	7.54	7.68	7.20	8.33	7.70
Managing/planning digital libraries	7.54	7.94	7.59	7.37	7.07	8.33	7.55
Experience with scholarly communication	7.86	7.63	7.12	7.03	7.07	7.00	7.25
Collaboration w/other campuses/ institutions	7.75	7.04	6.82	7.51	6.67	7.33	7.22
Experience with public relations	7.21	7.03	6.53	6.86	6.60	8.00	6.85
Experience with marketing services and resources	7.07	6.91	6.76	6.85	6.47	6.33	6.83
Expertise with distance education	5.86	6.99	5.56	7.44	6.60	6.00	6.72
Experience with facilities planning	6.89	6.93	6.29	6.40	5.60	5.33	6.48
Record of scholarly achievement	6.57	6.23	5.68	5.69	5.53	5.67	5.86
Planning/coordinating new library building	6.43	5.99	5.50	5.61	5.13	6.33	5.74
Experience with grant writing	6.50	5.89	5.54	5.38	6.07	6.67	5.68
Fund-raising and securing funding support	6.43	5.37	4.84	4.73	4.20	5.33	5.03

Note: 1 = unimportant, 10 = very important now and in the future. Sp = special, Tr = tribal.

Knowledge of library operations received the best scores probably because it is a general catchall that incorporates everything technical that a library director needs to know. The next two on the list both include those two hot words: information and technology. Doctoral administrators gave their lowest rating to expertise with distance education, which received a surprisingly low overall score of 6.72. Experience with scholarly communication scores were not much higher in the doctoral schools (7.86) than anywhere else (7.03–7.63) and likewise with a record of scholarly achievement (6.57–5.53), despite what one reads in many position announcements. Experience with public relations was unusually higher for tribal administrators compared to the others.

It is noteworthy that the doctoral and master's administrators awarded more points overall in all three categories signifying a tendency on their part to ascribe greater importance to all items. Also, participants' rating of many items may have been influenced by temporary circumstances, a possibility that will be investigated more thoroughly later.

Ranking the Attributes by Funding Type

Managerial Attributes

Additional variables collected in the survey allowed for the comparison of the lists of administrators in institutions of different funding types. Tables 10–12 show the means broken down in this manner. All three categories reveal how little difference there is in the ratings between the two funding types. The widest spread of any item in the managerial list (0.45, Table 10) was for commitment to diversity, with the spread for commitment to institutional mission, supervisory experience, and experience developing digital libraries (each at 0.41) being the only others that came close.

Personal Attributes

Table 11 shows even less variance overall for the personal attributes category with the single exception of the spread between the ratings for sense of humor which was only at 0.61. All others varied 0.28 or less between the ratings by the public and private funding types.

Areas of Knowledge

There was a little more variance between the ratings from the two funding types in the areas of knowledge category. The spread surpassed 1.5 points

Table 10. Means for Managerial Attributes by Funding Type.

Managerial Attributes	Public	Private	Both	Spread
Work in collegial, networked environment	8.84	8.94	8.90	0.09
Commitment to institutional mission	8.68	8.87	8.87	0.41
Firm commitment to quality	8.87	8.84	8.84	−0.04
Integrate print and electronic resources	8.55	8.59	8.59	0.09
Plan, implement, assess strategic goals	8.44	8.50	8.50	0.14
Personnel, fiscal, budget, program, management	8.44	8.30	8.30	−0.23
Supervisory experience	8.45	8.23	8.23	−0.41
Team building and participatory management	8.24	8.22	8.22	−0.05
Facilitative leadership skills	8.13	8.12	8.12	−0.06
Commitment to diversity	8.10	7.88	7.88	−0.45
Demonstrated ability to identify trends	7.87	7.82	7.82	−0.10
Record of innovative and effective leadership	7.85	7.73	7.73	−0.27
Positions of increasing responsibility	7.76	7.66	7.66	−0.19
Experience developing digital libraries	7.72	7.31	7.51	−0.41

Note: 1 = unimportant, 10 = very important now and in the future.

Table 11. Means for Personal Attributes by Funding Type.

Personal Attributes	Public	Private	Both	Spread
Integrity	9.54	9.56	9.56	0.02
Work collaboratively w/campus colleagues	9.15	9.13	9.15	−0.03
Exercise mature judgment	8.99	8.97	8.97	−0.03
Strong interpersonal skills	9.02	8.90	8.96	−0.12
Enthusiasm for work in educational environ.	8.87	9.04	8.95	0.18
Strong service orientation	8.83	9.06	8.93	0.23
Articulate vision for library w/in institution	8.90	8.90	8.90	0.01
Excellent oral and written communication	8.98	8.70	8.86	−0.28
Respect for scholarship and learning	8.73	8.96	8.82	0.22
Ability to serve as an advocate for the library	8.76	8.75	8.75	−0.02
Listening skills	8.85	8.57	8.73	−0.28
Have MLS degree	8.61	8.58	8.58	−0.03
Flexible	8.65	8.40	8.54	−0.25
Commitment to professional development	8.50	8.40	8.45	−0.10
High energy level	8.24	7.99	8.12	−0.24
Documented record of problem solving	8.12	7.84	7.97	−0.28
Creative	7.96	7.87	7.91	−0.08
Sense of humor	8.11	7.50	7.82	−0.61
Dynamic	7.67	7.43	7.55	−0.24
Second advanced degree	5.39	5.31	5.33	−0.08

Note: 1 = unimportant, 10 = very important now and in the future.

Table 12. Means for Areas of Knowledge by Funding Type.

Areas of Knowledge	Public	Private	Both	Spread
Knowledge of library operations	9.14	9.19	9.15	0.05
Current technology/info systems in libraries	8.98	8.94	8.95	−0.04
Experience with information technology	8.81	8.69	8.73	−0.12
Knowledge of collection development	8.31	8.26	8.26	−0.05
Experience with information literacy	7.99	8.01	7.98	0.03
Program assessment and evaluation	8.03	7.87	7.95	−0.16
Experience with long-range planning	7.95	7.94	7.93	−0.04
Knowledge of bibliographic control	7.79	7.82	7.79	0.03
Experience with change management	7.85	7.55	7.70	−0.30
Managing/planning digital libraries	7.67	7.43	7.55	−0.23
Experience with scholarly communication	7.32	7.20	7.25	−0.13
Collaboration w/other campuses/institutions	7.68	6.71	7.22	−0.97
Experience with public relations	7.14	6.53	6.85	−0.61
Experience with marketing services and resources	7.13	6.52	6.83	−0.61
Expertise with distance education	7.43	5.90	6.72	−1.53
Experience with facilities planning	6.73	6.22	6.48	−0.52
Record of scholarly achievement	6.13	5.59	5.86	−0.53
Planning/coordinating new library building	6.03	5.38	5.74	−0.65
Experience with grant writing	5.84	8.49	5.68	−0.35
Fund-raising and securing funding support	5.36	4.65	5.03	−0.71

Note: 1 = unimportant, 10 = very important now and in the future.

for expertise with distance education as shown in Table 12. The rest of the higher variances between the funding type ratings belonged to the more specific items on the bottom half of the list. Even these, however, do not appear to be great differences in terms of the overall ratings. Funding type appeared to have little influence on the ratings in any category.

Ranking the Attributes by Institution Size

The means according to size of institution are given in Tables 13–15. Interestingly, the administrators from the smallest schools (less than 1,000 FTE) awarded the least points overall to items in all three lists, while those from the largest schools (over 20,000 FTE enrollment) awarded the most. Although the ratio scale did not run perfectly from smallest to largest, those who tended to award higher scores to the items in one attribute category, did so for the others as well, which gives an indication of their tendencies.

Table 13.   Means for Managerial Attributes by Size.

Managerial Attributes	<1K	1K+	2.5K+	5K+	7.5K+	10K+	15K+	20K+	All
Work in collegial, networked environment	8.64	8.81	8.98	8.92	9.10	9.42	8.88	9.33	8.90
Commitment to institutional mission	9.13	8.75	8.88	8.83	8.60	8.53	8.25	9.27	8.87
Firm commitment to quality	8.71	8.77	9.02	9.21	9.00	8.84	8.38	9.00	8.84
Integrate print and electronic resources	8.48	8.53	8.77	8.75	8.60	8.68	7.75	8.80	8.59
Plan, implement, assess strategic goals	8.17	8.47	8.56	8.67	8.60	8.79	8.63	9.33	8.50
Personnel, fiscal, budget, program, management	7.53	8.41	8.56	8.50	9.10	8.79	9.00	9.33	8.30
Supervisory experience	7.27	8.25	8.63	8.54	9.10	9.05	9.13	9.33	8.23
Team building and participatory management	7.81	8.10	8.48	8.42	8.60	8.68	8.38	8.73	8.22
Facilitative leadership skills	7.58	8.02	8.38	8.25	8.30	8.47	8.50	9.07	8.12
Commitment to diversity	7.40	7.82	8.02	8.25	8.60	8.00	8.13	9.07	7.88
Demonstrated ability to identify trends	7.38	7.78	8.11	8.17	8.30	7.79	8.38	8.13	7.82
Record of innovative and effective leadership	7.03	7.75	7.92	8.13	8.60	7.89	7.88	8.80	7.73
Positions of increasing responsibility	7.12	7.67	7.78	8.33	8.60	7.58	8.13	8.20	7.66
Experience developing digital libraries	7.21	7.32	7.88	8.29	7.90	7.68	6.13	8.00	7.51

Note: 1 = unimportant, 10 = very important now and in the future.

Table 14. Means for Personal Attributes by Size.

Personal Attributes	<1K	1K+	2.5K+	5K+	7.5K+	10K+	15K+	20K+	All
Integrity	9.42	9.66	9.56	9.79	9.30	9.37	9.38	9.60	9.56
Work collaboratively w/ campus colleagues	8.95	9.23	9.05	9.42	9.20	9.47	8.50	9.40	9.15
Exercise mature judgment	8.83	9.05	8.84	9.21	9.10	9.26	8.75	9.20	8.97
Strong interpersonal skills	8.74	8.95	8.95	9.42	9.10	9.16	8.88	9.20	8.96
Enthusiasm for work in educational environ.	9.08	8.88	9.02	9.08	8.40	8.84	8.63	8.87	8.95
Strong service orientation	8.81	8.85	9.22	8.88	8.20	9.26	9.00	9.07	8.93
Articulate vision for library w/ in institution	8.68	8.93	8.95	9.21	9.00	9.11	8.38	9.07	8.90
Excellent oral and written communication	8.77	8.78	8.81	9.13	8.80	9.16	8.75	9.07	8.86
Respect for scholarship and learning	8.88	8.85	8.72	8.75	9.00	8.89	8.50	9.20	8.82
Ability to serve as an advocate for the library	8.69	8.69	8.81	8.79	9.10	8.95	8.50	8.87	8.75
Listening skills	8.40	8.77	8.77	9.04	8.70	8.89	8.63	9.13	8.73
Have MLS degree	8.45	8.62	8.91	9.00	9.00	8.05	8.00	8.00	8.58
Flexible	8.34	8.56	8.50	9.13	8.70	8.84	8.00	8.33	8.54
Commitment to professional development	8.23	8.48	8.48	8.54	8.40	8.53	8.38	9.07	8.45
High energy level	7.82	8.07	8.17	8.42	8.30	8.42	8.00	8.93	8.12
Documented record of problem solving	7.71	7.93	8.00	8.50	8.50	8.32	7.38	8.40	7.97
Creative	7.77	7.88	8.06	8.13	8.30	7.95	7.38	8.00	7.91
Sense of humor	7.25	8.11	8.00	8.04	7.50	8.32	7.50	7.80	7.82
Dynamic	7.29	7.55	7.67	7.58	7.90	7.79	6.75	8.47	7.55
Second advanced degree	4.60	5.25	5.83	5.54	6.20	5.26	6.00	6.57	5.33

Note: 1 = unimportant, 10 = very important now and in the future.

Table 15. Means for Areas of Knowledge by Size.

Areas of Knowledge	<1K	1K+	2.5K+	5K+	7.5K+	10K+	15K+	20K+	All
Knowledge of library operations	9.13	9.34	9.13	9.04	9.20	9.00	8.75	9.00	9.15
Current technology/info systems in libraries	8.81	8.96	9.09	9.08	9.00	9.21	8.25	9.07	8.95
Experience with information technology	8.53	8.78	8.89	9.04	8.70	8.89	8.00	8.87	8.73
Knowledge of collection development	8.30	8.34	8.30	8.38	8.30	8.05	7.75	8.27	8.26
Experience with information literacy	7.96	8.09	8.16	8.21	8.10	7.58	7.25	7.53	7.98
Program assessment and evaluation	7.55	8.08	8.08	8.50	8.10	7.95	7.63	8.07	7.95
Experience with long-range planning	7.57	7.93	8.14	7.92	8.70	8.16	7.50	8.33	7.93
Knowledge of bibliographic control	7.96	7.85	7.91	7.83	7.90	7.21	7.13	7.27	7.79
Experience with change management	7.09	7.79	7.89	8.13	8.40	8.16	7.63	8.00	7.70
Managing/planning digital libraries	7.42	7.23	7.92	7.83	7.80	8.00	6.38	8.20	7.55
Experience with scholarly communication	7.05	7.23	7.42	7.29	7.20	7.11	7.13	8.13	7.25
Collaboration w/other campuses/institutions	6.52	7.26	7.36	7.58	8.50	7.37	7.00	8.67	7.22
Experience with public relations	6.25	6.89	7.19	6.71	7.50	6.84	7.75	7.73	6.85
Experience with marketing services and resources	5.97	6.91	7.28	7.21	7.50	7.00	7.50	7.47	6.83
Expertise with distance education	6.27	6.26	7.42	7.21	7.80	7.16	6.63	6.80	6.72
Experience with facilities planning	5.70	6.46	6.91	6.75	7.70	6.58	7.13	7.33	6.48
Record of scholarly achievement	5.25	5.70	6.36	6.17	6.50	5.63	6.63	7.20	5.86
Planning/coordinating new library building	4.90	5.77	6.05	5.50	7.30	6.11	6.63	6.80	5.74
Experience with grant writing	5.31	5.62	6.09	4.96	5.80	5.68	6.75	6.67	5.68
Fund-raising and securing funding support	4.22	4.92	5.52	4.54	5.70	5.47	5.50	7.33	5.03

Note: 1 = unimportant, 10 = very important now and in the future.

Managerial Attributes

The administrators from each size designation who gave higher scores generally also tended to give higher scores to all items within the managerial attributes category depicted in Table 13. This means that there would be little rearrangement of the order of the attributes from one school size to another. The lack of a smooth or regular progression from lowest to highest indicates that institution size is not a reliable mathematical predictor of how important these qualities are deemed by their administrators. No other noticeable patterns were found in this category's scores.

Personal Attributes

Table 14 exhibits greater spreads (of up to 2.07) occurring in the personal attributes category, meaning that the order of some items would jump several places from one subgroup to the next, but there were no clear patterns from smaller to larger schools here either. The second-largest size schools usually had the lowest scores while the largest size schools often had the highest.

Areas of Knowledge

Although there are no clear patterns in the areas of knowledge category (Table 15) from smaller to larger institutions, there are several items rated lower by administrators from the smallest schools than most others and higher by those from largest schools than most others. Most notably, the item "fundraising and securing funding support" was rated lowest by the smallest schools (4.22) and highest by the largest schools (7.33). The middle school size (7,500–10,000) also rated most items on the high side.

Ranking the Attributes by Extenuating Circumstances

Managerial Attributes

Tables 16–18 give an idea of how extenuating circumstances (temporary conditions at the institution) may have affected the results for each of the three areas. Participants were asked about any temporary conditions that would influence their choice of important library director attributes right now. The largest spread between those who claimed such circumstances and those who did not in the managerial attributes category (Table 16) was also in the highest rated one – the ability to work in a collegial, networked environment – at only 0.34. Although development of digital libraries was given a few times as a circumstance, that item varied only 0.07.

Table 16. Means for Managerial Attributes in Institutions with Extenuating Circumstances.

Managerial Attributes	Yes	No	All	Spread
Work in collegial, networked environment	9.17	8.84	8.90	−0.34
Commitment to institutional mission	8.87	8.87	8.87	0.00
Firm commitment to quality	8.83	8.86	8.84	0.03
Integrate print and electronic resources	8.46	8.61	8.59	0.15
Plan, implement, assess strategic goals	8.65	8.48	8.50	−0.17
Personnel, fiscal, budget, program, management	8.41	8.32	8.30	−0.9
Supervisory experience	8.39	8.24	8.23	−0.15
Team building and participatory management	8.35	8.20	8.22	−0.15
Facilitative leadership skills	7.93	8.13	8.12	0.20
Commitment to diversity	7.93	7.89	7.88	−0.05
Demonstrated ability to identify trends	7.70	7.85	7.82	0.16
Record of innovative and effective leadership	7.59	7.75	7.73	0.16
Positions of increasing responsibility	7.50	7.70	7.66	0.20
Experience developing digital libraries	7.59	7.52	7.51	−0.07

Note: 1 = unimportant, 10 = very important now and in the future.

Personal Attributes

Table 17 shows that the highest spread for the personal attributes category was the MLS degree (0.60) with sense of humor second at 0.41. The two items here with the next widest spreads may have been slightly influenced by the eight administrators who cited a change in reporting structure: flexibility (a 0.32 spread) and dynamic (0.35).

Areas of Knowledge

The areas of knowledge category likewise displayed little effect as shown in Table 18, although the most often mentioned extenuating circumstance (given 32 times) was also the widest spread between the two subgroups – that of facilities planning for a new library or renovation of an existing one (0.54). Institutional libraries merging (given four times as a circumstance) may have affected the collaboration with other campuses and institutions attribute (a 0.50 spread). A rating 0.26 higher for expertise with distance education was given by institutions not claiming special circumstances, although eight of those in the other subgroup cited development of distance education as a circumstance affecting their choices. Other circumstances given, which may have changed ratings slightly include accreditation visits (given three times), expected high turnover in positions, and tough budget times. The overall effects of such circumstances may have been slight, but

Table 17.   Means for Personal Attributes in Institutions with
Extenuating Circumstances.

Personal Attributes	Yes	No	All	Spread
Integrity	9.65	9.53	9.56	−0.12
Work collaboratively w/campus colleagues	9.11	9.15	9.15	0.04
Exercise mature judgment	8.98	8.98	8.97	0.00
Strong interpersonal skills	8.76	9.00	8.96	0.24
Enthusiasm for work in educational environ.	8.80	8.97	8.95	0.17
Strong service orientation	8.76	8.97	8.93	0.20
Articulate vision for library w/in institution	9.00	8.88	8.90	−0.12
Excellent oral and written communication	8.70	8.87	8.86	0.18
Respect for scholarship and learning	8.78	8.85	8.82	0.06
Ability to serve as an advocate for the library	8.72	8.76	8.75	0.05
Listening skills	8.61	8.74	8.73	0.13
Have MLS degree	9.11	8.51	8.58	−0.60
Flexible	8.26	8.58	8.54	0.32
Commitment to professional development	8.52	8.44	8.45	−0.08
High energy level	7.96	8.15	8.12	0.20
Documented record of problem solving	7.83	8.02	7.97	0.19
Creative	7.70	7.96	7.91	0.26
Sense of humor	7.48	7.89	7.82	0.41
Dynamic	7.26	7.61	7.55	0.35
Second advanced degree	5.28	5.36	5.33	0.08

Note: 1 = unimportant, 10 = very important now and in the future.

they definitely occurred as documented by a medium-sized public two-year
institutional administrator: "We recently built a new library. We deliberately looked for someone with facilities experience. Also, we combined
the library position with institutional leadership for distance education.
In a community college setting, administrators wear many 'hats' and this
seemed to be a natural fit, although it substantially limited the number of
applicants."

Adding New Attributes

The possibility that someone might want to add attributes that were not pre-
defined was anticipated by offering blank items at the end of each attribute
category for participants to add attributes and rate their importance.
The 140 qualities that were added to the three sections resulted in only 60
unduplicated additions. The rest were either duplications of someone else's

Table 18. Means for Areas of Knowledge in Institutions with Extenuating Circumstances.

Areas of Knowledge	Yes	No	All	Spread
Knowledge of library operations	9.43	9.11	9.15	−0.32
Current technology/info systems in libraries	9.00	8.95	8.95	−0.05
Experience with information technology	8.59	8.78	8.73	0.19
Knowledge of collection development	8.48	8.25	8.26	−0.23
Experience with information literacy	8.04	7.99	7.98	−0.05
Program assessment and evaluation	7.98	7.95	7.95	−0.02
Experience with long-range planning	8.04	7.91	7.93	−0.13
Knowledge of bibliographic control	7.80	7.80	7.79	0.00
Experience with change management	7.89	7.68	7.70	−0.21
Managing/planning digital libraries	7.76	7.52	7.55	−0.24
Experience with scholarly communication	7.39	7.24	7.25	−0.15
Collaboration w/other campuses/institutions	7.65	7.16	7.22	−0.50
Experience with public relations	6.98	6.84	6.85	−0.14
Experience with marketing services and resources	6.80	6.85	6.83	0.05
Expertise with distance education	6.50	6.76	6.72	0.26
Experience with facilities planning	6.96	6.41	6.48	−0.54
Record of scholarly achievement	5.91	5.87	5.86	−0.04
Planning/coordinating new library building	6.74	5.55	5.74	−1.19
Experience with grant writing	5.74	5.67	5.68	−0.07
Fund-raising and securing funding support	5.04	5.03	5.03	−0.01

Note: 1 = unimportant, 10 = very important now and in the future.

addition (46 or 32.9%) or duplicated items in another section (34 or 24.3%). These were corrected for the tabulation of the means and the comparisons based on them.

The results of this process are shown in Tables 19–21. Each category's attributes are ranked first by the number of participants adding them and then by the mean of the rating given to them. When a participant added an attribute without a rating (such as in the comments section at the end of the survey), the participant was added to the count for that attribute, but no rating for that participant was figured into the mean. Most of the attributes added were requirements unique to one institution, although that one participant usually felt strongly about the attribute, rating it at the high end of the scale. It might be argued that many of these are actually included in the attributes that were pre-defined by the library directors. It was felt that there was enough difference to list these separately in the interest of accuracy and comprehensiveness. The scope of this research did not allow

Table 19. Added Managerial Attributes.

Managerial Attributes	Count	Rate
Professional activities	3	8.67
Ability to deal with both internal and external environments: see the big picture	2	10.00
Ability to manage multiple contra[di]ctory priorities	2	10.00
Managing difficult employees/work with difficult people	2	9.00
Ability to further cause of library sciences in environment of shrinking resources	2	
Record of fairness with staff	1	10.00
Ability to administer professional staff members	1	9.00
Ability to work with two institutions with different missions	1	9.00
Efficient use of personnel caused by changes in libraries	1	9.00
Pro-active	1	8.00
Able to focus on larger issues and delegate others	1	
Must be willing to be hands-on reviewer of holdings and acquisitions	1	

Note: Rate: 1 = unimportant, 10 = very important now and in the future.

for further refining of these lists the way Hernon et al. (2003) did with the library directors.

Managerial Attributes

Just as there were fewer added, the least agreement occurred in the added managerial attributes category (Table 19), the top one being professional activities.

Personal Attributes

For the personal attributes category (Table 20) the most agreed-upon items were being learning/student centered, having a strong work ethic that is self-directed and entails a sense of responsibility, and the ability to understand, relate to, and work effectively with all campus constituent groups. Some also included a positive personality and compatibility with the institutional mission, which includes any doctrinal statement for religiously affiliated schools as some respondents noted.

Areas of Knowledge

In the areas of knowledge category shown in Table 21, several wanted directors who had had specific experience in an institution of the same class, type, size, or a combination of those as their own, and some wanted experience in working with and reaching academically challenged students.

Table 20. Added Personal Attributes.

Personal Attributes	Count	Rate
Learning/student-centered	11	9.70
Work ethic/self-directed/sense of responsibility	9	10.0
Ability to understand/work effectively with/relate to all campus constituent groups	7	9.60
Positive personality	3	10.00
Compatability [sic] with institutional mission/doctrinal statement	3	10.00
Ability to handle stress	1	10.00
Ability to read and understand	1	10.00
Ability to teach	1	10.00
Approachable	1	10.00
Basic intelligence	1	10.00
Commitment to the educations function of library staff and faculty	1	10.00
Doctoral degree (or ABD)	1	10.00
Independent leadership: knows what to do and does it	1	10.00
Not thinking that library education for students is what the library is about	1	10.00
Professionalism	1	10.00
Punctuality	1	10.00
Record of continuing professional development	1	10.00
Young enough not to resist change: frustrated with how old-timers ran paper/print	1	10.00
Orientation toward computer rather than "books"	1	9.00
Tenatious [sic]	1	9.00
Patience	1	8.00
Empathic [possibly meant empathetic]	1	7.00
Must be advocate for personnel, not just the "library"	1	
Must be willing to work for $40,000 plus benefits	1	
Professional/personal qualities to be considered a "peer" by the academic deans	1	
Someone who can adopt [sic] to multiple Presidents and Provosts as they come and go	1	

Note: Rate: 1 = unimportant, 10 = very important now and in the future.

The desire for library directors who could change the culture of their library also appeared more than once.

Comparison with the ALD Lists

The final phase of this research is a comparison of the ratings by the administrators for each of the three categories of attributes with those of the

Table 21. Added Areas of Knowledge.

Areas of Knowledge	Count	Rate
Experience in their type of institution or academic library (all different)	6	9.00
Experience working with academically challenged students	4	9.75
Experience in changing the culture within a library	3	10.00
Experience with collective-bargaining workplace	2	8.50
Experience in grant administration	2	8.00
Ability to build traffic in the libraries through programs, services, collections	1	10.00
Facility with computer learning technologies	1	10.00
Experience as an instructor	1	9.00
Experience dealing with publishers	1	9.00
Experience in providing media services to the university	1	9.00
Experience with ADA issues and accommodations	1	9.00
Experience with bringing library services to dorms, classrooms, etc.	1	9.00
Experience with friends and other support groups	1	9.00
Record of working with faculty/students outside the library — county agent model	1	9.00
Work experience in tech and public services	1	9.00
At least an additional language	1	8.00
Experience with archives	1	8.00
Record of self-evaluations	1	8.00
Copyright issues	1	
Development of library resources for graduate programs	1	
Having background in the research, theories, and principles of librarianship	1	
Must be able to teach in some specialized field within our curriculum	1	

Note: Rate: 1 = unimportant, 10 = very important now and in the future.

ACRL ALDs. The set of Tables 22–24 presented here is a side-by-side listing of the original attributes as rated by the administrators and the library directors. The ranking system used is ordinal, but does not assign intervals; therefore, it cannot be said how much more important any attribute is than any other in the eyes of the participants of either the Hernon et al. research or of this research.

Managerial Attributes

In Table 22, the first four items on the administrators' list are rated in the same order by the library directors but further down on the list. The next three appeared at the top for the library directors and in reverse order. The next two on the administrators' list were only one notch higher for the library directors, and the next pair went a little lower while the pair after them moved somewhat higher. The last item stayed in the same slot.

Table 22. Comparison of Lists for Managerial Attributes.

List as Rated by Administrators		List as Rated by ALDs	
Work in collegial, networked environment	8.90	Supervisory experience	9.00
Commitment to institutional mission	8.87	Personnel, fiscal, budget, program, management	8.90
Firm commitment to quality	8.84	Plan, implement, assess strategic goals	8.70
Integrate print and electronic resources	8.59	Work in collegial, networked environment	8.70
Plan, implement, assess strategic goals	8.50	Commitment to institutional mission	8.70
Personnel, fiscal, budget, program, management	8.30	Facilitative leadership skills	8.60
Supervisory experience	8.23	Team building and participatory management	8.50
Team building and participatory management	8.22	Record of innovative and effective leadership	8.50
Facilitative leadership skills	8.12	Firm commitment to quality	8.50
Commitment to diversity	7.88	Integrate print and electronic resources	7.80
Demonstrated ability to identify trends	7.82	Positions of increasing responsibility	7.70
Record of innovative and effective leadership	7.73	Commitment to diversity	7.50
Positions of increasing responsibility	7.66	Demonstrated ability to identify trends	7.20
Experience developing digital libraries	7.51	Experience developing digital libraries	6.60

Note: 1 = unimportant, 10 = very important now and in the future.

The administrators' ratings put items that were more ideological in nature (having to do with professional orientation) at the top, whereas the library directors had items of experience there. The other ideological items ranked higher with the administrators in terms of order than the other experiential items as well.

Personal Attributes

Integrity was the overwhelming favorite for the category of personal attributes as seen in Table 23 for both groups and they both rated all of the items in this category higher on average than those in the other two categories. The items in the middle of the list moved both up and down

Table 23. Comparison of Lists for Personal Attributes.

Rated by Administrators		Rated by ALDs	
Integrity	9.56	Integrity	9.80
Work collaboratively w/campus colleagues	9.15	Strong interpersonal skills	9.50
Exercise mature judgment	8.97	Ability to serve as an advocate for the library	9.50
Strong interpersonal skills	8.96	Excellent oral and written communication	9.50
Enthusiasm for work in educational environ.	8.95	Work collaboratively w/campus colleagues	9.30
Strong service orientation	8.93	Articulate vision for library w/in institution	9.10
Articulate vision for library w/in institution	8.90	Exercise mature judgment	9.10
Excellent oral and written communication	8.86	Have MLS degree	9.00
Respect for scholarship and learning	8.82	Flexible	9.00
Ability to serve as an advocate for the library	8.75	Listening skills	9.00
Listening skills	8.73	Commitment to professional development	9.00
Have MLS degree	8.58	Respect for scholarship and learning	8.90
Flexible	8.54	Strong service orientation	8.50
Commitment to professional development	8.45	Enthusiasm for work in educational environment	8.50
High energy level	8.12	Sense of humor	8.40
Documented record of problem solving	7.97	Documented record of problem solving	8.30
Creative	7.91	Creative	8.00
Sense of humor	7.82	High energy level	7.90
Dynamic	7.55	Dynamic	7.50
Second advanced degree	5.33	Second advanced degree	6.60

Note: 1 = unimportant, 10 = very important now and in the future.

from the administrators' to the directors' list, while the last six items stayed essentially the same except that high energy level and sense of humor traded places. It is interesting to note that many attributes in this category that appear lower in the library directors' list were actually rated higher by them, since they handed out higher scores overall in this category. Therefore, a lower place on the library directors' list in this category does not necessarily mean that they assigned less importance to an item.

Areas of Knowledge

Once again in Table 24, both lists showed the same item (knowledge of library operations) at the top, probably because it is so broad and really includes some of the others. It is also possible that the library directors in the

Table 24. Comparison of Lists for Areas of Knowledge.

Rated by Administrators		Areas of Knowledge	
Knowledge of library operations	9.15	Knowledge of library operations	8.90
Current technology/info systems in libraries	8.95	Experience with change management	8.20
Experience with information technology	8.73	Current technology/info systems in libraries	8.10
Knowledge of collection development	8.26	Program assessment and evaluation	7.90
Experience with information literacy	7.98	Experience with information technology	7.80
Program assessment and evaluation	7.95	Experience with long-range planning	7.50
Experience with long-range planning	7.93	Collaboration w/other campuses/ institutions	7.50
Knowledge of bibliographic control	7.79	Experience with scholarly communication	7.30
Experience with change management	7.70	Experience with public relations	7.30
Managing/planning digital libraries	7.55	Knowledge of collection development	7.20
Experience with scholarly communication	7.25	Experience with marketing services and resources	7.20
Collaboration w/other campuses/ institutions	7.22	Record of scholarly achievement	7.20
Experience with public relations	6.85	Experience with facilities planning	7.10
Experience with marketing services and resources	6.83	Fund-raising and securing funding support	7.00
Expertise with distance education	6.72	Experience with information literacy	6.90
Experience with facilities planning	6.48	Knowledge of bibliographic control	6.90
Record of scholarly achievement	5.86	Managing/planning digital libraries	6.70
Planning/coordinating new library building	5.74	Experience with grant writing	6.40
Experience with grant writing	5.68	Planning/coordinating new library building	6.30
Fund-raising and securing funding support	5.03	Expertise with distance education	5.10

Note: 1 = unimportant, 10 = very important now and in the future.

medium-sized ACRL libraries who rated this list see some of these areas (i.e., collection development, information literacy, knowledge of biblio-graphic control, managing/planning digital libraries, and expertise with distance education) as being the responsibility of librarians working under them and rated such areas lower than the administrators, many of whom come from small institutions with only one librarian. The most notable difference in this category is higher importance placed on grant writing and especially fund-raising by the library directors. Perhaps this is an area where they perceive a demand being placed upon them that is not as strong as they think it is, although there were some comments given by the administrators that implied or stated directly that library directors needed to be able to do more with less.

In all three categories, the ratings for any particular attribute were only rarely different by more than a single point between the two groups on a scale of 1–10, indicating the considerable consensus on these attributes for ALDs. The top several attributes on each of the lists appear to be requirements for all ALDs in the view of both groups.

Correlation to ALD Ratings

The ranked attributes of the total group are compared to those of each of the subdivisions, then to those of the library directors, and then the ranked attributes of each Carnegie class, funding type, and institution size are compared separately to those for the library directors. Tables 25–27 show the correlations for each of these comparisons in each of the three attribute categories, respectively. The closer the coefficient is to 1.0, the more agreement there is between the rankings for the two groups being compared, and a score of less than .5 does not show significant agreement at any level.

As can be seen in Table 25, three administrator subgroups did not show as strong a correlation as the others with the overall set of ranks for the managerial attributes category. These are the tribal class, the 7.5K–9,999 institutional size, and the 15K–19,999 institutional size. This is not surprising, since these were the three smallest response subgroupings, having frequencies of 3, 10, and 8, respectively. These could be showing differences in the thinking of all administrators in tribal institutions and in schools of this size, but the possibility that at least some of these differences from the rest of the overall group are anomalies in the particular administrators who responded from these categories cannot be discounted. At any rate, they do not offer a reliable picture of these three subgroupings.

Table 25. Comparisons of Managerial Attributes Response Means.

Groups	Compare: Total with Groups			Compare: ALDs with Groups		
	CC	CL	S2	CC	CL	S2
All				0.636	0.05	0.014
PhD	0.887	0.01	0.000	0.739	0.01	0.003
MA	0.990	0.01	0.000	0.615	0.05	0.019
BA	0.922	0.01	0.000	0.539	0.05	0.047
AA	0.947	0.01	0.000	0.494	N/S	0.072
Spec'l	0.935	0.01	0.000	0.595	0.05	0.025
Tribal	0.599	0.05	0.024	0.453	N/S	0.104
Public	0.972	0.01	0.000	0.624	0.05	0.017
Private	0.978	0.01	0.000	0.579	0.05	0.030
<1K	0.903	0.01	0.000	0.366	N/S	0.198
1K–2,499	0.996	0.01	0.000	0.619	0.05	0.018
2.5K–4,999	0.965	0.01	0.000	0.601	0.05	0.023
5K–7,499	0.876	0.01	0.000	0.495	N/S	0.072
7.5K–9,999	0.616	0.05	0.019	0.705	0.01	0.005
10K–14,999	0.833	0.01	0.000	0.767	0.01	0.001
15K–19,999	0.464	N/S	0.095	0.794	0.01	0.001
20K +	0.679	0.01	0.008	0.885	0.01	0.000

Note: CC = correlation coefficient, CL = confidence level, S2 = significance (two-tailed), N/S = not statistically significant.

What this means in terms of the results of this research is that these anomalies may have skewed the overall rankings of the administrators to some extent, but again, because of the small number of responses in the three differing subgroups (even though they are not overlapping at all) they would not have skewed the results a great deal. That the rest of the subgroups agree so well with the overall rankings of the whole, offers some evidence that they do not contain anomalies. Testing the administrators' responses in this way pointed out where their rankings are probably the least reliable as a picture of all institutions of their class, type, or size.

Managerial Attributes

In the managerial attributes category (Table 25), the comparison of the library directors' responses to those of the overall group of administrators as well as to those of each subgroup do show some differences, even though, statistically, most of them line up as being closely positively related (i.e., close to agreeing with each other). The picture that the figures show seems to be that overall, administrators agree with library directors on what makes a good ALD, but with some notable differences here and there. The subgroups that agree the most are those in the doctoral class, and those in institutions with over 10,000 FTE in enrollment: the bigger the school, the closer the agreement. Here the tribal class showed no statistically significant agreement, neither did the schools of less than 1,000 FTE nor those in the 5K–7,499 FTE enrollment sizes, even though they showed no anomalies in the previously discussed test. All of the other subgroups were less in agreement with the library directors than the total group, but still showed the statistically positive relationship.

Personal Attributes

The comparison of the responses in the personal attributes category in Table 26 revealed no strong anomalies as were found in the previous category, although the tribal administrators were somewhat less in agreement with the rest of the group than anyone else. They turned out to be the least in agreement of any of the subgroups with the library directors as well. The overall agreement between the administrators and the library directors increased in this category over the managerial attributes

Table 26.   Comparisons of Personal Attributes Response Means.

Groups	Compare: Total with Groups			Compare: ALDs with Groups		
	CC	CL	S2	CC	CL	S2
All				0.778	0.01	0.000
PhD	0.917	0.01	0.000	0.674	0.01	0.001
MA	0.958	0.01	0.000	0.722	0.01	0.000
BA	0.950	0.01	0.000	0.684	0.01	0.001
AA	0.938	0.01	0.000	0.874	0.01	0.000
Spec'l	0.944	0.01	0.000	0.666	0.01	0.001
Tribal	0.520	0.05	0.019	0.511	0.05	0.021
Public	0.968	0.01	0.000	0.859	0.01	0.000
Private	0.964	0.01	0.000	0.683	0.01	0.001
<1K	0.946	0.01	0.000	0.685	0.01	0.001
1K–2,499	0.982	0.01	0.000	0.787	0.01	0.000
2.5K–4,999	0.934	0.01	0.000	0.712	0.01	0.000
5K–7,499	0.910	0.01	0.000	0.857	0.01	0.000
7.5K–9,999	0.782	0.01	0.000	0.881	0.01	0.000
10K–14,999	0.923	0.01	0.000	0.800	0.01	0.000
15K–19,999	0.892	0.01	0.000	0.737	0.01	0.000
20K+	0.822	0.01	0.000	0.664	0.01	0.001

Note: CC = correlation coefficient, CL = confidence level, S2 = significance (two-tailed).

Table 27. Comparisons of Areas of Knowledge Response Means.

Groups	Compare: Total with Groups			Compare: ALDs with Groups		
	CC	CL	S2	CC	CL	S2
All				0.626	0.01	0.003
PhD	0.902	0.01	0.000	0.744	0.01	0.000
MA	0.993	0.01	0.000	0.633	0.01	0.003
BA	0.989	0.01	0.000	0.611	0.01	0.004
AA	0.977	0.01	0.000	0.592	0.01	0.006
Spec'l	0.979	0.01	0.000	0.586	0.01	0.007
Tribal	0.782	0.01	0.000	0.548	0.05	0.012
Public	0.982	0.01	0.000	0.634	0.01	0.003
Private	0.995	0.01	0.000	0.634	0.01	0.003
<1K	0.982	0.01	0.000	0.529	0.05	0.017
1K–2,499	0.991	0.01	0.000	0.646	0.01	0.002
2.5K–4,999	0.979	0.01	0.000	0.535	0.05	0.015
5K–7,499	0.976	0.01	0.000	0.643	0.01	0.002
7.5K–9,999	0.873	0.01	0.000	0.650	0.01	0.002
10K–14,999	0.927	0.01	0.000	0.635	0.01	0.003
15K–19,999	0.792	0.01	0.000	0.765	0.01	0.000
20K +	0.800	0.01	0.000	0.774	0.01	0.000

Note: CC = correlation coefficient, CL = confidence level, S2 = significance (two-tailed).

category also, being quite significantly positive. It is notable, however, that this category had the largest number of added attributes, and more contributors to the additions than both other categories combined.

Areas of Knowledge
Once again, there were no anomalies or even much mild disagreement in the comparisons of the subgroups with the overall group relative to the areas of knowledge category displayed in Table 27. There was some disagreement from more of the subgroups of administrators with the library directors, and even the statistically positive (agreeing) subgroups showed less agreement overall than in the personal attributes category. A large number of attributes were added in this category also, although, as noted earlier, many of them were unique to one institution.

CONCLUSIONS AND RECOMMENDATIONS

When presented with the same list, the hiring administrators rated the items similarly to the ratings of the ACRL ALDs, although the administrators identified several additional characteristics that they look for in their library directors. Obviously, no one will have every single quality called for by all of these administrators, especially some of the attributes required to meet special needs arising because of the unique circumstances at particular institutions. But there is enough agreement to show the basic qualities and credentials that ALDs and their hiring administrators say every ALD should have.

Academic administrators felt more strongly about the personal attributes category than the others, especially integrity and the ability to work collaboratively with other campus colleagues. The general area of knowledge of library operations was the most important area of knowledge to them, and management abilities were more important than most of the items in the areas of knowledge category. Many administrators felt strongly about specific attributes that they added, in all three categories. There was some agreement in the additions in that several participants added the same items. These included professional activities in the managerial attributes category; being learning/student centered, having a strong work ethic, the ability to work effectively with all campus constituent groups, a positive personality and compatibility with the institutional mission for the personal attributes category; and specific experience in the same kind of institution as their own, experience in working with academically challenged students and the ability to change the culture of their library as belonging to the areas of knowledge category.

When compared to the library directors' ideas, the ratings by the administrators for any particular attribute were only rarely different by more than a single point, which illustrates the considerable consensus found in this research. However, there were also important differences in emphases that should be noticed by anyone interested in academic library directorships. These emphases are probably best illustrated by a section of the data that has not been heretofore extensively explored: the comments made in the comments section of the survey.

The Comments Section

Many of the differences between ALDs and their hiring administrators were expressed in the "comments" section of the survey, which bears special attention, because reading the exact wording of the administrators paints a vivid picture that enhances what can be gained from the responses that were so limited by the pre-structured wording in the attribute lists. For example, one participant said of the pre-defined list and wording, "Just a comment: For many of the areas where you say 'demonstrated ability,' I would settle for persuasive evidence of ability."

The comments of some of the administrators dealt with whether their perceptions matched reality. One administrator at a masters-level institution wrote: "being small and private, we sense that the attributes we would desire in a new director will differ signficantly [sic] from those at a larger institution." An administrator from a large public doctoral-level school was concerned with turnover: "Stabilility [sic] in library leadership helps the entire academic community. Someone who can adopt [sic] to multiple Presidents & Provosts as they come and go is an important consideration. I don't know the average term that Directors/Deans of Libraries serve but longer is defintely [sic] better."

It was obvious that many participants approached the survey from the standpoint of what they would be looking for in their next library directory (and consequently, how he/she should differ from the present one) as expressed this way by someone at a small private two-year institution: "My highest priority for our next library director is that we find a person who is able to provide leadership regarding the integration of technology into all aspects of the library program." The necessity of looking forward instead of backward was noted by one administrator at a medium-sized master's level school: "The library director needs to help create the library of the future, a place where students and faculty will come together even as traditional offerings become electronic." Participants in this research often expressed the need for an entrepreneurial spirit in their library directors, in order to deal with the continuing changes they will face: "The Director must also be able to manange [sic] the changing role of the library to maintain its central role in the academic setting" (small, private, doctoral-level institution). But management is not enough in this brave new academic library world. A library director "needs to be a 'leader' not just a manager" (small public community college). ALDs are going to have to learn to think outside the box, if they have not already done so. As one large public doctoral institution's administrator put it, "Flexibility to consider information technology broadly, and beyond the library, is essential. In the next decade the amount of interuniversity collaboration in libraries will grow markedly. The director must embrace this, with all of the attendant risks." This new academic library world will look quite a bit different for smaller academic libraries according to a respondent from a public master's level institution of that size: "I don't believe that many small libraries will be around in their current context. The digital age is almost complete and it tends to force most scholarly work on the Internet or to large institution's libraries." But some things will stay the same, such as the view that "the MLS is the 'union card.' Leadership and management skills are the new disciplines required for directors of libraries which are more than research centers and are now responsible for multiple learning resources" (medium public community college).

The trend of merging the library with information technology services was addressed by two respondents. One small public community college administrator noted, "At our institution, the library is a part of the IT organization. So our Library Director must embrace this relationship and must work extremely well with the IT staff." Another at a small public baccalaureate college wrote, "Ability to work in a merged library-ITS information services environment is extremely important to me."

The importance of the ALD's place and standing within the institution was recognized by one large, public master's level university administrator: "I think that the ability to collaborate with college deans is of critical importance. Our Library Dean is a full (and participating) member of the Deans' Council, and this has proven to be helpful time and again." Two administrators, one from a small public community college and one from a smaller private master's level school had the perspective of having been ALDs themselves before.

A participant from a large public community college discussed the difficulties in assessing the fit of candidates for library director positions:

> I have hired and supervised Library Directors at three different institutions. Candidates rarely appreciate that their professional qualifications are generally not the deciding factors when a search committee is reviewing the top 10 applications, all of whom have already met the search criteria. Ability to embrace the institutional mission and having talents/experiences that do not duplicate those already available on campus are usually more important and usually not visible to the candidate.

"All the characteristics you have identifed [sic] are highly desirable. Many are hard to assess," wrote an administrator from a similar medium-sized college. "One aspect that you might consider is personal/professional references."

A characteristic that sums up several of the original and added attributes was noted either directly or indirectly in several comments – adaptability. This characteristic was most often expressed in terms of personal qualities being most important, because they cannot be learned as qualities in the other two categories can. One administrator from a small public baccalaureate college put it this way: "I would prefer someone with a strong service and research orientation. Some things can be taught and I would rather have a teachable person with less experience than a well-qualified one with no indication of desiring personal improvement. Integritiy [sic] is utmost." Another who worked at a tribal college said, "Skills can be learned (how to organize a library, assess satisfaction) although some are more challenging than others such as online education. However, personality traits and personal integrety [sic] are inherent – not learned. Even management styles can not be easily changed. A willingness to adapt is more important to me than a second degree." A library director must be able to "Hold firmly to what they believe is best but recognize they need to cooperate with others and other initiatives," according to a small, public community college administrator. The library director must exemplify the Renaissance person who can do anything. As a small, public community college administrator put it, "She or he must be broadly capable and able to take on nearly anything among a diverse number of college-wide job responsiblities [sic]." This calls for someone who reaches outside the library, according to another small, public community respondent: "The director must be well versed in the issues affecting higher education – not just this college and particularly, not just the library. Libraries are in a fight for survival against formidable forces."

One provost gave an honest appraisal of why this research was needed to find out what hiring administrators look for in their ALDs: "I rated numbers 15 and 16 [experience with information literacy and knowledge of bibliographic control] as 1's because I don't know what they are. Librarians don't hire librarians, provosts do."

Recommendations for Further Research

The broader questions touched upon by this research – of what attributes are important for ALDs, who thinks they are important, how important they are, and why they are important – should be revisited. This study looked outside the profession of librarianship to see what attributes and credentials are important for ALDs to have in the eyes of those who hire them. There is more at work here than can be readily understood within the confines of this single study. Picking up where this research has left off, recommendations for future studies include the following:

1. The attributes added by administrators should be refined in a similar Delphi process to the one employed by Hernon et al. (2003) but perhaps with better representation of the population of hiring administrators.

2. Studies similar to this one which will match administrators and library directors of the same institutions or similar institutions to see how well they agree on what makes a good ALD, perhaps by using focus groups or some similar method.

3. Another constituent group who should be considered in future research about what makes a good ALD is students.

4. The more difficult task of studying the expectations of search committees for academic library directorships should be undertaken at length for all classes, types, and sizes of institutions of higher education.

5. Studies using focus groups involving all of the stakeholders would bring more understanding to the topic as well. Depending on how they operate, search committees themselves have the potential of serving as focus groups on the expectations of the perceived major stakeholders of the institutions in regard to their next library directors.

6. More understanding is needed of just how search committees operate at this level, how they are configured, and consequently how much influence each member wields in the final decision.

7. Other questions to tackle include how well those involved in the hiring process represent all of the stakeholders in that process and how savvy are upper-level academic administrators, CIOs, etc. when it comes to library operations and issues.

8. The work of Hernon et al. should be augmented and confirmed or denied by a broad-based research incorporating adequate representation from all types and sizes of academic libraries, especially those that employ only one professional librarian position to see what difference that makes in needed attributes. It would be interesting to see how much agreement there would be if the Delphi method were used with both administrators and library directors to attempt to condense the additions into the few most important ones.

9. Other studies are needed to take the understanding gained in this and similar investigations and apply it to how ALDs receive their training, which of these attributes can be learned, and how they can best be learned and, of course, taught. For those that cannot be learned, how can they be identified in individuals, and how can these individuals best be recruited, groomed, and guided in their library careers?

10. Librarianship needs a deeper understanding in general of its needs in terms of leadership in order to meet the challenges of providing that leadership for the coming generations.

11. All of these studies should be replicated for library directors in public, special, and school libraries.
12. Some useful lessons were learned in performing this research that may enhance other research in the future. When using the online survey method, e-mails with "clickable" links afford great convenience to computer-literate populations, speeding up the process and likely reducing some of the problems involved in using faxes. Research should be done to see which method of invitation to an online survey is most effective.

It is possible that such studies could alter many of the conclusions of this research, making them all the more necessary. A study with a larger sample of ALDs than the Hernon et al. (2003) research might show statistically significant differences between the ALDs and their hiring administrators' views, especially in very small or very large institutions. The views of other stakeholders could prove to be radically different also.

The need to develop leadership in the profession has been discussed at length (Martin, 1997; O'Brien, 1989; Orenstein, 1999; Sheldon, 1991; Totten & Keys, 1994), and librarians have even begun forming programs of many types to meet that need (Hardesty, 1997; Hiatt, Hamilton, & Wood, 1993), but they still do not have the full picture that takes into account all of the major stakeholders and their needs. This is critical for a service profession such as librarianship.

REFERENCES

Aldridge, B. B. (1992). *Creativity of selected library directors at private liberal arts colleges in the United States.* Unpublished doctoral dissertation, Texas Woman's University.

Allen, B. L., & Weech, T. L. (Eds). (1995). *Critical issues in library management: Organizing for leadership and decision-making.* Papers from the thirty-fifth Allerton Institute. Occasional Papers, nos. 198/199. ERIC, ED 386191.

Anonymous (1991). After the fall: Reflections on being fired. *The Journal of Academic Librarianship, 17*(5), 302–303.

Bailey, M. J. (1992a). Leadership characteristics of assistant/associate directors. *Journal of Library Administration, 17*(3), 43–54.

Bailey, M. J. (1992b). Leadership qualities of assistant/associate directors. *Library Administration & Management, 6*(4), 193–196.

Boccaccio, B. A. (1993). *A political systems view of the influence of faculty search committee members upon the presidential selection process.* Unpublished doctoral dissertation, The University of Connecticut.

Brittingham, B. (1997). The library, information, and institutional outcomes: Searching in a time of change. *Journal of Library Administration, 24*(3), 59–71.

Bromert, J. D. (1984). *The role of search committees in strengthening the effectiveness of colleges and universities.* Unpublished doctoral dissertation, University of South Dakota.

Bundy, M. L., & Wasserman, P. (1979). *The academic library administrator and his situation.* College Park, MD: School of Library and Information Science.

Cargill, J., & Webb, G. M. (1988). *Managing libraries in transition.* Phoenix: Oryx Press.

Carlson, M. A., Jr. (1989). *Leadership in the university library: Case studies of five directors.* Unpublished doctoral dissertation, Columbia University.

Carnegie Foundation for the Advancement of Teaching. (2001). *Carnegie classification of institutions of higher education* (Available online at http://www.carnegiefoundation.org/Classification/CHE2000/Tables.htm). Menlo Park, CA: Carnegie Foundation for the Advancement of Teaching.

Chapin, L. W., & Hardesty, L. (1995). Benign neglect of the heart of the college: Liberal arts college deans look at the library. In: G. B. McCabe & R. J. Person (Eds), *Academic libraries: Their rationale and role in American higher education* (pp. 29–41). Westport, CT: Greenwood.

Cohn, W. L. (1976). An overview of ARL directors, 1933–1973. *College and Research Libraries, 37*(2), 137–144.

Cooney, D. (1952). Management in college and university libraries. *Library Trends, 1*(July), 83–94.

Cottam, K. M. (1994). Directors of large libraries: Roles, functions, and activities. *Library Trends, 43*(Summer), 15.

Craddock, G. E., Jr. (1986). *The role of the library director in the small private liberal arts college.* Unpublished doctoral dissertation, The University of North Carolina at Chapel Hill.

Crawford, A. L. (1982). *Skills perceived to lead to success in higher education.* Unpublished doctoral dissertation, The University of Alabama.

Curran, C., & Davidson, R. (1999). Sometimes the roof doesn't just leak, it caves in! *American Libraries, 30*(2), 29–31.

Davis, J. S. (2002). *Perceptions of critical skills of chief student affairs officers.* Unpublished doctoral dissertation, University of Georgia.

DePew, J. N. (1984). Survey of academic library administration: Factors affecting academic library administration 1976–1981. *Journal of Library Administration, 5*(Summer), 13–57.

Eggleton, R., & O'Dell, J. (1981). Selecting library managers. *Drexel Library Quarterly, 17*(3), 1–13.

Euster, J. R. (1986). *The activities and effectiveness of the academic library director in the environmental context.* Unpublished doctoral dissertation, University of California, Berkeley.

Euster, J. R. (1987). *The academic library director: Management activities and effectiveness.* New York: Greenwood Press.

Faculty of Health and Social Care. (2002). *Spearman's coefficient of rank correlation* (Available online at http://hsc.uwe.ac.uk/dataanalysis/quant_spear.htm). Bristol, UK: University of the West of England.

Farey, R. A. (1967). *The American library executive: An inquiry into his concepts of the functions of his office.* Unpublished doctoral dissertation, University of Illinois.

Fowler, P. R. (2003). *Leading technology in higher education: An empirical investigation of the role of the chief information officer.* Unpublished doctoral dissertation, Kent State University.

Fowler-Hill, S. A. (2001). *Full-time faculty recruitment and selection strategies practiced by learning-centered community colleges.* Unpublished doctoral dissertation, Oregon State University.

Garten, E. D. (1988). Observation on why so few chief library officers move into senior academic administration. *Library Administration & Management, 2*(March), 95–98.

Hardesty, L. L. (1997). College library directors mentor program: "Passing it on:" A personal reflection. *The Journal of Academic Librarianship, 23*(4), 281–290.

Hernon, P. (1998). The library director as scholar-librarian. *The Journal of Academic Librarianship, 24*(2), 111–112.

Hernon, P., Powell, R., & Young, A. (2001). University library directors in the Association of Research Libraries: The next generation, part one. *College and Research Libraries, 62*(2), 116–145.

Hernon, P., Powell, R., & Young, A. (2002). University library directors in the Association of Research Libraries: The next generation, part two. *College and Research Libraries, 63*(1), 73–90.

Hernon, P., Powell, R., & Young, A. (2003). *The next library leadership: Attributes of academic and public library directors.* Westport, CT: Libraries Unlimited.

Hiatt, P., Hamilton, R. H., & Wood, C. L. (1993). *Assessment centers for professional library leadership: A report to the profession from the Career Development and Assessment Center for Librarians.* Chicago: American Library Association.

Holmes, R. C. (1983). *The academic library director's perceived power and its correlates.* Unpublished doctoral dissertation, University of Minnesota.

Hutchins, E. C. (1974). *The role of the community college division chairman as perceived by the dean of instruction, assistant dean of instruction, division chairmen, and instructors of a community college.* Unpublished doctoral dissertation, East Texas State University.

Ivy, B. A. (1984). *Academic library administration: Power as a factor in hiring and promotion within a feminized profession.* Unpublished doctoral dissertation, University of Pittsburgh.

Johnson, D. R. J. (1987). *Cognitions in university hiring practices: A case study.* Unpublished doctoral dissertation, The Pennsylvania State University.

Karr, R. D. (1984). The changing profile of university library directors, 1966–1981. *College and Research Libraries, 45*(4), 282–286.

Kaufman, P. T. (1993). Library leadership: Does gender make a difference? *Journal of Library Administration, 18*(3–4), 109–128.

Krasowski, M. K. (1997). *Perceptions of trust in two year colleges.* Unpublished doctoral dissertation, University of Minnesota.

Lary, M. S. (2005). The inadequacy of LIS classifieds. *American Libraries, 36*(2), 29.

Lin, C. (2001). Changes in stated job requirements of director positions of academic libraries in the U.S. *Journal of Information, Communication and Library Science, 8*(1), 9–25.

Martin, R. R. (1997). Recruiting a library leader for the 21st century. *Journal of Library Administration, 24*(3), 47–58.

Martin, S. K. (1998). The changing role of the library director: Fund-raising and the academic library. *Journal of Academic Librarianship, 24*(1), 3–10.

McAnally, A., & Downs, R. (1973). The changing role of directors of university libraries. *College and Research Libraries, 34*(2), 103–125.

McCracken, P. H. (2000). The presence of a doctorate among small college library directors. *College and Research Libraries, 61*(5), 400–408.

McElrath, E. (2002). Challenges that academic library directors are experiencing as perceived by them and their supervisors. *College and Research Libraries, 63*(4), 304–321.

McKee, C. W. (1993). Understanding the chief academic officer: Beginning point in the development of a partnership between academic and student affairs. *College Student Affairs Journal, 13*(1), 13–16.

Mech, T. (1990). Academic library directors: A managerial role profile. *College and Research Libraries, 51*(5), 415–428.

Metz, P. (1977). *The academic library and its director in their institutional environments.* Unpublished Master's thesis, University of Michigan.

Metz, P. (1978). Administrative succession in the academic library. *College and Research Libraries, 39*(5), 358–364.

Metz, P. (1979). The role of the academic library director. *Journal of Academic Librarianship, 5*(July), 148–152.

Moran, B. (1983). Career patterns of academic library administrators. *College and Research Libraries, 44*(5), 334–344.

Moran, B. B. (1982). *Career progression of male and female academic library administrators.* Unpublished doctoral dissertation, State University of New York.

Moskowitz, M. A. (1986). The managerial roles of academic library directors: The Mintzberg model. *College and Research Libraries, 47*(5), 452–459.

Myers, M. J., & Kaufman, P. T. (1991). ARL directors: Two decades of changes. *College and Research Libraries, 52*(3), 241–254.

Newman, C. G., Dibartolo, A. L., & Wells, M. R. (1989). Becoming an effective academic library manager: Preparation, process, and performance. *Library Administration & Management, 4*(1), 33–37.

O'Brien, P. (1989). Quality leadership for the 21st century. *Journal of Library Administration, 11*(1–2), 27–34.

O'Connor, T. F., & Duchon, M. I. (1993). The college library assistant director: Serving at the pleasure. *Journal of Academic Librarianship, 19*(1), 12–15.

O'Keeffe, J. (1998). Small college library directors: Getting in the door and surviving on the job. *College and Research Libraries, 59*(2), 140–153.

Olsgaard, J. N., & Olsgaard, J. K. (1981). Post-MLS educational requirements for academic librarians. *College and Research Libraries, 42*(3), 224–228.

Orenstein, D. I. (1999). Developing quality managers and quality management: The challenge to leadership in library organizations. *Library Administration & Management, 13*(1), 44–51.

Parsons, J. L. (1976). Characteristics of research library directors, 1958 and 1973. *Wilson Library Bulletin, 50*(8), 613–617.

Perez, M. (1990). Recruiting leaders: How the process works and how it fails. *Liberal Education, 76*(1), 14–19.

Person, R. J., & Newman, G. C. (1988). *Selection of the university librarian: An OMS occasional paper* (ERIC, ED 293556). Washington, DC: Association of Research Libraries, Office of Management Studies.

Person, R. J., & Newman, G. C. (1990). Selection of the university librarian. *College and Research Libraries, 51*(4), 346–359.

Piccininni, J. (1995). *Qualifications necessary to become a library director* (ERIC, ED 383348). Houston, TX: University of St. Thomas.

Plate, K. (1970). *Management personnel in libraries: A theoretical model for analysis.* Rockaway, NJ: American Faculty Press.

Prather, D. D. (1980). *Qualities chief administrators of selected community and junior colleges perceive as important in perspective administrative staff members.* Unpublished doctoral dissertation, Indiana University.

Pugliese, P. J. (1985). *The nature of managerial work: The extent Mintzberg's roles are required by the chief executives in academic and public libraries.* Unpublished doctoral dissertation, University of Pittsburgh.

Rooks, D. C. (1994). Terms for academic library directors: Current validity of the 1973 McAnally and Downs findings. *Library Trends, 43*(Summer), 47–61.

Sager, D. (2001). Evolving virtues: Library administrative skills. *Public Libraries, 40*(4), 268–272.

Shaughnessy, T. W. (1987). Making the boss more effective. *Journal of Library Administration, 8*(2), 5–14.

Sheldon, B. (1991). *Leaders in libraries: Styles and strategies for success.* Chicago, IL: American Library Association.

Sheldon, B. (1992). Library leaders: Attributes compared to corporate leaders. *Library Trends, 40*(3), 391–401.

Skipper, C. E. (1979). Indicators of administrative effectiveness. Paper presented at the annual meeting of the American Educational Research Association, San Francisco, April. ERIC, ED 172638.

Snyman, R. M. (2001). Do employers really know what they want? An analysis of job advertisements for information and knowledge managers. *Aslib Proceedings: New Information Perspectives, 53*(7), 273–281.

Stewart, G. (2004). Defining the enrollment manager: Visionary, facilitator, and collaborator. *Journal of College Admission, 183*(Spring), 21–25.

Stussy, S. A. (1989). The candidate and the library director search committee in small academic libraries. *Journal of Academic Librarianship, 15*(4), 223.

Suwannarat, P. (1994). *Library leadership in research university libraries.* Unpublished doctoral dissertation, Peabody College for Teachers of Vanderbilt University.

Sweeney, R. T. (1994). Leadership in the post-hierarchical library. *Library Trends, 43*(1), 62–94.

Totten, H. L., & Keys, R. L. (1994). The road to success. *Library Trends, 43*(1), 34–46.

Twombly, S. B. (1992). The process of choosing a dean. *Journal of Higher Education, 63*(6), 653–683.

Veaner, A. B. (1984). *The assistant/associate director position in ARL libraries SPEC Kit 103.* ERIC, ED 243492.

Williams, D. E. (1998). The library director as a campus leader. In: T. F. Mech & G. B. McCabe (Eds), *Leadership and academic librarians* (pp. 39–54). New York: Greenwood Press.

Winston, M. D., & Dunkley, L. (2002). Leadership competencies for academic librarians: The importance of development and fund-raising. *College and Research Libraries, 63*(2), 171–182.

Winter, P. A. (1996a). The application of marketing theory to community college faculty recruitment: An empirical test. *Community College Review, 24*(Winter), 3–16.

Winter, P. A. (1996b). Recruiting experienced educators: A model and a test. *Journal of Research and Development in Education, 29*(Spring), 163–171.

Woodsworth, A. (1989). Getting off the library merry-go-round. *Library Journal, 114*(May), 35–38.

DETERMINING THE RELIABILITY AND VALIDITY OF SERVICE QUALITY SCORES IN A PUBLIC LIBRARY CONTEXT: A CONFIRMATORY APPROACH

John Patrick Green Jr.

ABSTRACT

This study used confirmatory factor analysis to analyze the secondary data resulting from a service quality survey conducted by a large public library. The library outsourced the development of this survey, which was founded on the well-recognized SERVQUAL and LibQUAL+ service quality models. Applying structural equation modeling and recognized fit indexes to the secondary data, this study determined that the library model did not fit the data and that the data itself were neither reliable nor valid. This study developed a nine-step process for implementing the SERVQUAL model that enables the data derived from SERVQUAL-type implementations to provide superior information for decision making.

Advances in Library Administration and Organization, Volume 26, 317–348
Copyright © 2008 by Emerald Group Publishing Limited
All rights of reproduction in any form reserved
ISSN: 0732-0671/doi:10.1016/S0732-0671(08)00207-1

INTRODUCTION

Service quality is a primary concern for most American companies today. In a 1990 Gallup poll, US businesses rated improving product and service quality as their primary objectives in the foreseeable future (Parasuraman, Zeithaml, & Berry, 1990). With the percentage of workers in the services sector increasing from 55% in 1929 to 80% in 1999 and the gross domestic product in the same years being 54 and 78% (Zeithaml & Bitner, 2003), it is no wonder that service quality is the center of attention in US boardrooms.

Many companies have failed to understand that services are much different from products. Services are intangible, inseparable, and hetero-geneous (Parasuraman, Zeithaml, & Berry, 1985). Services cannot be inventoried and unlike products, where the customer is not involved in the production process, customers are intimately intertwined in the service consumption process, even to the point of self-service. But the most important difference is that service quality is determined by the customer at every moment-of-truth interaction point with the company's delivery system, which makes services almost infinite in variability. The result is ubiquitous pressure to customize services at the customer level. This innate variability of services is diametrically opposed to the generations of teachings by the founding fathers of production efficiency, such as Fredrick Taylor's one best way (Scott, 2003), or the newer models of production efficiency, such as six sigma (Lambert & Carnell, 2004), both of which are designed to reduce duplicity of effort and drive out variability. A process rated at six sigma represents 3.4 defects per million. Blakeslee (1999) found that manufacturing firms usually performed at three to four sigma, whereas service companies are often between one and two sigma.

Today's service-dominated economy has resulted in a true paradigmatic shift as depicted by Kuhn (1996), wherein capital has been replaced by the customer as the scarcest resource (Peppers & Rogers, 2005) and the creation of value is no longer the sole domain of the firm (Prahalad & Ramaswamy, 2004b). The determination of a firm's quality and value, as well as which firm is worth loyalty, is now totally in the domain of the customer. Parasuraman et al. (1990) succinctly describe this new paradigm: "The only criteria that count in evaluating service quality are defined by customers. Only customers judge quality; all other judgments are essentially irrelevant" (p. 16).

The consumer today has more leverage than at any time in history and is connected as never before with access to heretofore proprietary corporate information, facilitated by the power of the Internet and powerful search engines such as Google, thus making them more highly aware and increasing their leverage as stakeholders. Customers, now free from isolation, have access to pertinent and unbiased information with which to make more informed decisions. Companies must face the reality of choosing between efficiency and profits or focusing on the customer as a true partner (Arussy, 2005).

Many companies have been unable to make the transition this shift requires due to ineffective leadership and change-resistant cultures. Paradigmatic shifts in the perception of leadership have also occurred over the last few years (Gronfeldt & Strother, 2006). This fact was highlighted in research by Jamrog and Overholt (2004), who found that in the 3 years preceding 2004, 40% of the 2,500 global CEOs were terminated as a result of a failure to develop or execute any meaningful strategy. The primary reason for this failure was an inability or unwillingness by top executives to make a connection between how their companies actually operate, how the market actually operates, and how the ever-changing and complex global environment affects the needs of their customers (Charan, Burck, & Bossidy, 2002). This fact is supported in a Gartner (2005) study of executives, mid-level managers, and employees in customer-facing positions, which found:

1. Executives who believe their company deserves their customers' loyalty: 41%.
2. Those who state that their executives do not meet customers frequently: 65%.
3. Those who say their company will take any customer who is willing to pay: 46%.
4. Those who have compensation tied to quality of service: 19%.
5. Those who agree they have the tools to service and resolve customer problems: 31%.
6. Through 2006, organizations will continue to fail to understand the true value of [customer] feedback, throwing away most information collected from customers (p. 5).

Parasuraman et al. (1990) added to the management issue by stating, "The root cause of our quality malaise in America today – the reason service isn't better than it is despite the fruits of excellent service – is the insufficiency of service leadership" (p. 5). Some use the slogan, "The head leads the way" (Gronfeldt & Strother, 2006, p. 3) to describe the importance of changing organizational cultural values to instill a collective leadership mind-set, not by simple empowerment, but by developing a shared understanding of the role of the entire organization in co-creating a unique value proposition with the customer (Prahalad & Ramaswamy, 2004a).

A recent Gartner (2005) study based on interviews with 175 top executives found that "over 90% of enterprises don't understand the customer ... and lack cross-functional processes that strengthen the customer experience" (p. 4). Many firms today still think they can win their customers' share-of-wallet by price alone, concentrating on any cost reduction possible, including business process outsourcing, product and service off-shoring, and even off-shoring customer service functions to countries such as India and the Philippines. In the process, they may be alienating some of their customers who perceive inferior service quality and reject off loading of additional costs. This trend is continuing, even in light of recent studies by Gartner (2005) that showed that "60% of organizations that outsource parts of the customer-facing process will encounter customer defections and hidden costs that outweigh any potential savings they derive from outsourcing" (p. 5).

As the global market becomes even more competitive, some corporate executives are becoming concerned about falling customer retention rates and about how to build competitive advantage while remaining profitable. They are also finding that their satisfaction ratings do not tell the whole story, especially in light of research showing many highly satisfied customers still defect (Reichheld, 1993, 2003; Reichheld & Sasser, 1990). The theory that service quality equals profits was not embraced until the links between increased service quality and profits were established. Only then did some corporations take a renewed and keen interest in developing a service quality climate within their companies. The anticipated rewards are many.

Service quality has been shown to correlate positively with global performance measures such as repurchase intentions (Bolton & Drew, 1991; Boulding, Kalra, Staelin, & Zeithaml, 1993), customer retention (Reichheld & Sasser, 1990), market share (Anderson & Zeithaml, 1984; Kordupleski, Rust, & Zahoric, 1993; Phillips, Chang, & Buzzell, 1983), financial return (Anderson, Fornell, & Lehmann, 1994; Fornell, 1992; Rust & Oliver, 1994), and other measures of financial performance (Roth & Jackson, 1995). In their *Harvard Business Review* article, Reichheld and Sasser (1990) stated, "Companies can boost profits by almost 100% by retaining just 5% more of their customers" (p. 105).

Just as important as implementing customer quality programs is the development of means to measure service quality from the customer's perspective (Churchill, 1979). The most used and today the de-facto standard for measuring service quality is the SERVQUAL gap model and survey instrument developed by Parasuraman, Zeithaml, and Berry (1988a), commonly referred to in the literature as **PZB**. It was posited as being generalizable to many different service contexts. When using SERVQUAL, it is recommended that data derived from the survey instrument be assessed to make sure they fit the model and also that the data be assessed for both reliability and validity for the contexts for which they are used, if the data are to provide information which has "truth value" (Miles & Huberman, 1994, p. 278).

BACKGROUND TO THE STUDY

The SERVQUAL model (Parasuraman et al., 1988a) (see Appendix A) and the accompanying multi-item scale survey instrument has been the most implemented service quality measurement tool in the literature and has been implemented in almost every conceivable service context. The SERVQUAL survey instrument is comprised of two batteries of 22 questions each. One battery measures customers' perceptions of service quality (see Appendix B) using five quality dimensions – reliability, assurance, tangibles, empathy, and responsiveness – which Grapentine (1999) dubbed the RATER dimensions:

1. Reliability – Ability to perform the promised service dependably and accurately.
2. Assurance – Knowledge and courtesy of employees and their ability to inspire trust and confidence.
3. Tangibles – Appearance of physical facilities, equipment, personnel and communications material.
4. Empathy – Caring, individualized attention the firm provides its customers.
5. Responsiveness – Willingness to help customers and provide prompt service.

The second 22-question battery measures customers' expectations of service quality using the same quality dimensions. A gap score is obtained by developing composite scores of the five dimensions and subtracting the total expectations score from the total perception score. The resulting score, if negative, indicates that improvements may be necessary.

The SERVQUAL instrument has received much criticism for being posited as an industry generalizable instrument (Parasuraman et al., 1988a). Implementations in the academic library context, which is pertinent to this research, also failed to produce the SERVQUAL dimensions

(Andeleeb & Simmonds, 1998; Cook, 2001; Cook & Thompson, 2000; Hernon & Altman, 1998; Hernon & Whitman, 2001; Nitecki, 1996).

This inability to arrive at simple structures has been posited to be the result of failing to follow the same survey methodology as used by the SERVQUAL authors (Parasuraman et al., 1988a). The original authors followed the mixed-methods (qualitative–quantitative) survey methodology proposed by Churchill (1979). The Churchill process (see Fig. 1) is an eight-step approach that contains both an exploratory first phase to craft and purify the scales and a confirmatory second phase to determine if a

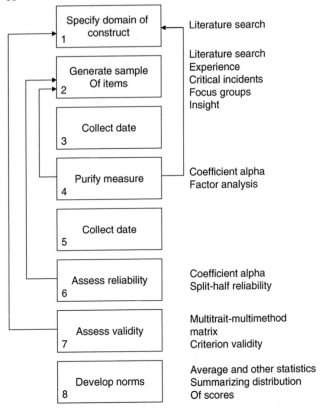

Fig. 1. Churchill's Eight-Step Survey Methodology. *Note:* From Churchill (1979, p. 66). Copyright 1979 by the American Marketing Association. Reprinted with Permission.

theoretical model is supported by the data from the sample (Byrne, 2001; Kline, 2005; Lomax & Schumacker, 2004). For example, when wording changes to the original SERVQUAL survey instrument's items were made to fit a particular context or when survey items were deleted and new items added, the resulting model may or may not have been subsequently purified through an appropriate and rigorous exploratory factor analysis first phase as described in Churchill's methodology (steps 1–4).

Additionally, few implementations in the literature subjected either the original SERVQUAL scale (if used in a new service context) or the context-customized SERVQUAL-type model to the second phase (steps 5–8), which was intended to assess the validity of the model. By not confirming that the model and its dimensions fit the data, the information derived may be of little business value.

NATURE OF THE PROBLEM AND CONTEXT

Public libraries today have certainly morphed from their early beginnings as the Royal Library of Alexandria in the Third Century B.C. At no time in history have the core services of libraries (quiet place for study; collection of books; newspapers and magazines and knowledgeable librarians) been added to as they have in the last few decades. Some added services to libraries include: digital collections of books, videos and, CDs, age-specific services, computers, Internet access, wireless connectivity, community information, and even amenities such as coffee shops. Most of these new services are the effects of socio-economic forces, the Internet and the ever-present effects of Moore's Law which doubles technology throughput every 18 months. Our industrialized system is generating more goods and services than any previous time in history, delivered through an ever-growing number of delivery channels. This burgeoning complexity of product and service offerings, as well as the associated risks, confounds and frustrates most time-starved consumers. Product and service variety has not necessarily resulted in better consumer experiences. Public libraries are not immune from these same revolutionary forces that much of the for-profit sector has been experiencing over the last couple of decades. These same socio-economic and technology forces may be eroding the customer-perceived value of the core historic services of libraries by providing alternatives and substitutes that are more relevant to the user population. Some studies have been undertaken to obtain a better understanding of the relevancy of public libraries in today's infosphere.

Based on results from a 2003 OCLC study (OCLC, 2003), *Environmental Scan: Pattern Recognition*, there appears to be dissonance between the environment and content that libraries provide and the environment and content that information consumers want and use. A later 2005 OCLC study (OCLC, 2005), *Perceptions of Libraries and Information Resources* reported that: (1) libraries were not the top choices for access to electronic resources, (2) libraries do not market services effectively, (3) the library is not the first or only stop for many information seekers, (4) library as place was based on nostalgia and still focused on books, (5) the highest number of negative associations had to do with service quality. The findings suggest that public libraries should rejuvenate the brand which is currently based on books and by conducting local polls and open-ended surveys.

In order for libraries to remain relevant they will be required to rethink how they use resources from various stakeholder groups in order to create value and provide patron-perceived quality services for their different customer/citizen/patron groups. To remain relevant, libraries will need to develop an assessment culture that continually assesses and measures how they are co-creating value and providing quality services through personalized experiences that are unique to each individual library user. To remain relevant libraries can no longer think or act unilaterally (Prahalad & Ramaswamy, 2004a). Libraries can learn from some of the methods that some forward-thinking for-profit, not-for-profit, and even other government organizations have been forced to implement to remain competitive, remain viable, or remain funded. Most of these methods are focused on the customer and have started to transition from a focus on outputs that focus on efficiencies of internal processes to a focus on outcomes that touch the customers they serve.

The most prominent assessment of service quality in the academic library environment is the research conducted at Texas A&M University by Colleen Cook, Fred Heath, and Bruce Thompson. They produced the LibQUAL+ scale to measure service quality specific to the academic library environment. Their scale was modeled after the original 22-item SERVQUAL scale developed by Parasuraman et al. (1988a) to measure service quality in the for-profit context. The LibQUAL+ model and its variables have been refined over the years with thousands of academic respondents and the scales have even been confirmed using structural equation modeling (SEM) techniques.

One of the first public libraries to develop a service quality model specific to the public library context using the SERVQUAL model is KCLS, the subject of this article. This library is a large public library system – in fact, "the nation's second-busiest library system behind Queens, NY" (Ervin, 2006, p. 1). This Library is comprised of 43 branches located throughout the largest county in the state. The Library provides myriad services to a diverse population of over 900,000 patrons who hold library cards. Unfortunately, the 11-step methodological approach advocated by the SERVQUAL authors (see Appendix E) was not followed by the vendors the Library hired, resulting in data that do not fit the model and that are not reliable or valid. Validating that the measures used in the SERVQUAL survey instrument adequately represent the constructs and their relationships in the model is of vital importance in producing useful data for developing information and aiding in the decision-making process. What is needed is a clearly defined process for implementing the SERVQUAL model in a public library, or any other environment, that will provide optimal data reliability, data validity, and model fit.

The survey methodology used by this library to assess library service quality was based on the SERVQUAL model. This library study also attempted to assess the impacts of service quality on patron satisfaction and loyalty which comprised the structural portion of the model (see Fig. 2). In this research, the library will simply be referred to as Library.

The overarching objective of this survey was to provide insights to aid Library management in transforming the organization so it can continue to offer services that patrons perceive as valuable. The Library is a quasi-government entity that uses public funds, yet is not accountable to the government for the use of these non-governmental funds. Oversight for the Library is the sole responsibility of the Library's board of directors. Public records show that the Library outsourced the development of the survey on January 5, 2005, to two separate organizations. It appears that only one organization was involved in the actual survey development process.

The survey was fielded using an intercept method during a 2-week period to current library patrons visiting the library. Non-users of the library were not included. For library website users a random self-selection method was utilized. The survey yielded 5,405 respondents with 1,800 with full row responses (answered all questions). Survey development took 7 months, and the survey was offered to patrons as a web-based instrument during a 2-week period starting on July 14, 2005. Library employees were employed in the survey delivery process. The data analysis and reporting phase ended with descriptive data and a report (KCLSm, 2005) which included the study's aims, methodology, and findings.

The report revealed that the survey architects stopped short of confirming that their hypothesized model (they fit the data to the model) and they

KCLS High-Level Conceptual Framework (model)

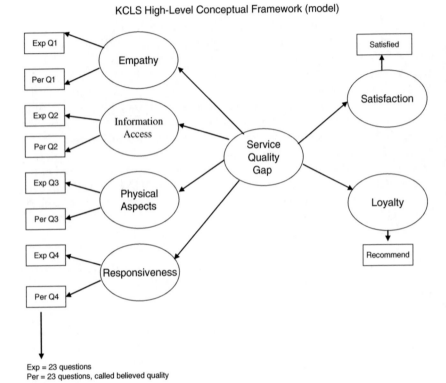

Exp = 23 questions
Per = 23 questions, called believed quality

Fig. 2.   Library Conceptual Framework of Service Quality.

presented no statistics regarding the reliability or validity of the data in their report to management (KCLS, 2005). The outsourced organization failed to respond to subsequent queries for information on the exact steps they followed, as outlined in both the SERVQUAL and LibQUAL+ models; according to the report they based their model development on these explicitly stated models using the term "on the shoulders of giants" (KCLSm, 2005, p. 1). In short, there is no way to reproduce or validate the findings, other than to begin with the raw data as this study purported to do. Good research dictates that any research report, especially if the data is to be used for decision-making purposes, should include enough information (such as correlation or covariance matrices, at the very least, etc.) so another researcher can validate their steps and findings.

The Library service quality model (Fig. 2) was posited by the Library's survey architects as resulting from factor analysis. It shows four dimensions, or constructs – empathy, information access, physical aspects, and responsiveness – two of which differ from the original SERVQUAL dimensions. It is not clear why the survey authors found it necessary to initially develop new dimensions not present in either the SERVQUAL or LibQUAL+ instruments. Had the Library authors simply implemented either the SERVQUAL of LibQUAL+ surveys as off-the-shelf instruments would the results be significantly different from an information standpoint, especially if used as part of an exploratory pilot program? These four constructs in Fig. 2 are referred to as the *measurement* model. Information access is reflective of a dimension obtained in the LibQUAL+ implementation of the academic library context (Cook, 2001). Information access "reflects the change from wholly print-based context to one without regard to format or location" (p. 264). Physical aspects closely resemble SERVQUAL's tangibles dimension and is described as "the physical evidence of the service" (Parasuraman et al., 1985, p. 47). Each of the four constructs has an average of five expectations and five corresponding perceptions measures (questions). When the composite scores for the expectations battery are subtracted from the composite scores from the corresponding perceptions battery of each construct, the resultant composite score forms the service quality gap. The larger the gap, the more inadequate is the perceived service quality from the patron's perspective. Service quality, in turn, is posited to affect both patron satisfaction and loyalty.

In Fig. 2 the satisfaction and loyalty variables comprises the structural portion of the model. These were implemented to show the relationship and impact of the service quality gap on both satisfaction and loyalty. Unfortunately, both the satisfaction and loyalty constructs (variables) used by the library consultants were single-item scales so the data produced cannot be validated.

The use of single-item latent variables (not composites of multiple items) can be used only if the error variance is known beforehand from research in similar context or if the error variance is set to zero. In addition, measurement models with only one factor must have at least three indicators to be identified (Kline, 2005). Measurement models with more than one factor must also follow the two-indicator rule suggested by Bollen (1989). Some SEM applications give error messages if single-items are used without these steps. It is unlikely that any latent variable in the social sciences can be perfectly measured without error (Fornell, 1996). As both the *satisfaction* and *willingness to refer* (loyalty) variables use single-item constructs with no mention of their error variance, it is highly unlikely that they have no error or that they could be used in a descriptive study as having no error, especially when measurement error in surveys is often much greater than the sampling error (Andrews, 1984; Fornell, 1996). Most implementations of conceptual frameworks, in the literature, that incorporate the SERVQUAL's dimensions' relationship to satisfaction and behavioral intentions (the loyalty variable is but one of the variables in the behavioral intentions battery – PZB (Parasuraman, Zeithaml, & Berry, 1996) incorporate models that have at least three items for each construct (Brady, Cronin, & Brand, 2002; Parasuraman, Zeithaml, & Berry, 1994a, 1994b; Yang, 2001). Therefore both the satisfaction and loyalty variables should have at least three items to be properly identified.

The library survey architects cited the article by Reichheld (2003) for the loyalty variable (recommend) which was coined the Net Promoter Score (NPS). The NPS used a 0–10 scale with endpoints "Not at all likely" and "Extremely likely." The wording was, "Would you recommend us to a friend or colleague?" The library survey architects used the wording, "How likely are you to recommend KCLS to others?" They also used a seven-point 1–7 scale with endpoints "Not at all likely" and 'Completely likely." Not using the exact wording, scale and endpoints may change the meaning to the survey respondent and therefore change the quality of the data produced.

In addition, the "recommend" variable did not appear to be relevant in all contexts. Reichheld stated, "In a few situations it [recommend] was simply irrelevant... [such as] in industries dominated by monopolies where consumers have little choice" (p. 51). From this, it appears that the loyalty may not be operationalized the same in a government context and it is in a for-profit context where consumers may have more choices.

The resulting model the Library used contained both an expectations and perceptions battery; however this research analyzed only the *perceptions* battery of the measurement model since the *expectations* battery was not subjected to factor analysis. These included the Library's four service quality dimensions: empathy, information access, physical aspects, and responsiveness. Table 1 shows the Library questions (measures), latent variables (dimensions), percent responses, rankings and other descriptive statistics.

The Library project did not appear to follow all the steps necessary for developing new scales or for validating currently available scales in a new context, according to the Churchill process. By failing to subject the results of the exploratory first phase to the confirmatory second phase, the Library model's fit to the sample data was not assessed. The failure to confirm the model's internal consistency (reliability) and convergent and discriminant

Table 1. Questions, Latent Variables, and Other Descriptive Information.

Question Number in Survey	Measure in Model	Description	Latent Variable Unobservable	Number of Respondents of 5,405 Total
2	PEM1	Respect for diversity	Empathy	3,660
13	PEM2	Putting customers' best interests at heart	Empathy	4,018
11	PEM3	Library as heart of the community	Empathy	3,929
3	PEM4	Polite and friendly staff	Empathy	4,487
19	PEM5	Caring staff	Empathy	4,206
17	PIA1	Variety and choice in the collections	Information access	4,176
18	PIA2	Access to library collections	Information access	3,897
5	PIA3	Programs, event and classes	Information access	3,011
15	PIA4	Communications with customers	Information access	4,113
4	PIA5	Online access from outside the library	Information access	3,769
23	PIA6	Overall convenience	Information access	4,333
10	PPA1	A space for quiet study	Physical aspects	4,174
1	PPA2	Having enough room	Physical aspects	4,268
22	PPA3	Overall safety	Physical aspects	3,841
21	PPA4	A comfortable and welcoming place	Physical aspects	4,345
7	PPA5	Building layout and design	Physical aspects	4,110
20	PPA6	Furnishings and equipment	Physical aspects	4,181
8	PRE1	Staff knowledge and accuracy	Responsiveness	4,260
6	PRE2	Understanding customer needs	Responsiveness	4,205
12	PRE3	Timeliness of service	Responsiveness	4,118
16	PRE4	Willingness to help	Responsiveness	4,329
14	PRE5	Taking time to help customers	Responsiveness	4,290
9	PRE6	Neat appearing staff	Responsiveness	4,292

Table 1. *(Continued)*

Question Number in Survey	Missing % Pairwise	Rank	Mean	SD	Standard Error	Skew	Cr.	Kurtosis	Cr.
2	32.28	4	6.27	1.041	0.017	−1.855	−30.914	4.478	35.390
13	25.66	11	6.05	1.098	0.017	−1.519	−24.075	3.204	24.404
11	27.31	21	5.51	0.032	0.021	−0.756	−13.127	0.294	3.099
3	16.98	1	6.38	0.963	0.014	−2.038	−33.356	5.216	39.160
19	22.18	7	6.20	1.201	0.016	−1.614	−25.271	3.466	24.759
17	22.74	19	5.64	1.100	0.019	−0.925	−16.467	1.016	8.960
18	27.90	14	5.99	1.147	0.018	−1.294	−23.315	2.328	21.627
5	44.29	18	5.65	1.111	0.021	−0.489	−14.223	0.703	7.027
15	23.90	15	5.96	1.139	0.017	−1.186	−17.778	1.648	10.117
4	30.27	9	6.10	1.031	0.019	−1.544	−26.556	2.852	22.969
23	19.83	12	6.04	1.491	0.016	−1.224	−20.149	2.019	17.266
10	22.78	23	5.23	1.321	0.023	−0.739	−12.885	0.054	0.765
1	21.04	22	5.44	1.024	0.020	−0.806	−12.183	0.472	2.273
22	28.94	5	6.24	1.015	0.017	−1.724	−26.388	3.911	26.847
21	19.61	8	6.16	1.209	0.015	−1.425	−24.266	2.726	23.357
7	23.96	20	5.64	1.057	0.019	−0.965	−16.526	1.219	10.383
20	22.65	17	5.80	0.930	0.016	−0.888	−14.653	1.111	8.099
8	21.18	6	6.23	1.107	0.014	−0.432	−19.819	2.846	10.991
6	22.80	16	5.94	1.057	0.017	−1.319	−20.358	2.381	16.823
12	23.81	13	5.99	0.938	0.016	−1.247	−20.914	2.222	19.375
16	19.91	2	6.36	0.990	0.014	−1.917	−29.808	4.972	32.434
14	20.63	3	6.27	1.012	0.015	−1.766	−28.377	4.251	32.550
9	20.59	10	6.07	1.025	0.015	−1.251	−23.591	2.127	23.714

and nomological validity poses the likelihood that the model may not have measured what it was purported to measure.

It was not mentioned whether an assessment as to unidimensionality of measures was undertaken by the Library, and therefore, addition of individual construct item scores to form composite scores was questionable. The Library survey architects reported using principle component factor analysis (PCA), yet only the "believed quality" (perceptions) battery scores of 23 questions were analyzed using PCA. The "expectations" battery of 23 questions was not subjected to PCA analysis. The Library methodology section (KCLSm, 2005) stated, "The four hypothesized Quality dimensions [also called constructs or factors] – responsiveness, empathy, physical aspects, and information access – were confirmed for the 'believed quality' scores by applying principal component analysis" (p. 9).

The fact that the "perceptions-only" battery, and not the "expectations" battery, was subjected to exploratory factor analysis added to the possible irrelevance of the difference scores and subsequent information relevance. In addition, the data screening portion of this study also revealed that the data did not meet the requirements of multivariate normality (skew and kurtosis, etc.) which is necessary to conduct factor analysis. In addition, upon conducting PCA and CFA analysis the four constructs in Fig. 2 could not be duplicated using any of the PCA techniques available in SPSS 15 or CFA techniques available using SPSS (AMOS), Lisrel, or EQS structural modeling programs.

The survey design used a convenience sampling strategy of patron interception and self-selection. Only patrons who were physically at the library during the 2-week survey period, who logged onto the library web site, or who took paper surveys home from the library were polled. Users or non-users who were not present during the 2-week period were not surveyed. As such, inferences would not be generalizable to the library population. The survey architects relied solely on the sample size of the convenience sample to provide generalizability: "A large sample size was planned (3,400 +), which would maximize generalizability of results" (KCLSm, 2005, p. 3). A large sample size, however, has other problems such as inflated significance. Had a random sampling survey design been utilized to incorporate all members of the Library population, a less biased sample might have been attained.

There is also some confusion as to the population and sample frame for the survey methodology approach. The definition of patron (user) was explicitly stated in the consultant's proposal (Furnow, 2005) as, "We'll start by defining users as anyone who uses either the libraries or the web site, regardless of whether they hold a library card (for example, teachers)" (p. 3). However, statements were made in the Report that the sample demographic proportions matched the population of the county (less one large city) which is certainly not "anyone who uses the library ... or whether they hold a library card."

This research adds value to upper management by determining if inferences can legitimately be made from the survey questions (Sharma, Netemeyer, & Bearden, 2003). Higher quality data that is shown to be both reliable and valid will lead to better-informed management decisions.

RESEARCH QUESTIONS AND HYPOTHESES

The purpose of this research was to assess the degree of fit of the proposed *measurement* model as posited in the conceptual framework in Fig. 2, to the data, using confirmatory factor analysis (CFA) incorporating SEM. This confirmatory approach added value to management as an improved tool for more informed decision making by providing an assessment of the reliability and validity of the survey data. This study adds knowledge needed to confirm initial use of newly developed survey instruments and validate use of currently available scales in a context different from that in which they were developed.

The research questions and associated hypotheses in this research were threefold: (a) to determine how well the hypothesized conceptual *measurement* model (the four dimensions on the left side of Fig. 2) from the Library survey of over 5,405 library patrons fit the survey data, (b) to determine the reliability of the survey data, and (c) to determine the validity of the survey data. This study's research questions were based on the purpose of the study:

1. How well does the measurement model, as identified in the conceptual framework in Fig. 2, fit the sample scores?
2. What is the reliability of the scores derived from the survey instrument?
3. What is the validity of the scores derived from the survey instrument?

The hypotheses for answering the three research questions, and the complete procedures for their answering them, are beyond the scope of this article but are available in the full dissertation (Green, 2007).

With increasing regularity, companies today have used the de-facto service quality measurement standard, SERVQUAL, to measure how customers perceive their firm's service quality. Some, like the Library project, have also used the SERVQUAL-type model as the foundation for measuring relationships, such as loyalty and satisfaction.

SUMMARY

Some academic and public libraries are adopting the SERVQUAL model and survey instrument to gain insights on how patrons perceive the quality of the library's services. Some have attempted to follow the same steps that the SERVQUAL authors used. However, some of these organizations are stopping at the exploratory phase and not confirming whether their newly developed service quality models actually fit the data derived from the survey instrument. In addition, when using the standard, off-the-shelf SERVQUAL instrument, many are not assessing the reliability or validity of the data. Validating that the measures used in a survey is of vital importance in producing useful data for developing information and aiding in the decision-making process.

The purpose of this research was to assess the degree of fit of the proposed measurement model to a secondary dataset from a large public library system. Appropriate fit indexes from the literature were used (Hu & Bentler, 1999; Kline, 2005; Lomax & Schumacker, 2004). This confirmatory approach incorporated the second phase of Churchill's survey methodology, and was enhanced by newer additions to the Churchill methodology (Anderson & Gerbing, 1988). In addition, this study assessed the reliability and validity of the data. As a result of this assessment, a 9-step process for implementing a potentially viable SERVQUAL-type model was constructed that could be used by others contemplating a similar implementation (see Appendix C).

The subject of this research study was a large public library system that had conducted a service quality analysis to gain insights on how patrons perceived the quality of the services. The objective of this survey was to provide insights to aid Library management in transforming the organization in order to offer more services that patrons perceive as valuable.

The survey development and implementation was contracted to an outside consulting firm. The survey methodology the firm used to assess library service quality was based on the SERVQUAL model developed by Parasuraman et al. (1988a) and the academic library context based LibQUAL+ model developed by Cook and Heath (Cook & Heath, 2001). Instead of implementing either the SERVQUAL or LibQUAL+ scales intact, a mixed-methods approach was utilized by the contractors that contained a qualitative first phase to develop scale items and factors and a quantitative second phase to confirm these factors.

Survey development took 7 months, and the survey was offered to patrons primarily as a web-based instrument during a 2-week period starting on July 14, 2005. The data analysis and reporting phase ended with descriptive data and a report that included the study's aims and findings.

An analysis of the report (KCLS, 2005) showed that the survey architects stopped short of confirming that the hypothesized model actually fit the data from the survey instrument. No statistics regarding the reliability or validity of the data were included in their report to management. In addition, no steps were presented by the survey architects for implementing the SERVQUAL model, as recommended by the SERVQUAL authors (see Appendix E). The report included no information on some critical aspects of this research and it did not present any reliability or validity assessments. As a result, a researcher had no clear methodology by which to reproduce or validate the report findings, other than to begin with the raw data, as this study did.

Methodology

This study used a deductive, fixed, quantitative design with qualitative underpinnings. The data analysis was based on Library secondary cross-sectional survey data. The research methodology employed in this project was primarily confirmatory and focused on the quantitative second phase of a mixed-methods approach. This research was ex post facto and non-experimental, and, therefore, no variables were manipulated. Analysis of the data resulting from the Library survey used the scientific method and principles of "good research" (Cooper & Schindler, 2003, p. 13). The data analysis method was based primarily on the use of CFA using SEM.

Findings from Independent Expert

In order to remain as unbiased as possible, the original Library raw dataset (5,405) was examined by an independent researcher who used the Lisrel SEM program with non-significant differences in findings. For example, both researchers found that the data did not meet multivariate normality necessary for conducting exploratory factor analysis. The data contained high skewness and kurtosis and should be transformed. Both researchers could not duplicate the dimensions seen in Fig. 2 using the raw data. In addition, both researchers found an inadmissible solution with a non-positive definite covariance matrix using the library data. The results of this independent researcher were not significantly different from the findings of this study, in that the model did not fit the data according to pre-specified cutoff points as determined by the literature. However, the fact that the Library model was rejected with this sample does not mean it would also be rejected using another sample from the Library population.

Causation must also be used guardedly in research assessment, including SEM. Causation requires three factors, as posited by John Stuart Mill: (a) the cause has to precede the effect in time (temporal precedence), (b) cause and effect have to be related, and (c) other explanations of the cause–effect relations have to be eliminated (Kline, 2005). None of these has been adequately accomplished with this study.

CONCLUSIONS

The SERVQUAL gap model of Parasuraman, Zeithaml and Berry has been the standard tool organizations could use to measure service quality and to modify their processes and technology to optimize the customer service experiences. Developed in 1984, the SERVQUAL model and instrument has received continual methodological refinements to now advocate the use of advanced statistical analysis techniques (SEM) to confirm that the SERVQUAL gap model actually fits the data in any context. Although the SERVQUAL gap model has its critics on both theoretical and operational grounds it still predominates as a service quality measure.

Many organizations implementing the SERVQUAL model, either as an off-the-shelf survey instrument with minor modifications (wording changes or adding and subtracting survey items) or by developing an individualized instrument through a mixed-methods approach similar to the how the SERVQUAL model was originally designed, do not follow the original model's 11-step process the SERVQUAL authors used to develop SERVQUAL (see Appendix E). In addition, many do not assess the psychometric properties of the 22-question perception and 22-question expectation scales individually before developing composite scores and then subtracting these composite scores to arrive at a service quality gap score. Unless both batteries are defined by the same unidimensional constructs, rational inferences from the resulting gap scores cannot be made (Carr, 2002).

Of equal importance is the fact that the SERVQUAL model is considered a total market survey, usually administered only once or twice per year, but is only one of the 12 research approaches for monitoring service quality in an organization. Other approaches such as transactional surveys (satisfaction and loyalty surveys), lost customer surveys, customer advisory panels, service reviews, customer complaint analysis, and employee surveys should be implemented to form a more iterative and holistic view of service quality. Furthermore, many forget the benefits of qualitative methods such as observations. One does not need to use surveys to ask if cell phone use is an issue when employees and management can visually see cell phone use is disrupting other patrons.

Many organizations also fail to realize that the SERVQUAL model consisted of five gaps (see Appendix D): Gap1: Customers' expectations versus management perceptions, Gap2: Management perceptions versus service specifications, Gap3: Service specifications versus service delivery, Gap4: Service delivery versus external communication, Gap5: The discrepancy between customer expectations and their perceptions of the service delivered (service quality gap). However, many still prefer to assess only the fifth gap which is actually a function of the other four gaps within the organization and their effect on the service quality gap. Without measuring and understanding the impact of the other organizational gaps and how they affect the fifth gap, the total market survey cannot disclose operational causal linkages that might be changed to improve service quality.

The primary benefits of this research were threefold:

1. In the specific case of the Library, the research disclosed that the model did not fit the data and that the reliability and validity of the data was not supported.
2. It developed a nine-step process that any organization attempting to implement SERVQUAL can use to assist in developing more viable models for their specific context, which have sound psychometric properties and whose reliability and validity is assessed and reported. These abbreviated steps are as follows: (1) screen data for multivariate normality (transform data), (2) check for missing values and outliers, (3) conduct PCA, (4) conduct CFA, (5) check for reliability (composite reliability, average variance extracted, Cronbach alpha), (6) check for unidimensionality, (7) check for discriminant validity, (8) check for convergent validity, and (9) check for nomological validity. The above steps assume that scale development and scale purification are conducted using sound survey methodology techniques.

3. The 9-step process can be used by others to validate previous findings of other SERVQUAL implementations and determine if inferences can be made from the results.

This research was significant in that it provided Library management with an objective assessment of the Library model's fit to the survey data. It also provided an assessment of the reliability and validity of the survey data as a tool for improved decision making. More importantly, this research provided a case study that demonstrated the necessity of adhering to all steps in the survey development methodology process if meaningful outcomes that facilitate better decision making are to be realized. Due to the high levels of missing data (some questions have up to 40% missing data) it was necessary to assess whether the missing data were missing systematically, which would reduce the reliability and validity of the results. High non-response rates might indicate issues with respondents' under-standing of the question or how the question was worded, to cite only two possible issues.

RECOMMENDATIONS FOR FUTURE RESEARCH

This study highlighted the need to develop a predictable process by which the SERVQUAL model and instrument can be successfully implemented within any organization, whether public or private and also allow another researcher to be able to duplicate the process and validate the findings of a study. A sample process is included in Appendix C. Management can also be more confident in using the resulting information for decision-making purposes.

As depicted in this study, the four-factor Library model in Fig. 2, using the same raw data and all available factor analysis techniques, could not be replicated. The results of this study have highlighted that implementing a mixed-method SERVQUAL approach is much more complex than many of its users believe. Since the bedrock of the SERVQUAL scales is the 22-question perception and expectation batteries, it is imperative that the psychometric properties of each battery be assessed before they are made into composite scores and subtracted from each other. This includes factor analysis to determine if the same factors exist in each battery and that the measures for each factor are unidimensional. Omitting this step may also be why many SERVQUAL implementations failed to replicate the original five-factor structure.

In many cases the results provided by statistical analysis can be flawed because the data was not properly screened to assess its applicability for the statistical tests contemplated. A thorough analysis of the data should be included as required by these tests. In this study the data was found to not meet multivariate normality standards. The findings of this study also posited that insufficient time was devoted to the qualitative phase which includes scale purification (steps 1–4 in Fig. 1). It is not unusual for quantitative researchers to feel uneasy in a mixed-methods setting. Since the qualitative phase forms the basis for the theory and relationships in the conceptual model, it is vitally important that adequate time be devoted to this phase and that researchers have the requisite skills to achieve the research objectives.

Since the SERVQUAL instrument is not generalizable in whole to all contexts, continued research should be devoted to refining the process by which the SERVQUAL model is implemented to arrive at useful information that is reliable and valid within the particular context. Implementation of the 9-step approach in this study may help maximize these criteria. More research should be also be committed to other aspects of service quality measurement, beyond simply focusing on the gap between expectations and perceptions. This includes implementing and evolving the extended five-gap SERVQUAL model within the organization. SERVQUAL may also be beneficial when implemented as part of the customer alignment portion of other organizational performance management and measurement toolsets such as the Baldrige Criteria or the Balanced Scorecard. However, without a viable methodology for effecting change in the organization to improve service quality, its measurement is a hollow exercise.

REFERENCES

Andeleeb, S. S., & Simmonds, P. L. (1998). Explaining user satisfaction with academic libraries: Strategic implications. *College and Research Libraries* (March), 156–167.

Anderson, C., & Zeithaml, C. P. (1984). Stage of the product life cycle, business strategy, and business performance. *Academy of Management Journal*, 37(March), 5–24.

Anderson, E. W., Fornell, C., & Lehmann, D. R. (1994). Customer satisfaction, market share and profitability: Findings from Sweden. *Journal of Marketing*, 58(July), 53–66.

Anderson, J. C., & Gerbing, D. W. (1988). An updated paradigm for scale development incorporating unidimensionality and its assessment. *Journal of Marketing Research*, 25(2), 186–192.

Andrews, F. M. (1984). Construct validity and error components of survey measures: A structural modeling approach. *Public Opinion Quarterly*, 404–442.

Arussy, L. (2005). *Passionate & profitable: Why customer strategies fail and 10 steps to do them right.* New York, NY: Wiley.

Blakeslee, J. A. (1999). Implementing the six sigma solution. *Quality Progress, 32*(7), 77–85.

Bollen, K. A. (1989). *Structural equations with latent variables.* New York, NY: Wiley.

Bolton, R. N., & Drew, J. H. (1991). A multi-stage model of customers' assessments of service quality and value. *Journal of Consumer Research, 17,* 375–384.

Boulding, W., Kalra, A., Staelin, R., & Zeithaml, V. A. (1993). A dynamic process model of service quality: From expectations to behavioral intentions. *Journal of Marketing Research, 30*(1), 7.

Brady, M. K., Cronin, J. J., & Brand, R. R. (2002). Performance-only measurement of service quality: A replication and extension. *Journal of Business Research, 55,* 17–31.

Byrne, B. (2001). *Structural equation modeling with AMOS.* Mahwah, NJ: Lawrence Erlbaum Associates, Publishers.

Carr, C. L. (2002). A psychometric evaluation of the expectations, perceptions, and difference scores generated by the IS-Adapted SERVQUAL instrument. *Decision Sciences, 33*(2), 281–296.

Charan, R., Burck, C., & Bossidy, L. (2002). *Execution: The discipline of getting things done.* New York, NY: Crown Business.

Churchill, G. A. (1979). A paradigm for developing better measures of marketing constructs. *Journal of Marketing Research, 26,* 64–73.

Cook, C. (2001). *A mixed-methods approach to the identification and measurement of academic library service quality constructs: LibQual+.* Unpublished Dissertation, Texas A&M University.

Cook, C., & Heath, F. M. (2001). Users' perceptions of library service quality: A LibQual+ qualitative study. *Library Trends, 49,* 548.

Cook, C., & Thompson, B. (2000). Reliability and validity of SERVQUAL scores used to evaluate perceptions of library service quality. *Journal of Academic Librarianship, 26,* 248–258.

Cooper, D. R., & Schindler, P. S. (2003). *Business research methods* (8th ed.). New York, NY: McGraw Hill.

Ervin, K. (2006). King County libraries may curtail key service to patrons from Seattle. *Seattle Times,* p. 4.

Fornell, C. (1992). A national customer satisfaction barometer: The Swedish experiment. *Journal of Marketing, 56,* 6–21.

Fornell, C. (1996). Customer satisfaction methodology: A summary of key issues. Retrieved August 8, 2005, from www.cfigroup.com

Furnow, L. (2005). *Fernow consulting library proposal.* In: KCLS (Ed.). Seattle, WA: Fernow Consulting, LLC.

Gartner, C. (2005). Enterprises with loyal customers generate profits up to 60% higher than those of competitors. Retrieved November 3, 2005, from www.perseus.com/survey/solutions/index.html

Grapentine, T. (1999). The history and future of service quality assessment. *Marketing Research* (Spring), 5–20.

Green, J. P., Jr. (2007). *Determining the reliability and validity of service quality scores in a public library context: A confirmatory approach.* Ph.D. dissertation, ProQuest Digital Dissertations database. Publication no. AAT 3241793. Retrieved February 23, 2008. Capella University, Minnesota.

Gronfeldt, S., & Strother, J. (2006). *Service leadership: The quest for competitive advantage.* Thousand Oaks, CA: Sage.

Hernon, P., & Altman, E. (1998). *Assessing service quality: Satisfying the expectations of library customers.* Chicago, IL: American Library Association.

Hernon, P., & Whitman, J. R. (2001). *Delivering satisfaction and service quality: A customer-based approach for libraries.* Chicago, IL: American Library Association.

Hu, L., & Bentler, P. M. (1999). Cutoff criteria for fit indexes in covariance structure analysis: Conventional criteria versus new alternatives. *Structural Equation Modeling, 6*(1), 1–55.

Jamrog, J. J., & Overholt, M. H. (2004). Building a strategic HR function: Continuing the evolution. *Human Resource Planning, 27*(1), 51–62.

KCLS. (2005). *King County library system patron experience transformation project – quantitative research (Final Report, 2005).* Seattle, WA: King County Library System.

KCLSm. (2005). *King County library system patron experience transformation project – quantitative research (Final Report – methodology section, 2005).* Seattle, WA: King County Library System.

Kline, R. B. (2005). *Principles and practice of structural equation modeling* (2nd ed.). New York, NY: The Guilford Press.

Kordupleski, R. R., Rust, R. T., & Zahoric, A. J. (1993). Why improving quality doesn't improve quality (or whatever happened to marketing?). *California Management Review, 35,* 82–95.

Kuhn, T. S. (1996). *The structure of scientific revolutions* (3rd ed.). Chicago, IL: University of Chicago Press.

Lambert, J., & Carnell, M. (2004). Organizational excellence through six sigma discipline. *Quality Focus, 4*(2), 18–25.

Lomax, R. G., & Schumacker, R. E. (2004). *A beginner's guide to structural equation modeling.* Mahwah, NJ: LEA Publishing.

Miles, M. B., & Huberman, A. M. (1994). *An expanded sourcebook: Qualitative data analysis* (2nd ed.). Thousand Oaks, CA: Sage.

Nitecki, D. A. (1996). Changing the concept and measure of service quality in academic libraries. *The Journal of Academic Librarianship, 22*(3), 181–190.

OCLC. (2003). *Environmental scan: Pattern recognition.* Dublin, OH: OCLC.

OCLC. (2005). *Perceptions of libraries and information resources.* Dublin, OH: OCLC.

Parasuraman, A., Zeithaml, V. A., & Berry, L. L. (1985). A conceptual model of service quality and its implication for future research. *Journal of Marketing, 49,* 41–50.

Parasuraman, A., Zeithaml, V. A., & Berry, L. L. (1988a). SERVQUAL: A multiple-item scale for measuring consumer perceptions of service quality. *Journal of Retailing, 64*(1), 12–40.

Parasuraman, A., Zeithaml, V. A., & Berry, L. L. (1988b). Communication and control processes in the delivery of service quality. *Journal of Marketing, 53,* 46.

Parasuraman, A., Zeithaml, V. A., & Berry, L. L. (1990). *Delivering quality service: Balancing customer perceptions & expectations.* New York, NY: Free Press.

Parasuraman, A., Zeithaml, V. A., & Berry, L. L. (1994a). Alternate scales for measuring service quality: A comparative assessment based on psychometric and diagnostic criteria. *Journal of Retailing, 70*(3), 201–230.

Parasuraman, A., Zeithaml, V. A., & Berry, L. L. (1994b). *Moving forward in service quality research: Measuring different customer-expectation levels, comparing alternative scales, and examining the performance-behavioral intentions link.* Marketing Science Institute, Report # 94–144.

Parasuraman, A., Zeithaml, V. A., & Berry, L. L. (1996). The behavioral consequences of service quality. *Journal of Marketing, 60*(April), 31–46.

Peppers, M., & Rogers, D. (2005). *Return on customer: Creating maximum value from your scarcest resource.* New York, NY: Currency.

Phillips, L. W., Chang, D. R., & Buzzell, R. D. (1983). Product quality, cost position, and business performance: A test of some key hypotheses. *Journal of Marketing Research, 47*(Spring), 26–43.

Prahalad, C. K., & Ramaswamy, V. (2004a). *The future of competition: Co-creating unique value with customers.* Boston, MA: Harvard Business School Press.

Prahalad, C. K., & Ramaswamy, V. (2004b). How to put your customers to work: It's getting harder for companies to sustain growth and create value on their own. It's time to loop customers into the act. *CIO, 17*(13), 1.

Reichheld, F. F. (1993). Loyalty-based management. *Harvard Business Review, 71*(March–April), 64–74.

Reichheld, F. F. (2003). The one number you need to grow. *Harvard Business Review, 81*(12), 46–54.

Reichheld, F. F., & Sasser, W. E. (1990). Zero defections: Quality comes to services, *Harvard Business Review* (Vol. 68, pp. 105), Harvard Business School Publication Corp.

Roth, V. A., & Jackson, W. E. (1995). Strategic determinants of service quality and performance: Evidence from the banking industry. *Management Science, 41*(11), 1720–1733.

Rust, R. T., & Oliver, R. L. (1994). *Service quality: New directions in theory and practice.* Thousand Oaks, CA: Sage.

Scott, W. R. (2003). *Organizations: Rational, natural, and open systems* (5th ed.). Upper Saddle River, NJ: Prentice Hall.

Sharma, S., Netemeyer, R. G., & Bearden, W. O. (2003). *Scaling procedures: Issues and applications.* Thousand Oaks, CA: Sage.

Yang, Z. (2001). *Measuring E-service quality and its linkage to customer loyalty.* Unpublished Dissertation, New Mexico State University, Las Cruses.

Zeithaml, V. A., & Bitner, M. J. (2003). *Services Marketing: Integrating customer focus across the firm* (3rd ed.). Boston, MA: McGraw Hill Irwin.

APPENDIX A. SERVQUAL MODEL

Gap 5: Service Impact on Firm's Competitive Advantage

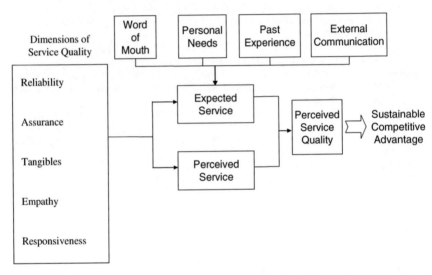

Note: From Parasuraman et al. (1985, p. 48). Copyright 1985 by the American Marketing Association. Reprinted with permission.

APPENDIX 1. SERVQUAL PERCEPTIONS BATTERY

Directions: The following set of statements relate to your feelings about XYZ Company. For each statement, please show the extent to which you believe XYZ Company has the feature described by the statement. Once again, circling a 1 means that you strongly disagree that XYZ Company has that feature, and circling a 7 means that you strongly agree. You may circle any of the numbers in the middle that show how strong your feelings are. There are no right or wrong answers – all that we are interested in is a number that best shows your perceptions about XYZ Company.

	Question	Dimension	Strongly Disagree 1	2	3	4	5	6	Strongly Agree 7
1	XYZ Co. has modern-looking equipment	Tangibles							
2	XYZ Co's physical facilities are visually appealing	Tangibles							
3	XYZ' Co's employees will be neat-appearing	Tangibles							
4	Materials associated with the service (such as pamphlets or statements) are visually appealing at XYZ Co.	Tangibles							
5	When XYZ Co. promises to do something by a certain time, they will do so	Reliability							
6	When you have a problem, XYZ Co. shows a sincere interest in solving it	Reliability							
7	XYZ Co. performs the service right the first time	Reliability							
8	XYZ Co. provides its services at the time it promises to do so	Reliability							
9	XYZ Co. insists on error-free records	Reliability							

APPENDIX B. (*Continued*)

Question	Dimension	Strongly Disagree						Strongly Agree
		1	2	3	4	5	6	7
10 Employees in XYZ Co. tell you exactly when services will be performed	Responsiveness							
11 Employees in XYZ Co. give you prompt customers	Responsiveness							
12 Employees in XYZ Co. are always willing to help you	Responsiveness							
13 Employees in XYZ Co. are never too busy to respond to your requests	Responsiveness							
14 The behavior of employees in XYZ Co. instills confidence in you	Assurance							
15 You feel safe in your transactions with XYZ Co.	Assurance							
16 Employees in XYZ Co. are consistently courteous to you	Assurance							
17 Employees in XYZ Co. have the knowledge to answer your questions	Assurance							
18 XYZ Co. gives you individual attention	Empathy							
19 XYZ Co. has operating hours convenient to all its customers	Empathy							
20 XYZ Co. has employees who give you personal attention	Empathy							
21 XYZ Co. has your best interests at heart	Empathy							
22 Employees of XYZ Co. understand your specific needs	Empathy							

Note: From Parasuraman et al. (1988a, pp. 38–40). Reprinted with permission.

APPENDIX C. NINE-STEP LIBRARY ANALYSIS PROCESS

1. Screen data for multivariate-normal (transform data?)
2. Missing values and outliers (per data screening flowchart)
   1. Listwise deletion to compare directly with KCLS approach
   2. Analyze if missing values MAR or MCAR[a] (SPSS MVA)
3. Conduct principle component exploratory factor analysis
   a. Use Mertler and Vannatta checklist for factor analysis
   b. Correlation matrix reveal many items >0.3 (any abnormalities)?
   c. Use orthogonal and oblique rotations (listwise deletion)
   d. Force 4-factors to conform to KCLS
   e. Examine screen plot. Which will be used (Cattell inflection or Kaiser-eigenvalues >1)?
   f. Determine if KCLS factors cleanly emerge (Varimax rotation)
   g. If not, does another "clean" model appear (Promax)?
   h. Check KMO >0.6?
   i. Bartlett's test significant?
   j. How many factors have eigenvalues >1?
   k. Report results and show pattern and structure matrix
4. Conduct confirmatory factor analysis (covariance-based)
   a. Skew present? (use both transformed and non-transformed data & compare)
   b. Specify model
   c. Identify model
   d. Estimate model
   e. Test null four-factor model (no correlations between factors); test single-factor model (all indicators load on one variable); test alternative model in 3(g) if any
   f. Assess using χ^2, and other appropriate fit indices (CFI >0.95; GFI >0.95; RMSEA ≤ 0.05 for close fit; PCLOSE >0.050; SRMR close to zero; NFI, etc.
   g. $H_0 1$: The service quality measurement model's $\Sigma(\theta)$ provides a "good or close fit" for the population, that is, $[\Sigma = \Sigma(\theta)]$ using parameters in (f) above
   h. Assess difference in KCLS and alternative model if one appeared in 3(g) above using ΔNFI and other changes in "fit" indices

APPENDIX C. (*Continued*)

---

    i.   Run KCLS model on all 5,405 (and alternative model) and report fit indices and any abnormalities (non-positive covariance matrix or Heywood cases?)

    j.   Model modification – Report possible cross-loading and error correlation issues through examining the modification index (MI)

5.   Reliability

    a.   Composite reliability: $H_0 2a$: Composite reliability = $(\Sigma\lambda)2/[(\Sigma\lambda)2 + \Sigma(1-\lambda j2)] = \geq 0.7$

    b.   Average variance extracted: $H_0 2b$ = Average variance extracted = $\Sigma\lambda 2/[\Sigma\lambda 2 + \Sigma(1-\lambda j2)] = > 0.5$

    c.   Cronbach alpha: $H_0 2c$ = Cronbach Alpha (α) = $p(r)/[1+(-1)r] = \geq 0.95$

6.   Unidimensionality (required if new measures are added to form composites as in the KCLS study)

    a. $H_0 2d$ = Unidimensionality = All indicators will load more highly on their intended variable than with other variables

    b.   Evaluate standardized covariance matrix (|values| > 1.96 or 2.58)

    c.   Evaluate MI for high-error correlations and indicator cross-loading

7.   Discriminant validity for measurement model

    a. $H_0 3a$ = Discriminant validity = All constructs should be more strongly correlated with their own measures than with other constructs using AVE/correlation technique

8.   Convergent validity

    a. $H_0 3b$ = Convergent validity = All indicator's standardized regression coefficients should be > 0.7

9.   Nomological validity for the measurement model

    a. $H_0 3c$ = Nomological validity = The chi-square statistic should be low with an insignificant p-value > 0.05 and with an RMSEA value ≤ 0.05

---

[a]MAR, missing at random; MCAR, missing completely at random.

APPENDIX D. EXTENDED MODEL OF SERVICE QUALITY

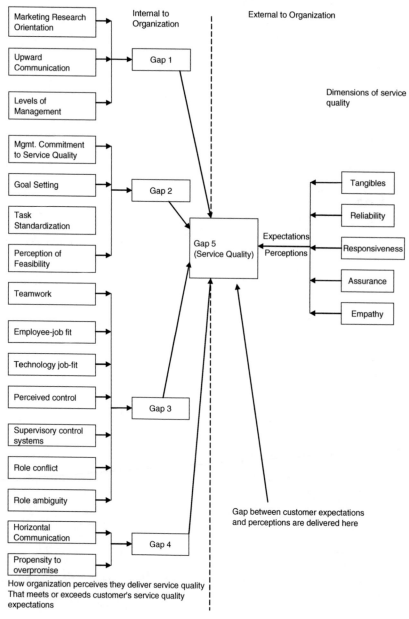

Note: From Parasuraman, Zeithaml, and Berry (1988b). Copyright 1988 by the American Marketing Association. Reprinted with permission.

APPENDIX E. SUMMARY OF STEPS IN SERVQUAL SCALE DEVELOPMENT

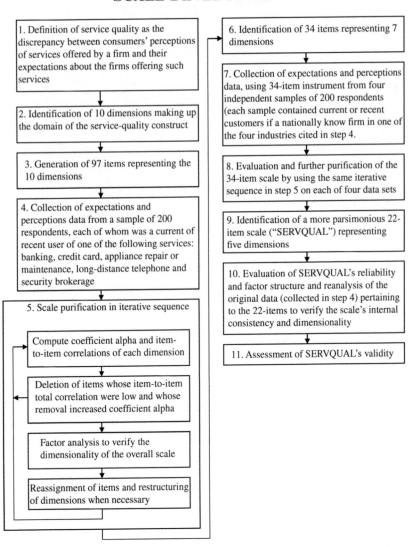

1. Definition of service quality as the discrepancy between consumers' perceptions of services offered by a firm and their expectations about the firms offering such services

2. Identification of 10 dimensions making up the domain of the service-quality construct

3. Generation of 97 items representing the 10 dimensions

4. Collection of expectations and perceptions data from a sample of 200 respondents, each of whom was a current of recent user of one of the following services: banking, credit card, appliance repair or maintenance, long-distance telephone and security brokerage

5. Scale purification in iterative sequence

  Compute coefficient alpha and item-to-item correlations of each dimension

  Deletion of items whose item-to-item total correlation were low and whose removal increased coefficient alpha

  Factor analysis to verify the dimensionality of the overall scale

  Reassignment of items and restructuring of dimensions when necessary

6. Identification of 34 items representing 7 dimensions

7. Collection of expectations and perceptions data, using 34-item instrument from four independent samples of 200 respondents (each sample contained current or recent customers if a nationally know firm in one of the four industries cited in step 4.

8. Evaluation and further purification of the 34-item scale by using the same iterative sequence in step 5 on each of four data sets

9. Identification of a more parsimonious 22-item scale ("SERVQUAL") representing five dimensions

10. Evaluation of SERVQUAL's reliability and factor structure and reanalysis of the original data (collected in step 4) pertaining to the 22-items to verify the scale's internal consistency and dimensionality

11. Assessment of SERVQUAL's validity

Note: From Parasuraman et al. (1988a, p. 12). Copyright 1988 *Journal of Retailing.* Reprinted with permission.

ABOUT THE AUTHORS

Belinda Boon is currently an Assistant Professor at Kent State University. Formerly, she was a Continuing Education Consultant with the Texas State Library and a small community library director. She earned an MLIS (1987) and PhD (2006) in Library and Information Science from the University of Texas at Austin.

H. Frank Cervone is an Associate Professor of Education and the Director of the Library, Information, and Media Studies program at Chicago State University. The author of numerous articles and four books on topics related to information technology, he has an MSEd with a specialization in online teaching and learning from the California State University, an MA in information technology management in libraries from DePaul University and a PhD in management from Northcentral University.

Gary Neil Fitsimmons earned his Master of Library Science degree in 1990 and his PhD in Library Science in 2005, both from Texas Woman's University. He has served as a practicum student at American Airlines corporate library; Acquisitions/Reference Librarian at Wayland Baptist University in Plainview, TX; Research/Reader Services Librarian at the Baptist Sunday School Board in Nashville, TN; Technical Services and Systems Librarian at New Mexico Junior College in Hobbs, NM; and as Director of Library Services at Cisco Junior College in Cisco, TX.

John Patrick Green Jr. is a consultant who helps non-profit and government organizations improve service quality and effectiveness. Prior to establishing his consulting business, Service Quality Partners, Dr. Green spent numerous years in various technical, operations, management, and business development positions with companies such as IBM, McDonnell Douglas, Bell Atlantic, and Gartner Consulting serving commercial, medical, education, and government clients. Dr. Green's current focus is helping public libraries remain relevant to the customers they serve. This includes implementing fact-based and actionable customer-focused strategies (a customer listening system) so libraries can more effectively compete with other channels of information, such as the Internet and You-Tube. Dr. Green received his PhD in Organization and Management from Capella University and is a senior Baldrige Examiner with the State of Washington (WSQA).

Deborah Lee is Professor of Library Science and Coordinator of the Library Instructional Services Program and the Corporate and Statistical Research Center at the Mississippi State University Libraries. She also serves as the Associate Director of the MSU Center for Teaching and Learning.

Charles B. Osburn is Dean and Professor Emeritus of University Libraries at the University of Alabama, where he teaches part-time in the School of Library and Information Studies. He is the author or editor of several books and a number of articles.

Jennifer K. Sweeney is a research analyst on the Minority Opportunities in Research and Education Project, School of Education, University of California, Davis. Prior to earning her PhD from UCLA, Dr. Sweeney was a program evaluator, analyst, and reference librarian at UC Davis and American University. Her research interests include evaluation of educational enrichment programs and library staff diversity and skill development (MSLS, Catholic University; BA, Stony Brook).

AUTHOR INDEX

351

SUBJECT INDEX